The History of Mary Stewart: From the Murder of Riccio Until Her Flight Into England - Primary Source Edition

Claude Nau

61

THE HISTORY OF
MARY STEWART

FROM THE MURDER OF RICCIO UNTIL HER FLIGHT
INTO ENGLAND.

BY CLAUDE NAU
HER SECRETARY

NOW FIRST PRINTED FROM THE ORIGINAL MANUSCRIPTS

WITH

ILLUSTRATIVE PAPERS FROM THE SECRET ARCHIVES OF THE VATICAN
AND OTHER COLLECTIONS IN ROME

EDITED, WITH HISTORICAL PREFACE, BY

THE REV. JOSEPH STEVENSON, S.J.

EDINBURGH:
WILLIAM PATERSON.
1883.

CONTENTS.

—————

INTRODUCTION.

THE tempest which swept over Europe during the middle of the sixteenth century, levelling in its career many a stately fabric which had been erected and preserved by the wisdom and affection of earlier ages, did not spare either the Church or the State of Scotland. The political changes which were effected by this movement seemed, at the outset, as if they would overthrow the sovereignty which had been established in the land for many centuries; and had these novel theories of government been carried out according to the spirit in which they were conceived and introduced, the necessary result would have been the establishment of a republic. The same democratic principles had freer exercise when they came to deal with the church; a body which, notwithstanding its more perfect organisation, had become so far fettered as to be unable to resist the pressure which at that time was made to bear upon it. Hence it came to pass that the movement, which, for want of a more accurate term, we are content to call the Reformation, had in Scotland a wider field than in England for its exercise, and left behind it a deeper impress of its character. Thus it is that the history of Scotland will always recommend itself as a favourite study to those enquirers who seek to understand the full meaning of the Utopia contemplated by the religious and political reformers of the sixteenth century.

If we limit our enquiry in this direction to the history of our own country, we shall find that its interest centres around two individuals, whose figures stand clearly defined and sharply marked off from the other actors. Two women claim our attention, Mary Stuart and Elizabeth Tudor. They are the representatives of the two distinct systems then brought into antagonism, and these they typify with sufficient precision. Although they are near of kin, yet there is a great gulf between them. Elizabeth is the symbol of national progress, intellectual activity, and material success, but these advantages are gained by the sacrifice of laws which ought to admit of no compromise. Mary Stuart is the embodiment of a different code of legislation; she keeps on the old path, she is willing to suffer rather than to temporise, and seeks to be directed by eternal principles rather than urged on by temporal expediency. Yet however widely these two women may differ in character, in sentiment, and in action, they are drawn towards each other by a sympathy which acts with the power of a destiny. The one follows the other like her shadow. Neither of them can be understood so long as she stands apart; there is always a mutual influence, sometimes by attraction, but oftener by repulsion. Each of them is worthy of a careful study, and each will repay it by the lessons which she teaches. The character of Mary Stuart is indebted for very much of its growth and firmness to the long training which she underwent at the hands of her cousin; and she has to thank Elizabeth Tudor more than any other human being for that undying interest with which her name has become associated.

The story of Mary Stuart has been often told, and told

well. It has been told by friend and by foe, by Protestant and by Catholic, by those who look upon her execution at Fotheringhay as a judicial murder, and by those who regard it as an act of tardy justice. So abundant and so varied is the biographical literature connected with the Scottish queen that it may reasonably be asked upon what grounds I venture to add yet another contribution to the store of materials already too extensive. My answer is that I offer this work to the public because I believe it to contain information which is at once new and important. I claim a hearing for a witness who has something to say on an interesting question which is yet undecided. It seems to me that no just estimate of queen Mary can be formed until the contents of the present volume shall be adduced in evidence, and their value duly sifted and ascertained. Upon these grounds I invite the attention of my countrymen to the present volume ; and I now proceed to state the nature of the documents which it contains, and from what sources they are derived.

By far the largest portion of this work is occupied by the fragment of a history of the reign of Mary Stuart, which I believe to have been composed by one of her French secretaries, named Claud Nau. I contend that it is in his handwriting, and that it was written while he was in her service, and an inmate in her household. The arguments upon which these conclusions are based will be given at considerable length in the Preface which follows; it is unnecessary, therefore, to do more than to refer to them here. To me the evidence appears to be conclusive, and I venture to hope that it will commend itself as such to the majority of my readers.

The narrative, as I have already stated, is unfortunately only a fragment, mutilated at the beginning, and apparently unfinished. It extends from the murder of Riccio (9th March 1566) to some uncertain date apparently in the year 1571.

An abstract of this narrative appeared in a periodical named " The Month." [1] The original French text is here printed for the first time, together with a notice of the various alterations which it has undergone at the hands of the author. It is accompanied by an English translation, which aims chiefly at giving a close rendering of the original without regard to elegance of diction.

Besides these " Memorials of the Reign of Queen Mary," Claude Nau proposed to make more extended researches into Scottish history. He seems to have intended to write an account of the royal house of Stuart, from the accession of king Robert the second to his own times. With that view he began his collections by translating into French the Latin history of bishop Leslie.[2] This version is extant,[3] but it possesses no interest, and may be dismissed without further notice. Nau, however, added to it a continuation, a few fragments of which survive, and are given along with a translation.[4]

Among the manuscripts which formerly belonged to sir Robert Cotton is one which certainly passed through the hands of Nau, and which most probably was seized at Chartley.[5] It is a treatise written in the French

[1] Vol. xvi. New Series.

[2] Lond., 1575. 4to. Romæ, 1578. 4to.

[3] MS. Cott. Vesp., C. xvi., fol. 41. It extends from A.D. 1436 to 1454.

[4] General Record Office, London, Scotland, queen Mary, vol. xxi. No. 46.

[5] MS. Cott. Titus, C. xii. fol. 1. It came into the possession of " Robertus Cotton Bruceus," as he is pleased to style himself, in 1599, probably by purchase from Phillipps, the decipherer.

language, in vindication of the claims of Mary Stuart to
the English throne, in preference to those of Elizabeth.
It is not in Nau's handwriting, but a single note by him
appears on the margin of one of the pages. The treatise
itself is the composition of a writer who was the author
of a history of his own times, a work apparently of considerable extent and value. A specimen of this treatise
is given in the present volume.

Nau seems not to have been aware that bishop Leslie
wrote an account of the reign of queen Mary, extending
from the 20th of August 1561 to the death of the regent
Lennox in 1571. Not only has this work never been
printed, but its existence was unknown until I had the
good fortune to discover a copy in the Secret Archives of
the Vatican.[1] It is written by a scribe who frequently
proves himself to have been careless and ignorant.
No other copy is known. The information furnished
by this history is valuable, and I have frequently
availed myself of it in illustrating the narrative here
published.

I have also derived considerable assistance from an
anonymous life of Mary, hitherto unprinted, of which I
have failed to discover the author. Whoever he may
have been, he possessed much curious information. The
work has not come down to us in its original form, but
as we now have it, it professes to be "An abstract and
compendium drawn up of a discourse that hath been
heretofore collected and framed upon certain notes and
observations of the diverse and sundry disasters and
adverse fortunes wherewith the late queen of Scots, of
glorious memory, was for a great part of her life afflicted."

---

[1] Politicorum Variorum, vol. xvi. 297. The title which it there
bears is, "Paralipomena ad historiam, comitia et annales Scotiæ
Joannis Leslei, episcopi Rossensis, eodem auctore."

The original author[1] tells us that "he speaketh partly of his own knowledge, having been a near beholder of a great part of the tragedy; and partly from the information and asseveration of those whose wisdom and upright consciences render them worthy of all credit; and lastly, upon such probabilities and demonstrations as the effects, sequels, consequences, and other circumstances prove." The original manuscript seems to have perished, and of the abridgment the only copy known is that already cited.[2] As it refers to the murder of king Henry IV. of France, it cannot have been reduced to its present form before 1614, but it contains many traces of having been written at a much earlier period.

The Secret Archives of the Vatican have also supplied me with several documents of great value, translations of which are given in the Appendix. For permission to examine this wonderful repository, and to transcribe these and various other papers of equal interest, I express my deep gratitude to the kindness of his late holiness pope Pius IX. The private Archives of the Society of Jesus have also contributed several letters of considerable importance connected with Scottish history. Others might have been added from the same precious collections could I have found room for their insertion. The rich library of prince Barberini in Rome has also added to our harvest. In the Supplemental Notes to the successive chapters of the Preface, I have not scrupled to

---

[1] Were I inclined to speculate I might conjecture that this work is founded upon " Sinclair's manuscript History of Scotland, which was written at the time, and remained in the Scots College at Paris until recent times," and which is quoted by Chalmers in his " Life of Queen Mary," iii. 67, ed. 1822. But the passage about Bothwell there quoted from the Paris MS. does not occur in the Cottonian copy.

[2] It is to be found in MS. Cott. Calig., B. iv. 137, the same volume which contains Nau's History.

print various documents derived chiefly from English
sources, which will be acceptable to the reader. But I
have been careful to avoid the repetition of papers which
have already appeared in works of frequent occurrence.

It is not for me to anticipate the judgment which will
be passed upon the volume now submitted to the public.
I may say, however, that, as far as I am conscious, I
have striven to write of men and their motives in the
spirit of charity rather than censoriousness, whenever it
was possible to do so. It has been my wish to avoid
prejudice, and yet at the same time to be faithful to the
principles by which I desire to be guided. I am anxious
it should be understood that my book is not a life of
Mary Stuart, still less that it is an apology for her
conduct. I do not come forward as her champion.
Doubtless she had her faults, her weakness, and her sins;
but, situated as she was, I wonder that they were not
more numerous, and of a graver character. I think that
much that she said and did has been misunderstood, and
much that she suffered has been concealed and forgotten.
If these pages enable us to realise more distinctly than
we hitherto may have done, the insults and indignities
to which she was exposed, the cruelty and violence in
the midst of which she lived, the brutal indifference of
her husband Darnley, the refined treachery of her brother
Moray, and the implacable malignity of her cousin
Elizabeth, painful as the revelation may be, it is not
without its lessons. In the case of Mary Stuart, the
name and the fame of a brave woman have been vilified,
because her ruin was necessary to the success of her
enemies. Nau helps us to obtain a partial insight into
the process by which this fraud was accomplished, and
we are grateful for the knowledge for which we are indebted to his Narrative.

England, was her Secretary Raullet. His health failed him early in the year 1574, and he died in the following August.[1] It was no easy matter to supply the place of one who for so long had occupied such a confidential position in her household. Nor was this the only difficulty; for about the same time Mary discovered that her finances had fallen into lamentable disorder. Her dowry from France was paid very irregularly; her revenues from Scotland had been seized by the regent for the time being; the contributions which had been promised by foreign princes had long since ceased;[2] and her treasurer, Dolu, had proved himself careless, or dishonest, or both.[3] Not only was a new secretary needed but a new accountant, and she was anxious that the duties of these two offices should for the future be

[1] Lab. iv. 215. Writing to Walsingham on 31st August 1574, Shrewsbury tells us how he conducted himself on the death of Raullet, "whereupon, in respect the said Rollet had, as I think, the whole knowledge of the whole secrets his mistress had dealt in these years past, and might have had some papers in his custody, considering the same I thought good to take occasion (in hope to find some things that might serve the Queen's Majesty) to take possession of the keys of his coffers, as I did immediately after the advertisement. . . . . Wherein after long search I could find nothing of effect, saving certain reckonings that already past through my hands, which I would not deal with, and some letters of the pope's, the Spanish ambassador, the cardinal of Lorraine, which, albeit it seemeth they are of old date, I thought best to retain and make this advertisement of the same, till I should know the Queen's Majesty's pleasure thereupon." Lodge's Illustr., ii. 40, ed. 1838.

[2] If sent they had been intercepted (see Lab. vi. 413; vii. 206), in the latter of which passages Nau assures Elizabeth that for twelve years no money had been received from this source by Mary. Respecting the losses which she had sustained by the non-payment of her dower in France see an important paper by Nau in MS. Cott. Cal., C. ix. 1.

[3] Lab. iv. 137, 217, 255, 302, 304; v. 2. In R. O. Mary, xiv. 22, Nau does not hesitate to refer to " Les voleurs de Dolu."

united in the same individual. At Mary's request the
Archbishop of Glasgow, her ambassador in Paris, placed
her requirements before her maternal relations, the Cardinal of Lorraine and the Duke of Guise. They offered
the appointment, such as it was, with its dangers and
responsibilities, to a young man of the name of Nau, and
Nau at once accepted the situation.

Mary wished it to be understood that the office of
secretary was no sinecure. Not only was the average
day's work heavy, but the whole of the work for some
months past had fallen into arrear. The pay was
small, the labour was irksome, and the life was dreary.
But Nau was full of zeal, and he was not easily deterred. He was young and enterprising; there was a
certain character of dangerous adventure about the proposal which made it attractive, and he was anxious to
please his patrons of the great family of Lorraine.
Early in the January of 1575 Mary had ascertained the
name of her new secretary, and she was urgent for his
speedy arrival.[1] Everything was done to expedite it.
By the Guises he was presented at the French Court,
and having been accredited by King Henry the Third to
the English sovereign as Mary's new secretary for her
foreign correspondence, he crossed over into England.

When Nau arrived in London Elizabeth was in a bad
humour, and she did not receive him graciously. She
permitted him, however, to pursue his journey, and that
was enough. An emissary sent from the house of Guise
to Mary Stuart could scarcely expect more, if so much.
We still possess the letter[2] which the new secretary
carried with him from London to Sheffield, where Mary

---

[1] Lab. iv. 260.

[2] This letter is dated at St James's, 29th March 1575, and is preserved in the Lansd. MS., 1236, n. 47. The queen's autograph

then resided. It was addressed to her keeper, the Earl of Shrewsbury, and as it was left open it was probably intended that Nau should read it. If he did so far gratify his curiosity, it would tell him that as Raullet had been guilty of "certain evil offices," the English queen had been in no haste to sanction the appointment of a successor, whose conduct might be equally offensive; but that the bearer, one Nau, "having been chosen and sent, hath promised that he shall carry himself in that even manner that becometh an honest minister." It would only be prudent, however, she thought, if the earl were to remind him from time to time of the duties of his position; and care should be taken that this new officer did not follow in the steps of his objectionable predecessor.

Claude Nau was born of a good family[1] which had originally settled in Lorraine, but which, following the for-

signature is prefixed and her signet is impressed. The document states that since the death of Raullet, the Queen of Scots, being destitute of a French secretary, has, by her own letters and by means out of France, desired her, Elizabeth, to suffer another to come to supply that place about her, which, continues her gracious Majesty, "we have hitherto forborn to grant for diverse good causes, and, among others, for the evil offices which her other secretary did there, whereof you are not ignorant." She is addressing the Earl of Shrewsbury, who at this time was Mary's custodian.

[1] The following summary of the dignities attained by Mary's secretary is given by M. de la Chenaye-Desbois, *Dictionnaire de la Noblesse*, tom. x., p. 698. (Paris, 1775, 4to.) Claude Nau de la Boisseliere, Counsellor of the King, Auditor of the Chambre des Comptes, Secretary of State and Finances to Queen Mary, on his return from her service was nominated Counsellor and Intendant of Finances; and lastly, Secretary in Ordinary of the Chamber of Henry the Fourth, by provision, 1st July 1600. By the same sovereign he was ennobled by letters dated at Fontainebleau, in May 1605, and registered in the Chambre des Comptes, 26th September 1605, and in La Cour des Aides, 26th January 1606, and again registered 12th September 1738. The family still existed when the work cited above was pub-

tunes of the aspiring house of Guise, had for some years past domesticated itself in Paris. The Cardinal of Guise had taken Claude under his protection and employed him as his own secretary, a position from which he had passed into the service of the king. Being ambitious, Claude aimed at a more public life ; he studied law and practised it in the Courts of Parliament in the French capital. At the time of his appointment to serve Mary Stuart he had attained a fair eminence in his profession, while higher promotion and increased wealth seemed likely to follow through the influence of his powerful patrons. Although still a very young man he must have stood high in the opinion of those who selected him to fill a position of such great delicacy and responsibility, and we shall see that he retained their good opinion to the end of his life. He was a Catholic, and his children did good service to the church after him.[1]

lished in 1775. See also L. Paris, *Indicateur*, ou Grand Armorial Général de France, par Charles d'Hozier, ii. 126, Paris, 1865, 8vo.

Claude Nau was not the only one of his family who served in the household of the Scottish Queen. In 1581 a commission was granted to Jacques Nau, who is qualified by Mary as " Conseiller et Secretaire de noz finances." R. O. Eliz., Scot., Mary, xi. 71. Ruisseau, Nau's brother-in-law, was Mary's Chancellor, and had the management of part of her revenues, MS. Egerton, 1639, fol. 62, Nau to Beale ; and several letters which passed between them are mentioned in Scot., Mary, xi. 39. Another brother-in-law, Fontenay, Secretary of Mary's Council, was employed in an important mission from the Court of France to James VI. in 1584. See Scot., Mary, xiii. 38, 45 ; Lab. vi. 80. She calls him " a young man of great resolution and wisdom," Ibid., p. 460, and left him 2400 francs in her will, Lab., vi. 488. See Supplemental Notes and Illustrations to Chapter I., p. lviii.

[1] Two of his sons became Priests of the Society of Jesus, and were men of mark in their generation ; Nicholas, born in Paris in 1603, and Michael, born in 1631. The latter was the author of several works illustrative of the history and antiquities of the Eastern Churches, which attained considerable reputation. See M. de la Chenaye-Desbois, x. 698, and De Backer, i. 508 ; vi. 396.

Nau entered upon the active discharge of his duties as secretary to Queen Mary in the early summer of 1575, and he served her in that capacity until a short time before her death in 1587. Recommended as he had been by her relatives of the house of Guise, doubtless he was well received by his new mistress, and soon found himself in a position of anxious trust and responsibility. His duties brought him into frequent and confidential intercourse with her. He deciphered the ciphered letters which reached her from the continent, and received her instructions as to the terms in which they should be answered. He discussed with her all her plans, and with very rare exceptions he was the only person to whom she could turn for advice in the management of the many delicate affairs which required her daily attention. Large discretionary powers were entrusted by her to him, she was often guided by his judgment, and upon many important occasions he had a direct influence upon her decisions.

Nau appears so frequently in Mary's correspondence that we are able to form a tolerably clear idea of his character and attainments. He was of polished manners and pleasing aspect; perhaps a little too fond of dress and show, for the display of which he could have had few opportunities while in her service.[1] He could speak and write good Italian, his Latin is accurate and easy,

---

[1] Walsingham draws a contrast between Mary's two secretaries, Nau and Curle, which helps us to understand the peculiarities of each. Of Curle he writes:—"He is nothing so quick-spirited nor so ready as Nau is, but hath a shrewd melancholy wit. She maketh great account of him as very secret and sure to her. This man shall go lightlier in post, with small show, and not with such pavado as the other would do for his reputation. Example his costly voyage to the Queen's Majesty. She cannot so spare Nau for her French affairs, happening oft." Feb. 1584. Sadler, ii. 523.

and he expressed himself in the English language with fluency.[1] A careful accountant and a practical lawyer he stood Mary in good stead in correcting and adjusting her troubled finances. In mental temperament he was quick and warm even to being impetuous ;[2] he was not the man, therefore, to witness in silence the slights and discourtesies to which his mistress was too frequently exposed at the hands of her keepers. Under the tyrannical rule of Elizabeth's ministers the severities of Mary's imprisonment had steadily been on the increase. Until Nau came, the jailer to whom she was consigned practically had his own way as to her treatment. The queen and her household of women could only complain, remonstrate, and submit. This did not satisfy her new secretary. He asked for explanations, and when they were given he examined their veracity and tested their probability. He made complaints to Cecil, Walsingham, and Leicester the omnipotent, and if these complaints were disregarded the French ambassador was induced to bring them into the presence of Elizabeth herself. Nau allowed no statement to pass unchallenged which touched the dignity or the honour of his mistress ; and his quick perception and ready power of rejoinder made him a dangerous antagonist.[3] Altercations took place from

[1] Writing to Walsingham from Sheffield, 16th April 1583, Beal says :—Shrewsbury understandeth little or no French, and therefore all our dealings with her [Queen Mary] and her ministers have been in English, which Nau and Curle speak well enough. MS. Cott. Cal., C. ix. 58, b.

[2] He sometimes pushed his own opinions too far, and disregarded those of his mistress. See Le Journal de Bourgoing, p. 526.

[3] "Nau was more earnest, and used a kind of protestation that if his mistress failed for want of such help, her Majesty would be answerable for the same before all the princes of Christendom." Beal to Walsingham, 23rd Nov. 1581. R. O. Q. Mary, xi. 69. See also B. M. MS. Harl., 290, fol. 135.

time to time between him and the Earl of Shrewsbury, whose harsh conduct arose not so much from his own deliberate unkindness as from Elizabeth's direct instructions. But when the earl was removed from his office and Sir Amyas Paulet succeeded him as Mary's turnkey, the collisions between him and Nau became frequent and furious. Paulet opened every letter and packet which was addressed to Mary or any of her household, and having read and copied them, he resealed them in the hope that the process of inspection through which they had passed would escape detection. But it did not. "Nau" (says he, writing to Walsingham), "Nau is very curious to observe seals; and finding that things have been opened hideth not his mind, but is as well answered."[1] Paulet unbosomed his troubles to Walsingham, and in the bitterness of his soul he expresses himself in the following terms. "I know Nau better than I may make known by writing, and I know him so well as I would be glad with all my heart he were removed and his place supplied with any two others whosoever, I care not out of what country or from whence they came."[2] A month afterwards the same feelings exist with increased acerbity. He writes :—"Nau hath a French busy head, more fit for France than for this country. This queen [Mary] would be governed with quietness and to her good contentation if his ambitious

[1] Scot., Mary, xv. 70. Somer, who was employed by Walsingham "to intercept letters which are coming hither out of Scotland," found that Nau was a troublesome member of the household. He writes in the following terms of him :—"Nau is very curious to open the seals upon boxes of things from the French ambassador (for such have been commonly sealed, but looked into for all that), and finding that they have been opened, will not hide his mind ; but is as well answered." April, 1585. Sadler Papers, ii. 542.
[2] Orig. in MS. Harl., 6993, fol. 90. Tutbury, 10th June 1585.

nature did not interrupt it. I call it ambitious, because
all his cavilling and quarrelling tends to none other end
than by finding faults with this and that to win credit
with his mistress, which no doubt he hath obtained in
so great measure as whatsoever she shall speak, write, or
do, it must be said to come from him and not from
her. . . . If he were removed from hence her Majesty
should be delivered from a French Guisard and a dangerous ghost, and her ministers here should enjoy some more
quiet than they now do." [1] We need not be surprised
then to find Paulet expressing his conviction that Nau
hath been, and is, best acquainted with all her affairs. [2]

Upon two occasions Mary employed her secretary
upon political missions of considerable importance.

Early in the year 1579 circumstances occurred which
induced Mary to believe that some impression might be
made upon her son through which he would consent to
act with her for their mutual interests, instead of neglect-
ing her and submitting, as he hitherto had done, to the
dictation of Elizabeth. But whom could she employ
upon such a mission? She would gladly have sent the
Archbishop of Glasgow, her ambassador in Paris; but
this being opposed by the French Government, [3] her only
alternative was to send her secretary. "After long suit
having obtained licence of the queen," [4] Nau set out
from Sheffield upon the 8th of June, and in due course
reached Edinburgh. His mission was a failure. He
was not permitted to see the young king. He had
reached home by the beginning of July, and on the

[1] Tutbury, 14th July 1585. R. O. Scot., Q. M., xvi. 10.
[2] R. O. Mary, xviii. 89. Thus also (xi. 66) Beale writes to Walsingham:—"She hath expressly signified unto me that she mindeth to
employ Nau in this service, who hath been, and is, best acquainted
with all her affairs."
[3] See Q. Mary to Henry III. of France, Lab. v. 80.
[4] Q. Mary to Sir George Bowes, Lab. v. 81.

fourth of that month his mistress gave an account of her secretary's adventures in a letter which she sent from Chatsworth on that day to the Archbishop of Glasgow. It tells us the following story.

As the despatch, of which Nau was the bearer, was addressed by the queen simply, "To my Son," without any recognition of his title as king, it was decided at the Court of Holyrood that it could not be presented to his Majesty. James pleaded hard to be allowed to receive it, and at one time it seemed as if his appeal would be successful. It had even been arranged, at a meeting of the council held late in the evening, that Nau should be admitted on the following morning; and this would have been done but for the unexpected arrival of the Regent Morton, who, warned during the night by the Laird of Tullibarden, appeared at Stirling, and over-ruled the former decision of the council. Mary's enemies succeeded in preventing any communication between James and her secretary. But from all that she could gather, she was firmly impressed with the conviction that her son still loved her. "Everyone assures me" (she writes to her ambassador in Paris) "that my son recognises infinitely his devoir towards me, and that the poor child dare not show it in the captivity he is, fearing therethrough, as there is great appearance, the hazard of his life."[1] But although he had not had any direct communication with James, his journey had been of no small service to the cause of his mistress. Unknown to Errington, who had been employed to watch him, Nau had conferred with the most faithful of the nobles who

[1] Lab. v. 95. At a later period Mary discussed with Beal the details of Nau's treatment by Morton, adding "that if Nau had then had access to do his message perhaps Morton's head had been on his shoulders now." See Beal to Walsingham, Sheffield, 28th Nov. 1581, R. O. Mary, xi. 71.

still adhered to her party, more especially Seton and Ogilvy, whom he had instructed as to her plans, and the course which she wished them to follow. His visit enabled Mary to understand the danger of her son's position and her own, as well as the real drift of the policy which Elizabeth was now pursuing towards Scotland.[1]

In 1584 Nau was again employed in the service of his mistress. She had again trusted the promises made to her by Walsingham and others so far as to believe that some compromise might even yet be effected between the Queen of England, James, and herself. Elizabeth, when she granted permission to Nau to visit the Court, "hoped that he would bring with him sufficient matter to work a thorough reconciliation between them."[2] The details of his journey were arranged with the most careful precision by the English Government. On Tuesday night (November 10) Nau was to sleep at Nottingham, on Wednesday at Leicester, on Thursday at Northampton, on Friday at Dunstable, at Uxbridge on Saturday, and on Sunday at Kingston. On the eighteenth M. Nau had his first conference with her Majesty, "who (says Walsingham) "seemeth to rest very well satisfied with

[1] A more detailed account of this attempted negotiation between Mary and her son is contained in a letter addressed to Walsingham by the officer into whose care, or custody, Nau was committed during his brief stay in Scotland. It is given in the Illustrative Notes appended to this chapter, Note the Second, p. lx.

An interesting letter addressed by Mary to her aunt, the Countess of Athol, furnishes us with some further particulars regarding this mission, and is an additional confirmation of the skill with which Nau carried out the instructions of his mistress where he could act according to his own prudence. This letter, which has escaped the researches of Prince Labanoff, has been printed and lithographed from the original by Mr Frazer in his most valuable work "The Lennox."

[2] Scot., Mary, xiv. 20.

him." We learn from the same authority that from the eighteenth to the twenty-fifth his "negotiation was private with her Majesty's self, the purpose of which did chiefly concern my Lady of Shrewsbury and her causes." Mary had a grave accusation to bring against her ladyship, an accusation in which it pleased Elizabeth to take so much interest as to bestow on it a personal investigation. The countess had gone so far as to charge her husband with having carried on a guilty intercourse with his prisoner, which had resulted in the birth of a child.

These reports had reached Mary's ears in the course of the year 1583. She promptly requested the French ambassador to protest against them in her name in the presence of Queen Elizabeth and her council, to demand an investigation, and to declare that unless justice were done to her, she would make her case known to every court in Christendom. Her demands having been disregarded for several months the calumniated prisoner at last made a direct application to the queen herself, which was followed up by the personal appeals of Nau, who insisted upon the immediate and public vindication of the honour of his mistress.[1] The urgency with which he pressed his suit admitted of no further delay, and at last

[1] Ibid. xiv. 28, 33, 42. Sadler, Mary's temporary custodian, at last (20th Oct. 1584) thought it was time to caution Walsingham of the probable result of this long disregard of Mary's complaints. He writes thus :—" She is marvellously grieved with the Countess of Shrewsbury, for the foul slanders of late raised upon her by the said Countess and some of hers, as she saith, which having touched her so near in honour and reputation abroad, she saith she can no longer sustain, trusting that her Majesty will suffer her to have justice."— Sadler Papers, ii. 422. Mary's own letters to Elizabeth, Mauvissière, and others, urgently demanding the vindication of her character, are given in Lab. vi. 33 seqq.

tardy justice was done to the maligned Queen of Scotland. The countess and her two sons, Charles and William Cavendish, were obliged to affirm on their oath their belief in "the chaste and honourable deportment of the Queen of Scots, and their disbelief in the scandalous falsehoods and reports which had been spread abroad against her."[1]

Having carefully investigated these cruel calumnies which had been circulated against her rival, and having been compelled to admit their falsity, Elizabeth's interest in Nau and his mission soon flagged and came to an end. He was directed to discuss with her privy council whatever questions yet remained undecided respecting the affairs of Mary and her son. Then followed the usual process of deliberation, delay, and disappointment. Paper followed paper in rapid succession; requests, articles, offers, "memoryes," cautions, and provisions,[2] kept the secretary busy, and made him suspicious. He saw that he was being tricked and beguiled, and that he had nothing to expect from the English queen or her council. Naturally, he was anxious, under such circumstances, to leave the Court, but he was not permitted to do so. Upon one plea after another he was detained in London, and for more than twelve days his letters to his mistress were intercepted and withheld from her. Even Sadler, her keeper at Wingfield, was annoyed at such disregard to ordinary civility, and he remonstrated with Walsingham, who thus excused himself :—"The not sending of Nau's despatches proceeded only of the negligence of my man, who forgot to send them with mine."[3] Nau had returned home by 29th December 1584.

They swore "Que jamais ilz n'ont congneu ny sceu que la royne d'Ecose aye eu aulcuns enfans depuis son arrivee en ce royaulme."— R. O. Scot., Mary, xiv. 111.

[2] Ibid. xiv. 46-63.　　　　　[3] Ibid. xiv. 81.

No benefit whatever resulted to the queen from these lengthened negotiations. She was removed from Wing-field to Tutbury during the depth of winter, and the harsh Puritan, Sir Amias Paulet, was appointed as her keeper.

The vigilance with which the royal household was guarded, and the severity with which their confinement was enforced, exceedingly stringent even from the first, was increased on the arrival of this new jailer. In an early letter he already finds it necessary to vindicate himself to Walsingham for undue rigour in the discharge of his office.[1] The walks of the inmates were limited within a narrow circle round the house ; even then they could have fresh air only for a brief time during the course of the day, and never without the presence of a keeper. None were suffered to go forth save in the company of some gentleman, or two soldiers.[2] For the

[1] R. O. Scot., Mary, xv. 74.

[2] Ibid. xiv. 103; Sadler's Memoirs, ii. 361. In May 1573, Shrewsbury's son, speaking of a conversation with a friend about Queen Mary, thus writes to his father :—"I told him what heed and care you had to her safe keeping, especially being there that good numbers of men, continually armed, watched her day and night, and both under her windows, over her chamber, and of every side of her, so that unless she could transform herself to a flea or a mouse, it was impossible that she should escape." Lodge, Illust. ii. 19, ed. 1838. And Shrewsbury himself, whose rule was gentle as compared with that of Paulet, thus expresses himself in answer to some questions addressed to him by Cecil. (Cott. MS. Cal. C. iii. fol. 208.) . . . " Truly I would be very loth that any liberty or exercise should be granted unto her, or any of hers, out of these gates, for fear of many dangers needless to be remembered unto you. I do suffer her to walk upon the leads here in open air, in my large dining chamber, and also in this court-yard, so as both I myself or my wife be always in her company, for avoiding all others talk either to herself or any of hers: And sure watch is kept within and without the walls, both night and day, and shall so continue, God willing, so long as I shall have the charge. . . ." Sheffield, 12th Dec. 1571.

women of the party there was the unfailing resource of
the needle, an occupation of which they never grew
weary ; and Mary has left behind her numerous proofs
of the skill and industry with which she exercised the
various arts of the sempstress.   She found amusement
in trying to rear turtle doves and Barbary fowls, and she
kept small birds in cages.   She asked to have two couple
of little dogs sent to her, " for," said she, " besides knit-
ting and sewing, my only pleasure is in getting all the
little beasts I can find."[1]   Upon another occasion she
begged to be furnished with the patterns of dresses such
as then were worn at Court, and cuttings of the choicest
silk and cloth of gold and silver.[2]   Even with such
pastimes as these the hours must have hung heavily
upon the hands of the imprisoned household ; it must
have been dull for the women, but for the men it must
have been almost unsupportable.

Thus pent up within four walls, nothing could be more
natural than that the queen and her little circle of attendants should find a pleasant occupation in the telling of
stories, real or fictitious.   History always possessed a
great attraction for Mary Stuart.   When she was a girl
her favourite author was Plutarch.[3]   There still exists
the fragment of an essay on adversity, written by her,
which " exhibits, in a remarkable degree, her strong religious convictions, and her extensive acquaintance with
history, both sacred and profane."[4]   What more probable
than that Mary and her friends should here find some
occupation to alleviate the weariness of the prison-house?
What more natural than that, as they gathered round

---

[1] Lab. iv. 183.   [2] Ibid. vi. 187.
[3] This author is very frequently quoted by her in her autograph
book of Themes, printed from the Paris MS., 8860.
[4] Hosack's Queen Mary, ii. 611.

the fire in the winter, or sat together in the summer
twilight, the Marys should ask their queen to tell them
some of the incidents of her early life ? What histories
could be more exciting than those which she had to
recount of the splendours of Paris and Fontainebleau, or
the terrors of Amboise, Holyrood, and Lochleven ? In
contrast with these it would be with a thankful heart
that she would recall the holy calm in which she had
spent the days of her early childhood and first widowhood at Rheims, a peaceful and happy home in which
she would gladly have passed the remainder of her existence. And next, we can imagine, that without any violation of respectful propriety, the little circle of questioning friends might turn the conversation so as to introduce
Moray and Lethington, Lindsay and Morton, Riccio,
Darnley, and Bothwell. Is it too violent a supposition
to imagine that her secretary, moved by the narration of
incidents at once so touching and so terrible, incidents
too in which she who was speaking had faced the chiefest
danger and endured the longest suffering, that he should
endeavour to give a permanent existence to the outline of
the history which she even then was telling them, and
while she was yet speaking that he should attempt to
reduce her words to writing ? That, at his earliest
leisure, he should bestow upon his unfinished draft the
revision, the correction, the expansion which he was conscious it needed ? That where he doubted he would ask
for information from the authority most capable of giving
it ? I see no difficulty in believing that some such mental relaxation as this would suggest itself to the imprisoned household, and that it would be gladly accepted
by them. The difficulty rather would lie in deciding
that such an obvious means of rational amusement
should not have presented itself, and should not have

c

been welcomed. Here, then, is the probable origin of the history of Queen Mary as designed by Nau, the faint outline of what he intended should in due time become the finished portraiture of his royal mistress. But he was not permitted to look upon its completion. The work at Chartley was rudely interrupted; and a few mutilated fragments are all that at present remain to us of Nau's *Memoirs of the History of Queen Mary.*

Such, then, was the author of this narrative; such apparently were the circumstances under which it was written, and such the claims which it has upon our attention. It is the production of a man who occupied a position of trust and honour in Mary's household, and who lived with her for eleven years beneath the same roof. And one step further,—my next assertion is that the manuscript copy of these biographical notes respecting Mary Stuart which we are now considering, is in the handwriting of Claude Nau.

This section of the enquiry will not detain us long, for the assertion which I have advanced rests upon evidence at once abundant and conclusive. The scribe, whoever he may have been, who wrote the Memoirs preserved in the Cottonian volume, has left behind him a mass of writing sufficiently large to afford ample material on which to speculate. Every handwriting has its own peculiarities which distinguish it from others; individualisms, which are easily recognised whenever and wherever it may happen to turn up. So it is with the Cottonian fragment. The style of the handwriting is marked. Certain letters, and certain combinations of letters, which occur in it over and over again, carry with them their proofs of ownership, with which we soon become familiar, and which we should detect at a glance even should we happen to meet them elsewhere, and under unexpected circumstances. Do we ever happen to meet with them elsewhere? Yes, frequently, and always in connection with the affairs of the Scottish Queen. The scribe who penned these Memoirs was assuredly in Mary's service during her imprisonment in England, and was employed by her in matters of the most confidential nature. His was the hand that penned the letters which she addressed to popes, cardinals, bishops, and her own confessor; to the queens of England and France, and the kings of France and Spain; to Cecil, Walsingham, and Leicester; to the English privy council; to her own ambassador in Paris, and the French and Spanish ambassadors in London, and which finally executed the draft of her last will, which she herself corrected with her own pen. Of these several statements it is unnecessary to give the proofs which might easily be cited from the original manuscripts in the British Museum and the General Record Office. A demonstration at once simpler and easier is at hand. The reader is invited to settle the question for himself. Let him compare together the two photographs with which he is here provided for the purpose of comparison.[1] One is a page of the Memoirs, the other is taken from the draft of a letter, the authorship of which is settled by the signature of Nau himself. Their identity is established at a glance. If further proof be required it can be produced. The two fragments which remain to us, that, namely, in the Public Record Office and one of those in the British Museum, each bears a certificate to the effect that it is in the handwriting of Nau. This fact is vouched for by Phillipps, the expert,[2] to whose examination Elizabeth caused to be submitted all the papers which had been seized at Chartley.

It becomes important to work out with some detail

---

[1] See the facsimiles.   [2] See R. O., xxi. 46.

this part of the inquiry, since the history of the seizure of the papers enables us to trace the successive steps in the process by which Nau's volume passed out of his own keeping into that of Sir Robert Cotton, the founder of the priceless library which bears his name, and of which it still forms a part. To do this we must return to Mary and her keeper, Sir Amias Paulet.

We have seen that the behaviour of Sir Amias towards the Scottish Queen was generally harsh and uncourteous; he disliked her, and it pleased him to show his dislike. His rule over her household was strict even to severity. All suffered from it; all pined for fresh air and exercise, for freedom and sunshine, but they were made to feel that they were prisoners in the hand of the enemy. Great was their surprise then when Sir Amias proposed to the queen that she and her whole household, male and female, should enjoy a day's sport by hunting the stag in the neighbouring forest.[1]

The invitation, of course, was gratefully accepted. Mary longed, with the yearning of the prisoner, for the exercise of which she had so long been deprived,[2] and

[1] This account of the seizure of Nau and of the change of Mary's residence is founded upon the journal of M. Bourgoing, who witnessed the incidents which he has described. It has been printed by M. Chantelauze.

[2] That Mary should be deprived of fresh air and exercise was of no moment to her custodiers, and her health suffered by the loss for eighteen years. Yet when Sadler was detained at Wingfield Castle, where he could have no exercise on foot or horse, and was compelled to keep within doors for a few days, contrary to his usage and pleasure, he was not a little vexed. See R. O., Queen Mary, xiv. 77. And herein he had Elizabeth's ready sympathy. Walsingham writes thus to Sadler:—" I have acquainted her Majesty with the coldness of that country, and of the foulness thereof by situation, whereby you are debarred of your wonted exercise, which hath been the chief and principal preservation of your health. . . . Her Majesty thereupon groweth to some resolution to take present order for your relief." 28th Oct. 1584. Sadler Papers, ii. 428.

which she knew to be essential to her health. Her young attendants were full of the anticipation of being allowed to enjoy a good gallop over the turf and a blithe dance on the green-sward; and even the more matured members of the household willingly accepted this unexpected invitation. All promised themselves a pleasant holiday, and young and old set out in high spirits. The party consisted of the queen, Paulet and his son, Nau and Curle, the two secretaries, and several others. They had not ridden far before Mary was informed that a special messenger from Elizabeth desired to speak with her in private upon important business. Knowing by the experience of twenty years the probable meaning of such a message, the heart of the prisoner must have prophesied evil tidings. Her worst fears were soon realized. Elizabeth's envoy, Sir Thomas Gorges, informed her that several grave accusations had of late been brought against her, of the truth of which her Majesty had satisfied herself by the evidence of her own senses. Mary therefore, he continued, need not be surprised if certain of her household, who were found to be implicated in this unhappy affair, were prevented from doing further mischief by being at once removed from her service. This was the message with which he had been entrusted by his royal mistress; Sir Amias Paulet would let her know the remainder of the queen's pleasure.

Quick of temper and prompt of action Nau anticipated mischief, for in the unexpected arrival of Gorges and his armed followers, he saw a plot for the murder of his mistress. He must for long have expected some such occurrence. Accordingly he attempted to ride up to her side for her protection, but Sir Thomas Gorges rudely pushed his horse betweeen them, and commanded him to hold back. Nau, though well mounted, was nearly unhorsed

in the confusion. Curle, the other secretary, was treated
with the same violence. For a moment it seemed as if
a skirmish were about to follow, but happily this did not
occur. To have offered any armed resistance would
have been not only useless, but actually dangerous to
the queen's safety. Had a skirmish ensued, a chance
thrust from a sword or the accidental discharge of a
pistol would have freed Elizabeth from many an hour of
anxiety; nor would either she or Paulet have inquired too
curiously whose hand it was that had done the deed in
this chance medley.[1] It was wise, therefore, for Mary's
friends to offer no opposition. Paulet and Gorges had
their own way, and Mary was separated from Nau and
Curle. They could do no further mischief to Elizabeth,
and they might even become serviceable to her. From
that hour Mary never saw them again. Prisoners in the
hands of the English government, they were at once sent
to London in order that they might be examined by the
privy council, and there they remained until the completion of the tragedy at Fotheringhay.

[1] In 1572, Shrewsbury, writing to Queen Elizabeth about Queen
Mary, then in his custody, thus expresses himself : — "I have her
sure enough, and shall keep her forthcoming, at your Majesty's command, either quick or dead, whatsoever she, or any for her, invent to
the contrary. And as I have no doubt at all of her stealing away
from me, so if any forcible attempt be given for her, the greatest peril
is sure to be hers."—Lodge's Illust. ii. 13. Twelve years afterwards
the same determination existed. Writing to Burghley on 5th July
1585, Paulet thus expresses himself. "Touching the safety and
forthcoming of this queen's person I will never ask pardon if she depart out of my hands. . . . If I shall be assaulted with force at
home or abroad, as I will not be beholden to traitors for my life
(whereof I make little account in respect of my allegiance to the
queen, my sovereign), so I will be assured, by the grace of God, that
she shall die before me." See the original letter in Harl. MS., 6993,
fol. 94.

After this interruption of their sport, the queen and her party set out on their way back to Chartley. So at least they thought, but they were mistaken. Too much excited to notice very closely the road they were going, they concluded that all was right. They saw Paulet and their keepers a little way in advance of them, and they naturally followed. Presently, however, they began to doubt; and Paulet, having been questioned on the subject, frankly admitted that he was now conducting Mary to a new place of residence.

Mary dismounted, and seating herself on the ground, declared that she would not advance one step further in that direction. Paulet attempted to persuade her, but in vain. He argued that she was losing her time and wasting her strength; that sooner or later she would be driven to yield to his wishes; that the house now provided for her was superior to that which she had left; and that Elizabeth and he were acting in the spirit of true kindness. Mary was unmoved. At last he gave her to understand that if she drove him to it he was prepared to resort to violence, and that go she should; if not willingly, then by force. At last she yielded to the arguments and entreaties of her people; and her own discretion told her at the same time that further resistance was undignified, and must be useless. As if at once to warrant his own conduct, and to apologise for it, Sir Amias now produced his instructions. They were signed by Elizabeth herself; they authorised the imprisonment of Mary's two secretaries, and the removal of herself from Chartley to some place of surer custody.

The house now selected for her confinement was Tixall, the residence of Sir Walter Aston. It stood at no great distance from Chartley, to which, in every respect, it was inferior. On her arrival she found that only the scantiest preparations had been made for her reception; that no change of clothing, not even the most necessary articles for daily use, had been provided; and she discovered at the first glance that in such quarters she would be exposed to the most annoying inconveniences. Ill, wearied, and agitated as she was, she asked for pen and paper, in order that she might make known to Elizabeth the many indignities to which she was being subjected. Paulet declared that she should not send from the house any communication of any kind whatever; and when she begged that he would come to her, or permit her to wait upon him, he returned for reply that he would do neither the one nor the other.

In the meantime, Elizabeth's agents were not idle at Chartley, from which Mary had been thus cunningly removed. On their arrival they secured such of her servants as had remained behind their mistress, and locked them up in separate rooms, so that they could not hold any communication with each other. They then searched every chest, drawer, desk, and closet which might be supposed to contain letters, papers, or other objects of importance. The investigation was afterwards renewed more carefully and thoroughly. Four justices of the peace were occupied in it for two long days, at the end of which three boxes, filled with documents, consisting chiefly of Mary's most private correspondence, were sent off to Windsor for the inspection of the English queen and her privy council.[1]

[1] On Oct. 7, 1586, Esneval gives the following account of the queen's treatment in a letter which he sends to Courcelles. Sir Amias Paulet, he says, invited her Majesty to go a-hunting. When she and all her attendants were on the way, along with Nau and Curle, her secretaries, she was met by the elder Gorges, who gave her to understand that he had it in charge from the Queen of England to conduct her to Tixall, a house about three miles distant from Chartley, which

This crowning calamity might apparently have been avoided, for the possibility of such an occurrence had long been foreseen. Knowing the character of the persons with whom she had to deal, Nau had more than once warned his mistress to be careful as to the safety of her papers, but he did not succeed in persuading her of the danger to which she was exposing herself. Not very long before this disaster, as many as twenty-one or twenty-two packets of letters, which had long lingered upon the road, reached her on the same day. All of them referred to matters of the highest political importance. At that time her prospects of escape had grown brighter, and she believed that the hour of her deliverance was near at hand. She even discussed with Nau what should be done with this bulky mass of compro-

---

belongs to Sir Edward Aston. He would also seize Nau and Curle. This treatment made her Majesty so angry that she spoke violently to him, and abused his mistress. She also wished that her people should act on the defensive. But as the party led by Gorges was the stronger, he carried off the secretaries, while Paulet conducted her to the place appointed. In the meantime a secretary of the council, named Wade, was busy at Chartley searching all the queen's papers, which he seized and carried off along with the prisoners, boasting that they were of the utmost secrecy and importance. Whether this be true, or whether it be an artifice (for they abound in such tricks), I cannot say. Master (*blank*) has just now told me that her will has been found, by which she gives England and Scotland to the King of Spain, which, as you will perceive, is for the purpose of exciting the King of Scotland against her. M. de Châteauneuf sent his secretary with a letter to Cecil, in which he reminded him that Nau and Curle were officially employed in the service of the French king, of which he cautioned Elizabeth and her council. Cecil said nothing, but handed the letter to Walsingham, who remarked that the Queen of Scotland was a very bad woman, that the secretaries were very wicked men, and that his sovereign would deal with them according to justice. The ambassador was not diverted from his purpose. R. O. Scot., Eliz., xli. 30.

mising paper when the moment for their escape should arrive. He advised that it should be destroyed without further delay. Mary thought otherwise, but her secretary seems to have had the best of the argument. "If," said he, "you escape, you must do one of two things. Either you must take these letters away with you, or you must leave them behind you. You cannot promise to yourself that, in the danger and excitement of the moment of your flight, you can do the former, or that your friends can do it for you. To leave them behind would be most imprudent. It would sacrifice the lives and estates of those who have put both in jeopardy in your cause; and it would reveal many plans and devices, past, present, and future, which should assuredly be kept secret. And if these letters happen in the meantime to be seized by our keeper, then Curle, Pasquier, and I will certainly be hanged."

Still Mary was not convinced. She could not bring herself to believe, she said, that her good cousin would condescend to meddle with her private letters, nor would she subject her to the indignity of causing her papers to be examined by others. Besides, she thought that she was sure of having such ample warning of the approach of danger as would give her time to remove, or secrete, or if necessary to destroy the fatal documents. We have seen that she was no match for Cecil and Walsingham, and that Paulet's device for the day's merry-making placed her letters and her life in the hands of her enemies.

When Elizabeth's personal curiosity had been satisfied, and this large mass of correspondence had been transferred to her privy council, the whole was subjected to a careful examination. The ciphered documents, of which the number was very considerable, was entrusted to one

of Walsingham's agents, named Phillipps, who supplied
his employers with what professed to be copies of such
as they needed, and these he had written out in ordinary
characters. The law officers then selected such documents as would be most useful in carrying out Elizabeth's
cherished plan for the trial and condemnation of her
rival. Through what hands these papers passed, to what
treatment they were subjected before they were produced
in court, it would now be impossible to affirm. It is not
easy in our day to discriminate between the genuine, on
the one hand, or those which have been interpolated, or
falsified, or forged, on the other. But this we know—
the evidence upon which Mary was condemned was derived from papers which were said to have been found
in her own custody.

After the more important legal documents had been
culled out by the law officers of the Crown, the remainder
underwent many vicissitudes. Cecil selected from the
mass of papers such as pleased his taste or gratified his
curiosity, and he deposited them in his own private
library in Hatfield House, where they still remain. Very
many were sent to the State Paper Office, and were in-
corporated with the Public Records of the United Kingdom. Some remained with Phillipps, and were disposed
of by him to Sir Robert Cotton.[1] Others, which appeared to be of no immediate interest or curiosity, were
for the time disregarded, and after passing from hand to
hand were ultimately absorbed in the collections of successive antiquarians. Besides these, a large number must
have been destroyed, either by design or accident.

[1] As late as 1621, Phillipps, then an old man, was in correspondence
with Sir Robert Cotton (see Harl. MS., 7000, fol. 64), who certainly
obtained from him some papers connected with Scotland. A note in
Cotton's hand in Cal. C. ix., fol. 32, describes this as "one of the
bundles I bought from Mr Phillipps."

This, then, is the early history of that collection of papers of which Nau's Memoirs of Queen Mary originally formed a portion. We can trace the volume from Chartley, where it was written, into the possession of Sir Robert Cotton, in whose library it still remains. It is somewhat remarkable that the exceptional importance of these papers, although they must have been inspected by hundreds of intelligent and inquisitive eyes, has never been recognised; and that it is only now, after the neglect of three centuries, that the evidence which they reveal has been permitted to obtain a public hearing. The reasons for this neglect are not far to seek. Nau could write a very beautiful and legible hand when he pleased, of which we have many specimens in the British Museum and the Record Office; yet when he was hurried his hand degenerates into a scrawl, which at times becomes almost impossible to decipher. Writing, as we believe he did when he penned these Memoirs, in the hope of keeping pace with the dictation of one who was speaking rapidly and under the excitement of the moment, we need not wonder that the penmanship should be no better than it is. The attempts subsequently made by Nau to correct the errors of his first rough draft too often increase the ultimate difficulty. Interlineations, cancels, and additions follow; the original construction of the sentence is lost, and the result is distraction and confusion. With such a page before him, we can scarce wonder that the student who inspected it should abandon the attempt to master its meaning, and should comfort himself with the thought that his time and eyesight might be elsewhere employed to greater advantage.

There is yet another reason not without its weight, which may help to explain the obscurity in which these Memoirs have been allowed to slumber on the shelves of our great national library. In the catalogue of the Cottonian Manuscripts the volume is entered under the uninviting title to which reference has already been made at the beginning of the present Introduction. There was little inducement to linger over a collection of papers, of which both the beginning and end are wanting, and the subject-matter of which is spoken of so slightingly by the principal librarian of the British Museum.

It has already been stated that Queen Mary's private correspondence was carried off from Chartley to London; and that, by virtue of a warrant from Elizabeth, it was accompanied thither by Nau and Curle. In themselves the papers were exceedingly valuable, but they might be made to become more precious still if interpreted by the help of her secretaries. Their assistance would be of the highest service in the preparation of the evidence which was now at last about to be produced in court against the great criminal. Nau and Curle knew the history of each single paper; they could explain every covert allusion; they could decipher every scrap of secret writing; they could interpret the many mysterious passages which, without the aid of such experts as her secretaries, would be unintelligible. All this they could do; but would they do it? Probably they would refuse at the first, but Elizabeth could employ many potent arguments when she pleased. She was bent upon the conviction of Mary, and the rackmaster,[1] the scavenger's daughter, and the

[1] We revolt from the thought of extorting evidence by the employment of the rack, but not so Cecil and Elizabeth. With his own hand the former drew up, and with her own hand the latter signed, a warrant authorising her commissioners to cause two of Norfolk's men, at that time in the Tower of London, " to be put to the rack and to taste thereof until they shall deal more plainly" in giving evidence against their master.—Cal. C. iii. fol. 229. Another document, also written entirely by Cecil, on the same subject, occurs in the same volume, folio 239.

hangman were at her call, and would help her to attain
her object.

Of Curle we have little to say; he does not fall within
the scope of our present enquiry.[1] Of Nau's behaviour
during his imprisonment, the details which have come
down to us are more abundant and more minute than
might have been expected; but the conclusions to which
they lead are not so decidedly in his favour as could
have been wished. The following particulars have
reached us as to the manner in which he is said to have
passed through the period of danger and trial which
intervened between his own seizure and the execution
of his mistress.

All direct correspondence between Nau and the household at Chartley was cut off from the moment of his
arrest. If any attempt was made on either side to
exchange letters it failed, and Mary's isolation from the
outer world was now complete. It was supposed for
some time that Nau had been put to death, a conjecture
which was by no means improbable.[2] Presently came
tidings that he was in safety, well treated and comfort-
ably housed with Walsingham's family; and that he had
bought these privileges by giving important information
against his mistress. Walsingham took good care that
the alleged treachery of her secretary should reach Mary's
ears, and he doubtlessly expected that it would produce

[1] While Curle was in custody, Walsingham placed before him
certain documents in cipher, of which he furnished copies in the ordinary character. See R. O. Mary, xvii. 7, 55, 56; xviii. 6.

[2] Phillipps, the decipherer, writing to Walsingham on July 19, 1586,
hopes that the queen will hang Nau and Curle. R. O. Mary,
xviii. 61. Writing to Courcelles, 15th Sept. 1586, Châteauneuf says
that Nau, Curle, and Pasquier are in prison, and in very great danger
of their lives. He had spoken to the queen on their behalf, but she
had shown herself "fort rigoreuse." R. O. Scot., Eliz., xli. 30.

a marked effect upon her future conduct. If, through
Nau's cowardice and treachery, the English law officers
had penetrated the mysteries of her correspondence with
the Pope and the King of Spain, with Morgan and Paget,
with Babington and " the six gentlemen who were to do
the deed," then Mary's position was indeed desperate.
In the face of such overpowering evidence, any further
denial of her guilt would only make her position yet
more dangerous. Would it not be wiser and safer for
her at once to admit her treason? to humble herself
before the woman whom she was said to have plotted to
dethrone and murder? to appeal to her cousin's known
generosity and tender heart, and sue for pardon? Possibly Walsingham thought that Mary might be driven to
do this through fear of Nau's revelations. Had she been
the criminal that Cecil and Walsingham wished to prove
her to be, this possibly might have been her line of action.
But she was unmoved, because she knew her papers
could make no such revelations; and no confession of
guilt, no cry for mercy came from the prison-house of
Chartley.

As time went on, so evil reports against Nau gained
ground. He still continued to reside in Walsingham's
family, where, as it was said, he was contented and
happy, despite the direct accusations which were brought
against him. The charge comes in its simplest form in
a statement to the effect that he and Curle had been
bribed with seven thousand pounds to betray their
mistress,[1] but the accuser is anonymous. Within a

[1] A paper, printed by F. Morris from one of the Stonyhurst manuscripts, states that proof of the bribe of seven thousand pounds having
been paid by Walsingham to Nau and Curle to betray their mistress
" was found in a bill in his study after his decease, as hath been
credibly reported." Sir A. Paulet, p. 387. The value of this evidence
is much weakened by finding Curle included in the accusation.

month previous to Mary's execution, the secretary of the French Legation in London, one Chérelles,[1] writes about him in these terms :—" M. Nau continues in good health and spirits, an inmate in Walsingham's house. I fear, however, that in the end he will pay dearly for his board and lodging. I suspect he is being cheated. This good treatment which he is receiving troubles me, and makes me uncomfortable. It would be far better for him if he had worse fare and more liberty." The impression continued to gain ground until it was very generally accepted, even among Mary's adherents. It was reported at Chartley that during all this time of his stay in London, Nau was employed in selecting and preparing the documentary evidence which was to be produced against his mistress at her so-called trial. Such seems to have been her own conviction, and if she believed it to be true, we cannot wonder that she felt it keenly. When it came to the last, and she was told that she was to be executed upon the following day, she enquired whether Nau was still alive, and on being informed that such was the case, she exclaimed with unusual vehemence, "What! shall I be put to death and Nau escape? Nau is the cause of my death. I suffer in order that he may go scatheless."[2] So strong was this impression on her mind that she recorded it in her last will. As originally drawn she had been liberal to her two secretaries,[3] but the payment of these bequests was now made contingent upon the proof of their fidelity and the re-establishment of their character from

---

[1] But Chérelles betrayed his trust to his master and his country, and was a spy and traitor in the pay of Walsingham, to whom he sent copies of her letters, several of which in his handwriting are still extant. See the Letter Books of Sir A. Paulet, by F. Morris, pp. 85, 86.

[2] La morte de la royne d'Escosse, in Jebb, ii. 621.

[3] Lab. iv. 537.

the charges which had been brought against them.[1] Nau had sent certain papers to her from London in proof of their falsity; these she now forwarded to the Duke of Guise, with the request that he would examine into the question to which they related. We shall presently see with what result.[2] Mary's last hours, therefore, were embittered by the thought that Nau, and Curle, and Pasquier had each and all deserted her, and by their treachery had helped on her condemnation.[3]

Nau's conduct after Mary's death was calculated to strengthen these suspicions. He did not visit his old friends during their protracted and enforced residence at Fotheringhay, not even upon the occasion of the funeral of their mistress at Peterborough. Long before the other members of her household were permitted to return to their respective homes, a passport from the English Government enabled him to reach France, not only in safety, but with comfort. Evil reports had preceded him, and worse reports followed him. It was stated that when he was taken prisoner at Chartley twenty thousand livres, all in hard cash, were found in

---

[1] Jebb, ii. 631.

[2] See La Mort de la royne d'Escosse, in Jebb, ii. 661. This treatise, printed in 1589, was written, as is stated by the author, from information derived chiefly from the servants of the late queen. Its hostility to Nau is very decided, see pp. 660, 661.

[3] Before Nau left England he drew up a paper, which he forwarded to one Mr Proby, in which, after referring to the importance of the calumnies and impostures which had been put into circulation against him by some of the servants of his late mistress, which also affected the honour of two of Elizabeth's chief secretaries, he requests that he may have the opportunity of clearing up the whole matter with his accusers before they cross over into France, and that they may have access to him for this purpose. This paper is in Nau's hand. See R. O. Mary, xxi. 22.

his wardrobe,[1] together with thirty costly mantles, each fitted for the wear of a nobleman.[2] He crossed over into France in a little boat of his own, taking with him ten thousand livres; and during the passage he was heard to lament the cruel necessity of having been compelled to leave behind him as much more in England. His property in France amounted to one hundred thousand livres. And these large sums he had contrived to amass, said his accusers, within the space of twelve years.[3]

[1] Nau seems to have acted as banker for the other members of the royal household, and at the time of his arrest had in his custody certain sums of money belonging to Mrs Beauregard and Mary's surgeon. See R. O., Mary, xxi. 30, 39. Hence, perhaps, an explanation of the above charge.

[2] On the 2d of December 1586, Nau sent to Walsingham a list of certain articles which he says he wanted "for his necessities." It is too long to be given entire, but the following extracts lead to the conclusion that at this time Nau felt pretty easy in his mind as to his own safety. He asked for six shirts, a dozen new handkerchiefs, a dozen collars with cuffs to match, half a dozen collars with six pairs of cuffs, a dozen pair of socks, a dozen large handkerchiefs, half a dozen new nightcaps, a jacket with wrought sleeves of velvet, a long mantle of black taffeta, furred throughout, a small mantle without sleeves, a long mantle of black cloth, a pourpoint of black satin, two pair of boots, two pair of shoes, four yards of black cloth, one hat of taffeta, one hat of black beaver, six pair of gloves, a silver cup and cover, a cup of silver, a book in Italian called "Dieci Veglie," two volumes of the Lives of Plutarch, in Italian, the smaller works of Plutarch, a book in English, "Of resolution of Lyffe," and a Breviary (R. O., Mary of Scots, xx. 36).

It should not be forgotten, however, that during this stay in London, Nau was paying his addresses to Elizabeth Pierrepoint, who had formerly been one of Queen Mary's attendants. See R. O. Mary, xv. 71; xviii. 7, 9; xxi. 17.

[3] These details are gathered from the charges against Nau contained in La Mort de la royne d'Escosse, in Jebb, ii. 661. How far these charges were true I do not take upon me to decide. In order that the reader may do this for himself, I have added to this chapter a translation of the more important passages of the treatise in which they occur. See Note the Third, p. lxii.

Nau did not submit to these accusations in silence, but proceeded to vindicate his character with the quiet resolution of a man conscious of his innocence. On his arrival in Paris, he presented himself, in the first instance, before his sovereign, and next before the princes of the family of Guise. He produced various letters and other papers in proof of the fidelity and honour of his conduct; and he begged that the charges which had been brought against him should be investigated. After a careful enquiry the Duke of Guise declared his conviction that Nau had been falsely accused, and he embodied his decision in a judicial document which is now before me. It states that the duke had carefully investigated the history of these recent transactions in England, and had inspected the many proofs which Nau had produced in evidence of his integrity. One of these was from Queen Mary, another from M. de l'Aubespine, the French ambassador at the Court of London. The duke expresses "his entire satisfaction" at the secretary's conduct, and his belief that these garboils had been brought about by English trickery. The accused, whom he had known from his youth, had always borne an excellent character, and had been well affectioned towards the house of Lorraine, in which he had been educated. "Therefore," continues his Grace, "let Nau have his salary, his pensions, and all his other rights as counsellor and secretary to Queen Mary. Let him also have all the moveable property which he can verify as his own, and which, at this present time, is in the hands of other persons, her late Majesty's servants. Especially let him have certain rings and other articles of gold which he had placed in her cabinet for greater safety at a time when she thought she was about to escape, and which these servants affirm to have been divided among them

by their late mistress, possibly in the belief that Nau
had been put to death by the English. In such case,
however, he must give an equivalent." At the same
time that the duke executed this legal document he
wrote to the Archbishop of Glasgow, Mary's ambassador
in Paris, highly commending the long and valuable
services of the secretary.[1]

It appears, then, from these instruments, that however
much Nau's integrity may have been questioned in
England, however open to suspicion may have been the
line of conduct which he was pleased or compelled there
to adopt, it was officially declared in France that his
character was unsullied. He there stood in the position
of a man who had been grossly calumniated, and whose
reputation had been restored to him by competent
authority after sufficient investigation.

Here at this point it might naturally be supposed
that our interest in Mary's secretary should cease, and
that we might leave him in the quiet possession of the
wealth and the honours which are said to have attended
him in his own country. To our surprise, however, Nau
appears among us once more, and at so late a period as
the year 1605.[2] In that year he addressed a memorial
to King James the First, in which he once more vindi-
cates his character from the charges which had been
brought against him nearly twenty years previously.
A copy of the paper which he presented, or was prepared to present, to the son of his late mistress is still

[1] A copy of this paper, authenticated by Nau, is preserved in MS.
Cott. Cal., D. i., fol. 89, *b*. Both of these documents are dated 15th
Oct. 1587, at the camp at Joigny.

[2] Before setting out from Paris he drew up and signed a certificate,
dated 2d March 1605, that the copies to which he refers had been
accurately copied, word for word, from the original documents. See
Cott. MS. Cal., E. v. 233:

extant, and from it we gather a few additional particulars respecting his former doings in England. We do not forget, however, while reading it, that however plausible, Nau is here telling his own story in his own vindication; nor ought we to forget, in justice to him, that the facts which he brought forward at this time were not disproved, and still remain uncontradicted.

Nau asserts that when he was brought up before the English privy council, and questioned as to certain facts tending to incriminate Queen Mary, he refused to admit the jurisdiction of the court, and demanded that if he had offended he should be put upon his trial before his own sovereign. This having been overruled, he stated that, in regard to the charges on which Mary was accused, she had incurred no guilt because she possessed no freedom of action. Ballard's plot was known to her only by letters written by Ballard himself, and as usual addressed to Curle. These letters did not speak of the design as something on which Mary was asked to deliberate, or decide, or approve. There was no room for deliberation—that period had already passed; Mary could neither approve nor disapprove; the time for action was at hand, and she could not stop it. The attempt about to be made on her behalf had already been agreed upon by Spain and the Netherlands, and by certain friends in France, all of whom were on the move. Everything, therefore, had been decided long before Mary, or any one near her, had heard one word upon the subject.

When at last Nau was compelled to plead, he disputed, he says, every inch of the ground. Upon one occasion he went so far in his obstinacy as to deny his own handwriting, which appeared in the draft of a letter given by him to Curle that he might translate it into English. Curle had imprudently left this draft in the

queen's cabinet, where it was found. When Nau denied
that this writing was his, Walsingham, who knew better,
became furious. He crossed over to that part of the
room where Nau was standing, insulted him grievously,
and shook his fist in his face more than once. The late
Lord Treasurer Cecil then interposed, and gently rebuked Walsingham for his violence.

Continuing his self-vindication, Nau next states that
he made no admission whatever upon any point which
could be prejudicial to the queen. He admitted nothing
which had not previously been proved by independent
evidence.[1] In his last appearance before the court he
impugned the justice and the legality of the sentence
which had been pronounced against her. Again Walsingham broke out into a tempest of fury, became
abusive, charged him with speaking against his conscience, and read certain confessions and depositions
made by criminals recently executed, and also of some
of Mary's servants, hoping thereby to make Nau retract

---

[1] In confirmation of what he here states, Nau might cite the evidence of Cecil himself, who, in a letter to Walsingham, entirely in his
own hand, writes thus :—" Nau offered on Tuesday to have opened
much ; and instead thereof he hath only written to have a pardon, as
yesterday, because it was the queen's birthday. I do send to Mr
Mills to challenge him, and to warn him to be sent to the Tower, if
he do not otherwise acquit himself of his promise. I think Curl will
be more open ; and yet Nau hath only confessed by his handwriting
to have written by the queen's inditing and by her own minute the
long letter to Babington ; but he would qualify his mistress' fault in
that Babington provoked her thereto, and that Morgan provoked her
to renew her intelligence with Babington." Dated 8th Sept. 1586,
in Calig., C. ix. 320. Francis Mills was the person who had Nau
and Curl in his custody. See R. O. Mary, xix. 54.

To this it may be added, that when Nau did make a long declaration of the proceedings of his mistress (which he did on Sept. 10),
Cecil was disappointed as to the nature of its contents, and described
it as a " long declaration of things of no importance sent privately to
her Majesty." R. O. Mary, xix. 98, Lab. vii. 196.

what he had shortly before asserted. But so far from
doing this, Nau repeated his arguments, and cited Walsingham to appear before the tribunal of God, there to
answer such calumnies and falsehoods as these were.
He requested that his protest might be engrossed in the
acts of the privy council, and frequently reminded the
registrar that he had done so, but with what result is
uncertain.

The last will of his mistress might be cited against
him, he said, and it might be urged that she had doubted
his fidelity to the last. Yes, she had doubted, because
she had been beguiled and misled; yet she had never
ventured to assert his guilt absolutely. She suspended
her judgment until the question should be cleared, a day
which she had not lived to witness. Had she believed
him guilty, actually and positively, she would have said
so; and such was her nobleness of character, that before
her death she probably would have sent him her forgiveness. But, in truth, she was cheated into these unhappy
doubts by the crafts of Walsingham, seconded herein by
the false reports introduced into her household by the
agents of Queen Elizabeth. One of her servants yet
alive may recall to mind how she has spoken of their
mistress in the presence of others at dinner and supper,
calling Mary "traitor and double traitor," and how she
repeated scandalous stories about her familiarities with
Sir Amias Paulet.

The idea, Nau proceeds, that he had been bribed by
Elizabeth is utterly without foundation. He protests,
upon his share in paradise, that the only thing which
she ever gave him was a little portrait of herself, framed
in ebony, worth about ten crowns, after he had resided at
her court for some months. On his return he gave it to
his mistress. As to Mary, he cannot charge her with
want of liberality; but perhaps it might be found that

in the end she owed more to him than he did to her.
He can say with truth that during the whole of the
eleven years he had the honour of serving her, he never
received so much as a thousand crowns " extraordi-
narily." He did not neglect her interests. Under his
management her finances greatly improved ; she cleared
off more than four hundred thousand livres of old debts ;
she paid all her servants' wages, with scarce any re-
trenchment ; she made handsome gifts to many friends
in England and Scotland ; and at her death she left a
large sum of ready money in her coffers.

From these facts Nau proceeds to deduce certain in-
ferences, which are obvious and reasonable, but upon
which it is unnecessary to enlarge, as having no direct
bearing upon the history of Mary Stuart.

Here, then, we bid adieu to Claude Nau, for at this
point his manuscript ends, as far at least as it is at the
present known to us by the autograph draft in the
British Museum. We part from him with regret—regret
mingled with the feeling that under happier circumstances
we might have profited yet further by the information
which it was in his power to have communicated. If
his Narrative was continued beyond the period at which
the Cottonian manuscript ends, that continuation has
perished, or, at least, its present place of concealment is
unknown. It is difficult to believe that in its original
condition it extended no further than the execution of
the Duke of Norfolk in the year 1572. Many considerations lead to this conclusion. Mary's French secretary
evidently had planned a work, which, when completed,
should embrace the history of the Royal Family of
Scotland, from the death of King James the First until
the latest event in the life of his imprisoned mistress.
As Nau was an inmate of Mary's household until A.D.
1586, we are all but compelled to believe that he carried

on his Narrative as far as that date, and that, consequently, we have to lament the loss of the most authentic portion of his literary labours.   It seems most improbable that, having undertaken a work of which the outline was so distinct and the limits so definite, Nau should have grown tired of it, and have cast it aside unfinished. There was every inducement to persevere.   He had now reached the period at which his history of his own time could be carried on with the least trouble to himself and the greatest advantage to his royal mistress.   He could henceforward explain and vindicate the line of action which she had thought fit to adopt.   He could now speak with the authority of an eye-witness, and his testimony as to matters of fact could not be disputed. Why should we imagine that he should be indifferent to all these considerations ?

But while we are compelled to lament the loss (whether temporary or final is uncertain) of a considerable portion of these precious materials, we are not the less grateful for the recovery of the pages which have come down from his day to ours.   They have a significance which our readers will not be slow to discover and to appreciate. They throw light upon certain moving incidents connected with our national history, which too long have been misinterpreted by ignorance or perverted by prejudice.

Summing up, then, the various branches of the argument respecting the authorship of the present Narrative, I venture to hope that I have shown, in the first place, that certain papers here printed are in the handwriting of Secretary Nau ; and, further, that they were written by him while he resided in the Queen's family, and possibly were corrected by her authority and under her direction.

We are now in a position to enquire into the bearing of this new information upon the history of Scotland in general, and the history of Mary Stuart in particular.

SUPPLEMENTAL NOTES AND ILLUSTRATIONS TO CHAPTER THE FIRST.

NOTE THE FIRST.   (See p. xxii., Note.)

Some of Fontenay's observations made during this mission, and sent by him to Nau, are sufficiently curious to merit preservation.   He makes the following remarks upon the young King of Scotland.[1]

I have been well received by the king, who has treated me better in reality than in appearance.   He gives me much credit, but does not show me much kindness.   Since the day of my arrival he has ordered me to live in his house along with the earls and lords, and that I shall have access to him in his cabinet just as the others have.   On the Saturday after my arrival he directed an esquire to bring me one of his horses, in order that I might accompany him to the hunt, and afterwards gave me an excellent and handsome hackney.   By the letters to the queen [2] you will see that he has promised to do all I have asked him, even as to the points which I had to dispute with the Earl of Arran, yet he takes very little notice of me, that he may avoid suspicion.   Yet, in spite of every precaution, many persons are offended at these frequent conversations.

One thing surprises me much.   The king has never spoken about his mother, neither about her health, nor of her treatment, nor of her servants, nor of her mode of life, nor her food, nor of her recreation, nor anything of the kind.   Yet I know he loves and honours her much in his heart.

To tell you truly what I think of him :—I consider him

[1] From R. O. Scot., Eliz., xiii. 45.

[2] On the same day M. Fontenay wrote to Queen Mary in cipher. The packet was intercepted, and was deciphered by Philippes.   The letter to Nau was a P.S. to that addressed to the queen.

the first prince in the world for his age. He has the three parts of his soul in perfection. He apprehends and conceives quickly, he judges ripely and with reason, and he retains much and for a long time. In questioning he is quick and piercing, and solid in his answers. In any matter which may be under discussion, religious or secular, he always holds and believes that which to him seems to be the truest and most just. For instance, in several disputations about religion I have seen him take the side of M. de Fentray,[1] and defend it boldly against his own party. He is learned in many languages, sciences, and affairs of state, more so probably than any one in his realm.

In a word he has a miraculous wit, and moreover is full of a noble glory and a good opinion of himself. Having been brought up in the midst of constant fears, he is timid, and will not venture to contradict the great lords; yet he wishes to be thought brave. Nothing is too laborious for him to attempt on the side of virtue. Having heard that my Lord Doun had been two days and two nights without sleep, he passed three. If ever he is beaten in any of these laborious exercises, he dislikes them ever afterwards. He hates dancing and music in general, and especially all the mincing affectations of the court, such as love talk, or daintiness in dress, especially earrings.

From want of proper instruction his manners are boorish and very rough, as well in his way of speaking, eating, dress, amusements, and conversation, even in the company of women. He is never at rest in one place, but takes a singular pleasure in walking; but his gait is very ungainly, and his step is wandering and unsteady, even in a room. His voice is thick and very deep as he speaks. He loves hunting better than any other pleasure in the world, and occupies himself in it for at least six hours at a time, going at full speed over mountains and valleys. He is weak of body, but not dainty. But to sum up in one word, he is an old young man, resembling the Sirens of Socrates. I have noted in him three

---

[1] This was Graham of Fintry, an earnest Catholic, who had recently arrived in Scotland with letters from the Duke of Guise to the young king. See R. O. Scot., Eliz., xxxii. 110.

qualities which are assuredly injurious to the stability of his State and Government. He misunderstands the real extent of his poverty and weakness; he boasts too much of himself, and he despises other princes. In the second place, he disregarded the wishes of his subjects; and lastly, he is too idle and careless in business, and too much addicted to his own pleasures, chiefly hunting. He leaves all his affairs to be managed by the Earl of Arran, Montrose, and the Secretary.

I know, continues Fontenay, that these faults are excusable in a youth, but it is to be feared that they will increase with his age. He told me that he really gave greater attention to business than he seemed to do, for he could get through more work in one hour than others could in a day; that he was the true son of his mother in many things, chiefly in that his body was weak, and that he could not attend to business for long at one time. But, said he, when he set to it he could do more than six others; that he could even sit at the desk for six days in succession, but afterwards was sure to be ill. He told me, in short, that he resembled the Spaniards, who make but one gallant charge, and that to continue in it is fatal. These were the exact words he used.

NOTE THE SECOND. (See p. xxviii., Note 1.)

LETTER from Nicolas Errington to Secretary Walsingham, 23d June 1579.[1]

My most humble duty remembered. I have received your honour's letter unto me of the xviijth of May for the conduction of Mr Naw, secretary to the Scottish queen, to the Scottish court; which accordingly I have done with such good regard and diligence as in duty appertaineth, and with no less courtesy than I could show unto him, your honour's instructions always respected. But notwithstanding our coming to the Scots king's court there was none would take knowledge of his coming, which he thought very strange; looking

[1] From the MS. Cott. Cal., C. iii. fol. 539.

rather to have been met with some of quality on the way than so cold a suit.

I was glad at his request to make his way for to have presence with the king, which, with some travel, I did procure the council to send unto him ij gentlemen to demand of his affairs and coming into that country. He answered that he was come from the Scottish queen, his mistress, to visit her son there. It was answered that they knew none such, but if he came to the king with direction from the queen his mother, they thought he should be welcome ; but if he would not acknowledge the king, they were not to deal with him any further.

He did alledge that he used such terms as his mistress did command, thinking that there should have been no difficulty between the mother and the son ; but always he craved his answer, which was promised.

The king and the counsel being advertised of the manner of his direction, sent to him the next day, that if he had no other language to speak than yet they perceived, that the king's pleasure was that he should presently avoid the country ; and to give thanks unto the gentleman that was his conductor that he was not made understand of his fault and presumption to enter the country, not acknowledging a king. He offered, rather than he would depart without having his presence, he would for his particular, acknowledge him king, but that would not take place ; so that taking very unquiet rest for that night, which I obtained, and taking advice of his pillow, requested me to solicit his cause to have presence, offering to acknowledge him king in his mistress her name ; which I did. But in no wise would he be heard, but willed to content himself with his answer, and so returned discontented, without presence of the king, or any of the counsel, or delivering of his tokens.[1]

I perceive that he had ij letters ; the one in French and the other in Italian ; the one directed " to her dear and well-beloved son in Scotland," the other " to her dear and well-beloved son the prince of Scotland." The first he confessed

[1] Tokens, namely, of Mary's affection, of which Nau was the bearer. They consisted chiefly of her own needlework.

to have, but not that [in] which [the] title was prince. There was none of them both seen unto them.

Thus he is returned to Berwick very discontented, and this day takes his journey towards the queen, his mistress, seeming to me that he thinks the queen's majesty my sovereign and all other princes will be offended with their doings in that case.

I must confess that he was careful of his mistress her promise made to the queen's majesty for doing or speaking with any during his abode there, as well there was few or none as did press to speak with him, except some poor men that had been servants, of no value, for such wages and pensions as had not been well paid by her treasurer, and yet in my hearing and sufferance.

Some occurrences of that country I send herewith in Mr Robert Bowes his letters for consideration, which your honour will receive ; humbly craving pardon of your honour for this my boldness and rude hand, referring to your honour's good judgment not this profession to be much used by me. I shall humbly pray to God for your honour's long and good health to continue to His good pleasure with much encrease of honour.

Berwick, this xxiij of June 1579.—Your honour's humbly ever to command,   NICOLAS ARRINGTON.

To the Right Hon. Francis Walsingham, Knight, Chief Secretary to the Queen's Majesty of England.

Orig. hol. with mark of seal in red wax.

NOTE THE THIRD.   (See p. l., Note 3.)

It is important that the reader should have the means of forming his own estimate as to the weight of the charges brought against Nau ; and with this object I subjoin a translation of the chief passages in which they are recorded.

The author of the anonymous work descriptive of the death of Queen Mary from which these extracts have been made tells us that he had left nothing unnoticed, in Scotland, in England, and in France, which might further the object he had in view.

"More especially have I availed myself," says he, "of the help of such persons as could bear witness from their own personal knowledge by having taken part in the whole of the incidents connected with the life, death, and funeral of her Majesty. I have enquired into the details of the reports verbally made by the servants of the late queen to the King of France and the great lords of the realm, herein fulfilling the charge imposed upon them by their mistress." [1]

On the morning of her execution "she charged Elspeth Curle to carry the letters and papers which Nau had sent to her from the prison of London, and to show them [to the Duke of Guise] in order that it might be seen that he was cheating her." [2]

"After her Majesty's burial at Peterborough, her servants, being unable to obtain their passports, were detained more than a fortnight in London, at their great changes, and all that they said and did was pried into by the English. This was done to gratify an imprisoned secretary, who was so far in Walsingham's good graces, that so long as he remained in his house, he received from him all the courtesy and good treatment that one friend could show to another; while at the same time these same persons were heaping every imaginable indignity and cruelty upon his mistress, and at last put her to death. They sent Nau his passport that he might return into France; and having persuaded three of his attendants to accompany him (men who were always at his devotion), he and his friend Pasquier crossed over before the other servants, who were detained in London, and told the King of France whatever tale they pleased. And in order that he might cross over the more easily, and be less closely looked after, he assumed the title of an ambassador. He embarked in a small boat, taking with him ten thousand livres; and when he knew that he was out of danger, he lamented the other ten thousand livres which he had left behind him in England, as some of the persons who crossed over along with him in the boat are reported to have heard. This agrees with what the English said of him, when they examined and inspected his luggage at the time when he was made

[1] Jebb ii. 609 (bis).   [2] Ibid. 631.

prisoner. These persons declared publicly, that within his coffers were twenty thousand livres in hard cash, to say nothing of his jewels, his silver plate and dresses, among which report affirms that he had more than thirty clokes, the meanest of which would not have been unbecoming for any lord in England. He had dresses and other garments of silk in great numbers, strangely rich. At all events, he conveyed into France from twelve to fourteen chests filled with his own property. It is within the scope of the subject to mention that the ready money and the annual rents which he has in France may be fairly reckoned at one hundred thousand livres, of which he became the possessor during the twelve years he was in England."

"As soon as he and his party arrived in France, he told his own tale to the king, in which, I suppose, he was not hard upon the English, from whom he had derived so many advantages. But I cannot understand how he could justify himself without accusing his own mistress, for he was her chief adviser, and he could do anything he pleased upon his own authority, so much so, that if he had taken anything in hand, he could have done it without her Majesty's knowledge, as his own admissions prove. If then the late queen was guilty (which could not be the case) why was not he punished as well as she? There was no reason why he should escape and she be put to death. The only explanation is that he had made his peace with the English. The queen, therefore, was justified in saying that he was the cause of her death."

Passing to the consideration of the charges against Mary, founded upon the papers seized at Chartley, the French author from whom we are quoting proceeds thus :—"It is a fraud to say that her Majesty had them in her custody. If it be true that any such discovery was ever made it was made in the chamber of a secretary, and consisted of nothing more than some memoirs and rough drafts, or the crazy speculations of one of the most presumptuous men in the world, to whom every dream was a reality. All this happened by the fault of his clerk, a young fellow, who kept copies of them for his own instruction and that he might use them afterwards. The English wished for nothing better than this, or possibly were aware of it; and now, thinking that they had a firm footing on which to proceed, they pushed on the matter in such wise that the persons who had written these papers thought it necessary to affirm that they had acted under the orders of their mistress, for unless they had done so they could not have saved themselves. Here we see the reason why her Majesty said that Nau had brought about her death to save his own life."

" Nau's supporters affirm that all that her Majesty said was not true ; that when she spoke in these terms of her secretary she was agitated and transported by anger and impatience. Such people are unworthy of having been in the service of such a mistress. Her words and her behaviour at the time of her death sufficiently declare their falsehood and ill-will,—according to the estimate even of her greatest enemies.

" They also assert that her Majesty dealt more gently with Nau in her own writings than her servants have reported in what they have said. But if we look at the terms of her will where he is mentioned, we shall find her ordering that neither wages nor pensions shall be paid to him, a sufficient indication of what her wishes really were. These, however, she expressed with all possible moderation, for she feared that if she had given vent to her feelings against Nau the English would have prevented the removal of the will, and would have kept it, or destroyed it. Thus her Majesty would have been thwarted in the execution of her last wishes, which she explained verbally and very fully to her attendants, with the request that they should be believed in what they reported about such matters that she did not dare to commit to writing."

After some very severe remarks upon Nau, who is described as being, in the opinion of all the English and Scotch, " the most impatient, the most audacious, and the most presumptuous man in the world," the narrative proceeds thus :—" I hope that God will give him the grace to make amends and confession of his own free will, so that laying his hand upon his heart he will speak the truth as to what he has seen and known ; and thus become the principal means by which this good princess may be liberated, declared innocent, and avenged on all these wicked and lying heretics. Now that he has escaped from the danger of his former position, let him confess that he has been surprised, circumvented, deceived, and cheated by the craft, the cunning, the imposture and the falsehood of the English ; who, in order to get from him what they wanted, have spared neither false reports, nor forged letters, nor lying witnesses, nor promises nor civilities, nor good entertainment, nor menaces and threats, to induce him and his fellow to put into writing and to sign a statement to the effect that the papers which were shown to them had been written by the express orders of their mistress."

" But is it not a piece of intolerable arrogance in this person to say that if the princes did not cease to report the words against him which her Majesty uttered at her death, he would be compelled to say what he did not wish to repeat against the dead ? What can he say or do worse than he has already done ? After her death he could do nothing worse against her honour than he had done against her life while she was yet alive. His deposition is extant, without which, and that of his companion, the English could not have had sufficient subject matter on which to condemn her to death. . . . He has been so long accustomed to play the master within the prison that he thinks he must needs be as much regarded out of it as he wished to be within it. He wished to be considered the first councillor, the king's agent, the great master, the great treasurer, the chancellor, the controuller, the banker, the master of the household, the physician, the master of the wardrobe, the esquire, second only to the queen ; all the others were nothing, if they were not his deputies."

These extracts might be enlarged, but the passages here given may suffice to show the principal charges brought against Nau. Although I do not venture to decide how far they are true or false, I cannot but remark that the tone of bitterness with which they are urged detracts, in my opinion, from their credibility. Be that as it may, I have thought it my duty to give the reader the opportunity of weighing the evidence for himself and coming to his own conclusions.

CHAPTER THE SECOND.

THE FLIGHT FROM HOLYROOD.

WE now reach the point at which Queen Mary's Secretary begins his narrative, and as long as he continues to be our guide we shall find ourselves upon firm ground. It might seem that he plunges abruptly into the very heart of his story, and some introductory information might naturally have been expected. The fault does not lie with Nau; it arises from the mutilated condition in which his papers have reached our hands. In the portion which is lost he had already begun to describe the incidents which took place at a conference which was being held by Riccio's murderers, and which had not yet broken up. We do not know the precise time when it was held, nor the place of meeting, nor the names of all those who were present; but we cannot be far from the truth if we assume that they met within the walls of Holyrood, possibly in Darnley's apartment, and very shortly after the completion of the bloody tragedy. All who had taken a prominent part in it probably met together to discuss the questions which now demanded their further consideration. Darnley was there, so was Lennox, so was Ruthven, for their names are mentioned in our history. As to the others we have no certain evidence; but as the safety of the entire party demanded a resolute unity of action, we may take it for granted that of its members few ventured to absent themselves upon such a momentous occasion.

The chief question which claimed their attention touched the person of the queen. She stood in their way, and hindered their onward progress. How was she to be dealt with? It was a plain question, and was discussed without reserve. Although upon this point the lords had already come to a tacit understanding among themselves, although they anticipated no formidable opposition from Darnley, however sweeping might be the scheme which might be proposed, still it was important that his express approval of their plans should be obtained. It was necessary that the king should identify himself with them so completely as to make his reconciliation with his wife an impossibility. It was necessary for their present safety as well as for their future operations. They knew the irresolution, the timidity, and the treachery of the person with whom they were acting, and they dealt with him accordingly. He should be made to understand the true nature of his present position; he ought to comprehend the force of the obligations which he had incurred, and the duties which were henceforth required of him. They observed that he had already begun to waver. He had discovered the danger of his position as the associate of rebels, traitors, and murderers, and they noticed that he would gladly have escaped from further dealings with them, were it possible. But it did not suit the plans of the conspirators that he should do so. As he had begun, so must he continue. He had cast his lot with theirs, and they resolved that now there should be no looking backwards. Even that much was not enough, he must advance a step further. Not only must he be one with them, but he must be their leader; they must be able to quote his name and appeal to his authority. In one word, he must head the movement which aimed at the deposition of the queen.

Knave and fool as he was, Darnley had sense enough to perceive the danger which lurked in such a proposal, and willingly would he have escaped from the dignity thus thrust upon him. But it was too late, and it was not safe to offend such men as he knew these to be. The confederate lords were urgent with him, and they supported their resolution with the following arguments :—

They appealed, in the first place, to his ambition. The crown matrimonial of Scotland was the object of his legitimate aspirations, and they promised that they would help him to secure it. It was his by right, and he had been kept out of it unjustly. Hitherto a mean and selfish jealousy had barred his elevation, but now it was in his own power to remedy past grievances, and to secure future advantages. But he must show himself worthy of it. The crown was now within his reach; he had but to put forth his hand and grasp it. So far their party had been successful. Influenced by Riccio, the queen had refused to grant him this most reasonable request; but where was Riccio now? Where would the queen be to-morrow? The power was in his own hands. Already he was their leader, and would soon be their sovereign. Let him march at their head, and they would follow wherever he led them. There was, indeed, no alternative; he *must* do so. Their common safety demanded it. Should he play the coward, should he waver or attempt to draw back, he would find that they at least were in earnest. They were united and resolute; they would stand by each other without regard to consequences, and with them there should be no respect of persons.

If Darnley was the servant of his ambition, he was the slave of his fears. Nau tells us that he lacked courage in the hour of danger. Alone, and in the midst of such a

f

blood-stained assembly, his scanty stock of resolution failed him; and he felt that he needed the guidance of a firmer will and a clearer judgment than his own. He had been wont to rely upon his wife, but he could do so no longer; he had separated his interests from hers; and in this very question which was now being discussed, his elevation was to be built upon her overthrow. The only person to whom he could turn was his father, and in him he had no great confidence. Yet he asked that the Earl of Lennox might be admitted into the conclave. The confederates could have no objection; he was one of themselves. He had made common cause with them against the queen, and had busied himself in arranging the preliminaries of Riccio's murder.[1] They knew Lennox to be as weak and as timid as Darnley; so the earl, and a few others with him, were admitted. Who they were we know not, but their presence made no change in the deliberations of the meeting. The conspirators proceeded to discuss the question as to the disposal of the queen, and Darnley had no word of remonstrance or protest to offer on her behalf. He seems to have listened unmoved to the recital of the insults and the violence to which she was about to be subjected.

The meeting then pursued its deliberations. Mary's ultimate fate had already been all but decided, so there was no great difference of opinion as to the mode of her immediate disposal. Yet there had been some hesita-

---

[1] For the evidence against Lennox see Chalmers, II. 516. The king and his father, says Knox (II. 521), subscribed to the bond, for they durst not trust the king's word without his signet. Lennox had obtained from Henry VIII. a grant of the manor of Temple Newsome, near Leeds (which had been forfeited by Thomas Lord Darcey in consequence of the share he had taken in the Pilgrimage of Grace), where Darnley was born, in 1545. See Douglas's Peerage, II. 97.

tion as to the time. It was now agreed, without a
dissenting voice, that for the present she should be sent
to Stirling Castle, there to await the hour when she
should give birth to her child. The meeting did not
raise the question as to her final lot,—that would follow
in due course,—and there was no need at present to give
it unnecessary prominence. So it was decided that she
should be deposed and imprisoned, and that sufficed for
to-day. Lord Lindsay seems to have taken the lead in
discussing this matter, in which he exhibited his usual
ferocity. With cruel mockery he attempted to depict
the happy life which the captive would lead within the
walls of her prison. She could amuse herself, he said,
by rocking her baby's cradle, or by singing it to sleep
with her lullaby, or by shooting with her bow in the
garden, or indeed by any amusement she might like.
And while the queen was thus enjoying herself, their
sovereign the king, aided by his faithful nobles, would
devote himself to the affairs of the kingdom.

At this point the conversation was interrupted by the
suggestion of a possible difficulty, by whom proposed we
know not. "But what if some of the nobility of the
royalist party should happen to interfere in the queen's
behalf, and come upon us at the head of an armed force?"
The question was a reasonable one; nothing was more
probable than that the nation would rise in arms in
behalf of its sovereign. The answer is instructive, as
depicting the character of the men with whom Mary
Stuart had to deal. Lord Ruthven was prepared for the
occasion, and he suggested his remedy without any hesitation. "In such a case," said he, "we know what we
shall do. Let the persons you speak of give us the
slightest trouble, let them make but the faintest disturbance by their endeavour to regain possession of her

Majesty, and then they shall see what will happen. She shall be cut into gobbets, and tossed to them from the top of the terrace." No one dissented. The conversation then turned upon the probable sex of the coming child. Ruthven expressed his conviction that it would be a girl; and he maintained this opinion with such vehemence as to warrant the supposition that the rejection of the female line from the throne of Scotland had already been discussed and decided.

The conference was now drawing to a conclusion. There was nothing more to do: the two points which pressed for an immediate solution had been considered openly, and unanimously agreed upon. The queen's fate had been decided, and Darnley's permanent adhesion to the party of the confederate lords had been secured. The road to victory now lay open before the conspirators. It was resolved that all questions of detail should be suspended until the arrival of the earls of Moray and Rothes, to whose opinion and authority everything was to be referred. The delay would be trifling; for it was well known to the meeting that these two noblemen had found their way back from Newcastle, and already were in safe hiding within the city of Edinburgh.[1]

Before the conspirators separated they thought it well to give the king a parting admonition. "If," said they, "you wish to secure the crown which we have promised to give you, be careful to obey our directions. So long as you keep with us you are safe, but no longer. Fail in this respect, and then your troubles will begin. Be assured of one thing: we know how to take care of

---

[1] "It is said that the king sent word to James, earl of Moray, eight days before the committing of the said slaughter, to England, to cause him to come down from Newcastle to Berwick, to be in readiness there when he sent about him."—Diurnal, p. 90.

ourselves, and we will do so, happen what may to others." Hereupon the company broke up into little knots, and talked among themselves in mysterious whispers. Darnley and his father were thrown into agonies of terror, for they did not think their throats safe so long as they were in such company. There was a depth of degradation lower even than this; for as the young king was hurrying out of the room, he was forbidden to speak with his wife, save in the presence of his new masters. His own private attendants were no longer permitted to wait upon him; they were removed, and a guard was placed near the door of his chamber. By courtesy Darnley might be styled a king, but in fact he was a prisoner.

The excitement which had been occasioned by the meeting now began to subside, and in the quiet and solitude of his own chamber Darnley had leisure to review the events of the evening. His thoughts naturally reflected the most marked features of his own character—a character in which selfishness, fraud, and cowardice predominated by turns. The crime of murder, planned by himself, and carried out with such revolting brutality in his presence by his associates, seems to have weighed but lightly upon his conscience; while the thought of his own position, his own dangers and his own interests, stirred the depths of his soul. The condition in which he found himself was alarming. He was a prisoner in his own palace, and his door was surrounded by a guard of armed men who did not acknowledge his authority. The confederate lords styled him their master, and treated him as their slave. He had so far compromised himself that to retrace his steps seemed all but impossible. He had bartered away the affection of his wife for the assistance of these rebels, and now he had discovered the price which they demanded for it. To continue in the course on which he had entered would be ruin, prompt and certain; for the men who had begun by making him their tool would end by making him their victim. All things considered, might not it be safer to try the other alternative, if it were yet open to him, and attempt to regain the confidence of his wife? When he had offended her upon previous occasions, he had always found her generous and forgiving: might not he appeal once more to the tenderness of her woman's nature? It would cost him little to acknowledge his fault, he could easily profess sorrow and promise amendment; and even if it should end in a failure, the attempt could do him no harm. There was a reasonable chance of success, so he resolved to hazard the experiment.

Darnley mounted the narrow winding stair which then, as now, led from his apartment to that immediately above it, which at this period was occupied by the queen. On attempting to enter he found that the door was barred on the inside. To his earnest and repeated entreaties for admission no reply was vouchsafed, nor did any voice from within tell him that his presence was either desired or recognised. In vain he urged that he had business of the deepest importance to discuss with the queen, matters which concerned her safety, as well as his own. Mary was unequal to the effort. After the scenes through which she had been made to pass, during which her nervous system had been strung to its utmost degree of tension, there followed a corresponding period of depression. Attended only by a few faithful women, Mary passed the night in tears and silence.

An estimate of the value of Darnley's repentance, and

of the sincerity of his promises of amendment, may be formed by observing the way in which he occupied himself when he returned to his own apartment. Alone, or in company with the rebellious lords, he was employed in drawing up a proclamation which forbade the meeting of parliament, and ordered the peers, under pain of death, to leave the city of Edinburgh. This document runs in his own name, and was issued by his sole authority, thereby virtually announcing to her subjects that Mary Stuart was no longer Queen of Scotland.

Having, by this act, conciliated the lords and secured his own safety, as far as they were concerned, Darnley's next care was to regain the place which he had lost in his wife's affections. Here he comforted himself by the thought that even if she continued inexorably obdurate, she would not long enjoy the power of showing her resentment. Before daylight then, on the morning of Sunday, the 10th of March, he once more asked permission to enter Mary's bedchamber, and it was granted. We are indebted to Nau for the details of the conversation which then took place between them.

As Darnley was preparing to throw himself on his knees before the queen, she anticipated the movement, and prevented him. And then ensued the following conversation, which was begun by the returning prodigal:—

"My Mary," said he (for this was the form in which this young hypocrite familiarly addressed his wife), "though the confession which I make is tardy, believe it at least to be sincere. I acknowledge my fault, and I ask pardon for it. I will do my best to atone for it. As my excuse, I plead my inexperience and my great want of judgment. Now at last I have discovered how miserably cheated and beguiled I have been by the persuasion of these miserable traitors. They have dragged me into conspiracies against you, against my-self, and against our entire family. At last I see, and that right clearly, what their real design is; they are aiming at the ruin of the whole of us. I take God to witness that I never could have believed that men could have sunk into such a depth of wickedness. If I am blameworthy, attribute my errors to imprudence rather than to deliberate malice. Ambition has blinded me; I confess it. But since God has given me the grace to halt in my onward career, before going yet further,— since I have recovered the use of my senses before it is too late; since I hope to repent for what I have done, —I entreat you, my Mary, to have pity on me, on our child, on yourself. Unless we take some steps to save ourselves, we shall all be ruined, and that very shortly."

When the king had thus spoken, he gave the queen the Articles which had been drawn up and signed between the conspirators and himself; and at the same time he warned her that if it were ever known that he had made her acquainted with them, he was but a dead man. He protested that he did all this to free his conscience from what would otherwise become to him an intolerable burden.

The queen answered the appeal thus made to her with her usual frankness of manner and expression; for, as Nau tells us, " she had never been trained to dissemble, nor was she in the habit of so doing." " Sire," said she, " you have done me so grievous an injury within the last twenty-four hours that I shall never be able to forget it; and neither the memory of our past friend-ship, nor the hope of your future amendment, can win me ever to do so. I have no wish to hide from you what my real convictions are; I may tell you, there-fore, that I think you will never be able to repair the

mischief you have done. You have thoroughly misunderstood the nature of your position. You have been
trying to assume to yourself an authority independent
of mine, forgetting that without me you have no
authority whatever. These very persons whom you
have been courting are playing you false. Are you
aware that I have already asked them, nay, urged them,
to grant you the matrimonial crown, and that they have
refused to do so? I have been more anxious for your
elevation to that dignity than you yourself have been.
Have I ever denied you any reasonable request, provided
it were consistent with your real good? These persons,
who are trying to get both you and me into their power,
in order that they may tread us under their feet, have
they been more liberal? Look within, sire! Examine
well your own conscience, and mark that blot of ingratitude with which you have stained it. You tell me you
are sorry for what you have done, and this gives me
some comfort. Yet I cannot but think that this admission has been wrung from you by necessity, rather
than won by true and earnest affection. Had I inflicted
upon you the deepest of all imaginable injuries, you
could not have revenged yourself upon me with more
ingenious cruelty. But I thank God that neither you
nor any man living can charge me with ever having said
or done anything which could justly displease you,
unless indeed it were for your own real profit. Your
life is dear to me, and God and my duty oblige me to
watch over it as carefully as my own. You have dragged
both yourself and me to the brink of the precipice; it is
for you, therefore, to deliberate and to act in such a way
that we may mutually escape the danger."

"Have pity upon me, my Mary," said the poor prince;
"I assure you that this misfortune will make me a wiser

man for the future. Never will I rest until I have revenged you upon these wretched traitors, if we can but escape out of their hands."

I have purposely refrained from interrupting this remarkable conversation by any comments of my own, in order that the reader, having it before him in its unbroken sequence, may the more easily form his opinion of its real value. The information which Mary's secretary here gives us is absolutely new, and we need have no hesitation in accepting his statements. In no respect are they incredible in themselves, nor do they clash with any document of acknowledged authority. The two speakers express themselves naturally, just as we might expect they would do under the circumstances in which they were placed at the time. The habitual candid good sense of the queen sits upon her as naturally as the habitual arrogance, cowardice, and falsehood of her contemptible husband.

Nau proceeds with his story, and its interest does not flag. From him we learn that the queen now read the "Articles," which shortly before Darnley had placed in her hands. He had done this as a proof of the sincerity of his repentance, and as a token of that perfect confidence which for the future was to exist between them as husband and wife. Under such circumstances most men might have been trusted, but not so Darnley. Even in this action he was deceiving her. The fraud was a deliberate one. During the progress of the arrangements which preceded the murder of David Riccio, certain papers connected with that crime had passed between the confederate lords and Darnley. Two of these documents he now showed to Mary, and one he kept back, and that which he suppressed was the most startling of the three. It was that which, if produced, would have convicted him of having planned the slaughter of the Italian. That he did not produce it is clear from the terms in which he endeavours to exculpate himself. He would have Mary believe that he had been betrayed into a guilty connivance in the crime, almost without forethought, certainly without deliberation, on his part. The suppressed document proved the contrary. Darnley was weak enough to imagine that by such a transparent fraud as this he could keep his wife in ignorance of his share in the plot from the beginning. At all events, the lie would serve a present purpose, and he left the future to take care of itself.

Yet although Darnley suppressed this one special paper, the evidence which he produced against himself was sufficiently damnatory. To have read the two sets of "Secret Articles," as she did at that time, must have taxed to the uttermost all Mary's firmness and self-control, as well as her affection. These documents showed that her husband had consented to her deposition and imprisonment, in other words, to her death, and that he was ready to overthrow the Catholic Church and to place Calvinism in its stead. All this she was now ready to forgive, for she believed once more in Darnley's assurances of amendment, and in this conviction she promised that she would join with him in attempting to escape from Holyrood. She next reminded him that his active cooperation was necessary for the success of the undertaking, and that his first act should be to remove some soldiers who had been sent to keep watch over her. He too had a suggestion to make. He advised her to pardon the conspirators, who, doubtless, would make this request before long ; and he explained himself by remarking that this act of grace upon her part would mollify them and tend to bring about a general reconciliation. Mary dissented. Darnley saw things as they affected his personal safety. Mary saw them as they affected her own personal dignity and the welfare of her subjects; she refused, therefore, to promise compliance with his advice. "I can never bring myself to stoop so low," said she, "as to promise the thing which I have no intention of performing; nor can I do such violence to my conscience as to tell a lie; not even to such traitors as these men are, who have used me so disgracefully. With you the case is different; you can, if you like, promise them anything you please in my name. As for me, I will never pledge them my word." The king was satisfied; and then he and the queen parted, without their interview having been discovered by the conspirators.

After Darnley had gone, and while the morning was yet early, the earl of Moray came to visit his sister, to whom he made his excuses and explanations, with that plausible ease which sat so gracefully upon him. As usual, she believed him, and she expressed her unchanged confidence and affection with a simple earnestness which would have touched the conscience of most men. But Moray was satisfied by speaking a few words of meaningless comfort, and he left her in the same humiliating bondage in which he had found her; he, whose slightest wish would have restored her to her true position. He assured her that he did not approve of such "disorders" as those which had recently been enacted, and that he would remonstrate with the lords upon the subject. The queen, therefore, might hope that the murder of one of her servants in her presence would not be an every day occurrence. He advised her to invite the lords to pay her a visit on the morning of the following day; in other words, to

pardon the murderers of her secretary. This she refused
to do, and although he repeated his request, the queen
was steadfast in rejecting it.

During the course of the same morning proclamation
was made at the Market Cross of Edinburgh to the effect
that the parliament, which had been summoned to meet
on that day, would not be held; and every one who was
entitled to vote in it was commanded, under pain of
death, to depart from the city. So great had now become the terror occasioned by this reign of lawlessness
that, according to Mary's letter to the Cardinal of Lorraine,
of the whole body of the Estates only three members had
the hardihood to remain in the capital. This treasonable
proclamation, drawn up by command of the rebellious
lords and subscribed by Darnley, instantly announced
that Mary was no longer queen of Scotland. It cleared
the road for Moray and his followers, who on the following day went in procession to the Parliament House,
and there protested that they were ready to answer
every charge that might be brought against them. There
was no one who dared to raise a voice or a hand against
them, and they were safe. The majesty of the law had
been vindicated, and the lands and dignities which had
been in peril of forfeiture were once more their own.
It was a great triumph, and for it they had paid
nothing more costly than the blood of a stranger and an
idolater.

In the meantime the queen was guarded with the
most jealous vigilance. The lords dreaded a rescue, and
not without good reason. Nau tells us, quite incident-
ally, that upon one occasion during this period of terror,
the queen, happening to stand near the window, was recognised by some of the townspeople, among whom were
a few of her own officers. They expressed their sym-

pathy with their sovereign and their anger against her
rebels by shouts and threats. Lord Lindsay heard the
outcry, and with that brutal harshness which was habitual
to him, he rushed into the room and dragged the queen
from the window ; warning her, at the same time, that
if by her presence, or in any other way, she excited a
tumult among the people, it would be as much as her
life was worth.

Mary did not break her fast until four o'clock on the
afternoon of Sunday. It does not appear whether this
was of her own will or of necessity. On this occasion
the food with which she was supplied was carefully
examined by her noble turnkey, lord Lindsay, who
feared that some word of advice or consolation might
reach her from the outer world. Probably the dowager
lady Huntley brought her the nourishment which she so
much needed, for at this time she certainly gained permission to visit the prisoner. She found the opportunity
of letting her know that the loyal nobles had collected
some troops, and were preparing to strike a blow for her
deliverance. But this could not be done, consistently
with her safety, so long as she remained in the hands of
the ruffians who now had her in their keeping ; for they
would assuredly put her to death if any attempt were
made for her liberation.

The plan which her friends proposed for her escape
was this :—that she should let herself down from the
window of the chamber in which she was imprisoned,
and that they, for their part, would be in waiting and
would carry her off to a place of safety (apparently Dunbarton Castle), where she could await the result of the
impending struggle. Lady Huntley had brought with
her a ladder of ropes, which she had succeeded in conveying into the room between two plates, as if they

contained a part of the queen's supper. Mary saw at once that this plan was impracticable. The window from which it was proposed that she should descend by the rope ladder was in full view of the room immediately opposite, and this room was now occupied by the guard who were placed to watch over her. She found time to discuss the question with lady Huntley, and to suggest a safer plan, of which her friend approved. A few lines explanatory of the proposed change were then written by her Majesty to the earl of Huntley and the other loyal noblemen. Judging by the abstract which Nau has given of its contents it must have been a paper of some length. Mary stated, in the first place, the reasons why she did not accept the plan which they had suggested, and then she explained her own. She asked them to wait for her at the village of Seton, where she hoped to join them during the following night. She desired them to encourage the earl of Mar to persevere in holding out Edinburgh Castle for her, and to assure him that she would soon be at liberty. Mar had been a good friend to Mary, by giving a safe place of refuge at this time to Huntley and the others who continued faithful to the Scottish crown.

Lady Huntley's adventures, however, had not yet ended. When she received the letter which Mary had written she placed it between her chemise and her body. Shortly afterwards, while the two women (herself and her mistress) were in private together under circumstances which should have protected them from all intrusion, lord Lindsay had the indecency to burst into the closet, and ordered lady Huntley to leave the room. Before she was allowed to depart she was searched, but the paper upon which so much depended was not discovered. It reached the hands of her son, and the nobles prepared to do their part in carrying out the plan which it suggested.

And what was that plan? Nau enables us to answer this question pretty accurately. From him we learn that it originated with the queen: its conception was due to her ingenuity, and its success to her courage. He tells us further that Mary's first step was to procure an interview with the laird of Traquair, who was captain of the guard, whom she instructed as to the part he was to enact in the approaching enterprise. This conference took place in Darnley's chamber, to which it would seem that the captain was admitted on pretence of some official duty. The details of the escape were to be as follows. First of all, as to the time; it was resolved that the attempt should be made during the following night. Leaving her own apartment on the first floor, the queen would descend the winding stair which led to that of her husband, and then the two would pass into the offices belonging to the butlers of her own household. As all of them were French, she knew that she could depend not only upon their silence, but also upon their assistance, if it should happen to be required. From these offices a low gate (about the height of a man) led into the church-yard. It was seldom used, and its fastenings were so insecure that it could be forced open without difficulty. Mary directed the captain of the guard to arrange that Arthur Erskine, the chief equerry of her stables, should wait at this spot, mounted on a stout gelding, which should be provided with a pillion. Erskine had long been in the queen's service, and she determined that she would ride behind him on this midnight journey. He was directed to bring with him two or three other horses for the use of Darnley and his attendants.

These arrangements were judicious and gave the promise of success, but not the certainty. Dangers might arise at any moment, against which no forethought, no courage, could offer any security. Before sunset Mary might be on her road to Stirling or Lochleven. Yet she had done all that she could do, so she was contented to leave the issue in higher hands than her own. And now, her arrangements having been completed, Nau has something to tell us about Darnley.

In the course of his matrimonial confidences Darnley had more than once referred to the unhappy state of mind in which he found his father, the earl of Lennox. We can easily understand why he should feel the reverse of comfortable. The earl was not popular, and his son was hated. He was living in an atmosphere of violence and treachery, of which he might at any moment become the victim. The impression produced upon his mind by that conference with the nobles at which he had been permitted to assist confirmed his terror; and these convictions were still further increased by the return of Moray, whom he disliked and feared. From these dangers, partly real and partly ideal, Darnley thought it was his duty to rescue his father, and he hinted as much to the queen. As she did not respond to these remarks he spoke in plainer terms, and even ventured to propose that Lennox should be permitted to join them in their flight from the palace. Here, remarks Nau, with quiet sarcasm, the young king showed more than his usual affection towards his father, whom upon most occasions he treated with no great respect. But be that as it may, Mary gave a prompt refusal, and then stated the reasons why she did so. She said that she could not trust Lennox, especially on such a momentous occasion as the present. He had played the traitor too often already. Not only had he

g

been false to herself, but also to her late parents.[1] The slightest act of indiscretion on his part might endanger the lives of all of them. She had little confidence either in his courage or his fidelity. She reminded Darnley that out of her regard to him she had treated his father with greater respect than he himself had done. She had given him a seat at the royal table, she had consulted him on matters of consequence, and she had behaved to him as if he had been one of themselves. And what return had he made? He had forgotten all these obligations, and had made common cause with her rebels. If anything should go wrong with him he had brought it upon himself. In short, she had no intention of taking him into her confidence.

Mary was right, for Lennox was untrustworthy. To secure his own safety or advance his own interests he would not have scrupled to betray her to her enemies. He had played the traitor's part already, and he was ready to do so again. That her estimate of him was correct was proved by his subsequent conduct, in which he showed himself false not only towards his sovereign, but also to his religion and his country. To secure the elevation of his weak son to the throne of Scotland he would have sanctioned the public execution or the private murder of his daughter-in-law. Mary therefore did wisely in holding firm to her resolution. Her stronger will prevailed, and Darnley submitted to her decision in silence.

Yet it might seem that he made an indirect attempt to effect a change in her determination. During the

[1] Probably Mary was thinking of that memorable occasion when Lennox, having received 60,000 crowns from France for the support of the national cause in Scotland, converted them to his own use. He also served in the English army in the invasion and harrying of his own country.—See Sadler, i. 314, 318, 319, 323; and Lesley, in Jebb, i. 152.

course of the day—the precise time is unknown to us—
Darnley brought his father into the queen's presence, in
order, it may be presumed, to try the effect of a personal
interview. If so, it was a failure. Mary received Lennox
coldly, and nothing of importance took place during the
interview. The earl remained in ignorance of the intended flight from Edinburgh. About the same time
she found the opportunity of acquainting the friendly
nobles in the castle, that so far at least her plans had
succeeded to her entire satisfaction. But one more
difficulty had yet to be encountered, and that a most
formidable one. It was necessary that she should grant
an interview to the lords of the Congregation. They
had demanded it, and their request had been enforced
by Moray and Darnley. She would gladly have avoided
it, for it could not but be agitating and dangerous. The
men who had risen in arms against her authority, who
had murdered her secretary before her eyes, and had
threatened her own deposition, now came to solicit their
pardon, and the restoration of their estates and dignities.
How was she to act under such circumstances as these?

The interview between Mary and the lords took place
in her ante-chamber.[1] The confederates were introduced
by the earl of Moray, who throughout the entire meeting
affected to conduct himself as an independent mediator.
He wished it to be understood that in this matter his
interests were distinct from those of the lords. They
were pleading a cause which did not touch him. In his
private interview with his sister, she had practically
freed him from all complicity in the murder of Riccio,
and he took care to maintain the vantage-ground which
she had given him. Thus, all having knelt on their

---

[1] According to the "Diurnal," p. 92, this meeting took place in the
evening.

first admission into the presence of their sovereign, as soon as that act of dutiful homage had been rendered, Moray arose and continued to stand upright during the remainder of the conference. The others remained on their knees, and confessed themselves to be offenders, penitents, and suppliants. The scene, as represented by Nau, must have been most impressive. In the presence of their dethroned queen knelt, in mocking humility, the men by whom she had been insulted, deposed, and imprisoned. The room in which they were then gathered together had lately been the scene of a cowardly assassination; and the blood of their victim was scarcely yet dry on the spot where now knelt the chief criminal. On one side of the queen stood her miserable husband, the tool of the conspirators, and already doomed to be their next victim; and on the other side stood her unworthy brother, the author of all her sufferings and sorrows, past, present, and yet to come. For Darnley there was left in Mary's heart as much love as a woman has to give to the husband she despises; for Moray as much as she can feel for the brother whom she trusts and yet fears. Her only confidence was in the justice of her own cause; so she girt herself for the conflict, and bravely faced the danger which now it was too late to avoid.

The lords had deputed the earl of Morton to act as their advocate, and his experience in the courts of law had taught him how to make the worse appear the better cause. It was his own cause, as well as theirs, for he was deeply implicated in the murder; and had the parliament met, as was intended, the large possessions which he had secured to himself out of the plunder of the church would have reverted to the queen. It was supposed that this act of restitution had been warmly advocated by Riccio, and the earl hated him accordingly.

Interest and revenge are powerful motives, and they urged him to do his best in pleading with the queen for the pardon of the conspirators.

Kneeling, then, on the spot where David had fallen, and from which his blood was crying to heaven for justice, the chancellor of Scotland began his address to his sovereign. He admitted that the nobles had not acted as obedient subjects, but in no respect had they been disloyal to her person. He propounded the remainder of his argument with a simplicity of diction which is startling. The death of Riccio, said he, had become a matter of necessity—it was dictated to the lords by the instinct of self-preservation. Had this obnoxious parliament been allowed to meet, there was nothing before them and their children but ruin and starvation. The course which they had adopted was an extreme one, but the same thing had happened before now, and pretty frequently too. After all, to what did it amount? The death of a single individual, and he a mean man and a foreigner; what was that in comparison with the ruin of so many lords and gentlemen? Let her majesty look at the men now kneeling before her; they were her own liege subjects, and they were ready to do her true and loyal service. If she would promise them that she would forget the past, they, on their part, promised by him, their spokesman, that for the future they would serve with all devout fidelity.

The next speaker was Moray. From the moment of Riccio's murder it was felt that, directly or indirectly, the earl was implicated in it, and none were misled by the fact that he was absent from Edinburgh at the moment of its perpetration.[1] As yet, however, Mary

[1] An interesting letter from Morton and Ruthven to Leicester, now for the first time printed, may be seen among the Illustrative Documents appended to this chapter. See p. xcviii.

did not suspect him, and it was important for the
success of his plans that she should continue in this
delusion. With this end in view he swore by his God
that he knew nothing of the crime before his arrival in
the capital. Next, he very humbly entreated his sister
to forgive his presumption in venturing to return home
without her knowledge or permission.

Having thus pleaded his own cause, Moray began to
plead the cause of his friends. He reminded the queen
that the present investigation was of the highest national
importance, and that every one within the realm had a
direct interest in its decision. Among the accused were
some of the chief nobles of the land, and in dealing with
such men clemency should be observed. Moray then
discoursed at some length upon the virtue of clemency.
For crowned heads it was something more than an
advantage, it was a necessity. It conduced not only to
their personal safety, but to the benefit of the republic.
He concluded his address by advising the queen to restore
these eminent noblemen to the position which they had
held in her court, so that she might in future profit by
the great affection which they felt for herself and the
king.

This language contrasts strangely with that which the
same noblemen had shortly before addressed to the
queen, and the change is so abrupt and so decided as to
ask for an explanation. Nau affords it by telling us
that a new plan of action had been decided upon by the
confederates at a recent meeting of the Scottish peers.
It had become clear to all, be he of whatever party he
might, that Darnley was utterly untrustworthy. No
one could depend upon his word, or his promise, or his
bond, or his oath. He had neither courage nor constancy; he would betray each in turn, whoever it might

be who gave him the opportunity. The lords of the Congregation felt that in this indecision and general worthlessness of the young king's character lay their greatest strength. They could no longer work through Darnley; his help was not worth the having. If they could no longer shelter themselves under his authority, they must depend upon their own. For the moment it was necessary to delay. Lindsay had said that nothing should be done without the approval of Moray, whose wishes and plans had not yet been ascertained. For the present, then, it was necessary to temporise. For a while, at least, the queen should be treated with some show of decent respect, and in the meantime there would be leisure to deliberate upon their future proceedings.

After this interruption, which we pardon because of its importance, we resume Nau's account of the conference between the queen and the confederates.

It was now Mary's turn to speak. In her reply to the addresses of the two earls, she expressed herself with her usual calm good sense and courage, thereby showing herself mistress of the position into which she had been driven, difficult and hazardous as it confessedly was.

Dealing, in the first place, with Morton's remarks about the murder of her secretary, she asked him, and the lords whom he represented, to understand that they had been guilty of crimes of no small magnitude. She would mention a few of them. They had attacked her authority as a queen, and thereby had become guilty of rebellion. They had plotted against the state, consequently they were chargeable with treason. They had injured her as a wife, by weakening the tie which bound her to her husband; nay, perhaps they had ruined it entirely. Surely these were crimes of no small account.

They had spoken of the murder of her secretary as a trifle ; in her way of thinking, it was a crime of the blackest dye ; and they who now knelt before her were the ringleaders in the guilt. She reminded them of the relation in which they stood to each other : they were her natural subjects, and she was their rightful sovereign. Let them think, too, of the benefits which she had lavished upon them. If the expression were permitted, she might say that she had even shared her crown with them ; and whenever any kindly action had been shown to her by them, she had always acknowledged it with gratitude.

So far she had addressed them collectively ; now she spoke to them individually. She reminded Morton of his former rebellion against her late mother, the queen Regent of Scotland, and against her husband, the late king of France. In mentioning the obligations under which Morton lay to herself personally, a curious fact comes to light and is worthy of being here noticed. Mary reminded him that when it became known that he had joined the party of which Moray was the leader, she had been urged by her husband and his father, Lennox, to cause him, Morton, to be beheaded ; and that he owed his life to her refusal. She also reminded him that to her liberality he was indebted for the earldom of Morton and the dignity of the chancellorship of Scotland.

Turning then to her brother she spoke a few words to him, in reply chiefly to his laudation of clemency. A tinge of sarcasm is perceptible in what she said. She thanked him and certain others of her nobles and people for the lessons which they had taught her about this virtue, and for the many opportunities which they had given her of practising it. They had made her familiar with the word. By nature she was by no means inclined to severity ; in fact she had been blamed for being too lenient. And what had been the result? Many of them, encouraged by past impunity, had persevered in their evil courses up to the present time, and perhaps were ready to advance a step onwards in the same direction, led by the hope that they would escape as easily now as they had upon former occasions. " I owe justice," continued Mary (and it might seem that here Nau reports her very words); " I owe justice to every one, nor can I refuse it to those persons who demand it in the name of a murdered man. Whatever may have been his rank, he was my servant, and that was enough to have protected him from every outrage, especially in my presence. I do not think, therefore, that I can promise you a full pardon on the very first moment you ask me to do so. But I can promise you that, provided you endeavour to blot out past delinquencies by the fidelity of your future conduct, I will endeavour to forget the crime which you have just committed."

A promise of pardon upon the condition of future good conduct did not suit such men as Morton and Moray. It was more liberal than would have been made by any government which could have enforced its laws, but it did not satisfy the lords of the Congregation. It gave no security against a criminal prosecution for the murder of Riccio, nor did it guarantee in perpetuity to the present occupants the lands which they held by the plunder of the Church. The chancellor of Scotland knew that when the queen should attain her legal majority, all the ill-gotten wealth which these men had secured during the general scramble might revert to its lawful owners. The queen might have good intentions, but what were they worth in a court of law? Her proposal, therefore, was rejected, decidedly and unanimously.

Mary felt that the supreme moment had now arrived,

and that upon the course which she must now take hung the fortunes of herself, her family, and her kingdom. Her courage and presence of mind were taxed to the uttermost, for danger threatened her on the right hand and on the left. Could she pardon these traitors and murderers, and yet style herself queen of Scotland? If she refused, she was aware what would be the issue of the refusal. Even were she to do so, she knew that she could not enforce her decision, for these ruffians would take by force what they now asked as a favour. Her decision would not control their action, and in this sense nothing would be gained. As regarded herself personally, the case was even clearer. Her refusal would be succeeded by her immediate imprisonment and probably by her death, which would be followed in rapid succession by that of her husband and her child. The government of her kingdom would pass into the hands of the earl of Moray, who would buy the protection of England upon such terms as Elizabeth might be pleased to dictate. Scotland would lose at once her ancient independence and faith, and would become an English colony. All these contingencies arose in her mind, and each demanded to be heard. One of the alternatives must be chosen; which of the two should it be?

The mother-wit of the young queen saved her from being impaled on either horn of this ugly dilemma. She interrupted the proceedings of the meeting at this point by telling the lords that she suddenly felt ill, and that the moment had arrived when she was about to give birth to her child. Such an announcement could excite no surprise, especially in the minds of men who well knew the scenes of agitation through which she had passed so recently. Mary requested that the midwife might be summoned, accompanied by whom she hurriedly went to her bedroom, into which she was followed by her husband. After a short absence, he returned to the meeting and attempted to resume the conversation at the point where it had been broken off. He entered more fully than she had done into the terms of the pardon ; and although his concessions were more liberal, the lords were not disposed to treat with him. Their suspicions were aroused, and they held a conference among themselves, to which Darnley was not admitted. They decided that the terms offered did not guarantee their safety, and they therefore rejected them. They had no faith in Darnley, whom they could not trust, and they resolved to treat only with the queen. They sent a message to her, demanding to be admitted into her presence. She refused to receive them, assuring them that it was impossible. The midwife confirmed Mary's report as to her condition, and as this woman had been nominated by themselves, they believed what she stated. According to Nau, there was no deception on her part—she had spoken in all honesty, and firmly believed what she said. The lords were now constrained to break up the meeting, which they did, with the intention of reassembling on the following day.

Freed from the presence of the confederates, Mary proceeded with the arrangements which were necessary for her escape from Holyrood. They were carried out in strict accordance with the plan which had already been settled with the earl of Huntley. Nau has chronicled a few of the incidents which occurred during the flight, and they are worth recording here. The party consisted of the queen and her husband, the captain of the guard, and Arthur Erskine, a servant of the king's bedchamber (whom we know to have been Anthony Standen), and two or three soldiers. In crossing the burial ground, in

which lay the body of the murdered secretary, Darnley
showed such marked signs of agitation that the queen
asked what ailed him.   Darnley replied, with one of his
stupid falsehoods, "Madam, we are just now passing by
the grave of poor David.   In losing him I have lost a
good and trusty servant, the like of whom I shall never
see again.   I shall regret him every day of my life.
I have been miserably cheated."   He would have continued in this strain, but his lamentations were effectually silenced by the remark that possibly they might be
overheard by the watchmen of the confederates.

The laird of Traquair and Arthur Erskine had carefully followed out the queen's instructions.   At the spot
which had been agreed upon, the horses were waiting for
the arrival of the royal fugitives.   Mary rode upon a
pillion behind Arthur Erskine.   Why not behind her
own husband?   Nau is silent.   As soon as the party
had gained the open country they pushed on at full
speed.   When near Seton, some soldiers were noticed,
who had been posted on the road by the loyal nobles, in
order to protect the queen in the event of pursuit from
Edinburgh.   Darnley, in his blind terror, imagined that
they were enemies, and spurred on his horse to its utmost
speed, at the same time flogging that upon which Mary
was seated.   While he was doing this he cried out,
"Come on!   Come on!   By God's Blood, they will
murder both of us, if they can but lay hands on us!"
To a woman in the queen's critical condition, such continued violent exertion was an impossibility.   She reminded him of what he seemed to have forgotten, that
the result would be a miscarriage.   To fall into the hands
of such men as Lindsay and Morton would be a calamity,
but a still greater calamity would it be to endanger the
life of their child.   But Mary appealed to sentiments

about which Darnley was indifferent; and the brutality of his character shows itself in language which was at once profane and indecent. "Come on!" repeated he; "Come on, in God's name! If this child dies we can have another."

The queen's power of endurance was now exhausted, and she could hold out no longer. She told her husband that if he so pleased he might look to his own safety, without regard to hers. He took her at her word and left her. But she was not unprotected; the earls of Huntley and Bothwell, the lords Fleming, Seton, Livingston, and a few others, closed around her, and conducted her in safety within the walls of the royal castle of Dunbar.[1]

A few only of the facts recorded in this have hitherto been known to us, and that in their barest outline. We are indebted to Nau's manuscript for the curious details now for the first time published.

[1] Nau's account of Mary's flight from Holyrood to Dunbar receives some important illustrations from two papers which are printed among the Illustrative Documents appended to this chapter. See p. c.

NOTE THE SECOND. (See p. xcvii., Note 1.)

PETITION AND STATEMENT OF FACTS by Sir Anthony Standen, Knight, and Anthony Standen, Gentleman, presented to King James the First.[1]

The humble petition of Sir Anthony Standen, Knight, and Anthony Standen, Gent., brothers.

To the King's Most Excellent Majesty,

In most humble wise do show unto your majesty, Anthony Standen, the elder, knt., and Anthony Standen, the younger, gent., brothers, your majesty's loyal subjects and humble servants, that where in the year of our Lord, 1565, the elder brother, being then in the service of our late sovereign lady of worthy memory, and by that means placed in her royal court, became inwardly acquainted with the late king Henry, your majesty's most noble father, the said king having occasions to follow into the realm of Scotland, Matthew, earl of Lennox, his father, about the restitution to them both of that state and earldome. And whereas within three months after it pleased Almighty God to effect a liking and consequently a marriage between the queen, your majesty's most noble mother, and the king, your highness's father, the lady Margaret Douglas Lennox, your Majesty's grandmother, understanding hereof, and having a desire to settle near unto her dearly beloved son some one of trust and confidence, made a motion to the said sir Anthony that he would be contented, for the love he bore unto her son and herself, to relinquish his country, parents, court, and service, and to dedicate himself and his best endeavours to those two noble princes; which the said sir Anthony did soon effect, and by way of the Low Countries did conduct with him to accompany him, the younger Anthony, his brother; and upon their arrival were by that noble queen most humanely received, and the knight immediately placed in the office of first escuyer of the king her husband's stable. The younger brother her majesty ordained in the room of cup-bearer to the king, with a stipend to the elder of two hundred French crowns yearly, and

[1] Public Record Office, State Papers, Domestic, James I., Vol. I. No. 100.

pose direct by our sovereign to the queen's majesty of England for the same effect, that he getting credit may make us odious by his untrue dealing. We doubt not (so assured by your good lordship's favours shown heretofore to our brethren and all those that tender the true religion of Jesus Christ and mutual intelligence betwixt the realms) but you will cause the queen's majesty understand the simple truth of that action, according as we have written and sent the same to Mr Secretary,[1] to be communicated with your lordship, so as we will before the whole earth, upon our honour, defend it against all that will sinisterly in hatred of us labour otherways to misreport thereof; and for that your lordship shall be the more fully assured that that which we have written is the very and undoubted truth of that action, the earl of Moray, who has already written to our good lord the earl of Bedford,[2] in favour of us, as by his lordship you will understand, immediately after his return from Argyll, where as yet he remains, shall inform you so that your lordship shall find (the truth tried) our action founded upon a just ground, and to have hitherto proceeded so uprightly that it is able enough in the self to convince the enemy.

Thus we commit your lordship to the protection of the Almighty.

From Berwick, the ix. day of April,

Your Lordships,

MORTONE.
RUTHVEN.

To the Right Hon. our very good lord the earl of Leicester.

Mark of small seal in red wax. Original signatures.

[1] This report by Morton and Ruthven upon the circumstances connected with Riccio's murder was sent to Cecil on the second of April. The letter which accompanied it is in the Record Office, under the date just mentioned.

[2] The fact of Moray having written to Bedford in favour of the fugitives into England is now for the first time made known to us. Moray's journey to Argyll is confirmed by Knox, II. 527.

liking) by sir James, Robert, and Andrew Melvin, all three knights and men of honour, and by James Hudson, who then served the king, your majesty's father, under the knight's charge.

May it therefore please your majesty . . . according to the 65 leaf of your Book to our lord the prince, to take compassion of the said two poor afflicted brothers, your so ancient and dutiful servants, in causing to be paid unto them the arrearages of their said pensions, and to continue unto them some means to succour and relieve the small rest of their aged years. . . .

Two contemporary copies.

MEMORIAL from sir Anthony Standen presented to king James the First.[1]

It is notorious to many yet living how sir Anthony Standen, being in the court and service of queen Elizabeth of high memory, and how by that occasion growing inwardly acquainted and favoured by the king's majesty's father, then also a courtier, out of his love and word given to the said king, Standen and a brother of his in the year 1565 both together left court, fortunes, and country, and departed this realm into Scotland to the marriage of the king and queen, where, upon their arrival, the elder was placed in the office of the first escuyer of the king's escuyrie, and the younger cup-bearer of the king, with extraordinary favours and welcomes from both their Majesties.

Within four weeks after the queen began to discover to be with child, whereupon fell out a practice most dangerous, contrived by certain lords, amongst which wicked Ruthven was the chief, which most barbarously they put in execution by murdering in the queen's majesty's bedchamber and presence one David Riccio, a servant to both their majesties. In this bloody tumult and press one of Ruthven's followers offered to fix his poinard in the queen's left side, then very great bellied with the king's majesty, our now sovereign lord, which Standen, by his nearness to her well advising, turned aside

[1] Record Office, State Papers, Domestic, James I., Vol. I. No. 102.

to the younger of one hundred crowns a year. But so it afterwards befell that upon the practices and conspiracies of James,
earl of Moray, against his sovereign and sister, divers troubles
and afflictions were raised, whereby ensued her majesty's
long imprisonment, and so after many years her life's end.

Upon the birth of your majesty it pleased the queen to
make choice of the said sir Anthony for her messenger into
France to Charles IX., then reigning there, and to the duke
and famous princes of the family of Lorraine, her cousins,
and to some of them then in France, and from her to declare
unto them your majesty's happy coming into this world,
wherein the said elder brother consumed a whole year, at the
end whereof, being ready to return into Scotland, the unfortunate news of the death of the king, his lord and master,
was brought to Paris, and soon after the restraint by Moray
in Lochleven of the queen, whereby the said sir Anthony was
forced to pass his life in exile, as well from Scotland as from
England, having incurred by his departure from her service
his sovereign's highest indignation. This banishment endured
thirty years and more, wherein what your Majesty's servant
passed and suffered God Almighty and some men do know.
The younger brother remained in Scotland until the death
and durance of the king and queen, his master and mistress;
who a little before her majesty's adverse fortune, assigned to
us both to be paid out of the revenues of the crown of Scotland the said two hundred crowns yearly to the elder, and the
said hundred crowns a year to the younger, as a pension or
stipend during their natural lives, whereof sithence their
departures out of Scotland after the first two years they never
received hitherto more of their entertainment. And as the
elder brother suffered those pressures and banishments abroad,
so the younger was not exempt of his crosses at home by being
imprisoned a whole year in Berwick, and in his native
country bearing all the disgraces ever sithence might be
heaped upon him merely for his loyal duty, love, and affection
to the queen and her service. The truth whereof, and of a
great deal more than here is laid down (to avoid tediousness)
is sufficiently to be witnessed (if it stand with your majesty's

liking) by sir James, Robert, and Andrew Melvin, all three knights and men of honour, and by James Hudson, who then served the king, your majesty's father, under the knight's charge.

May it therefore please your majesty . . . according to the 65 leaf of your Book to our lord the prince, to take compassion of the said two poor afflicted brothers, your so ancient and dutiful servants, in causing to be paid unto them the arrearages of their said pensions, and to continue unto them some means to succour and relieve the small rest of their aged years. . . .

Two contemporary copies.

Memorial from sir Anthony Standen presented to king James the First.[1]

It is notorious to many yet living how sir Anthony Standen, being in the court and service of queen Elizabeth of high memory, and how by that occasion growing inwardly acquainted and favoured by the king's majesty's father, then also a courtier, out of his love and word given to the said king, Standen and a brother of his in the year 1565 both together left court, fortunes, and country, and departed this realm into Scotland to the marriage of the king and queen, where, upon their arrival, the elder was placed in the office of the first escuyer of the king's escuyrie, and the younger cupbearer of the king, with extraordinary favours and welcomes from both their Majesties.

Within four weeks after the queen began to discover to be with child, whereupon fell out a practice most dangerous, contrived by certain lords, amongst which wicked Ruthven was the chief, which most barbarously they put in execution by murdering in the queen's majesty's bedchamber and presence one David Riccio, a servant to both their majesties. In this bloody tumult and press one of Ruthven's followers offered to fix his poinard in the queen's left side, then very great bellied with the king's majesty, our now sovereign lord, which Standen, by his nearness to her well advising, turned aside

[1] Record Office, State Papers, Domestic, James I., Vol. I. No. 102.

by laying a grip upon the dagger, wrested of this traitor, by which means (though with exposing his own) Standen saved two lives together, a service by both king and queen taken such notice of as after, while they lived, their majesties esteemed and valued accordingly.

These two thus distressed princes, upon the execution of so detestable an act, finding themselves captives to their rebellious subjects, sought means to wind out and to save themselves the next night following, which, by God Almighty's great mercy, was happily put in practice, and as fortunately succeeded, wherein Standen's fidelity was by the queen chiefly made proof of, and three others besides were also to be trusted and used, [that is] to say, John Steward, laird of Traquair, captain of the guard, William his brother, and Arthur Erskin. These, seven in number, secretly stole away after midnight from Holyrood House toward the castle of Dunbar, twenty long miles from thence, into which strength being entered, after some difficulty these princes' lives were by God's blessing miraculously put in safety.

Within three days after the subjects of the counties of Lothian and Edinburgh assembling themselves in arms, their royal persons were by these troops conducted safe to the castle of Edinburgh; within which place, three months after, her majesty was most happily delivered of our then lord the prince, and our now most gracious king and sovereign. At which time, in acknowledgment of Standen's services, it pleased the king, by the queen's appointment, to honour him with the order of knighthood; and also it liked her royal majesty, some days after the childbirth, to cause the knight to be called unto her bedchamber, where the infant prince laid asleep, a cross of diamonds fixed on his breast. Upon this cross her majesty commanded the knight to lay his hand, to whom it was her pleasure herself to give the oath of fidelity to her only son, even then ordaining him his first servant, saying he had given the prince the first faith and homage of the crown of England, with these words of comfort, " For that you saved his life;" using other more noble speeches before the king and ladies of the ominous casting his princely hands open immediately upon his coming into this world, with such

They now saw in him nothing more dignified than the individual whom the queen had honoured by giving him her hand in marriage; out of respect to her they had hitherto treated him with a certain amount of deference and obedience, but they vowed that now they would do so no longer. They were no more bound to him than he was to them. None of them had ever accepted him as their king, and they would not do so now. Darnley might have learned many a useful lesson from these remarks, but he did not profit by them; and the only effect which they produced was to make him hate yet more bitterly the men by whom they were uttered.

From Dunbar we return to Holyrood. When it was understood that the queen and her husband had escaped from the custody of the lords of the Congregation, the excitement in Edinburgh was extreme. The fact became generally known on the morning of Tuesday. The earl of Lennox, who resided within the palace, when he heard the tidings broke out into many bitter imprecations against his son, whom he denounced as a traitor for having abandoned him to his fate in the midst of such manifold dangers. Lethington was made aware of the fact by the ladies of the queen's chamber, who fled to him for protection against the mob which, as they had been told, was about to sack the royal apartments. Nau remarks that whatever might be Lethington's outward obedience to Mary, he was at heart a traitor at this time, but that he conducted himself with such skill that his duplicity escaped detection. Thus, when others, not more guilty than himself, sued for their pardon, he kept aloof from the party; leaving it to be inferred that as he had committed no crime so he needed no forgiveness.

The effect produced upon the nation at large by the queen's escape from Holyrood was remarkable. It broke

CHAPTER THE THIRD.

FROM THE QUEEN'S ESCAPE FROM HOLYROOD UNTIL THE BIRTH OF THE PRINCE.

WHEN the excitement and fatigue of this midnight ride were at last ended, the queen discovered that nature was exhausted and demanded food and repose. She ordered a fire to be lit, at which she cooked some eggs, and having partaken of this frugal meal, she lay down to rest herself for a short time. She then wrote several letters addressed to her relatives in France, which were immediately despatched by a vessel which at that time happened to be lying in the offing.[1]

The five days which the queen spent within the walls of Dunbar to her were days of great consolation. They enabled her in some degree to recover from the mental prostration which followed the multiplied terrors of the previous week. When she calmly surveyed her position she saw no reason for despondency. She had escaped from a cruel and treacherous blow aimed at her own life and the life of her child. She had defeated a formidable conspiracy formed against her government by her traitorous nobility; and it seemed to her that she had broken up the combination so effectually that she had no further cause to dread its reconstruction. The power of

---

[1] An abstract of certain letters from Mary to the cardinal of Lorraine, dated March 13, 14, and 18, may be seen in Teulet, ii. 260. See also the Memoire in Lab., vii. 78.

When Mary returned to Edinburgh she went to reside in the town house of the bishop of Dunkeld,[1] where she remained until Holyrood was ready for her reception. Hitherto she had entrusted the management of her affairs too confidingly to Moray and Lethington, but she determined that henceforth she would exercise a more immediate control over them herself. With this view she frequently presided at the meetings of the privy council, thus making herself familiar with the transaction of public business.[2] These meetings were attended by men of every shade of politics: by Royalists and Republicans, by Catholics and Calvinists. Of course Moray was there, and he was well supported by his numerous followers; Darnley too found time to favour these meetings with his presence and advice. He made no secret of his hostility towards both Moray and Lethington, whom he disliked, feared, and calumniated. He could not have committed a more dangerous mistake; for to provoke the enmity of such men as Moray and Lethington was to court destruction. The hostility of Darnley was fostered by Bothwell and Huntley,[3] who hoped to find in him a convenient tool whom they could employ in the carrying out of their own designs. Thus encouraged Darnley ventured to make a public attack upon Maitland, the details of which reach us through Nau's manuscript. Darnley wished to deprive him of

[1] The tenement in which the queen resided at this time had formerly been the palace of the bishop of Dunkeld, but at the time specified was occupied by the lord Hume. It was situated "anent the salt trone." See Diurnal, p. 94.

[2] Mary's attention to business receives a pleasing confirmation from an unexpected quarter. See Supplemental Note iii., p. cxxiv.

[3] This intimacy between Huntley and Bothwell was considered to be a matter of sufficient importance to warrant the issue of a proclamation on 21st April 1566. See Diurnal, p. 99.

no pains to disguise their sentiments. They expressed their contempt in his presence, and even to his face they told him what they thought of his behaviour. In this respect lord Fleming was especially frank and outspoken. Some of the other noblemen of the same party declined to hold any intercourse with him. They said (and truly) that in betraying his wife's cause he had betrayed theirs, and that the life of every one of them had been imperilled by his conduct. They hinted that he had begun with Riccio, and that unless he were curbed he would go further on the same road. Their feelings are intelligible; and we can imagine that the terms in which they expressed them were forcible rather than elegant.

Darnley was a coward, and he acted according to his nature. He shrank before the expression of the contempt and anger with which he was regarded.[1] He was not ashamed, but he was alarmed, and he fled for protection to his wife. He carried to her the pitiful tale of the jibes and slights to which he had been exposed, and he asked her to stand between him and the angry barons who surrounded her. What a moment of humiliation for the woman who called this man her husband! But she bent her pride to intercede for him, and to a certain extent she succeeded in effecting a reconciliation, although the respect of the nobles for Darnley had gone for ever. They began to discuss not only his personal character but his true official position in the court.

[1] He went so far as to publish a declaration (dated Edinburgh, 20th March 1565-6) to the effect that he "plainly declared, upon his honour, fidelity, and in the word of a prince, that he ever knew of any part of the said treasonable conspiracy whereof he is slanderously and saklessly traduced; nor never counselled, commanded, consented, assisted, nor approved of the same." See Cal., B. ix., fol. 213; Goodall, i. 280. See, further, the Letter of Darnley in the Notes and Illustrations appended to this chapter, Note the Second, p. cxxiii.

friend, and he wished to substitute Leslie, because he thought that in him he would find an agent devoted to his own personal interests, a man at once bold, pliant, and unscrupulous. Nau tells us how Darnley set about the execution of his scheme, and how it failed.

Taking advantage of the queen's absence from an ordinary meeting of her privy council, Darnley introduced the measure which he had so deeply at heart. The members who were present agreed to accept the draft of a minute which he laid before them. In it the bishop of Ross was nominated to the office of secretary of state, which was said to be vacant by the resignation of Maitland. Darnley affixed his signature to this document as king, in the belief, as it would appear, that it needed no further authentication to make it operative. How many additional signatures he obtained to this paper, if any, is unknown; certainly it was a document which his enemies would sign much more readily than his friends. But whether they were few or many was of small account with the queen. When she was aware of what had taken place during her absence, by an act of her supreme authority she overruled the nomination of Leslie, and she forbade him to accept the office of secretary, even though it might be offered to him. Maitland, against whose political honesty she had no definite charge to bring forward, was reinstated in his former position. How far she consulted her own interest in doing so may possibly be questioned; but that she acted according to justice and equity is beyond a doubt.

Thus defeated, Darnley broke out into one of his frequent fits of bad temper, and on the following night he sent an angry message to his wife by one of his servants. This attendant gave her some information respecting the mental condition of her wayward husband, which filled her with no little anxiety ; and she went to visit him in his own apartment. She tried to soothe him, and apparently she succeeded. When she left him she carried away with her the loaded pistols which he kept at the top of his bed, and next day she handed them over to the lords of the council. At the same time she explained to them the motives by which she had recently been guided, and endeavoured to remove from their minds the impression that her husband was the enemy of Lethington.

These outbursts of violence naturally alarmed Mary, and all the more so as she gradually became aware by sad experience that she was fast losing whatever influence she might once have possessed over her unmanageable and unreasoning husband. She tried to remove his antipathy towards Moray and Maitland, or at least to induce him to act towards them with greater moderation and self-restraint ; but she did not succeed. His hostility remained as it had been, and he made no attempt to conceal it. She knew them both too well to conclude that because they showed no outward token of resentment, therefore they felt none. As to the final issue of this trial of strength, if it were permitted to run its course, she could have no doubt that it would end in the overthrow of her husband, possibly in her own. With a temper so unloving and so unreflecting as that of Darnley, neither entreaty nor argument had any power. All she could do was to attempt to bring the rivals to a better understanding with each other before some actual collision should make peace an impossibility. But how this was to be done was a difficult question. To prepare the way for the reconciliation, she employed the influence which the laird of Traquair was supposed to have acquired over Darnley ; and she treated Moray

When Mary returned to Edinburgh she went to reside
in the town house of the bishop of Dunkeld,[1] where she
remained until Holyrood was ready for her reception.
Hitherto she had entrusted the management of her
affairs too confidingly to Moray and Lethington, but she
determined that henceforth she would exercise a more
immediate control over them herself. With this view
she frequently presided at the meetings of the privy
council, thus making herself familiar with the transaction
of public business.[2] These meetings were attended by
men of every shade of politics : by Royalists and Republicans, by Catholics and Calvinists. Of course Moray
was there, and he was well supported by his numerous
followers ; Darnley too found time to favour these meetings with his presence and advice. He made no secret
of his hostility towards both Moray and Lethington,
whom he disliked, feared, and calumniated. He could
not have committed a more dangerous mistake ; for to
provoke the enmity of such men as Moray and Lethington was to court destruction. The hostility of Darnley
was fostered by Bothwell and Huntley,[3] who hoped to
find in him a convenient tool whom they could employ
in the carrying out of their own designs. Thus
encouraged Darnley ventured to make a public attack
upon Maitland, the details of which reach us through
Nau's manuscript. Darnley wished to deprive him of

[1] The tenement in which the queen resided at this time had
formerly been the palace of the bishop of Dunkeld, but at the time
specified was occupied by the lord Hume. It was situated "anent
the salt trone." See Diurnal, p. 94.

[2] Mary's attention to business receives a pleasing confirmation from
an unexpected quarter. See Supplemental Note iii., p. cxxiv.

[3] This intimacy between Huntley and Bothwell was considered to
be a matter of sufficient importance to warrant the issue of a proclamation on 21st April 1566. See Diurnal, p. 99.

his office as chief secretary of state, and in his place to appoint John Leslie, better known as the bishop of Ross.

Viewed in itself and apart from its probable results this change had something to recommend it. Leslie was an honest man, and he had given many proofs of his devotion to the interests of Scotland. He was a man of some standing and experience in the foreign and domestic politics of his country. He had faithfully served the late queen dowager, and his constancy to his present sovereign had never been questioned. He had already spent some years in her service, and had gained her respect and confidence. He was trusted by the catholics of Scotland, France, and England; and it was felt that through him it might be possible to renew the communications which had been interrupted with the courts of Rome and Madrid. The principles and conduct of Maitland on the other hand were something more than questionable. He had made common cause with Elizabeth and Cecil, in union with whom he was now working the overthrow of Mary as an independent sovereign. He was a liberal in religion, and like all freethinkers he disliked the catholic faith as being the only form of belief which infidelity had cause to fear. It is obvious then that the change in the cabinet at which Darnley aimed by the appointment of Leslie as secretary of state would have been a real advantage to Mary's cause, provided it could have been safely and justly carried into effect. But the king was not guided by considerations of safety and justice; nor would they have had much weight even if they had been recommended to him. He acted from personal motives only; and unfortunately for his wife as well as for himself, nothing higher than self-interest gave the direction to his conduct. He disliked Maitland because Maitland was Moray's

Mary Stuart took up her permanent residence in Edinburgh castle, there to prepare for the coming event. She was anxious also to make such arrangements as would thwart a design of which some indistinct warnings had reached her. She had been told that an attempt to deprive her of the custody of her infant would be made ; that certain of the lords had determined to seize the child as soon as it was born, that they would baptize it according to the rites of their own faith, and then bring it up according to their own principles. They would do so, they said, because the baby, as heir to the throne, belonged to the realm at large, and not to the parents, neither of whom, being papists, ought to be allowed to exercise any influence upon its education. The queen very naturally found herself in a difficult position. She did not know to whom to turn for advice or protection. She had no confidence in her husband.[1] He had already shown himself so weak and wayward, so obstinate and so faithless, that to her he had become a broken reed.[2]

[1] The anonymous life of Mary tells us that at this time the queen, for Darnley's "more security, if haply she should miscarry at the birth of her son through the fright and fears she had conceived and sustained in the garboils and the pains of her journey, she giveth him her letters patents, according to the custom of the country, under the great seal, for shunning his being in future time called in question to the depriving him possibly of the tutorship of his child after her death." MS. Cott. Cal., B. iv., 148, *b.*

[2] The great object of Darnley's ambition was the possession of the crown matrimonial, with which, and the power which it implied, Mary hesitated to invest him. Even her habitual censor Randolph thought she was right. He thus expresses himself in a letter which he addressed to Cecil : "I cannot tell what misliking of late there hath been between her grace and her husband. He presseth earnestly for the matrimonial crown, which she is loth hastily to grant, but willing to keep somewhat in store, until she know how well he is worthy to enjoy such a sovereignty." Cal. B. ix., 220.

She could not trust her brother, whose schemes in regard to the crown of Scotland were now sufficiently plain, and whose sympathies were identical with the originators of the hostile movement. Standing thus in her solitary estrangement from surrounding interests, she determined that she would try to reconcile all feuds and settle all disputes among the nobility, whom she recognised as the lawful guardians of the Scottish crown, and thus unite them in one common bond of interest. To succeed would be most difficult, but the effort was worth the trial, for even failure itself could do her no harm. The attempt was well nigh a desperate one; it ought to have been successful, but it proved in the end to be a disappointment. But Mary is not to be blamed for its want of success.

With this design of a general amnesty and compromise, about the end of April Mary sent for the earls of Moray and Argyll, and effected a reconciliation between them and the rival earls of Athol, Huntley, and Bothwell.[1] All differences and disputes were to be referred to her arbitration. This having been done, they continued to reside in attendance upon her during the whole of the ensuing summer, and once more the queen restored them to her favour and confidence.

Nau has some remarks to offer upon the pardon granted by Mary to her brother, and they deserve our consideration. Moray assured Mary that Darnley, and Darnley alone, was the cause of the recent disturbances during which the Congregation had risen against their sovereign. He compelled them by the extravagance and harshness of his conduct to act upon the defensive. They had no complaint, they assured her, to make

[1] Upon this reconciliation of the nobility see a letter from Randolph to Cecil, 7th June 1566. R. O. Scot., xii. 68.

against her majesty personally; and they submitted that she had none to make against them save, perhaps, the single offence of having failed to appear before her in her court in obedience to her simple summons. They wished to remind her that this citation had been obtained from her by their inveterate enemies, by whom she was surrounded, men who had gained her confidence, and by whom she had permitted herself to be unjustly influenced. These men aimed at nothing less than the overthrow of the speakers, their fortunes and their families. With ruin before them, the lords were driven, they said, as of necessity, to employ those extreme measures in which alone lay any chance of safety for either life or property. They had no alternative but to disperse as they best might the parliament which had been called for their destruction. They assured her that they had no share in the insults and indignities to which she individually had been exposed. The murder of the late David was a personal matter which belonged solely to lord Ruthven and his adherents. The lords of the Congregation had nothing to do with the death of Riccio; it was an affair with which they had no connection whatever.

Such statements as these, untenable as they were in point of fact, may be supposed to have had some degree of weight in forming Mary's judgment. She admitted that at the beginning of those unhappy disputes between her nobility and herself the only plea of overt enmity which she could urge against Moray had been suggested to her by her husband. And now she had good reason to suppose that every cause of ill-will, real or ideal, between these rivals for the ascendency had been removed. Darnley had forgotten his former jealousies, whatever they might have been; and now Moray had been reinstated in his former position in the court by the sanction of Darnley. It was easy for her to follow in the road in which her husband had thus preceded her, and to complete the reconciliation which he himself had begun. She did this with the greater confidence, because she had remarked that whenever she wished to take any steps against the lords of the Congregation, of whom Moray was the chief, she received but feeble encouragement from the king, her husband. Such was the process of reasoning which at this time passed through the mind of the queen of Scotland, and on which she seems to have acted.

There is much truth in these observations, and they help us to understand at once the difficulties of Mary's position and the line of action which she was driven to adopt under the circumstances. Let us bear in mind, first of all, that this young woman stood alone. She had no one at hand who was able and willing to give her advice, no one to whose wisdom and honesty she could turn with confidence. The cardinal of Lorraine, her mother's brother, lived at a distance, and he was ignorant of the ever varying complications of Scottish politics. She knew that she was surrounded in her court by traitors and enemies; and that, by reason of her religion, she was unpopular with an active and influential body of her own subjects. All these hostile elements were encouraged and fomented by the personal jealousy of Elizabeth, and the national hostility of England. She had no comfort where most of all she had a right to expect it; her married life was not happy. Darnley was unkind and brutal, a drunkard, a profligate, and fond of low company. Politically he was to her a source of daily anxiety, weakness, and danger. He had no fixed principles of conduct, and therefore no fixed line of action. The attitude of hostility which he had assumed towards Moray was the source of continued embarrassment to her. It changed from day to day, according to the passing impulse of the moment, and in his folly the young king expected that his wife should be as wayward and as infirm of purpose as himself. When fear predominated over Darnley, then Moray was to be courted and caressed; but when hatred and arrogance resumed their sway then he and his party were to be crushed and exterminated.

Thus circumstanced, Mary felt it to be her duty to do what she could in order to provide, not only for present difficulties, but also for the still greater dangers which lay before her in the immediate future. The possibility of her death, and the certainty of her enforced absence during several weeks from all control over the affairs of State, compelled her to deliberate upon that future without regard to personal duties, family feuds, or private affections. She could not afford to look at any one single interest apart from the others. She must now aim at comprehension. The court of Holyrood for long had been split up into several rival factions. At the head of one was her husband, and at the head of another was her brother. There was an English party and a national party, a party which clung to the old faith of the church of Rome, and a party which preferred the new teaching and discipline of Geneva. In the event of her death, the fate of a motherless child among such discordant elements might easily be predicted. She could not leave him with any confidence in the keeping of his father. Mary did what she could for the safety of her unborn baby. She collected her disunited nobles around her in Edinburgh castle, and herself set the example of that great coalition which she hoped to effect among them, by pardoning the wrongs and the

She could not trust her brother, whose schemes in regard to the crown of Scotland were now sufficiently plain, and whose sympathies were identical with the originators of the hostile movement. Standing thus in her solitary estrangement from surrounding interests, she determined that she would try to reconcile all feuds and settle all disputes among the nobility, whom she recognised as the lawful guardians of the Scottish crown, and thus unite them in one common bond of interest. To succeed would be most difficult, but the effort was worth the trial, for even failure itself could do her no harm. The attempt was well nigh a desperate one; it ought to have been successful, but it proved in the end to be a disappointment. But Mary is not to be blamed for its want of success.

With this design of a general amnesty and compromise, about the end of April Mary sent for the earls of Moray and Argyll, and effected a reconciliation between them and the rival earls of Athol, Huntley, and Bothwell.[1] All differences and disputes were to be referred to her arbitration. This having been done, they continued to reside in attendance upon her during the whole of the ensuing summer, and once more the queen restored them to her favour and confidence.

Nau has some remarks to offer upon the pardon granted by Mary to her brother, and they deserve our consideration. Moray assured Mary that Darnley, and Darnley alone, was the cause of the recent disturbances during which the Congregation had risen against their sovereign. He compelled them by the extravagance and harshness of his conduct to act upon the defensive. They had no complaint, they assured her, to make

[1] Upon this reconciliation of the nobility see a letter from Randolph to Cecil, 7th June 1566. R. O. Scot., xii. 68.

NOTE THE THIRD.   (See p. cx., Note 2.)

Sir Thomas Craig, who well knew queen Mary, being one of her privy councillors, speaking of her says : " I have often heard the most serene princess Mary, queen of Scotland, discourse so appositely and rationally in all affairs which were brought before the privy council that she was admired by all.   And when most of the councillors were silent, being astonished, they straight declared themselves to be of her opinion, she rebuked them sharply and exhorted them to speak freely, as becomes unprejudiced councillors, against her opinion, that the best reasons only might overrule their determinations.   And, truly, her reasonings were so strong and clear that she could turn their hearts to what side she pleased.   She had not studied law ; and yet, by the natural light of her judgment, when she reasoned of matters of equity and justice, she ofttimes had the advantage of the ablest lawyers.   Her other discourses and actions were suitable to her great judgment.   No word ever dropped from her mouth that was not exactly weighed and pondered.   As for her liberality and other virtues they are well known."

Craig's Answer to Dolman, cap. 10, p. 84, quoted in Mackenzie's Scot. Writers, iii. 353.

NOTE THE FOURTH.   (See p. cix., Note 1.)

The anonymous Life of queen Mary[1] gives us some information as to the spirit in which Mary received Elizabeth's intercession in favour of the rebels who had fled from Scotland and found a refuge in England.

The queen of England, when she perceived that the drift of this complot took not all the effects that in reason were to be expected and without question intended, as the ruin of both mother, child, and father, and that her partizans were dispersed, sendeth greeting to the queen of Scotland by a captain of Berwick, called Carew,[2] congratulating her escape, con-

[1] Cal., B. iv. 148, b.

[2] Captain Carew, of Berwick, is mentioned in the monthly charges of that garrison, 27th June 1563.   See R. O. Foreign, No. 946.

been reinstated in his former position in the court by the sanction of Darnley. It was easy for her to follow in the road in which her husband had thus preceded her, and to complete the reconciliation which he himself had begun. She did this with the greater confidence, because she had remarked that whenever she wished to take any steps against the lords of the Congregation, of whom Moray was the chief, she received but feeble encouragement from the king, her husband. Such was the process of reasoning which at this time passed through the mind of the queen of Scotland, and on which she seems to have acted.

There is much truth in these observations, and they help us to understand at once the difficulties of Mary's position and the line of action which she was driven to adopt under the circumstances. Let us bear in mind, first of all, that this young woman stood alone. She had no one at hand who was able and willing to give her advice, no one to whose wisdom and honesty she could turn with confidence. The cardinal of Lorraine, her mother's brother, lived at a distance, and he was ignorant of the ever varying complications of Scottish politics. She knew that she was surrounded in her court by traitors and enemies; and that, by reason of her religion, she was unpopular with an active and influential body of her own subjects. All these hostile elements were encouraged and fomented by the personal jealousy of Elizabeth, and the national hostility of England. She had no comfort where most of all she had a right to expect it; her married life was not happy. Darnley was unkind and brutal, a drunkard, a profligate, and fond of low company. Politically he was to her a source of daily anxiety, weakness, and danger. He had no fixed principles of conduct, and

CHAPTER THE FOURTH.

FROM THE BIRTH OF JAMES THE SIXTH UNTIL THE MURDER OF KING HENRY DARNLEY.

DURING the period of Mary's seclusion from public life, occasioned by her confinement, the conduct of her husband formed a continual source of misery to herself and of scandal to her friends. Regardless of her happiness and of his own reputation, he led a life which was far from respectable, and associated with companions who encouraged him in his profligacy. In vain his wife remonstrated and entreated; he was deaf to reason and unmoved by affection. Whatever she did, or did not do, offended him. He was offended because she would not join in his quarrel with Lethington and Moray. He was offended because she had asked the Queen of England to become sponsor to his child. He ceased to cohabit with his wife, and went to reside with his father in Glasgow, who encouraged him in his estrangement, and still further embittered his feelings already more than hostile. It was impossible to know how to deal with a temper at once so jealous, so fickle, and so irritable. Mary comforted herself in the thought that the majority of her councillors sympathised with her in her trouble, and were resolved to support her. She devoted herself therefore to her public duties as the readiest mode of enabling her to overcome her domestic misfortunes.

A piece of fraud upon a small scale came to light about this time which, however insignificant in itself, is worthy of notice as illustrating the system of petty deception to which Elizabeth's ministers condescended to resort. They were apprehensive of an outbreak among the catholic population of the north of England, who, goaded to desperation by the sufferings to which they were exposed for their faith, were said to be upon the point of rising in open rebellion. It had been rumoured that they were encouraged by the queen of Scotland, who promised that she would assist them. It was important that the truth or falsehood of this report should be ascertained. For this purpose Cecil employed the services of a gentleman connected with the respectable Yorkshire family of Rokeby. This personage presented himself at the court of Holyrood, bringing with him letters of introduction to the queen, with which he had been furnished by sir Henry Percy and his brother, the earl of Northumberland. Rokeby professed to be a catholic, in token of which he offered for the acceptance of her majesty a carving in ivory which represented the sufferings of our blessed Lord. She accepted the gift.[1] Having thus gained her confidence he gradually unfolded the real object of his mission. He gave her to understand that many of the English nobility, especially the catholics, were weary of Elizabeth's rule, and would gladly make the attempt to throw it off, provided they might count upon her approval of the undertaking. He was urgent with her that she should signify her sanction of their design, and mentioned the names of certain families of distinction who would assuredly make common cause with the insurgents upon receiving from her a few words of encouragement.

Mary was too discreet to be caught by such a state-

[1] Possibly the "Histoire de la Passion," which is mentioned in the inventory of the queen's jewels given in Lab. vii. 243.

ment. She disclaimed any feeling of hostility towards the queen of England. She refused to furnish Rokeby with the letter which he solicited. Disappointed but not discouraged Cecil's agent returned to England, and succeeded in obtaining from the unwary Percys certain documents which seemed to prove that he was employed by them in the way he had stated. Furnished with these he returned to Edinburgh, but an unexpected reception there awaited him. During his absence Mary's suspicions as to his real character had been confirmed, and as soon as he set foot in the Scottish capital he was arrested. His papers revealed the nature of the plot, of which he intended to have made her the victim, but which had proved his own ruin. Among these papers was one by which Cecil promised to Rokeby, in the name of his mistress, a grant of land to the annual value of one hundred pounds, on the production by him of letters, signed by Mary and addressed to the Percys, establishing the charge of her complicity in the intended rising against Elizabeth.

Rokeby experienced the usual fate of traitors. When he had served his turn he was disowned and forgotten by his employers. Mary's indignation, largely mingled with contempt, was satisfied with a very moderate punishment. She banished him to Spyney castle, a residence of the Bishop of Moray, where he remained in neglected obscurity for eighteen months. We can pity the tool thus thrown aside when no longer useful for mischief, but what shall we think of the honesty of the person who condescended to use it?

The details with which Nau has supplied us respecting Mary's visit to Bothwell, who was lying in Hermitage castle dangerously wounded, and the illness by which she herself was attacked upon her return to Jedburgh, are so minute and at the same time so important that they claim our careful attention. Interesting in itself this part of her history becomes doubly so from the fact that upon it has been engrafted one of the most successful of Buchanan's slanders against his royal benefactress.

The outline of the story is briefly this. Mary left Edinburgh on 8th October 1566, and on the evening of the same day she reached Jedburgh. There she remained for a week, engaged along with her council in discussing the various questions which had arisen during the assizes. The condition of the Borders was such as to occasion no little anxiety to her government. That unquiet district had become more than usually troublesome by reason of the intrigues of Cecil, who had encouraged some of the more turbulent of the "broken men" to wage a harassing warfare upon such of their neighbours as remained true in their allegiance to Scotland. To curb these marauders was the official duty of Bothwell, who with this object went to reside in the castle of Hermitage. On the day on which Mary left Edinburgh Bothwell was severely wounded by one of the clan of the Elliots, whom he had attempted to capture, and for some time his life was in danger. The intelligence must have reached Mary immediately upon her arrival in Jedburgh, yet there she remained, intent upon the duties which had brought her thither. It was not until the 16th, when the assizes had closed, that she took her famous ride to sympathise and condole with the nobleman who had been wounded in the discharge of his duty as her servant.

Concerned as the queen naturally must have been in the welfare of one of her nobility who was suffering from a severe injury, it is gratifying to learn that she did not undertake the journey simply in obedience to her own personal feelings. Nau tells us that she was " requested and advised " to do so. And the object which induced her to undertake this expedition is also recorded by the same authority. It was in order that she might receive his report upon the condition of that part of Scotland of which he was the lord warden. What could be more natural than that the queen should pay an official visit to a trusted servant who had nearly lost his life in her service ? As such it was understood by her attendants. Fortunately for herself she was accompanied by Moray and several others of her courtiers. The party therefore must have been tolerably numerous, and presented nothing of that suspiciously private character with which it has been invested by some of Mary's calumniators.

When the queen reached the Hermitage she found that Bothwell was convalescent, and that he was able to converse with her upon matters of business. Her stay was not a long one. When we consider the length of the journey, the nature of the ground which had to be traversed by a party on horseback, and the shortness of daylight in the middle of October, it will be evident that the time actually spent by Mary within the walls of the Hermitage could not well have exceeded the two hours to which lord Scrope limits it in a letter which he addressed to secretary Cecil.

On the day which succeeded this memorable ride to Hermitage castle the queen was seized with a sudden and alarming attack of illness. It might be attributed naturally enough to the fatigues to which she had so recently been exposed, to her growing consciousness of the gravity of her position, and to her distress occasioned by the heartless misconduct of her husband. Of all these possible causes Nau must have been fully aware, and yet he does not hesitate to ascribe the attack to the administration of a dose of poison. By whom given he does not say. But if his suspicions are admitted to be correct, then the whole drift of the story as told by him leads to. the conclusion that Moray was the poisoner. Nau has recorded the symptoms with a precision of detail which makes it probable that they are derived from notes taken by one who was present on the occasion, possibly the bishop of Ross. Suspicion was always on the alert, and the medical science of the time was so imperfect that these notes are of no great value; but as far as they illustrate the case, the symptoms which they record are scarcely consistent with any known disease, and would rather point to the action of some irritant poison.

Mary was conscious of her danger, and, like a wise and good woman, she prepared herself to meet that which she saw at no great distance before her. She was anxious upon three points, and to these she now turned her attention while as yet she had the command of her intellect and the power of speech. One was as to the future government of her kingdom; the second related to the safety and education of her child; and the third concerned her own soul. The way in which she proposed to deal with these three urgent questions is detailed in a most interesting paper which of late has been ably edited by the learned keeper of the library of the university of Edinburgh, but which has not as yet attracted the attention to which it is entitled. With the object of extending the knowledge of a document so valuable in itself, and which leads to conclusions of such importance respecting the queen, it is here given among the Illustrative Notes appended to this chapter.[1]

Neither during the period of Mary's severe illness, nor that of her lingering recovery, did her husband exhibit

---

[1] See p. cxxxvii. A reference, however, to "Mackenzie's Scottish Writers" (iii. 281, fol., Edinb., 1722), shows that this, or a similar document, was known to the antiquarians of last century.

CHAPTER THE FOURTH.

FROM THE BIRTH OF JAMES THE SIXTH UNTIL THE MURDER OF KING HENRY DARNLEY.

DURING the period of Mary's seclusion from public life, occasioned by her confinement, the conduct of her husband formed a continual source of misery to herself and of scandal to her friends. Regardless of her happiness and of his own reputation, he led a life which was far from respectable, and associated with companions who encouraged him in his profligacy. In vain his wife remonstrated and entreated; he was deaf to reason and unmoved by affection. Whatever she did, or did not do, offended him. He was offended because she would not join in his quarrel with Lethington and Moray. He was offended because she had asked the Queen of England to become sponsor to his child. He ceased to cohabit with his wife, and went to reside with his father in Glasgow, who encouraged him in his estrangement, and still further embittered his feelings already more than hostile. It was impossible to know how to deal with a temper at once so jealous, so fickle, and so irritable. Mary comforted herself in the thought that the majority of her councillors sympathised with her in her trouble, and were resolved to support her. She devoted herself therefore to her public duties as the readiest mode of enabling her to overcome her domestic misfortunes.

A piece of fraud upon a small scale came to light about this time which, however insignificant in itself, is worthy of notice as illustrating the system of petty deception to which Elizabeth's ministers condescended to resort. They were apprehensive of an outbreak among the catholic population of the north of England, who, goaded to desperation by the sufferings to which they were exposed for their faith, were said to be upon the point of rising in open rebellion. It had been rumoured that they were encouraged by the queen of Scotland, who promised that she would assist them. It was important that the truth or falsehood of this report should be ascertained. For this purpose Cecil employed the services of a gentleman connected with the respectable Yorkshire family of Rokeby. This personage presented himself at the court of Holyrood, bringing with him letters of introduction to the queen, with which he had been furnished by sir Henry Percy and his brother, the earl of Northumberland. Rokeby professed to be a catholic, in token of which he offered for the acceptance of her majesty a carving in ivory which represented the sufferings of our blessed Lord. She accepted the gift.[1] Having thus gained her confidence he gradually unfolded the real object of his mission. He gave her to understand that many of the English nobility, especially the catholics, were weary of Elizabeth's rule, and would gladly make the attempt to throw it off, provided they might count upon her approval of the undertaking. He was urgent with her that she should signify her sanction of their design, and mentioned the names of certain families of distinction who would assuredly make common cause with the insurgents upon receiving from her a few words of encouragement.

Mary was too discreet to be caught by such a state-

[1] Possibly the " Histoire de la Passion," which is mentioned in the inventory of the queen's jewels given in Lab. vii. 243.

ment. She disclaimed any feeling of hostility towards the queen of England. She refused to furnish Rokeby with the letter which he solicited. Disappointed but not discouraged Cecil's agent returned to England, and succeeded in obtaining from the unwary Percys certain documents which seemed to prove that he was employed by them in the way he had stated. Furnished with these he returned to Edinburgh, but an unexpected reception there awaited him. During his absence Mary's suspicions as to his real character had been confirmed, and as soon as he set foot in the Scottish capital he was arrested. His papers revealed the nature of the plot, of which he intended to have made her the victim, but which had proved his own ruin. Among these papers was one by which Cecil promised to Rokeby, in the name of his mistress, a grant of land to the annual value of one hundred pounds, on the production by him of letters, signed by Mary and addressed to the Percys, establishing the charge of her complicity in the intended rising against Elizabeth.

Rokeby experienced the usual fate of traitors. When he had served his turn he was disowned and forgotten by his employers. Mary's indignation, largely mingled with contempt, was satisfied with a very moderate punishment. She banished him to Spyney castle, a residence of the Bishop of Moray, where he remained in neglected obscurity for eighteen months. We can pity the tool thus thrown aside when no longer useful for mischief, but what shall we think of the honesty of the person who condescended to use it?

The details with which Nau has supplied us respecting Mary's visit to Bothwell, who was lying in Hermitage castle dangerously wounded, and the illness by which she herself was attacked upon her return to Jedburgh, are so minute and at the same time so important that they claim our careful attention. Interesting in itself this part of her history becomes doubly so from the fact that upon it has been engrafted one of the most successful of Buchanan's slanders against his royal benefactress.

The outline of the story is briefly this. Mary left Edinburgh on 8th October 1566, and on the evening of the same day she reached Jedburgh. There she remained for a week, engaged along with her council in discussing the various questions which had arisen during the assizes. The condition of the Borders was such as to occasion no little anxiety to her government. That unquiet district had become more than usually troublesome by reason of the intrigues of Cecil, who had encouraged some of the more turbulent of the "broken men" to wage a harassing warfare upon such of their neighbours as remained true in their allegiance to Scotland. To curb these marauders was the official duty of Bothwell, who with this object went to reside in the castle of Hermitage. On the day on which Mary left Edinburgh Bothwell was severely wounded by one of the clan of the Elliots, whom he had attempted to capture, and for some time his life was in danger. The intelligence must have reached Mary immediately upon her arrival in Jedburgh, yet there she remained, intent upon the duties which had brought her thither. It was not until the 16th, when the assizes had closed, that she took her famous ride to sympathise and condole with the nobleman who had been wounded in the discharge of his duty as her servant.

Concerned as the queen naturally must have been in the welfare of one of her nobility who was suffering from a severe injury, it is gratifying to learn that she did not undertake the journey simply in obedience to her own personal feelings. Nau tells us that she was " requested arrangement for his convenience she went to reside in Holyrood, along with the baby James, where, of course, the infectious nature of her husband's disease made it impossible that he should accompany her. He was unwilling to be seen by any one; he wore a covering of taffeta before his face, and would not permit his windows to be opened. He was upon the most confidential terms with his wife as to the past doings and future intentions of some of his previous associates, and promised that in due time he would make disclosures yet more startling. He warned her especially to be on her guard against Lethington, who at that time was bitterly opposed to her. He seemed to be conscious of his past misconduct, and to be anxious to atone for it. But Darnley did not live to carry his good intentions into execution, for about three or four o'clock on the morning of the 10th of February 1567, he was murdered by the explosion of gunpowder placed in a mine driven under the house in which he was sleeping. According to Nau, the murder was planned by the earls of Bothwell and Morton and James Balfour, whose complicity in the crime was established by a bond, written by Alexander Hay, one of the clerks of the council, and signed by the earls of Moray, Huntley, Bothwell, and Morton, along with Lethington and some others. The murderers pretended that in putting the king to death they were acting for the public good, and that their object was to free the queen from the bondage in which she was held by her husband. They maintained, moreover, that their own lives would be in danger should the king gain that ascendency in the government at which he was aiming. These men, who were the actual murderers, were the persons who afterwards were the loudest in demanding an investigation, and the most active in endeavouring to throw the guilt upon her majesty the queen of Scotland.

does not say.   But if his suspicions are admitted to be correct, then the whole drift of the story as told by him leads to. the conclusion that Moray was the poisoner. Nau has recorded the symptoms with a precision of detail which makes it probable that they are derived from notes taken by one who was present on the occasion, possibly the bishop of Ross.   Suspicion was always on the alert, and the medical science of the time was so imperfect that these notes are of no great value ; but as far as they illustrate the case, the symptoms which they record are scarcely consistent with any known disease, and would rather point to the action of some irritant poison.

Mary was conscious of her danger, and, like a wise and good woman, she prepared herself to meet that which she saw at no great distance before her.   She was anxious upon three points, and to these she now turned her attention while as yet she had the command of her intellect and the power of speech.   One was as to the future government of her kingdom ; the second related to the safety and education of her child ; and the third concerned her own soul.   The way in which she proposed to deal with these three urgent questions is detailed in a most interesting paper which of late has been ably edited by the learned keeper of the library of the university of Edinburgh, but which has not as yet attracted the attention to which it is entitled.   With the object of extending the knowledge of a document so valuable in itself, and which leads to conclusions of such importance respecting the queen, it is here given among the Illustrative Notes appended to this chapter.[1]

Neither during the period of Mary's severe illness, nor that of her lingering recovery, did her husband exhibit

---

[1] See p. cxxxvii. A reference, however, to "Mackenzie's Scottish Writers" (iii. 281, fol., Edinb., 1722), shows that this, or a similar document, was known to the antiquarians of last century.

either concern or affection. He visited her once, remaining one night at Jedburgh, and on the following
day he returned to Glasgow, which had now become his
usual place of residence.   On her convalescence the
queen, attended by a large body of her nobles, made a
tour of inspection through the unsettled border districts.   Moray was with her, and so was Bothwell in
virtue of his office. Attended by a guard of five hundred
horsemen, the cavalcade halted on the high ground which
looks down upon the formidable stronghold of Berwick,
where she was welcomed by the English governor of the
town, and the garrison.   She then returned to Holyrood
with restored health and spirits, ready and willing to
devote herself to the responsibilities of her position.

The next matter which claimed her attention was the
baptism of the young prince.   It had been decided some
time previously that this ceremony should take place at
Stirling, and that it should be carried out in accordance
with the impressive ritual of the catholic church.
There was no reason why it should not be so.   The
catholic religion had for centuries been the religion of
the state, and was so still.   It was the religion which
was professed by the father and mother of the child, and
in which they intended that the future king of Scotland
should be educated.[1] Two of the sponsors who had been

[1] Darnley was not always steadfast in his religion, but at times he
was earnest.   Thus, Randolph writing to Cecil, on 25th December
1565, says : "The queen's husband never gave greater token of his
religion than this last night. He was at matins and mass in the morning, before day, and heard the high mass devoutly upon his knees,
though she, herself, the most part of the night sat up at cards, and
went to bed when it was almost day." R. O. Scot. Eliz., xi. 103. See
also Cal. B. ix., 214, Bedford to Cecil : the lord Darnley and this
queen fall still to popery, for on Candlemas day last, they carried
their candles, and since that time seek further to advance it. Berwick, 8th February 1565-6.

invited to assist on the occasion were catholics. Yet with a singular inconsistency of which it is not easy to approve, Mary invited the protestant queen of England to become godmother to the prince, and with equal inconsistency Elizabeth accepted the invitation. Her ingenuity soon discovered a cheap and easy method of mortifying her rival through this very interchange of civilities. She sent on this occasion as her ambassador one of the extremest calvinists in her court, the puritanical earl of Bedford. So little did she care to make his visit acceptable, that he was instructed to press Mary for the ratification of the obnoxious treaty of Leith. As her proxy in the baptismal office she selected a lady whose opinions were so pronounced, that when her services were required at the font she refused to assist at a catholic function or even to enter a catholic church. And in order that nothing might be wanting to complete the humiliation which was to be heaped on Mary and her husband, and on an occasion when it was known that she would be surrounded by her nobility, every member of the English court was forbidden, by the express orders of Elizabeth, to offer any token of respect to Darnley, or to address him by the title of king. In proof of the stringency with which these regulations were carried out by Bedford and his retinue, reference may be made to a curious narrative appended to this chapter. It is evidently derived from trustworthy information, and is in harmony with the spirit which is painfully conspicuous in Elizabeth's intercourse with the queen of Scotland.[1]

Darnley would have been an object of pity had not he been so meddlesome and so mischievous. Mary trusted much to the friendship of the catholic powers

[1] See p. cxlv.

k

of Europe as affording her something of a protection
against the undisguised ill-will of England. Her husband did his best, or his worst, to ruin this her last
stronghold. The continuator of Knox tells us that,
"desolate and half desperate, by the advice of some
foolish Cagots, he wrote to the pope, to the king of Spain,
and to the king of France, complaining of the state of
the country, which was all out of order, all because that
mass and popery were not again erected, giving the
whole blame thereof to the queen as not managing the
catholic cause aright." [1] A copy of these letters fell into
the queen's hands, and must have added in no small
degree to the difficulties of her position. Du Croc [2]
addressed a report to the queen of France, in which he
explained the unmanageable character of Darnley; but
the mischief had been done. With Darnley's letter in
her hands, Catherine de Medicis had become possessed of a
formidable instrument, by which she could effectually
cripple the hated queen of Scotland; and there seems
reason to believe that she employed it for this purpose.
It is certain that from about this time we hear less of
the sympathy and the assistance of these former allies of
the queen of Scotland.

On Christmas Eve (24th December 1566) Darnley left
Stirling without bidding farewell to his wife, and returned to his usual abode in Glasgow. Early in January
he was seized with an illness which was found to be
small-pox, which at that time was rife in the neigh-

[1] Knox, ii. 533. The Cagots were "an unfortunate race of people in
the Pyrenees, included by French writers among the *races maudites*."

[2] See Teulet, ii. 289. About this time Darnley amused himself
with forming schemes for the invasion of England, for seizing the
Scilly Islands, for taking possession of Scarborough Castle, &c. Of
course his plans were known to Cecil, to whom they must have
afforded no little amusement. See R. O. Scot. Eliz., xii. 82, xiii. 6.

bourhood.   Hearing of his attack, Mary sent her
own physician[1] to attend upon him, and shortly afterwards she joined him herself.   Sickness teaches many a
lesson, and under its influence Darnley felt that he had
been unjust to his wife.   He confessed his faults and
promised amendment, and in token of his wish to atone
for the past he determined that he would return with
her to Edinburgh.   Mary believed that she had recovered
his affection, and along with it her influence, and the
reconciliation between the husband and the wife now
appeared to be complete.   They left Glasgow on
27th of January, and reached Edinburgh on the last
day of that month.

According to the plan which had been settled between
the queen and Darnley, it was originally intended that
he should have gone to reside at Craigmillar,[2] but this
arrangement had been set aside "upon the report of
James Balfour and some others," who induced the king
to lodge in the ill-omened Kirk of Field.   Nau tells us
that her majesty was opposed to the change, but her
objections were overruled.   After having made every

[1] R. O. Scot. Eliz., xiii. 3 ; 9th January 1567.

[2] The following passage is a translation of the account of Darnley's
murder given by the bishop of Ross in his unprinted manuscript
preserved in the Secret Archives of the Vatican.

Darnley having gone to Glasgow to visit his father, the earl of Lennox, was there attacked by an illness which confined him to his bed.
Leaving Edinburgh the queen went to him and comforted him so much
by her words and her presence that he somewhat rallied, and so far
regained his strength as to be able to return to Edinburgh along with
her.   He did this by the advice of the nobility and physicians.
He was taken to the house of the Provost of Saint Mary's in the
Fields.   Although it was a humble building, and perhaps scarcely
adapted for the abode of royalty, yet by the advice of the doctors it had
been furnished and decorated with the royal furniture and hangings
for the use of his majesty, as being the most healthy spot in the whole
town.   The queen paid him a daily visit, accompanied by many of her
nobles ; and sometimes the conversation lasted till midnight.

This singularly interesting narrative receives an important confirmation from a letter written shortly afterwards by a well informed member of the Society of Jesus, at that time resident in Paris. This document is as follows :—

LETTER from F. Edmund Hay, S.J., to S. Francis Borgia, Father General of the Society of Jesus, dated at Paris, 6th November 1566.[1]

Very Reverend Father in Christ.
The Peace of Christ.
The purpose for which the reverend Nuncio[2] sent me into Scotland before his own journey thither is doubtless already known to you from his letters. The F. Provincial has written

[1] From the original, in the Secret Archives of the Society of Jesus. The original is in Latin.

[2] The bishop of Mondovi. See Labanoff, ii. 20; vii. 107. The following extract from the unpublished Memoirs of Bishop Leslie, preserved in the Secret Archives of the Vatican, furnishes us with some new information upon the mission of this Nuncio:—
"About this time the most Reverend the bishop of Mondovi was sent to console the queen in Scotland by pope Pius the Fifth as a Legate a Latere, together with a present of 150,000 crowns of gold, that she might wage war with the heretics. His aid had been requested in her name by the bishop of Dumblane and Master Stephen Woltar [Wilson]. The pope further promised that he would never desert her; but, on the contrary, would render her yet more efficient assistance, if it were needed.
"The queen did her best, as well directly as by the bishop of Ross and others, to induce the nobles to give free entrance into the kingdom to the papal legate. The catholic nobility were most anxious for this. No argument, however, could move the sectarian nobles, and especially the earl of Moray, to assent. It became necessary, therefore, for the queen to send John Beton into France, to offer her excuses to the legate on this head. Beton (who was a person of good rank, an excellent catholic, and a man of high character in every respect) brought back with him a portion of the money." Leslie's Paralipomena, fol. 354.

SUPPLEMENTAL NOTES AND ILLUSTRATIONS
TO CHAPTER THE FOURTH.

NOTE THE FIRST.   (See p. cxxxi., Note 1.)

THE DECLARATION of the Will of the most mighty and virtuous princess, Mary Queen of Scotland, Dowager of France, during the time of her extreme malady, with the prayers and exhortations made by her.[1]

My lords, who are presently near unto me, since it has pleased God to visit me with this sickness, and yet of His infinite goodness has given me time and leisure to declare unto you my will and intention, and "syk lyke" to cry to Him for mercy for many and most great offences which I have committed against His Majesty, I will not forget to make this discourse in your presences of the desire which I have as well towards the common weal of this country and business of this world, as of my duty unto my Lord my God.

And first, ye have known the good will and affection which in all times I have borne unto the common weal and rest of this realm, and also the love and most earnest affection which I have unto ye all in general, and every one in particular, travailing by all occasions "till enterteny" you together in the like love, charity, and concord.   And for this cause I require of you the like love[2] and affection of heart and common accord (such as I have always wished to be amongst you, by the which we all, as members of one body

---

[1] From the original in the possession of the University of Edinburgh, for the use of which I am indebted to the courtesy of John Small, Esq., Librarian to that learned body.   Mr Small has already printed this document in a volume entitled, "Queen Mary at Jedburgh in 1566."   Edin. 1881.   Quarto.

[2] The word "love" is an interlineation.

of this common weal, may put yourselves together), for to hold this same belief and obedience, due as well to God as unto the civil society and common rest, with administration of justice among the subjects of this realm. You know forsooth that by the diversity of governors, provinces and regions are troubled and molested; and contrary by agreement and unity stablished, pacified, and advanced. Wherefore, above all things, I require you to have charity, concord, and love amongst yourselves.

Secondly, I commend my son, your natural Prince, unto you, praying you most earnestly to have respect to bring him up and nourish him in the fear of God and all virtues and godly exercises, as you will answer unto God and the common weal of this realm. And that you suffer no evil company to be near him during the [*time*][1] of his youthhead, which by wicked companies may be induced to "misknaw" his duty towards his God and the world, and that he be corrected in his youth, to the end that he may reign as a Christian and virtuous Prince in this realm.

My lords, you know the goodness that I have used towards some whom I have advanced to a great degree of honour and pre-eminence above others; who, notwithstanding, has used more "nor" ingratitude towards me, which has engendered the displeasure that presently most grieves me, and also is the cause of my sickness. I pray God mend them.

Also there is some that has grievously offended me, and of whom I desire no great vengeance, but remits them to the will of God, for I am sure that He will have regard to my just cause. Yet for all aventures I pray you[2] if it come to pass that after my decease they return to this realm, you suffer them not to have any access near my son, nor government, nor authority near his person.

And since it[3] has pleased God to shorten my days, and that I have lived in great honours and triumphs to this present, now I "lightly" such vanities, and think me one of

---

[1] Here added to supply an accidental omission in the text.
[2] *You*, added above the line.
[3] The word *it* was omitted at first, but supplied on revision.

the most humble and poor creatures of the earth, and casts me at the feet of my Creator, ready to embrace His will. Nevertheless, after my decease (if you please) ye shall have regard to cause " earde " my body.

You know also, my lords, the favour that I have borne unto you since my arriving[1] in this realm, and that I have pressed none of you that professes the religion by your conscience. I pray you also on your part not to press them that make profession of the old faith catholic. And if you knew what it were of a person that is in extremity, as I am, and that it behoved him to think that he " man " render count of his faults, as I do, you would never press them. I pray you, brother, earl of Moray, that you trouble[2] none.

My lords, you know that before I took bed[3] I made my testament in such sort as was convenient, the which I have sealed and subscribed with my hand, and closed with stamp, which presently is in Sterling. I beseech you altogether[4] most affectiously and for the honour of God, that you open it, and take pain that the points contained intil it may be kept and put to execution ; holding myself most certain that that which is within it is noways prejudicial to the laws of this realm. And if peradventure things be not so well established as were necessary, I pray you with one accord to provide to the best for the government of this realm and according to the laws of this same, the which I have never desired prejudge.

Hereafter returning to my lord the ambassador of France, called Monsieur Du Croc, who then was present, said unto him, Monsieur Du Croc, you see how it has pleased God to visit me with this malady, whereby it is evident that the hour of my death approaches, and that it pleases my God to call me out of this life to His mercy. For this cause I will speak of four things unto you.

As touching the first, you shall testify to the king, my

[1] Originally, arrival.
[2] The sentence at first stood thus :—That you never trouble none.
[3] Originally, before my dying.
[4] Altogether, an interlineation.

already been made. The writer, whoever he may have been,
thus tells what he has to say :—

Things standing at this point, ensueth the christening of
the prince, whither was deputed for ambassador of the queen
of England's part, the earl of Bedford, governor of Berwick,
a chief pillar of the puritans, wholly at Cecil's the secretary's
devotion, mightily against the queen of Scotland's pretence to
the crown of England. Notwithstanding, of her part there
was nothing wanting for well entertaining of him ; she commanding the lord Hume, warden of her East Borders, with
five or six hundred horse, to accompany him unto Dunbar ;
and the next day by her like commandment another troop met
with him and convoyed him to Edinburgh ; from whence he
was conducted by the lord of Arbroath, the duke of Châtelherault's son, and his troop to Lithgow ; between which and
Stirling met with him the earls of Argyll, Bothwell, Athol,
Moray, and Morton, with many more earls and noblemen ;
and, finally, all the gallants of the court with a train of
followers, according to the quality and numbers of the nobility ; and so led him in orderly array to his lodging appointed
for him in the town of Stirling, the place assigned for the
christening, and where the queen made her residence.

She immediately for further compliment sendeth to give
him the welcome, and to observe other courtesies in such
case required ; and desiring it might stand with his liking to
permit the young gentlemen of his train to come that night
to pass their time in the court in dancing and other conversation. Hereunto the earl yielded, and these gentlemen
being most respectively entertained that night, the next day
the earl presented himself in person and declared his commission ; a thing of his part well discharged, and of hers in
like sort gratefully accepted, as appeared by her countenance
and all other her actions liked of all the world that beheld
them, and especially by the other ambassadors of France and
Savoy. And this the carriage of her person and her intention to entertain them in all honourable sort was confirmed
by the feasts, banquets, pageants, fireworks, and what else
belonging to triumph and joy.

pardon. Grant me mercy, for I seek not long life in this world, but only that Thy will may be fulfilled in me. O my God, Thou hast appointed me above the people of this realm, to rule and govern them. If, therefore, it be Thy pleasure that I remain to them in this mortal life, albeit that it be painful to my body, so that it please Thy divine[1] goodness, I will give myself to Thy keeping. If Thy pleasure and purpose be to call me from hence, so I come and with good will I remit myself to Thy pleasure, and is as well deliberate to die as to live, desiring that Thy will be fulfilled. And as the good king Ezechias, afflicted with sickness and other infirmities, turned him to Thy divine will and pleasure, so do I the like.

O most merciful Creator, I confess that I have not used Thy gifts to the advancement of Thy glory and honour, and good example of life to my people that has been committed under my charge as I ought to have done, but rather has been transported by the fragility of . . . and . . . I have offended Thy Majesty, not using my eyes as my duty required, for the which cause presently Thou most worthily hast taken from me the power of them. But my God, who of Thy goodness and infinite grace healed the man who was born blind and gave him power to see, grant unto me so long as I live in this mortal life that not only I may have the fruition of "thir" corporeal eyes, but also that with the eyes of faith and spirit I may behold Thy divine Majesty, or otherwise take this life from me according to Thy pleasure and will. I have diverse times offended Thy divine goodness, but yet have I no ways declined from Thy faith, but still continued and constantly persevered in the catholic faith, in the which I was instructed, brought up, and nourished, and of the which, before Thy divine goodness and in the presence of all that understands me, I make profession, desiring Thee of Thy infinite goodness to grant me the strength and constancy to persevere in this same unto my last sobs, and that I decline not from it, but constantly to continue.

[1] At this point the writing is very indistinct, and many of the words given in the text are uncertain.

This singularly interesting narrative receives an important confirmation from a letter written shortly afterwards by a well informed member of the Society of Jesus, at that time resident in Paris. This document is as follows :—

LETTER from F. Edmund Hay, S.J., to S. Francis Borgia, Father General of the Society of Jesus, dated at Paris, 6th November 1566.[1]

Very Reverend Father in Christ.
The Peace of Christ.
The purpose for which the reverend Nuncio[2] sent me into Scotland before his own journey thither is doubtless already known to you from his letters. The F. Provincial has written

[1] From the original, in the Secret Archives of the Society of Jesus. The original is in Latin.

[2] The bishop of Mondovi. See Labanoff, ii. 20; vii. 107. The following extract from the unpublished Memoirs of Bishop Leslie, preserved in the Secret Archives of the Vatican, furnishes us with some new information upon the mission of this Nuncio:—

"About this time the most Reverend the bishop of Mondovi was sent to console the queen in Scotland by pope Pius the Fifth as a Legate a Latere, together with a present of 150,000 crowns of gold, that she might wage war with the heretics. His aid had been requested in her name by the bishop of Dumblane and Master Stephen Woltar [Wilson]. The pope further promised that he would never desert her ; but, on the contrary, would render her yet more efficient assistance, if it were needed.

"The queen did her best, as well directly as by the bishop of Ross and others, to induce the nobles to give free entrance into the kingdom to the papal legate. The catholic nobility were most anxious for this. No argument, however, could move the sectarian nobles, and especially the earl of Moray, to assent. It became necessary, therefore, for the queen to send John Beton into France, to offer her excuses to the legate on this head. Beton (who was a person of good rank, an excellent catholic, and a man of high character in every respect) brought back with him a portion of the money." Leslie's Paralipomena, fol. 354.

That done, he was carried into a stately chamber of his own side, where the French ambassador presented his master's gift, which was a carkanet of rich work, with other jewels.

Then he went with the queen into the hall, where she supped at one board with all the three deputies. Every one was served with his mess of meat, and all at one instant, by her majesty's four servers, earls, to the board. At another table, which held sixty persons, at one side was a Frenchman and a lady, and on the other an English gentleman and a lady. The service was great, and great welcome.

After supper, the queen, with a great many, danced for the space of two hours; after which there came a device of three or four men coming like hobby-horses and yet sitting as upon a tailor's shop-board, cutting out silk to make something, and so sung five Italian songs. After that the dancing began for a while.

The 18th they had in the park the hunting of the wild bull, at which the queen was present.[1]

The 19th the two ambassadors came into the hall where the queen was, and sat down to supper at a round table like Arthur's; at each side the queen and ambassador, and so a lady and an earl, to the number of thirty persons, served by two masters of the household. There came from the end of the hall a stage drawn up by twelve satyrs, and sitting upon the stage six nymphs singing; and so against the bridge of the board at a place that did ascend the stage stayed, the satyrs delivered the torches to standers by, the nymphs arose and delivered the first service to the satyrs, who carried it to the board, fully as much as did serve it plentifully for the first course. The stage was garnished with laurel. The second course was served with the same stage, satyrs and nymphs as

---

[1] In 1570 the men of the regent were accused with "having slain and destroyed the deer in John Fleming's forest of Cumbernauld, and the white kye and bulls of the said forest, to the great destruction of police and hinder of the commonweal; for that kind of kye and bulls has been kept there many years in the said forest, and the like was not maintained in any other part of this Isle of Albion, as is well known." See Calend. 1570, No. 1418.

before, saving it was garnished with a . . . rock; the third
course with a conduit; the fourth with a child coming out of
a globe let down from the top of the hall to light upon the
stage, and so rendered an ovation by words and writing, with
another device, which could not be brought to pass, because
the stage broke after supper. That done, they took their
leaves and went their way.

CHAPTER THE FIFTH.

FROM THE MURDER OF DARNLEY UNTIL THE QUEEN'S IMPRISONMENT IN LOCHLEVEN CASTLE.

No better exponent of the circumstances connected with the murder of Darnley, and of the behaviour of his widow upon the occasion can be found than the report drawn up by the French envoy Clernault.[1] As he was in Edinburgh at the time of the king's death, his evidence is of the highest value. He tells us that entire confidence had been established for the previous three weeks between Mary and her husband, thereby confirming the statement of our narrative. According to Clernault, Mary went to visit her husband about seven o'clock on the evening of the 9th of February, remained with him for two or three hours, and probably would have stayed longer had not she promised to appear at a festival which was to be given at Holyrood that evening in honour of the marriage of Bastian, one of her French servants. When at last the party broke up, she retired to rest, from which she was aroused by a loud explosion, " equal to a volley of twenty-five or thirty canon," says Clernault, who must have heard it. She sent some of her household to ascer-

[1] Clernault was a confidential agent employed in the conveyance of letters and messages between the Courts of France and Scotland. See Lab. i. 191, 241. Upon the present occasion he was the bearer of a letter from Mary to the Archbishop of Glasgow, her ambassador in Paris. Clernault's letter is so important that a translation of it is given at the end of this Chapter. See Note the First, p. clxi.

tain whence it proceeded.   The town was already in
commotion.   Joining in the crowd they soon found
themselves amid the smoking and blackened ruins of the
Kirk of Field.   The body of Darnley was discovered
lying in the garden, distant some sixty or eighty paces
from the house.   After having been judicially inspected
for the purpose of ascertaining the cause of his death, it
was embalmed and interred on the 15th of February in
the burial-ground of Holyrood, close by the body of the
queen's father.

Suspicion fell immediately upon Bothwell, and justly.
The evidence against him was so abundant and so conclusive that his guilt was unquestionable from the night
of the murder.   The evidence against Moray was not so
decisive at the first, for with his usual prudence he had
absented himself from Edinburgh at the time of the
catastrophe; but before long the proofs which rose
against him became so weighty as to amount almost to a
demonstration.   Nau speaks without hesitation as to the
earl's complicity, and here doubtless he echoed the convictions of his mistress.   He goes on to state that after
having carefully planned each successive step in the de-
velopment of the conspiracy which was to consign his sister
to a perpetual imprisonment or an early grave, Moray
thought it would be more discreet if he should appear
to take no personal share in the events which were about
to follow. He left their execution in the hands of
Grange and Lethington, who thoroughly understood all
his plans, while he himself asked permission from his
sister to spend some time in France.   With her usual un-
questioning confidence Mary granted his request; and not
only did she do so, but she gave him letters of recommendation to her relations there, and authorised him to
draw upon the sums due to her from her marriage

portion. She seems to have had no suspicion as to the honesty of Moray's agents; but before long Maitland exhibited himself to her in his true character. And that the feelings of Grange were those of intense hostility is clearly established by the letters addressed by him to the Earl of Bedford, which still are in existence to speak for themselves.[1] But of this Mary was so entirely ignorant that she selected Grange as the one individual to whom she could trust herself with confidence when she gave herself into the hands of her enemies at Carberry Hill.

Nau then goes on to recount the mode by which the confederates brought about the next step in the series of events which were to end in the destruction of the queen. It was necessary for her ruin that she should be provided with a husband, and that this husband should be Bothwell.

The members of her Privy Council waited upon her, in due time, and represented to her the disorganised condition of the realm and the difficulty of bringing it into a state of tranquillity. Of this no one could be more fully convinced than the queen herself, and she easily assented to their statement. But they had a remedy to propose; they told her that she must marry. She listened, and then next arose the question as to the personage whom they could suggest as her husband. A foreign prince was impossible, an Englishman was equally objectionable, to both the difficulties at home and abroad were insurmountable. They and she would not accept Leicester—the proposal was too degrading. They ruled that she must marry a Scotchman, and that among her own nobility there was none who would fulfil the requisite conditions so well as Bothwell. Mary

---

[1] See R. O. Scot. Eliz. xiii. 35, 40, 43. See Illustrative Documents, Note the Second, p. clxiii.

was surprised, startled, and shocked; and she at once gave an absolute refusal.

That she should be indignant at the suggestion is very intelligible. There was not much to recommend Bothwell as a husband, and he laboured under many disqualifications. He was coarse in manner, ungainly in appearance, brutal in language, and dissipated in conduct. The only recommendation that could be urged in his favour, was that he had always been true to the national cause, and had never soiled his hand by touching English gold. But a queen is not obliged to marry one of her subjects because he is not a traitor. Moreover, and chiefly, he had a wife already, and he had been charged with having been a principal actor in the murder of Darnley. Influenced by these considerations, Mary refused to listen to the suggestions of her Privy Council when they recommended Bothwell as her husband.

The lords of the Congregation, however, were not easily discouraged. They held a meeting at Bothwell's house in Edinburgh, from which a deputation waited upon the queen. It consisted of Lethington, the Justice-Clerk, and a third, whom Nau does not specify, and these three conveyed to the queen the decision at which, as they informed her, the whole body of her nobility had arrived. The state of the realm was such that some prompt remedy for its disordered condition had become absolutely necessary. The only person who was able to cope with its difficulties was Bothwell.[1] He was a man of energy and decision, and as such they recommended

---

[1] The lords of the Congregation together with eight bishops drew up and signed a declaration to the effect that they believed in Bothwell's innocence of Darnley's murder, and they recommended him as the fittest husband for the queen. See Keith ii. 562. It is dated 19th April 1567.

That done, he was carried into a stately chamber of his own side, where the French ambassador presented his master's gift, which was a carkanet of rich work, with other jewels.

Then he went with the queen into the hall, where she supped at one board with all the three deputies. Every one was served with his mess of meat, and all at one instant, by her majesty's four servers, earls, to the board. At another table, which held sixty persons, at one side was a Frenchman and a lady, and on the other an English gentleman and a lady. The service was great, and great welcome.

After supper, the queen, with a great many, danced for the space of two hours; after which there came a device of three or four men coming like hobby-horses and yet sitting as upon a tailor's shop-board, cutting out silk to make something, and so sung five Italian songs. After that the dancing began for a while.

The 18th they had in the park the hunting of the wild bull, at which the queen was present.[1]

The 19th the two ambassadors came into the hall where the queen was, and sat down to supper at a round table like Arthur's; at each side the queen and ambassador, and so a lady and an earl, to the number of thirty persons, served by two masters of the household. There came from the end of the hall a stage drawn up by twelve satyrs, and sitting upon the stage six nymphs singing; and so against the bridge of the board at a place that did ascend the stage stayed, the satyrs delivered the torches to standers by, the nymphs arose and delivered the first service to the satyrs, who carried it to the board, fully as much as did serve it plentifully for the first course. The stage was garnished with laurel. The second course was served with the same stage, satyrs and nymphs as

[1] In 1570 the men of the regent were accused with "having slain and destroyed the deer in John Fleming's forest of Cumbernauld, and the white kye and bulls of the said forest, to the great destruction of police and hinder of the commonweal; for that kind of kye and bulls has been kept there many years in the said forest, and the like was not maintained in any other part of this Isle of Albion, as is well known." See Calend. 1570, No. 1418.

rather than counselled her, they governed her rather than obeyed her. She could not but see the ascendency which Bothwell had contrived to gain, or which had willingly been conceded to him. All the lords of the Council professed that they were contented to abide by his directions. Some were his friends, and acted as such from motives of friendship. Others did so from constraint, and out of fear for their lives. Others joined his party as affording them the readiest mode of furthering their own interests. Thus from one motive or another Bothwell seemed as if he held the supreme power in his own hands, and he resolved to avail himself of it. While the queen waited, and debated, and hesitated, and deliberated, he took violent possession of her person, carried her off into the Castle of Dunbar where he detained her for nearly a week.[1] At the end of that time can we wonder that she was aware that the only escape which was left from a ruined reputation was by a marriage with the man who had made her the victim of his brutal violence? This is the conclusion to which we are unavoidably led by the way in which Nau tells his tale. Considering the circumstances under which it was written, and the hearers for whose information it was primarily intended, it was impossible for him to have been more explicit. But the history is given with sufficient precision to make us sympathise with the condition in which this poor injured woman found herself, and to understand how she consented to patch up a marriage on any terms with the man who might become the father of her children. It is a horrible story at best; but while it is the story of horrible brutality on the part of the man let us not forget that at the same time it is the story of horrible suffering on the part of the woman.

[1] She was in the hands of Bothwell from the twenty-fourth to the twenty-ninth of April 1567.

No sooner was the crime accomplished, no sooner had
Bothwell's conduct rendered it a matter of necessity that
the queen should make him her husband than the scene
changed as if by magic.   The deference which the lords of
the Congregation had consented to yield to the will and
the words of the earl were suddenly withdrawn and he was
proclaimed to be a rebel, a traitor, and a murderer.   His
former friends now became his avowed enemies, and they
marshalled their forces against him.   The queen, of course,
had to share the fortunes of the man with whom she had
united her lot, and she did not shrink from doing so.
A large proportion of her subjects, aware of how matters
stood with her, still preserved their fidelity, and were
ready to prove it by fighting under her banners.   The
men of Aberdeen were among the foremost ; she had but
to speak the word and they were ready to march to her
assistance.[1]   She was speedily joined by a considerable
body of troops, at the head of which she marched boldly
forward to meet her rebellious subjects in open warfare.

The two armies stood face to face at Carberry Hill on
Sunday the 15th of June.   The combat, for which both
seemed anxious, was delayed from hour to hour by the
presence of the French envoy, M. du Croc, who attempted
to negotiate between them.   The sincerity of his motives
is open to doubt.   He was the acknowledged follower of
the Queen Dowager of France, consequently he had little
sympathy with Mary Stuart.   He had followed the
insurgents from Edinburgh that morning, with whom he
had so far openly identified himself that his mediation
ought to have been disregarded.   But Mary listened
to what he had to say, and was moved by his arguments.
He entreated her to come to terms with her subjects, and

[1] See the Illustrative Notes appended to this Chapter, Note the
Fourth, p. clxxii.

to believe their assurances of loyalty and allegiance.
She was always anxious to avoid the effusion of blood;
always ready to believe in the honesty of men who appealed to her as such.   In an evil hour, Mary listened to
the representations of Du Croc, and she resolved to act
upon his advice. Bothwell offered no opposition, but
he declined to follow her when she proposed to trust herself in their hands.   After she had made every arrangement in her power for his safety, the unhappy couple
parted from each other, never again to meet in this life.
He rode to the castle of Dunbar, where he remained in
unmolested safety as long as it pleased him to make it his
home.   Mary surrendered herself into the hands of
Grange,[1] and by him was conducted into the hostile
camp.   He was authorised by his party, he said, to
assure her that she should be treated with the respect due
by subjects to their sovereign.   Grange was considered to
be an honest and an honourable man, and Mary trusted
herself to his promises.   Her army was disbanded, and
she herself returned to Edinburgh, a prisoner in the
hands of the men who were in arms against her.

Mary soon discovered the spirit of the party to whom
she had so rashly entrusted herself. Grange was either
unwilling or unable to fulfil his promises; he was a

---

[1] The anonymous Life (Cal. B. iv., fol. 159, b.) says " some write that
as they were ready to join, she sent the French ambassador that was
in her company to propound, for the shunning of bloodshed, conditions
of peace.   But she, not liking the answer that he brought, should go
out of the squadron herself, for the respects beforementioned, and
William Kirkcaldy, the baron of Grange, to be sent to her, and upon
conference with him should go to Morton, who led the vanguard of the
enemies' side, and that he retained her against her will, and would not
suffer her to return again to her own army."
Mary's anxiety about Bothwell's safety is confirmed by other
authorities, see Hosack, i., 331.

portion. She seems to have had no suspicion as to the honesty of Moray's agents; but before long Maitland exhibited himself to her in his true character. And that the feelings of Grange were those of intense hostility is clearly established by the letters addressed by him to the Earl of Bedford, which still are in existence to speak for themselves.[1] But of this Mary was so entirely ignorant that she selected Grange as the one individual to whom she could trust herself with confidence when she gave herself into the hands of her enemies at Carberry Hill.

Nau then goes on to recount the mode by which the confederates brought about the next step in the series of events which were to end in the destruction of the queen. It was necessary for her ruin that she should be provided with a husband, and that this husband should be Bothwell.

The members of her Privy Council waited upon her, in due time, and represented to her the disorganised condition of the realm and the difficulty of bringing it into a state of tranquillity. Of this no one could be more fully convinced than the queen herself, and she easily assented to their statement. But they had a remedy to propose; they told her that she must marry. She listened, and then next arose the question as to the personage whom they could suggest as her husband. A foreign prince was impossible, an Englishman was equally objectionable, to both the difficulties at home and abroad were insurmountable. They and she would not accept Leicester—the proposal was too degrading. They ruled that she must marry a Scotchman, and that among her own nobility there was none who would fulfil the requisite conditions so well as Bothwell. Mary

---

[1] See R. O. Scot. Eliz. xiii. 35, 40, 43. See Illustrative Documents, Note the Second, p. clxiii.

the queen received a visit from the earl of Morton. As he
came, he said, to conduct her to the Palace of Holyrood,
she could not but obey him, so she arose and followed.
The procession down the Canongate was a repetition on
a larger scale of the march from Carberry into Edinburgh. On her arrival at the Palace she found that
supper had been prepared for Morton, a meal of which she
was afraid to partake, dreading poison, although she had
eaten nothing during the whole of the day. Before
supper was over, Morton told her it was time for her to
mount on horseback. When she asked where she was
to be led, he gave her to understand indirectly that she
was about to visit her son, doubtless with the idea of
reconciling her to the removal. Her destination was the
Castle of Lochleven, to which she was conducted by
Lords Lindsay and Ruthven. On the edge of the loch
she was met by the laird and his brothers. Enclosed
within the walls of that impregnable state dungeon, it
seemed to Mary as if she was at last and finally in the
power of her enemies, and that before her there was only
a speedy and a violent death or a lifelong imprisonment.[1]

[1] She was removed from Holyrood House (which she never again
saw) on the night of 16th June. The anonymous Life quoted above
tells us that on this occasion " they clothed her with a baggage grey
peticoat, coming little lower than her knees, and so set her upon a
cairon jade, found by chance in the pasture, and not worth 5s.; and
in this array, with the banner spoken of carried before her, they transport her straitway to the castle of Lochleven."—Id. fol. 160.
Thus also in an anonymous popular ballad (MS. Cott. Cal., C. i.
270) occurs the following stanza :—

> " The traitors, not therewith content,
>   Did lead her thence away,
>   And changed all her brave attire
>   Into a frock of gray."

SUPPLEMENTAL NOTES AND ILLUSTRATIONS TO CHAPTER THE FIFTH.

NOTE THE FIRST.   (See p. cli., Note 1.)

REPORT by the Seigneur de Clernault upon the death of King Henry Darnley.[1]

The Seigneur de Clernault states in the account which he has brought of the death of the King of Scotland, that the said king having been lodged at one end of the city of Edinburgh and the queen at the other, the said lady went to visit him on the evening of Sunday the 9th of this month, about seven o'clock, along with all the principal lords of her court. After having been with him for about two or three hours she left him in order that she might be present at the marriage of one of her gentlemen, as she had promised; but for which promise it is thought that she would have remained until midnight or one o'clock, regard being had to the good understanding and union in which she and the king had been living for three weeks.

When she arrived at the marriage festivities she did not stay there long, because of the late hour at which she had come, and as it was growing late every one began to depart, which occasioned the said lady to go to bed. About two o'clock after midnight, or a little later, there was heard a very great noise, as if twenty-five or thirty cannon had been fired in a volley, so that every one awoke. The queen, having sent to enquire whence came such a noise, her messengers followed the crowd until they came to the king's residence, which they found to be entirely overthrown. Having sought to find where he was, they discovered him sixty or eighty paces from

[1] Translated from the original French in R.O. Scot. Eliz., xiii. 13. It is written in a foreign hand, and is dated 16th February 1566.

the house.   He was dead and lying in a garden, as were also
a valet-de-chambre and a young page.

Any one may imagine in what pains and agony this poor
princess was when the matter was reported to her, especially
as it had occurred at a time when her majesty and the king
were on the best possible terms, in such sort that the said
Seigneur de Clernault left her so much afflicted as to be one of
the most unfortunate queens in the world.   It is very clear
that this wicked enterprise was occasioned by an underground
mine ; yet it has not yet been discovered, still less is it known,
who is the author of it.

Note the Second.   (See p. clii., Note 1.)

Letter from Randolph to the Earl of Leicester, 10th May 1567.[1]

Seeing that I cannot attend upon your lordship where your
lordship is, I think it my duty to let your lordship understand
such occurrences as are here amongst us.

First, that the Queen of Scotland is fully resolved to marry
the Earl Bothwell, and that the banns are already asked
between them.   That she is now minded to make Leith a
free borough, where before it was under the liberties of Edinburgh, and mindeth to name the same Marienborough, and to
create the Earl of Bothwell duke of the same name ; and if
that she cannot bring that to pass, then shall he be created
Duke of Ross, as her former husband was.

These news it pleased her Majesty to tell me this day
walking in her garden, with great misliking of that queen's
doing, which now she doth so much detest that she is ashamed
of her.   Notwithstanding, her Majesty doth not like that her

---

[1] This letter is here reprinted from the rare volume of Scottish
Miscellaneous Papers (of which the impression was limited to fifty
copies) edited by Mr William Stevenson Fitch, at Ipswich, in 1842,
quarto.   One copy is in the British Museum and another in the
Bodleian Library.

subjects should by any force withstand that which they do see her bent unto. And yet doth she greatly fear that Bothwell, having the upper hand, that he will reign again with the French, and either make away with the prince, or send him into France, which deliberation her Majesty would gladly should be stayed, but is very uncertain how it may be brought to pass.

Her Majesty also told me that she had seen a writing sent from Grange to my Lord of Bedford, despitefully written against that queen in such vile tenor that she could not abide the hearing of it, wherein he made her worse than any common woman. She would not that any subject, what course so ever there be proceeding from the prince, or whatsoever her life or behaviour is, that any man should discover that unto the world, and thereof so utterly misliketh of Grange's manner of writing and doing that she condemneth him for one of the worst in that realm, seeming somewhat to warn me of my familiarity with him, and willing that I should admonish him of her misliking.

Note the Third. (See p. cliii., Note 1.)
Bothwell's Divorce.

Very little information respecting the process by which Bothwell procured what he called a divorce from his wife has come down to us. It was a subject which could not but be unpalatable to all who were concerned in it, and the revelations which it brought to light were of such a nature that it was soon found to be objectionable reading. But in any enquiry into the history of Mary Stuart it becomes important that the leading facts of the case should be noticed, and the evidence which it affords should be laid before the public. Until the present time this has been impossible, for it is generally supposed that all the papers connected with it had perished. Such, however, is not the case, for a copy is to be found among the treasures of the Bodleian Library at Oxford.[1]

[1] Bodl. Addit. MSS. c. 27, fol, 1, a transcript of last century. There is reason to believe that the original from which this copy was made is at Hatfield House.

Unfortunately it throws no light upon the conduct of Mary, and only confirms what is too well known already as to the depravity of Bothwell's moral character. For the reasons already given I do not think it expedient to print these documents as they stand, but the reader may be assured that the following abstract contains all the particulars which possess any historical value.

THE PROCESS of Lady Jean Gordon, daughter of the late George Earl of Huntley, against James, Earl of Bothwell, begun 29th April 1567.

The libel presented by Lady Jean states that the marriage was solemnized in face of the kirk in the month of February 1565, and that the parties dwelt together several months. That the earl committed adultery with Besse Crawfurde, servant to the said noble lady, in May and June 1566, diverse times within the Abbey of Haddington, in a part thereof called Saint Paul's Work. That therefore the said Lady Jean requires to be no longer repute the bone of his bone nor flesh of his flesh, but that she be decerned to be free to marry in the Lord where she pleases. The commission to sit on 29th April.

Dated Edinburgh, 26th April 1567.

THE CERTIFICATE of the serving of the citation before three witnesses.

The FIRST ACT, Edinburgh, 29th April 1567.

For the pursuer, Henry Kynros, procurator; for the Earl of Bothwell, Edmond Hay, procurator.

Procuratory for Lady Bothwell, dated Edinburgh, 20th March 1566, before Adam Gordon, her brother, Patrick Whitlaw of that Ilk, Masters George Hacket and Alexander Leslie, notaries public.

Procuratory of Bothwell for Edmond Hay, dated Dunbar, 28th April 1567, before George, Earl of Huntly, William Newton of that Ilk, and Sir James Cockburn, knight.

The SECOND ACT, Edinburgh, ult. April.

Witnesses produced and sworn.

The THIRD ACT, Edinburgh, 1st May.

Adjourned until Saturday, 3rd May.

MAY THE THIRD.

Before Robert Maitland, dean of Aberdeen, and Edward Henryson, two of the Senators of the College of Justice, Clement Little, and Alexander Syme, advocates.

"The rights, reasons, and allegations of both the said parties by us heard, seen, considered, and understanded, and we being there with reply advised together, with the depositions of diverse famous witnesses produced, sworn, received and admitted in the said cause, the said noble lady compeiring by Master Henry Kynros, her procurator, and the said lord by Master Edmond Hay, his procurator, the said commissioners declares the said noble lord to be separate, cut off and divorced *simpliciter* from the said noble lady, and she to be free to marry in the Lord where she pleases, as freely as she might have done before the contract and solemnisation of marriage with the said noble lord. . . .

"Extracted forth of the Register of the said Commissary by me, Michael Marjoribanks, clerk thereto. Witnessing the same this my handwriting and sign-manual.

"MICHAEL MARJORIBANKS."

DEPOSITIONS of Witnesses Examined for Lady Gordon, ult. April 1567.

PATRICK WILSON, dwelling in Haddington, married, aged thirty-six, merchant, sworn, depones that he has served my lord, but has got no reward. Has dwelt in Haddington since the siege of Leith. Saw the parties married in the kirk of Halirud House before Fasternseven was a year. "Saw ilk ane had other in handis togidder." Saw the Bishop of Gallo-

way executor thereof. No one was in the pulpit. Knows
not who made the sermon to them that day, nor yet heard
the words of the marriage spoken, by reason there was many
people betwixt him and them.

Knows that Bothwell had carnal company with Besse
Crawfurde only in May. That she dwelt with my old Lady
Huntly of before she came with Lady Bothwell the time she
was married. She is a woman of twenty years of age, " and
that she then werit her hair, and yet weris." That she is a
bonny little woman, black haired, and that she is a " sewis-
ter," and had a black gown upon her, and sometimes a taffety
upon her head ; that she is a pale hued woman, and is a
smith's daughter. Her father is William Crawfurd. ·

The adultery was committed in May, about a month before
the prince was born. Saw Bothwell and the woman both in
Saint Paul's Work, which is in the east end of the close
without the cloister, of two house height. " She had gotten
her leave of before fra my lady, by reason of suspicion with
my lord."

THOMAS CRAIGVALLIS, dwelling with the laird of Skirling
in the castle of Edinburgh, and before the laird came to the
castle. Before then dwelt with Bothwell as his porter at
Haddington. Was not present at the wedding, but at the
banquet at " Kynlouchis the Sunday before Fasternseven was
a year." . . .

THOMAS CRAIGVALLIS, the younger, dwelling in Leith, aged
thirty. ·Was Bothwell's servant. Was in the house all the
time of the banquet, and therefore passed with his lord to
Creighton. . . . Saw Bothwell have company with the said
Besse in the place at Creighton, before the time of the passing to the abbey.

JOHN ROBERTSON depones to the marriage only.

PAREIS SEMPILL has dwelt with Bothwell twelve years.

GEORGE DALGLEISH, tailor, servant to Bothwell. " My
lady had put the said Bess away, for suspicion of my lord that
she had of her."

WILLIAM SCOTT, notary. Bothwell came to Haddington
about 17th May.

Everything connected with the question of Mary's divorce from Bothwell is at once so interesting and so obscure, that I make no apology for here bringing together some information respecting it, which may possibly contribute to its solution.

In September 1570, sir Henry Norreys, then resident in Paris as the English ambassador, informed his mistress that a divorce between queen Mary and the earl of Bothwell had been granted by the pope, who at that time was Pius V. He repeats the same information, nearly in the same words, to Cecil. I give the text of the two letters, as far as they relate to our subject.

" . . . . Whereas aforetime I have given your honour to understand of some likelihood of the marriage to be sought twixt mons. d'Anjou and the queen of Scots, it may now like you to consider of the likelihood thereof, since the pope hath made a divorce between the said queen and the earl of Bothwell, and that long since the cardinal, her uncle, had promised to cause her to yield to the said duke her right of Scotland and England. And considering his ambitious mind, as also how easy a request to be obtained to have a dispensation for the marriage between her and mons. d'Anjou, and finding how dangerous this should be both to the state of her highness and country, and in these of so great importance afraid anyways to wade therein by advice, I pray God so to inspire your hearts, as in these great heaps of dangers, His will direct you to choose the least. . . .

" From Paris this 29th of September 1570,—Your honour's most assured, HENRY NORREYS."

R. O. Foreign, Eliz., vol. cxiv. fol. 67. Sir Henry Norris to Cecil, Paris, 29th September 1570. An original, sealed with sir Henry's armorial seal.

"May it like your most excellent majesty, that using all the means I possibly can to understand of sundry practices and devices in hand by the queen of Scotts' fautors and ministers here, amongst others, I have learned that in the month of July last, one William Keyr, servant to the queen of Scots, was sent in post to Rome, and by the solicitation of the bishop of Dunglene,[1] her ambassador there, the pope hath

---

[1] So in the MS., an obvious mistake for Dumblane.

made a divorce between the said queen and the earl of Bod-
well, whereby, upon dispensation, the marriage between her
and monsieur d'Anjou to be intended: which cannot be, all
things considered, but dangerous to your estate. . . ."

R. O. Foreign, Eliz., vol. cxiv. fol. 65. Sir Henry Norris
to the queen, Paris, 30th September 1570. A contemporaneous copy, but unfinished.

We hear nothing more of the Bull for a couple of months,
at the end of which time the subject reappears in a form
which reflects no great credit upon the common sense of the
English ambassador. According to him the Bull not only
divorced Mary from the earl, and banished him from Christendom and all Christian company, but further ordered him to
be executed for his heinous offence committed upon the
queen. He tells us that the Bull had lately been sent from
Paris into Denmark, there to be put in execution. I give
the document, of which the object is patent. It was intended
to irritate and terrify Elizabeth by suggesting the possibility
of a marriage between the queen of Scotland—then a close
prisoner, be it remembered—and this duke of Anjou.

"Most gracious sovereign. Whereas I gave your majesty to
understand by my letters of the xxix of September that,
amongst sundry practices and devices in hand by the queen
of Scotts' fautors and ministers here, amongst others, that in
July last, one William Keyr, servant to the queen of Scots,
was sent post to Rome, and by the solicitation of the bishop
of Dunglene,[1] her ambassador there, the pope hath made a
divorce between the said queen and the earl of Bothwell, so
that now she may marry where she list. Since which time
it is known the dissolution to be granted, as appeareth by the
Bull sent hither, under the pretence of a rape committed to
the queen of Scots.[2] Wherefore by the pope's sentence he is

---

[1] So in the MS., an error obviously for Dumblane.

[2] According to the Council of Trent (Sess. xxiv. c. 6) this would
form an Impedimentum dirimens, inasmuch as between the capture
of the queen by Bothwell and the marriage she was never out of his
power. See Sanchez de Matr., C. vii., disp. xiii., sec. 2. S. Liguori,
1107. Gury, ii., 761.

banished Christendom and all Christian company, and the Bull is lately sent hence by a gentleman into Denmark, there to cause the said earl to be executed for his heinous offence. . . . ."

R. O. Foreign, Eliz., vol. cxv. fol. 59. Sir Henry Norris to queen Elizabeth, Nov. 29, 1570. The above is a copy in the hand of Norreys's clerk.

In the letter just cited, the English ambassador refers to William Keyr, " servant to the queen of Scots," as the agent employed in this mission. I find no trace of any such personage so employed ; but in the Secret Archives of the Vatican[1] occurs a document which professes to be " a copy of certain instructions to be declared to his holiness pope Pius V. on the part of the queen of Scotland, dowager of France, by her faithful servant and secretary, Henry Keir." They do not touch upon the divorce, but they seem to be incomplete. Is this mission the origin of Norrys's story ?

But that the queen made an application to the pope for a divorce is beyond a question. In one of the Cottonian manuscripts[2] are the heads of the business which she commissioned the bishop of Ross to transact for her at the apostolic See. They are undated, but we may safely ascribe them to the year 1575, the year of the papal jubilee, upon which occasion bishop Leslie visited Rome,[3] as he himself tells us. The document is sufficiently important to warrant its insertion ; I give, therefore, an English version of the whole.

EXTRACTS from the heads of the matters which the queen of Scotland has entrusted to the bishop of Ross on being sent to the pope.

Thank the pope as earnestly as it is in your power to do for his kindness towards me, which is truly that of a father, as he has shown by many tokens to my late uncle of good me-

[1] Politica Varia, tom. lxxi. fol. 465.
[2] Calig., C. ii. 189.
[3] See Leslie's Autobiography, in Anderson's Collections, i. 8.

mory, the cardinal of Lorraine,[1] to whom also his holiness promised that he would exert himself to the utmost for the recovery of my liberty, and that my son should be brought up as a catholic.

You may add that I am in constant fear of death, partly by the extreme closeness of my imprisonment, by reason of which I can scarce draw a breath of fresh air, and am all but deprived of bodily exercise. Consequently it would be all the more easy to remove me by poison, and my enemies, under whose power I now am placed, hate me very bitterly. Many attempts have been made to do so, but they have been thwarted by the prudent watchfulness of others, or happily prevented by the careful and faithful oversight of the earl of Shrewsbury, in whose custody I am. Hereupon my enemies, finding themselves prevented by the earl's diligence from thus murdering me, invent fictitious reasons for having me removed from his custody, and wish me to be handed over to the keeping of the earl of Bedford, or the earl of Hertford, or the earl of Huntingdon, which would be like consigning a sheep to the charge of a wolf, &c.

I have a good hope that many of the English are on my side. In the first place, not only all the catholics, but many others also, influenced by the justice of my title, have the honesty to profess their intention of firmly siding with my party when the opportunity offers itself. They see that by no other agency than through me can England recover the catholic faith.

Ask the Holy Father to permit me, out of his goodness, to try to conciliate Elizabeth by letters written by me in a kindly spirit, and by sending some other tokens of my goodwill, which shall be neatly wrought, and by some other marks of the same good will. Let him know that it is only by such means that her anger can be softened, or my liberty be recovered, or that I can hope for any mitigation of the severity of my imprisonment. And this I ask the rather because in these my trials no catholic princes can help me.

[1] This was Charles, cardinal of Guise, who died at Avignon, 26th December 1574.

Tell him also that there is nothing which I desire more earnestly than the total uprooting of heresy, and the restitution of the catholic faith in the whole of Britain. But I must leave the entire execution of this great project to those who are moved thereto by the love of God, and the desire of promoting virtue.

Take good heed that the Holy Father shall publicly announce that the pretended marriage contracted between me and Bothwell, without any legality but by a pretended procedure, is of no [force]. For although there are many reasons which, as you know, make it clearly invalid in itself, yet the matter will be much clearer if his holiness, acting as the most certain lawyer of the Church, will come forward to annul it.[1] And in order that nothing may appear to be wanting in this matter, I ask you, my father, to act for me in every proceeding which is required for the valid prosecution of the entire cause in the court, and through the whole process, as well in its introduction as its prosecution. Let this caution, however, be carefully observed ; let the entire proceeding be conducted as secretly as possible, for if it gets abroad, it may occasion me much trouble and annoyance.

Let the Holy Father know that the English, who favour my cause in England, have acquainted me privately, that it would conduce much to my advantage if foreign princes would write to Elizabeth asking for my liberation, or at least for a mitigation of the severity of my imprisonment. But this I will not do without the approval of his holiness. And yet the grave insults which have been offered to a catholic princess, if they remain unpunished, seem to reflect disgrace upon all catholic princes. You may urge the Holy Father, therefore, by his letters, to incite other princes to aid my cause. These letters may conveniently be given to their ambassadors resident in the English court. I have no doubt that if they be written in a friendly spirit they will do much good by producing, if not my liberty, at least some favour and benevolence.

[1] "Ad illud dirimendum." The use of this phrase seems to point to the fact that the marriage was null in consequence of an " impedimentum dirimens," namely, " raptus."

Note the Fourth.   (See p. clvii.)

Letter from the Nobility and Subjects of Aberdeen to the Queen, Aberdeen, 27th April 1567.[1]

Please Your Majesty,—It is bruited and spoken in the country that your Majesty should be ravished by the Earl Bothwell against your will.   When we your Majesty's nobility and subjects think ourselves most highly offended if so be, and therefore desire to know your Highness's pleasure and will,. what we shall do toward the reparation of that matter, and in what manner we shall use ourselves.   Which being known, there shall nothing be left undone that becomes faithful and loving subjects to do to the advancement and forthfilling of their prince's honour and affairs.   We will look to be certified of your Grace's mind by the bearer hereof.   And so after our humble commendations we commit your Majesty to God.

From Aberdeen, the xxvij of April 1567.

Note the Fifth.   (See p. clix.)

Plunder of the Royal Property at Holyrood.

" They encamped in the royal palace (writes Mary's anonymous historian), where all the night they occupied themselves in ransacking of it, seizing upon her apparel, moveables, and jewels, which could not but be many and rich, she having been the wife of a king of France, and daughter and heir of a king of Scotland, and she nor her son, as the bruit is, never recovering but a small portion of them, some being reserved for the bastard Moray, others presented to the queen of England and her councillors."   MS. Cott. Cal., B. iv., fol. 161.

The more precious of the jewels were sent by Moray, through Throckmorton, to London, where they were inspected

[1] From the privately printed volume of Mr W. Stevenson Fitch. Ipswich, 1842, 4to.

by Elizabeth on 1st May 1568, in company with the earls of
Pembroke and Leicester. They were considered to be "of
unparalleled beauty" (Lab. vii. 129). The feeling excited
by this act of spoliation was very general, and "acolded so
many of their stomachs," that Moray thought it well to
obtain the authority of Parliament. (See R. O. Eliz. xiv.
78 B., and Scot. Mary i. 46.) As late as 3rd Aug. 1570
a memorial was presented to Cecil, which recites that "certain apparel, costly hangings, and jewels, pertaining to the
queen of Scotland, transported and carried forth of her realm
by some of her disobedient subjects to be sold and disponed
without her majesty's knowledge or consent, whereof one part
is arrived at Hull and other ports of this realm." (See B. M.
Cal., C. ii., fol. 2, and R. O. Scot. Mary v. 59.)

CHAPTER THE SIXTH.

QUEEN MARY'S IMPRISONMENT IN THE CASTLE OF LOCHLEVEN.

WHEN the gates of Lochleven Castle closed upon Mary
Stuart, the conspirators felt that they had nearly attained
the great object of their ambition. The Queen of Scotland was in their power, and they could deal with her
according to their pleasure. They had but to propose
their own terms, and of necessity she must accept them.
So far they had done their work with consummate skill
and unscrupulous daring, and it had prospered in their
hands, or at least had seemed to prosper. Having advanced so far on the road, they were not the men to
pause, and hesitate, and retrace their steps. One bold
effort would place within their grasp the prize for which
they had striven so boldly. Two lives only stood between Moray and the crown, and both were insecure
even to a proverb—the life of a little child and the life
of a deposed sovereign. And the mother and the baby
were both in Moray's keeping.

At the time when Lochleven became Mary's prison,
its nominal mistress was Margaret Erskine, daughter of
John, Lord Erskine, one of the many mistresses of James
the Fifth, by whom she had become the mother of James
Earl of Moray. She had afterwards married Sir Robert
Douglas, and their son, William Douglas, was at this
time the proprietor of the castle and its keeper. A
second son, named George, resided with his mother and

brother, as did also a young foundling, to whom had been given the family name of William Douglas. A confidential servant, James Drysdale,[1] and several men servants, or soldiers, completed the garrison. William Douglas, the laird of Lochleven, as he was styled, was a married man, and his wife resided with him on the island, together with several female servants. Two young girls, relatives of the family (one being the laird's daughter and the other his niece), acted as spies upon the queen, and slept in her chamber. The castle was well fortified and amply provided with artillery, and at the same time its natural position made it almost impregnable. Mary's retinue, when at its fullest number, seems to have consisted of the two female servants who had accompanied her from Edinburgh, three of her ladies who had afterwards joined her, a cook, and her physician.

On her arrival at Lochleven, the queen found that no preparation had been made for her reception. She was placed in a room on the ground floor, provided with nothing better than the scanty furniture of the ordinary household. Nothing in it corresponded with the state and etiquette to which she had been accustomed from her infancy, and the absence of which was regarded as a token of degradation. When she arrived she was nearly unprovided with the common necessaries of daily life, for her departure from Holyrood had been so abrupt that she could carry with her only a single nightdress. In the midst of such desolation as this, the Queen of

---

[1] The queen tells us that this worthy, being evil content with the good service which little Willie Douglas had done for her, said that if ever he met with him " he should put his hands in his heart blood, whatever might follow thereupon."—See Lab. ii., 264 ; Goodall, ii. 299.

Scotland spent more than a fortnight, without holding
any communication with a single member of the household.

Mary's position, which for long had been one of dif
ficulty and danger, might now be regarded as all but
hopeless. Everywhere enemies, friends nowhere. Probably she was not fully aware of the gravity of the
dangers by which she was surrounded. She did not
realise the fact that her enforced marriage with Bothwell
had induced many of her former adherents, both at home
and abroad, to believe that to a certain extent she was
implicated in the murder of Darnley. She still had
some lingering faith in the honesty and affection of
Moray, who at this very time was busily employed in
ruining her cause on the Continent. She deluded
herself with the belief that in the King and Queen
Dowager of France she had allies whom she could
trust in every emergency.[1] When Elizabeth lavished
on her professions of friendship and promises of assistance, Mary was credulous enough to think her sincere.
She outlived all these hopes, and awoke from all these
visions, but at the time when she entered Lochleven
they had not ceased to be vivid and influential. They
gave her strength and comfort and patience ; and thus
supported by them, she endured, with the constancy of

[1] Mary was cheated on all sides. Lethington writing to Randolph
on 1st May 1566 (Cal. B. iv., fol. 244), tells him that " De Mauvissier
is spoken with by my Lord of Moray, who hath promised to declare
our cause to the queen's majesty of England and to his master." The
Spanish Ambassador resident at this time in the Court of Paris states
that as soon as the tidings of Mary's seizure at Carberry reached Paris,
the queen dowager sent a messenger to make Moray acquainted with
the fact. He was at that time resident at Lyons. On his homeward
journey he took London on his way, in order to confer with Elizabeth.
—See Teulet, iv. 27, 30.

an honest heart and a strong will, the dangers, the insults and the trials to which she was exposed during the eleven months of her imprisonment.

At this point the narrative of the queen's French secretary becomes exceedingly valuable. It reveals many circumstances, some of which are entirely new to us, while others, known hitherto only partially or through a false medium, are now for the first time placed before us in their true light. Until now Moray and his agents have had the telling of their own tale, and however questionable might seem their statements, they have been admitted, because no one could contradict them. At last, however, we are permitted to produce new evidence on the side of the prisoner, and we now ask a hearing for what Nau has to tell us of the incidents which occurred within the walls of Lochleven.

Nau states that shortly after the queen's arrival in Lochleven an attempt was made to poison her; and he has recorded the symptoms which exhibited themselves. It is impossible to decide how far this impression was correct, and the question must remain unsolved. In those days medical knowledge was in its infancy, and every unexpected attack of illness was attributed to poison. On the other hand, knowing as we do from Throckmorton and other sources that the queen's life was at this time in extreme danger, we may reasonably conclude that poison would probably be resorted to. It is certain that she thought so herself. Nau has referred to it more than once already.

Among the other revelations made to us by this narrative is one which takes us by surprise, the fact, namely, that shortly after her arrival in Lochleven[1] the queen gave birth to twins, which, however, were still

[1] It must have occurred not long before 24th July.

born. Yet that such should have been the case might
have been expected, for she herself had declared that she
was about to become a mother. Considering the rare
intercourse which at this time took place between the
ordinary household of the castle and the queen's attendants, it is by no means incredible that the birth of these
children was never know to the laird of Lochleven and
his family. It is never referred to in the correspondence
of the period. I may add that I discredit the story
told by Castelnau,[1] who would have us believe that
Mary had a daughter by Bothwell, who became a nun at
Soissons. This child must have been born within the
walls of Lochleven, and its existence must have become
a matter of notoriety.

In her midnight ride to Lochleven from Holyrood,
Mary was accompanied by the Lords Lindsay and
Ruthven, who had been commissioned to reside within
the castle as her keepers. How long they continued
there in that capacity is uncertain. Ruthven was
removed in consequence of having been guilty of an
act of the most scandalous indecency. Early one
morning he came into the bedroom of his captive
and made indecent proposals to her, offering to procure
her liberty as the payment of her sin. A complaint,
forwarded to the Lords of the Congregation, produced
Ruthven's dismissal from a post of which he had
shown himself so unworthy. But he presented himself before her on the afternoon of July 24th 1567 in
company with Lindsay, who urged her to sign three
documents which he produced, and which he gave her
to understand contained the formal act of her resignation
of the crown of Scotland. A detailed account of what
passed upon the occasion is given in the anonymous

[1] In Jebb. ii. 610.

History of Queen Mary, which I here adopt as the basis
of the account which follows.

That Lord Lindsay was the bloodiest and most furious
that could be found in the whole troop,[1] and altogether
brutish and without civility, was now witnessed by his
behaviour.   He came into her presence without doing
her any honour or reverence, and rudely told her that he
had been sent to her by the nobility, who would have
her sign certain articles which he produced, threatening
that if she refused, they would constrain her by other
means to do so.   Mary's reply is given at considerable
length in this narrative.   Lindsay interrupted her with
change of countenance, and became so transported with
rage that the hair of his head stood on end, seeming as
a man possessed.   He used many vile and reproachful
words in derogation of her honour, telling her with
execrable oaths and often renouncing of God, that if she
put not her hand immediately to the articles he would
sign them with her blood and seal them with her heart,
and afterwards throw her out of the window into the
lake at the house foot, to feed fishes.   Mary then signed
the papers without reading them, or demanding what
they contained, or by what means she should be from
henceforth in her private life sustained, only she required
him, as she did Robert Melvin, a man of credit among
them, to tell the nobility from her, that she besought it
might be permitted her at the least to be heard in her
justification at their Council Board, or in the presence of

[1] The Anonymous Life (Cal. B. iv., fol. 197), speaking of Lindsay,
tells us that "he was said to be one that haunted in his country
taverns and alehouses, and as forward as the other with his head and
hand in all rebellions and treasons, and when he was in England was
observed little better than a furious brute beast, and therefore choice
had been made of him to do the message to the queen when she was
in Lochleven."

CHAPTER THE SIXTH.

QUEEN MARY'S IMPRISONMENT IN THE CASTLE OF LOCHLEVEN.

WHEN the gates of Lochleven Castle closed upon Mary Stuart, the conspirators felt that they had nearly attained the great object of their ambition. The Queen of Scotland was in their power, and they could deal with her according to their pleasure. They had but to propose their own terms, and of necessity she must accept them. So far they had done their work with consummate skill and unscrupulous daring, and it had prospered in their hands, or at least had seemed to prosper. Having advanced so far on the road, they were not the men to pause, and hesitate, and retrace their steps. One bold effort would place within their grasp the prize for which they had striven so boldly. Two lives only stood between Moray and the crown, and both were insecure even to a proverb—the life of a little child and the life of a deposed sovereign. And the mother and the baby were both in Moray's keeping.

At the time when Lochleven became Mary's prison, its nominal mistress was Margaret Erskine, daughter of John, Lord Erskine, one of the many mistresses of James the Fifth, by whom she had become the mother of James Earl of Moray. She had afterwards married Sir Robert Douglas, and their son, William Douglas, was at this time the proprietor of the castle and its keeper. A second son, named George, resided with his mother and

Queen Mary—enabled them easily to act in concert. The Queen Dowager disregarded the warning which she had received as to the real object of Moray's journey to France, and not only permitted him to visit the leaders of the Huguenots, but forwarded his designs and watched over his safety.[1]   The Guises having been informed of the true character of Moray's proceedings and his real intentions, resolved to have him arrested and detained in France as a guarantee for the safety of the Scottish queen.   Their plans were frustrated by the prompt treachery of the Queen Mother, who apprised Moray of his danger, and defeated the arrangements which had been made for his arrest before his arrival at the French coast.   Moray reached England in safety, and after an interview with his allies in the English Court, arrived at Edinburgh on the eleventh of August.

During the whole of this period Mary's position was one of extreme danger.   It was admitted on all sides that she was in the hands of men to whom her death had become a political necessity.   Moray lingered in France longer than his friends expected, in the hope that the work would be done during his absence ; and his return was hastened by the alarming information affecting his own personal safety which had been communicated to him by the Queen Mother.   When he arrived in Scotland, the confederates lost no time in requesting him to become guardian to the young prince and Regent of the Kingdom.   He affected to hesitate,

[1] On 31st March 1567, Mary contrived to write to the Queen Mother from Lochleven, warning her of the great intelligence which existed between the Scottish rebels and the Admiral de Coligny and the Prince of Condé.   See Lab. ii. 64.   His identity of interest with the Huguenots became more and more conspicuous, as will appear by a document printed among the Illustrative Papers appended to this chapter.   See p. clxxxiv.

and `said that he could not act without the consent of
his sister. We have been taught to believe that he
actually did consult her upon the subject in all good
faith and true kindness ; and that when the question
had been discussed between them in all its bearings, she
not only advised, but entreated him to accept the proposals made to him by the confederates as being most
advantageous to herself. Nau tells us a different tale ;
one more consistent with Mary's character, and more in
keeping with her previous and subsequent principles of
action. The account which he gives is too valuable and
too interesting to bear compression, and too long to
permit its insertion here. The same remark applies,
even in a greater degree, to the whole of the remainder
of this chapter. We read with breathless interest the
details of the origin and progress of the various plans
which were suggested for the queen's escape, how each
in turn was found to be impracticable and was abandoned,
until at last the earnest devotedness and the cool daring
of "little Willie Douglas" gave her one more opportunity
of attempting to vindicate her rights as Queen of
Scotland.

SUPPLEMENTAL NOTES AND ILLUSTRATIONS TO CHAPTER THE SIXTH.

LETTER from the Archbishop of Glasgow to the Cardinal of Lorraine, 8th December 1567.[1]

(See p. clxxxi, Note 1.)

The affairs of the queen, my sovereign, do not improve, but they rather grow worse from day to day, if one may trust the information which I receive from my brother and others. The Earl of Moray, having got into his possession the Castles of Edinburgh and Dunbar by surrender, has succeeded so well that the greater part of the nobles have signed his appointment as Regent, with the exception, however, of the Earl of Huntley, the sons of the Duke of Châtelherault, and five or six poor catholic prelates, whom he has summoned for having infringed the queen's edicts by having sung mass, or caused it to be sung. His object in doing this is only to lay hold of their persons, or, if they do not appear personally, to seize their goods and benefices. And he states that on the fifteenth of this month he will declare by the Parliament that the tithes of the said benefices shall be forfeited.

The Earl of Huntley and Lord Fleming are cited; the former that he may learn that the restitution of his lands and goods which had been made to him by the queen is null; and Fleming shall be required, under pain of treason, to surrender into Moray's hands the Castle of Dumbarton, which is the only fortress in the whole realm of Scotland which at the present time holds out for her Majesty. She remains in the

[1] Translated from the original French in the Sloane MS., 3199, fol. 158b. It is one of a series of transcripts, made for Dr Robert Gray, from the manuscripts which formerly existed in the Scottish College in Paris, and which perished in the great Revolution.

same place where she was. I have stated the above facts to
the Queen Mother, and in several audiences I have especially
urged upon her how important it is to have a letter from the
king, or from herself to Lord Fleming, recommending him
to do his duty towards his sovereign and the fortress which
he holds.   In consequence of the difficulty of the times, this
was refused me, although I offered to let the queen have the
opportunity of opening two packets of the Earl of Moray and
Throckmorton written to Stuart, which were sent to me
by the Duke of Châtelherault, who is still at Dieppe waiting
the issue of these troubles.   He does not dare to return by
way of England.   By these papers the said Earl of Moray
declares that he is fully on the side of the insurgents here,
and asks to be informed if anything is likely to be done
against them by the king, the Queen Mother, or your house ;
in which case he will do all he can to help them.   He also asks
that M. the Constable, and Montmorency should be assured
that he, Moray, will never forget the good offices which
they did him when he was here.   This gave me the opportunity of saying to the queen :—" You perceive, Madame,
that all has not been done as I wished."   Her answer was
that truly Moray was much obliged to the Constable.   In like
manner Throckmorton writes to him to prevent by every
means in his power help from being given to the Duke of
Châtelherault, in which matter he would also employ all his
friends, but in which everything would tend to the advantage
of Moray.   The short of the story is this, that all that he has
done in Scotland, and all that he is doing at the present time,
is to forward the said earl, and to advance this unhappy sedition
and heresy.   The ill will of both the one and the other of them,
and particularly toward their Majesties, has been of no service
or advantage to me in this affair.

   As to other matters ; M. de Pasquier having let me know
what has resulted from his commission, I refer back to what
you have written on that point, namely, that the Queen of
England complains much of never having received from yourself, or from any prince of your house, either letter or recommendation in favour of the queen my sovereign. Hereupon,

I have despatched a special messenger to the Duke of Châtelherault with the letter which you should write for him to keep, and to state the evidence which he has received from you. If you think that there is anything else which ought to be added according to the notice which I shall recover, I would not fail to follow it; and I will send you the report made to me by the person whom I have sent to be present at the said Parliament. And the last remark which I have to make is this, that I am compelled, my lord, to entreat you not to forget, in the midst of the many labours and misfortunes which press upon you at this time, this poor unfortunate princess, of whom, under God, the help seems to depend upon yourself alone. For I see very little appearance of aid from any other quarter.

The following important letter contains the Bishop of Glasgow's subsequent report on the state of affairs in Scotland, and forms a valuable commentary upon Nau's remarks.

LETTER from the Archbishop of Glasgow to the Cardinal of Lorraine, 6 February 1568.[1]

My Lord,—If I have not satisfied you in the matter of which you had the goodness to inform me in the letter which I received from your secretary Gatinois, and of which he told me verbally, the fault is due to the individual who left this place to go to you without my knowledge. But if the business had been of the consequence which at that time I wished to write to you, I would not have failed to send you an express messenger. As at this present time I have the advantage of forwarding my letter by Captain Hay, the bearer, I could not but send you the contents of the letters which I have lately received from Scotland, especially from the person whom I sent for the express purpose of being present at the Parliament which was held by the Earl of Moray last December. The sum of the whole is this. The queen, my sovereign, your

---

[1] From the Sloane MS. 3199, fol. 159.

the States assembled, to whose arbitrament she would willingly submit herself, in whatsoever she should be charged with. Furthermore, she protested by the word of a prince, that if she should be found in any sort culpable of her husband's death, she would, without challenging any authority or privilege of a sovereign prince, submit herself to the punishment that is due to the poorest malefactor in the world. Although this request was often reiterated, they mocked and scorned at all that was spoken in that behalf, which is confirmed by letters in Moray's own hand. Such is the information which is furnished by the well-informed author of this history, who adds, that the Lords of the Congregation, having so far attained their end, now resolved to await the return of Moray from his continental expedition, before taking any further measures as to the disposal of their imprisoned sovereign.

When Moray left Edinburgh on the 9th of April 1567, on his way to France, he found it convenient to go round by London, in order to confer with Cecil and Elizabeth. He wished to be guided by their advice; and their approval and assistance were necessary to his success. These having been obtained, or at least the promise of them, Moray crossed over into France, and at once visited the Cardinal of Lorraine, to whom he presented the letters of recommendation with which his sister had the simplicity to furnish him. He expressed his great indignation and sorrow at the treatment to which the queen had been subjected since he had left Scotland, and promised that he would use all his influence with the Lords of the Congregation to obtain her liberty. The Cardinal seems to have believed him. To the Queen Mother he spoke in a different language; and the bond which united them—hatred to prisoners in the Orkney Isles by M. of Holyrood, one of the queen's bastard brothers, who at present has been created lord of the said islands. They were compelled to land by stress of weather, after which they were taken to Edinburgh, and having been charged with murder, were condemned to death. Yet they were executed in prison, because some of them having asked the favour of being heard by the Earl of Moray, while they confessed that they had amply deserved the punishment of death, yet declared the queen's innocence, and accused the greatest and chiefest of his council, who were at the time sitting beside him; especially the Earl of Morton, Secretary Lethington, and Balfour, who was captain of Edinburgh Castle, and their own master the earl, at that time in Denmark.

Besides this, there has lately arrived at this court one Leslie, a son of the late Earl of Rothes. He came through England, but did not bring me a single line, although he had a packet from the king, which he received from his ambassador in London. He called upon M. de L'Aubespine, by whom he was conducted to the Queen Mother. Next day he paid me a visit and explained the reason which had brought him here, the zeal, namely, which he has for the queen's service. He thinks that if he were so far favoured by their Majesties as to be supplied by them with some letters of credence to some of the lords in Scotland, he might find the opportunity of doing some good service. But (speaking for myself) as I have a great suspicion of this man, I have done nothing in the matter other than what the queen has ordered me to do, namely, to come here to me, where I have heard from him what I have written above. The chief of the nobles to whom the letters are addressed are the Lords Fleming and Hume, the one for the safe keeping of Dumbarton Castle, the other about the feud which has of late sprung up between him and Morton.

As I do not expect any great result from this project, I have been careful not to mix myself up with it any further than I have already told you. By so doing I wish to obey you, wishing herein to follow the instructions given by the said Gastinoys, and further because he was brother to the person who murdered my late uncle and lord, the Cardinal of Albrocht.[1] He has set out on his journey, and has a warrant for twelve hundred pounds of pension, as well as a hundred crowns sols to pay his travelling expenses. This is all that I can write for certain of this dispatch.

The Castle of Dumbarton is safe; how, I will make you acquainted when I shall have the happiness of seeing you, if it please God, although letters of recommendation for that purpose have been refused me, as I have already written to you. This is all I have to say at present. Paris, this 6th of February 1568.

I ought not to forget to let your lordship know that the Queen of England has ordered her deputies on the frontiers to meet those of Scotland who have only their commission from the prince, which until this last meeting she has refused to do; having commanded them to be present at no meeting, nor to treat about any restitutions upon the borders except with commissioners directly appointed by the queen.

[1] David Beaton had been abbot of Arbroath; hence the error in the text. See Keith's Scot. Bishops, p. 36.

CHAPTER THE SEVENTH.

FROM THE QUEEN'S ESCAPE FROM LOCHLEVEN TO THE END OF THE NARRATIVE.

ON her escape from the castle of Lochleven, under the circumstances related by Nau, Queen Mary pushed on with all speed to Hamilton, which she reached early in the morning of the 3rd of May.[1] She had every reason to congratulate herself on the strength of the party by which she was already surrounded. The Hamiltons had joined her in a body, an important acquisition, and many of the principal clergy and nobles flocked to tender their allegiance. In the course of a very few days she found herself at the head of an army of 6000 men, and reinforcements were being collected for her in the north by Lords Huntley and Ogilvy, the arrival of which was daily expected. Public opinion seemed to have decided that now at last the queen's cause was about to triumph.

But the royalists had to deal with an enemy who was at once skilful, wary, and resolute. The intelligence of his sister's escape from prison had fallen like a thunderbolt upon Moray, and for a time he hesitated upon the course which he would pursue. His first intention seems to have been to fall back upon Stirling, but upon consideration, and possibly by the advice of Grange, he abandoned that idea. He concluded, and wisely, that such a movement would be construed as a confession of weakness, which would discourage his followers and animate his opponents. He rejected the offer of pardon

[1] See Note the First, p. cxcix.

made to him by his sister upon his submission,[1] and he resolved to make Glasgow his headquarters, and (for a time at least) to act upon the defensive.[2]

After an injudicious delay of several days at Hamilton, vainly awaiting for the arrival of the troops under Huntley, the order for march was given on the 13th of May.[3] It had been decided in a council of war held on the previous evening that the queen should be placed in Dumbarton Castle, where she would be safe, happen what might. Her troops, thus relieved from all anxiety about their royal mistress, should then march against her enemies. The route from Hamilton to Dumbarton passed at no great distance from Glasgow, but it would seem that the leaders of Mary's army did not expect to be molested on their journey. But they were mistaken. The conference of the previous evening, at which the tactics of the next day had been decided, was attended by a traitor, who immediately forwarded to Moray the important information of which he thus had become possessed. Kirkaldy placed his troops accordingly. The queen's forces were attacked at disadvantage and defeated, and she herself was compelled to seek safety by flight.[4] It was impossible to reach Dumbarton,[5] so she

[1] See Note the Second, p. cc.

[2] On May 13, Mary appointed Archibald, fifth Earl of Argyll, to be her lieutenant of Scotland, with power touching the defence of her person, and generally, to do all usually done by any lieutenant of this realm. A facsimile of this important document is given in " The Lennox," by W. Fraser, p. 436, vol. xi., Ed. 1874, a work of very great historical value.

[3] See Note the Third, p. cci.

[4] See the Illustrative Notes. Note the Fourth, p. ccii.

[5] An account written immediately after the battle, in the R. O. (Scot., xv. 21) contains the following passage, the words enclosed within brackets having been cancelled :—" The queen beheld this conflict within half a mile distant, standing upon a hill, accompanied with Lord Boyd, the Lord Fleming, and the Lord Harris's son, with

turned her horse's head towards Dumfriesshire. On the
15th of the same month she had reached the Cistercian
Abbey of Dundrennan, near the Solway. Hence she
despatched a letter to Elizabeth, in which she told her of
her misfortunes, and further, that it was her intention to
seek the assistance which had been so frequently proffered
by "her good sister" the Queen of England. This plan
was earnestly opposed by her attendants, who understood
better than their mistress the dangers to which it would
expose her. But all was in vain. Mary was resolute in
her determination, and, attended by a small body of her
followers, she crossed over the Solway Firth, and landed
in Cumberland.

Near the spot where the party now found themselves
resided a gentleman of good family, named Curwen,
with whom Lord Herries was on terms of intimacy.
Lord Herries sent a message to his friend, which exhibits
some ingenuity of invention. Mr Curwen was given to
understand that his lordship had eloped from Scotland
with a young heiress, whom he carried off as being an
excellent match for the future head of the family of
the Curwens. Could she remain in safe hiding until
matters were arranged? When the messenger arrived
he found that Mr Curwen was absent from home; but
the chief of the household declared that he was willing
to receive the lady who possibly might become the
future mistress of the mansion. She arrived, accompanied by Lord Herries, both of them so weary and
travel-stained as to confirm the story of the elopement.
If the queen thought that at last she was safe, the delu-

thirty others, who seeing the company overthrown took the way [to
Dumbarton, who was so near pursued that she could not take the
boat that should bring her into Dumbarton, but was driven to take
the way to Dumfries, where she as yet remaineth]."

sion was soon broken.   No sooner had she crossed Curwen's threshold than she was recognised by a Frenchman, who was one of the establishment; and this person
remarked to Lord Fleming that he had formerly seen
her Majesty in better plight than she was at that
moment.   The news soon spread, and further concealment was impossible.[1]

Defeated but not crushed, the queen's adherents in
Scotland prepared themselves for another effort.   The
popular feeling was strongly excited in her favour.   An
ultra-Protestant named Willock tells Cecil that the west
borders are rising under Lord Herries, and that Huntley
was up and doing in the north.[2]   The Earl of Argyll,
acting as the queen's lieutenant, issued a proclamation
ordering all persons between sixteen and sixty years of
age to be in readiness by the 10th of August, to assist
against the enemies of their sovereign.[3]   A report,
drawn up in the beginning of October, tells us that in
the previous August Huntley had 1500 men at Aberdeen, Argyll had marched upon Glasgow with 2000
Highlanders, Lord Claud Hamilton had surprised the
castle of Hamilton, which he still kept, Lord Fleming
had a garrison of eighty or a hundred hackbutters in
Dumbarton Castle, and various others, lords and lairds,
carried on a private warfare, each man for himself.
"The whole country," says Willock, " is in such state

[1] The Curwens were settled at Workington from an early period.
See Hutchinson's Hist. of Cumb., ii. 137 ; Nicolson and Burn, ii. 55.
"The chamber in which she slept at Workington Hall is still called
the Queen's Chamber."

[2] R. O. Scot., xv. 29, 30.   Willock to Cecil.   He wrote in the same
strain on 8th July.   Id. 45.   This Willock was superintendent of
the west of Scotland, and is frequently mentioned by Knox in his
History, ii. 482-484.

[3] R. O. Scot., xv. 50.

that no man cometh to his parish church in all the west without his armour, company, and weapons; and every man is ready to avenge his old and new quarrel."[1] This report afforded Moray the opportunity of punishing such of the landed proprietors as still adhered to their sovereign, and this he did with no small severity. Marching through Clydesdale, Galloway, Nithsdale, Annandale, and Tweeddale, he ravaged the lands and ruined the houses of his opponents. Nau has chronicled a few instances of his cruelty; and a journal of his proceedings, which is printed at the end of this chapter, enables us still further to understand the spirit of his administration.[2]

Yet it was not simply to the exertions of her friends in Scotland that Mary looked for the vindication of her rights against her rebellious subjects. Regarding herself as the representative of Catholicism and royalty in Europe she appealed for assistance to the kings of Spain and France, to the princes of the family of Guise, and to the pope himself, on the assumption that the interests of them all coincided with her own. She wrote to her early friend, Elizabeth of Valois,[3] Queen of Spain, entreating

[1] R. O. Scot., xv. 45. Willock to Cecil, July 8.

[2] See the Illustrative Notes. Note the Fifth, p. cciv.

[3] Mary and Elizabeth had been educated together, and their attachment to each other was very deep. The young wife of Philip II. died at Madrid, 3rd October 1568, four months after the date of the letter cited in the text, a copy of which occurs in the Corsini Library at Rome, 33 E. i. fol. 143. It is addressed by Giulio Acquaviva to the Cardinal Alessandrino, and is dated 5th June. Another letter written by the Papal Nuncio in Paris to the Nuncio in Spain (11th June 1568) urges the necessity of prompt assistance being given by Philip, suggests that a special messenger should be sent by him to Elizabeth, asking her to permit the Queen of Scotland to pass into France, and mentions the interest which the pope felt in her welfare. This letter is in the Secret Archives of the Vatican, Nunciatura Hispaniæ, vol. iii., p. 39.

person who murdered my late uncle and lord, the Cardinal of Albrocht.[1] He has set out on his journey, and has a warrant for twelve hundred pounds of pension, as well as a hundred crowns sols to pay his travelling expenses. This is all that I can write for certain of this dispatch.

The Castle of Dumbarton is safe; how, I will make you acquainted when I shall have the happiness of seeing you, if it please God, although letters of recommendation for that purpose have been refused me, as I have already written to you. This is all I have to say at present. Paris, this 6th of February 1568.

I ought not to forget to let your lordship know that the Queen of England has ordered her deputies on the frontiers to meet those of Scotland who have only their commission from the prince, which until this last meeting she has refused to do; having commanded them to be present at no meeting, nor to treat about any restitutions upon the borders except with commissioners directly appointed by the queen.

---

[1] David Beaton had been abbot of Arbroath; hence the error in the text. See Keith's Scot. Bishops, p. 36.

of the hope and the strength which were hers when she entered it.

One of the last circumstances connected with the history of his mistress to which Nau refers is her intended marriage with the Duke of Norfolk.[1] He tells the story indistinctly upon the whole, but he affirms very distinctly indeed that Elizabeth was cognizant of the proposed alliance, and that Mary refused to listen to any such proposals until she was assured that such was the case. The author of the Anonymous Life, to which reference has been made so frequently, appears to have been well informed upon every point connected with Norfolk's designs from the beginning. They first showed themselves during Elizabeth's dangerous illness of 1562, when the question of the succession was warmly debated in the English Parliament. The duke then advocated the superior claims of the Scottish line over every other. During the festivities at Stirling, on occasion of the baptism of the young prince, he is said to have informed her, by a special messenger, " that in default of issue of the Queen of England's body, he and diverse others of the principalest of the nobility were to stand for her and hers." Again, he proved himself her friend at the conferences, first at York and then at Westminster, in which her cause was tried before the commissioners. He opposed some of Elizabeth's favourite designs even when she was present in the council, and refuted the arguments which had been advanced under her sanction for granting a loan to Moray. It would appear, however, that the duke was no match in statecraft either to Lethington or Morton, by both of whom he is said to have been overreached, to the great injury of the Scottish queen and his own de-

[1] See Illustrative Note, p. ccx.

struction.   From the same authority we learn that shortly after Moray's homeward journey from the meeting at Westminster, "and not before, her marriage with the Duke of Norfolk was propounded unto her by the Earls of Arundell, Pembroke, and Leicester, with the consent and liking of many other of the nobility; Leicester himself being the inditer and writer of the letter with his own hand.   It was sent to the queen to the insinuated effect, though afterwards one of the chiefest that persecuted both her and the duke."   The letter was then submitted to Mary, who resolutely declined to have anything to do with the proposal until it had been sanctioned by Elizabeth.   Cecil, at the request of Leicester, undertook to lay it before his mistress, by whom an undecided and indefinite answer was given.   Nau, however, seems to have thought that it was sufficiently precise to warrant the continuance of the engagement between Mary and Norfolk, and the queen herself evidently was of that same opinion.

Mary's last appearance in Nau's pages is one in which she shows herself to advantage.   Queen Elizabeth had given the Earl of Shrewsbury, who was Mary's custodian, to understand that several of the powers in the continent of Europe, regarding her as the centre of Catholicity, and as such the source of every political disturbance, would gladly have purchased their own tranquillity by her execution, but that she, Elizabeth, had magnanimously scorned to listen to any such proposal.   Mary, therefore, he argued, was indebted for her life to the grace of his sovereign.   The statement was too important to be disregarded; Mary requested to see the papers referred to, but the earl refused to produce them, and laid himself open to the rebuke which she administered to him.   She assured him that so far from being ashamed turned her horse's head towards Dumfriesshire. On the 15th of the same month she had reached the Cistercian Abbey of Dundrennan, near the Solway. Hence she despatched a letter to Elizabeth, in which she told her of her misfortunes, and further, that it was her intention to seek the assistance which had been so frequently proffered by "her good sister" the Queen of England. This plan was earnestly opposed by her attendants, who understood better than their mistress the dangers to which it would expose her. But all was in vain. Mary was resolute in her determination, and, attended by a small body of her followers, she crossed over the Solway Firth, and landed in Cumberland.

Near the spot where the party now found themselves resided a gentleman of good family, named Curwen, with whom Lord Herries was on terms of intimacy. Lord Herries sent a message to his friend, which exhibits some ingenuity of invention. Mr Curwen was given to understand that his lordship had eloped from Scotland with a young heiress, whom he carried off as being an excellent match for the future head of the family of the Curwens. Could she remain in safe hiding until matters were arranged? When the messenger arrived he found that Mr Curwen was absent from home; but the chief of the household declared that he was willing to receive the lady who possibly might become the future mistress of the mansion. She arrived, accompanied by Lord Herries, both of them so weary and travel-stained as to confirm the story of the elopement. If the queen thought that at last she was safe, the delu-

thirty others, who seeing the company overthrown took the way [to Dumbarton, who was so near pursued that she could not take the boat that should bring her into Dumbarton, but was driven to take the way to Dumfries, where she as yet remaineth]. "

her religion.   Elizabeth Tudor took care that the world should know that Mary Stuart was thoroughly in earnest in the expression of these sentiments.   Twenty years of cruel captivity and a bloody death did for the Scottish queen what she could not have done for herself; and they are another proof, if any such were wanting, that every truly noble character is made perfect through suffering.

SUPPLEMENTAL NOTES AND ILLUSTRATIONS TO CHAPTER THE SEVENTH.

NOTE THE FIRST.   (See p. clxxxix., Note 1.)

The Anonymous History has here some observations which are worthy of being recorded.[1]   They are to the following effect:—

"After the Queen was thus escaped, she took the right way to the Hamilton's territory, and put herself into their hands, who, with other persons of mark at her devotion, gathered incontinent a strong army in her defence. Against which her enemies, as desperate folks, made head with all the forces they could ; and notwithstanding they were inferior in number, yet upon the Laird of Lethington's motion she was content to temporise and come to some composition, and this only to save the blood in question. But as her fortune would, her answer to Lethington's motion came not in time to his hands, whether by mischance, or the messenger having no mind the battle should be shunned ; who, in all likelihood, was either a Hamilton, or of the Hamilton's faction. And they, presuming of their number and the goodness of their cause, with desire to be revenged of the injuries they had before sustained by the adverse party, as to have the government in their hands, might be enemies to reconciliation; or that some of the traitors about the Queen had intercepted this letter,—by the non-coming to Lethington in time of the answer to the said motion, in all probability she was deprived of her estate, and in process of time of her life. For Lethington, by his not hearing from the Queen, felt in account that she had no mind to hasten the pacification, and forthwith imparted his conceit with his trusty friends the Lord

[1] From the Cott. MS. Cal, B. iv. 166 *b.*

Hume and Kirkcaldy, laird of Grange; who then demanding of Lethington what their part should be the next day in the battle they expected, his answer was that of two extremes the least was to be chosen, which he thought to be to fight on the side and party where they were; for at the Hamiltons' hands, if they become victorious, there was no mercy for them to be expected for causes that occurred betwixt them. It being certain that Hume's troops and Grange's direction won the battle, and as certain that thereupon the Queen took the preposterous cause intimated. For if the answer had come in time to Lethington's hands, either he would have turned Hume and Grange to her side, or have found some device that the battle should not have been fought, or have advertised the Queen of their lying wait for her where they did fight the battle, and so she thereby might have by some other way put herself into Dumbarton, a thing above all others she endeavoured; and then her enemies must either have come to composition or dispersed and abandoned Moray, whereunto many were prone, disliking his proceedings, suspecting them to tend unto usurpation; and Morton himself brooked not Moray's being not altogether by his manner *privados*, as John Knox the patriarch, George Buchanan the poet, James Magill the lawyer, David Lindsay the minister, and master John Wood the Machiavellian."

NOTE THE SECOND.   (See p. cxc., Note 1.)

MARY's message to the earl of Moray.

Writing to Cecil from Berwick on 7th May,[1] Drury tells him that "the queen, the day after she came to Hamilton, where now she resteth, sent a gentleman to the earl of Moray and other the lords to declare that she was delivered by God's providence out of captivity; and albeit she had consented to a certain kind of approving thereunto, she was thereunto for defence of her life compelled; which now, seeing that God had thus mercifully relieved her, she desired them that if they

[1] MS. Cott. Cal., C. i., fol. 56.

would restore her with quietness to her former dignity and estate, she would in like manner wholly remit and pardon all manner of actions committed against her honour and person.

"Whereunto the earl hearkened and sent one Patrick Hume to her grace to know if the same messenger was sent by her order and commandment. But what thereof followed I know not . . . Though at the first the earl was minded to retire to Stirling, he is now determined to stay in Glasgow."

NOTE THE THIRD.   (See p. cxc., Note 3.)

Mary's march to Dumbarton.

There occurs a curious passage in Sir George Mackenzie's "History of the Family of Mackenzie," which should be here quoted. We are told that Colin Mackenzie, Rory's eldest son, entreated the queen to retire to Stirling, there to await the arrival of the troops which were known to be on their march from the north, "the place being situated commodiously for such a rendezvous, there being no pass to hinder any from coming to it, whilst it was the only pass that could stop the combination of her enemies that were divided by the Forth." "The French ambassador was the great instrument of that fatal advice for placing the queen in Dumbarton." Mackenzie went to the north to hasten Huntley's march, but before the troops which he had collected could be of any service, Mary had passed over into England. See Frazer's "History of the Earls of Cromarty," ii. 497.

I have been so fortunate as to recover an authentic copy of the order of the Council of War at which Mary presided at Hamilton on 12th May, and which settled the plan on which the movements of the army on the following day were to be conducted. This order is entered on a nearly defaced page of an official register of the queen's acts,[1] and is as follows:—

"Copy of the act and warrant for the transport of the queen's majesty's most noble person from Hamilton to Dumbarton, the xij of May 1568."

[1] B. M. MS. Reg., 18 B. vi. fol. 282 *b*.

" Apud Hamilton, xij May 1568.

" [On the] which day it is thought expedient by the lords of
our sovereign lady's council that our sovereign lady's most
noble person be surely transported to Dumbarton with [the]
whole army, aye, and while her grace be placed therein. And
that being done the [whole army] to return together to
Hamilton, and there to remain while the lieutenant Ce . . . . .
horsemen and footmen, hackbutters and spearmen, to [re]main
and do such service as the lieutenant shall command."

MARIE.

" This was the bishop's dyting and writing with his own
hand, and subscribed with the queen's."

Note the Fourth.   (See p. cxc., Note 4.)

Every piece of authentic information about Langside is
precious; I therefore gladly print the following letter written
on the Sunday before the battle. The transcriber has omitted
the name of the writer and the person addressed.[1]

Copia. Pleaseth your honour. Having understand by your
servant Richard Fraunch that you cannot get the sure advertisement of the proceedings in this country, I have thought good by
these few lines to let your lordship understand the same.

Upon the second day of this instant May, a servant
of the place in Loughleven, who hath since his birth been
nursed in the same place, and by reason thereof having
credit thereintill, privily stole the keys in the time of supper,
and thereafter passed and rescued the king's mother forth of
her chamber and conveyed her to the boat, and locked all the
yetts upon the rest who was at supper, and spoiled the rest
of the boats of their furniture so that none was able to follow
them. And when they were comed to land, George Douglas,
brother to the laird of Loughleven, who was in fantacy of love
with her, and had provided this money of before, met her at
the lough side, accompanied ·with the laird of Riccarton, a
friend of the lord Bothwell's, and with them in company ten
horse. They took away with them all the horse which per-

---

[1] R. O. Sc. Mary, xv. f. 45.

tained to the laird of Lochleven, so that he should not be able to follow. Within two miles or thereby, my lord Seton, together with James Hamilton of Ormiston, met her. In their company was xxx horse. In this company they came to the ferry. Being passed the same Claud Hamilton, second son to my lord duke of Châtelherault, met her, and with him xx horse, and conveyed her to ane place of my lord Seton's, called Niddry, where she made some despatches, with her own hand written, namely, one to John Betton to send into France, and directed him away with the same; another to the laird of Riccarton, commanding him to take the castle of Dunbar. He passed to have done the same, but he failed of his enterprise. At her departure from Niddry my lord Herries met her, accompanied with xxx horse, and all together conveyed her to Hamilton, to the castle thereof, where she now remains, accompanied with all such as was of the motion of this conspiracy, which are not a very great number, and earnestly at this present repent that ever they had melling therewith.

The principals that are of that faction are, my lord bishop of Saint Andrews, the Hamiltons, Herries, and Seton. Sensyne they have drawn unto them Eglinton and Fleming, with some mean gentlemen, friends of my lord Bothwell, that would gladly be quit of the matter. Their force is not great and very evil frayed. They mean to have all their force about Monday or Tuesday together in Hamilton. They cannot agree who shall be lieutenant, because it is laid to sundry of their charges and refused. My lord regent's force will be ready against that day, which will exceed their number very far in number, and likewise in goodness of men. After Wednesday my lord regent takes the fields. It is supposed the other party dare not abide the matter, but will steal away and do what they can to put the king their master's mother in Dumbarton, if to them it be possible. Always I think it shall not be able for them to do it. Within few days I believe you will hear this matter will be sooner at an end; for all the whole nobility of Scotland is already with my lord regent, save the few number already nominated, that are together neither of great foresight nor force. Your servant Haies sent his writings to Glasgow; he is remained

Hume and Kirkcaldy, laird of Grange ; who then demanding of Lethington what their part should be the next day in the battle they expected, his answer was that of two extremes the least was to be chosen, which he thought to be to fight on the side and party where they were ; for at the Hamiltons' hands, if they become victorious, there was no mercy for them to be expected for causes that occurred betwixt them. It being certain that Hume's troops and Grange's direction won the battle, and as certain that thereupon the Queen took the preposterous cause intimated. For if the answer had come in time to Lethington's hands, either he would have turned Hume and Grange to her side, or have found some device that the battle should not have been fought, or have advertised the Queen of their lying wait for her where they did fight the battle, and so she thereby might have by some other way put herself into Dumbarton, a thing above all others she endeavoured ; and then her enemies must either have come to composition or dispersed and abandoned Moray, whereunto many were prone, disliking his proceedings, suspecting them to tend unto usurpation ; and Morton himself brooked not Moray's being not altogether by his manner *privados*, as John Knox the patriarch, George Buchanan the poet, James Magill the lawyer, David Lindsay the minister, and master John Wood the Machiavellian."

NOTE THE SECOND. (See p. cxc., Note 1.)

MARY's message to the earl of Moray.

Writing to Cecil from Berwick on 7th May,[1] Drury tells him that "the queen, the day after she came to Hamilton, where now she resteth, sent a gentleman to the earl of Moray and other the lords to declare that she was delivered by God's providence out of captivity ; and albeit she had consented to a certain kind of approving thereunto, she was thereunto for defence of her life compelled ; which now, seeing that God had thus mercifully relieved her, she desired them that if they

[1] MS. Cott. Cal., C. i., fol. 56.

fries to the Hoddom, and burnt the Tynwald belonging to
Robert Maxwell's wife, of Towhill, and syne burnt the laird of
Hownam's place, with certain steeds about, and camped that
night in the woode of Hoddom, within shot of gun of the castle,
and laid siege to the castle that night, and lay in camp
and sieged while Monday at ten hours, and then the
house was rendered, and servants of the laird of Drumlanrick put into the house to keep it.   And the rendering of the
house was under condition that the house and men's lives,
which was into it, should be safe.   And on the afternoon there
rode forth certain hosts of horsemen to seek pricking, and
burnt the kirkhouse, which was the young laird of Hume's.

Tuesday the xxij at four hours in the morning my Lord
Regent's host rode a mile beyond Annan, and met my Lord
Scrope with a small company of Englishmen by eight hours,
and talked with him while four hours afternoon; and in the
meantime be sent four gentlemen of England to their camp to
see the number of the vanguard and fashion of their camp,
who gave them the musters; and on my Lord Regent's
coming backward again, the house of Annan was rendered,
and men put in the castle at my Lord Regent's command.

Wednesday the xxiij they removed camp at three hours in
the morning, and thereafter burnt certain steeds in Annerdale
while they come to Lochmaben castle, which was rendered,
and put servants of the laird of Drumlanrick into it.   And
thereafter past forward to the house of Louchwode, pertaining
to the laird of Johnston, which are rendered to the Lord Regent, and given in keeping to the laird of Buckleuch that
night, and thereafter past forward and camped in Tasshowme,
fornent Loganwood.   And word come to the camp that night
that the lord of Towhill came after them to Lochmaben castle,
and put out the men that my Lord Regent put into it, and
left his own servants in the castle, which the lords was evil
content of; and was in purpose once to have ridden backward
again, and put new men into the same, and was a great time
at council of the same; and by cause of scarceness of
victuals and time of proclamation of furnishing worn out, they
stayed purpose.

Thursday xxiiij, at morne they raised camp and come in at

a ryk stane, and down Tweed to Peebles and remained there that night. And so far as I can get knowledge they purpose rather to Edinburgh nor to turne in Tevidale at this time.

JOURNAL of the Regent Moray's expedition into the west of Scotland, in June 1568 :[1]

THE progress of the Regent of Scotland, with certain of his nobility, beginning the xi. day of June, anno 1568.

Imprimis, the xviij day of May anno 1568, the Regent of Scotland made a Proclamation that the shires of Mernes, Angus, Fife, Merse, Lothian, Argyll, and Carrick should provide 15 days' victual, and to meet him the x. day of June in Biggar, to ride in the southwest of Scotland for punishing of disobedient persons and thieves.

The xj day of June, the Regent of Scotland with certain of his nobility, marched forth of Edinburgh, and that night come to Biggar, where they received the castle of Boghall, pertaining to my lord Fleming. They had casten it down, but these reasons stopt them :—First, he was in England and at that present could get no word of them ; Secondly, he had the castle of Dunbarton in his hand, which they were in hope to receive, they sparing his place. The army journied this day xx. miles.

The xij day, the Regent caused cast down the castle and place of Skirling, a notable building, upon this consideration that others might hear and fear ; and that night he marched forward to a place called Crawfordjohn, pertaining to Sir James Hamilton, and received the castle thereof, but cast it not down because they had the man in their own hands. They journied this day x. miles.

The xiij day of June they marched to Sancher and lay there all night, but cast not down my lord's place because he hath made a promise to come in to the Regent to Edinburgh at a day, and surety found therefor. They journied this day xij miles.

[1] From the original in R. O. Scot., xv. 44.

tained to the laird of Lochleven, so that he should not be able to follow. Within two miles or thereby, my lord Seton, together with James Hamilton of Ormiston, met her. In their company was xxx horse. In this company they came to the ferry. Being passed the same Claud Hamilton, second son to my lord duke of Châtelherault, met her, and with him xx horse, and conveyed her to ane place of my lord Seton's, called Niddry, where she made some despatches, with her own hand written, namely, one to John Betton to send into France, and directed him away with the same; another to the laird of Riccarton, commanding him to take the castle of Dunbar. He passed to have done the same, but he failed of his enterprise. At her departure from Niddry my lord Herries met her, accompanied with xxx horse, and all together conveyed her to Hamilton, to the castle thereof, where she now remains, accompanied with all such as was of the motion of this conspiracy, which are not a very great number, and earnestly at this present repent that ever they had melling therewith.

The principals that are of that faction are, my lord bishop of Saint Andrews, the Hamiltons, Herries, and Seton. Sensyne they have drawn unto them Eglinton and Fleming, with some mean gentlemen, friends of my lord Bothwell, that would gladly be quit of the matter. Their force is not great and very evil frayed. They mean to have all their force about Monday or Tuesday together in Hamilton. They cannot agree who shall be lieutenant, because it is laid to sundry of their charges and refused. My lord regent's force will be ready against that day, which will exceed their number very far in number, and likewise in goodness of men. After Wednesday my lord regent takes the fields. It is supposed the other party dare not abide the matter, but will steal away and do what they can to put the king their master's mother in Dumbarton, if to them it be possible. Always I think it shall not be able for them to do it. Within few days I believe you will hear this matter will be sooner at an end; for all the whole nobility of Scotland is already with my lord regent, save the few number already nominated, that are together neither of great foresight nor force. Your servant Haies sent his writings to Glasgow; he is remained thousand men, was in Dumfries two days before, and spended all the meat and drink that was ready ; as also consulted what was best to be done against the Regent's coming. It was thought that my lord Maxwell should have come in if Cowhill, Johnson, and Lochinvar had not stopped him, and counselled him to the contrary. They journied this day xiiij miles.

The **xx** day they marched towards Hoddom, a place of my Lord Herries, the which was maintained by men of war against the Regent on Herries's behalf, and was a strong fort. This night they held it and shot many shot of great ordnance from off the place, and slew of horse and men. This night the broken traitors and thieves gathered to the number of a thousand men, and broke athrice after some of our men that was going forth of the camp. The which when the Regent's men perceived, sent forth a chase after them and took two or three, and one of them was the Laird Johnstone's father's brother. They lay within half a mile of the camp. This day they journied x miles.

The xxj day the house was given over to the Regent, the which they might have holden long enough, if they had been good fellows within it ; and upon this condition only, that the men should have their lives, and no more ; all bag and baggage to remain in it, and it was delivered to the laird of Drumlanrig to keep, who is appointed warden in those parts of Scotland fornenst England. This day the Regent sent forth a thousand men with my Lords Hume and Morton, to have drawn a chase on the thieves and rebels, but they fled and would not prick. This day (as oft of before and after) there was a great hunger in the camp ; for the Scottish pint of wine was at vijs. Scottish, and no bread to be had. Some died for hunger in the camp. This day and before they burnt diverse gentlemen's places about, that would not come in nor obey.

The xxij day the camp remained ; but the Regent, with a thousand horsemen, went to Annan, and received the castle thereof, and put one Edward Urwine to keep it. And there met my Lord Scrope of England, and talked with him a long while, and that night returned to the camp to Hoddom. They journied this day vj miles.

The xxiij day they marched to Lowmaben, and received the castle thereof and gave it to Drumlanrig; but some of the Maxwells remained in a close house or vault within, and took the house again after the Regent was gone, and so they have the house again.   This day they received a place of the laird of Johnston called Lokat and another called Bewthouse, but they cast them not down, for he hath promised to come in at a day and surety for the same find.   This day they took away cattle and furnished the camp.   This night also they slew two of the thieves by a shot of great ordnance shot at threescore of them.   This night they hanged one of the thieves that was taken in the camp stealing horses.   This night they lay at a place called Milton Holme.

The xxiiij day they come to Peebles and remained all night, and took order with that country ; for they come all in to the Regent.   They journied xxvij miles.

The xxv day the Regent went to Edinburgh, and the rest of the army to their own country and bounds.   They journied xij miles.

The countries the Regent passed through :—

He passed through Clydesdale, Galloway, Nidsdale, Annerdale, Tweedale.

The order of his army :—

First, Alexander Hume of Manderston and Hutton Hall, went before all the army a mile with cornet of two hundred men ; and they were appointed to show the fields.

Then followed them the vanguard with Wat Hume and Morton, with a thousand men and more.

Next after them came the carriage, and behind the carriage the Regent's self, with the rest of the army, and behind the Regent went the Laird of Cessford with a cornet and a company with him.   At every side of the army went a cornet ; to wit, on the one side the Lairds of the Merse, on the other side the Lord of Buccleugh.

THUS ENDS THE PROGRESS AND ORDER.

NOTE THE SIXTH.

QUEEN MARY's correspondence with the duke of Norfolk.

(See p. cxcv., Note 1.)

That Mary considered herself pledged to marry the duke of Norfolk cannot be doubted by any one who has had the opportunity of reading the letters which she sent to him. A few only have been printed, to which I make the following additions.[1]

On 17th May (1570), she writes :—"Come what so will, I shall never change from you, but during life be true and obedient, as I have professed; and so I pray you think and hold me in your grace as your own." And she professes herself to be, "Your own faithful to death, who shall not have any advancement or rest without you."

On the last of January :—"You have promised to be mine and I yours." . . . "As you please command me; for I will for all the world follow your commandment, so you be not in danger for me." . . . "This last of January. Your own faithful to death, Queen of Scots. My Norfolk."

In a letter which is dated 29th March, and which refers to the death of the earl of Pembroke (1569), occurs the following expressions :—"If you mind not to think at the matter, I will die and live with you. . . . Neither prison the one way, nor liberty the other, nor all such accidents, good or bad, shall persuade me to start from that faith and obedience I have promised to you."

Chatsworth, 13th June (1570). She assures him that she will be true and obedient to him as long as she lives, and signs herself, "Your own, faithful to death."

[1] From the contemporaneous copy in the Harl. MS. 290, fol. 89, *seqq.*

VINDICATION of the title of Queen Mary Stuart to the throne of England. [1] (See pp. iv., v.)

A remonstrance to the Pope and all Christian kings, princes, and potentates, containing evident proof and demonstration as to the right of succession to the crown of England, which has fallen to the most illustrious and virtuous princess, the Lady Mary Stuart of Scotland, widow of Francis, the second of that name, King of France, by the death of Mary, the late queen, deceased without issue : With a sufficient answer to all the claims of right unjustly preferred to the said crown by Elizabeth, born of king Henry and Anne of Bullen, during the lifetime of Catherine of Aragon, the king's first wife ; and an account of the means by which the said Elizabeth made herself mistress of the said kingdom, by the strength of those English who held the faction of the new opinions in religion, in order to obtain for them the free exercise of the same : And how not content with this, she has planned to get possession of the person of the said legitimate queen, and has kept her since in pitiful captivity, in order to take from her all means and hope of seeking to be acknowledged by the kingdom aforesaid.

For that I have lately published a small treatise concerning the history of Scotland, at the prayer and solicitation of certain worthy persons in Scotland devoted to the service of their captive queen, having extracted it from the 35th chapter of the ninth volume of my history of all the memorable events that have happened in Europe since 1558, I cannot be satisfied by simply showing the truth concerning the calumnious proceedings which certain rebel subjects of the Lady Mary Stuart, queen of Scotland, and queen dowager of France (worked upon by Elizabeth, daughter of Anne of Bullen, who at present holds the kingdom of England, to preserve herself in the wrongful occupation of the same),

---

[1] The following extract, a translation from the original French, is sufficient to show the scope of this treatise. It gives us no exalted idea of the genius of the author. No other copy is known besides that here used, in the collection of Sir Robert Cotton (Titus, C. xii. fol. 1), who probably obtained it from Phillips.

have employed against their queen to deprive her of her two kingdoms, and by the same means, of her liberty; having pretended to nothing else throughout my discourse, but by a true narration of facts to preserve her honour to her, and in order to do this to lay bare the more abominable impostures and calumnies by which she, the said queen Mary, has been oppressed; therefore, as the reader cannot be otherwise instructed as to the principal cause for which this legitimate queen of England and Scotland is still so tyrannously detained prisoner by the said Elizabeth, I have not spared either trouble or expense in order that I may be fully instructed as well concerning the manner by which the crown of England came to her, as concerning the rights pretended to it by Elizabeth, who still enjoy the same. The mere devotion which it has pleased God to excite in me to put in evidence the undoubted right of that unhappy queen, widow of my good master and my king, which is not known to most, has caused me to undertake the publication of this treatise, to make known to all who will read it, how by the disposition of all rights divine, human and positive, and even, by the mere understanding of the truth of English history, the succession of the said kingdom is fallen to her by the death of Mary, wife of Philip of Spain, dying without issue—without the said Elizabeth, who still occupies it (under pretext that she is the issue of Henry the Eighth and Anne of Bullen), being able to pretend any claim to it : To the intent that, the right of the said queen-widow being acknowledged, and after her the right of her son, prince of Scotland, like her a prisoner in the hands of his rebel subjects, the Pope and all Christian kings and princes recognizing that by express command of God they are above all others obliged to the protection and defence of that hapless queen-widow, and the prince her orphan son, may aquit themselves of their duty, by employing all their forces and all means to their deliverance, in order to reinstate them in the enjoyment of their kingdom of England, now tyrannically withheld from them.

King Henry VII. having conquered and expelled Richard III., who by violence had seized on the kingdom, before all else, according to the custom of the Athenians, proclaimed "the law of forgetfulness" of all past events, which the Greeks called amnesty, and afterwards he married Elizabeth, eldest daughter of Edward the Fifth,[1] and consequently his heiress, from which marriage ensued the entire pacification of the kingdom of England, in as much as by these means the two houses of Lancaster and York, which being the most noble, the richest, and the most ancient families in England, had for so long contended for the sovereignty, to the great detriment of all the kingdom, were reconciled.

The treatise concludes with the following passage :—

Therefore, O generous English people, at last acknowledge the fraud of her who so tyrannically holds by force the sceptre of your kingdom, and who has until now cheated you in order that you may not perceive her wrongful occupation of it to the prejudice of the illustrious princess Mary, hereditary queen of the kingdoms of England and Scotland, and dowager of France, who as in natural beauty of person she surpasses by far all the most perfect ladies which in this age we have been able to see in all the world, so also by the rare virtues with which it has pleased God to adorn her soul, she has hitherto not found her like in sweetness and humanity, as any one may have sufficient proof by what I have related in my history of Europe, regarding the admirable patience with which her majesty endured the cruel attempts of some of her rebellious subjects at divers times against her person and estate, by the instigation of her who still retains possession of her English kingdom and her person; which by her natural and incomprehensible goodness she has preferred to dissemble and to pardon, hoping so to bring her rebellious subjects to repentance, rather than use the power which God had given her to enforce exemplary punishment; the consideration of which forbearance ought to incite you to render her willingly the duty of submission and obedience to which divine and human law

---

[1] "Cinquissme" in the original text. Opposite this last sentence, in the margin of the text, occurs this note in Nau's hand, with his signature :—*quatrissme*, le mot est de moy, mais sur ma conscience je ne ma puis souvenir quel livre est cestuycy.—NAU.

p

obliges you towards her and her posterity, so that it may not
come to pass that the king of France, by many considerations
bound to the defence and protection of this queen-widow, so
tyrannously oppressed and deprived of the enjoyment of her
royal heritage, and with him all other Christian potentates and
princes, who cannot without greatly offending God and tarnish-
ing their honour, refuse him their assistance in so just a cause,
shall be constrained to unite their forces to bring exemplary
punishment for her violence and tyranny upon that woman,
who not content with usurping another's kingdom, still keeps
her person in a wretched and cruel slavery. And all you, ye
other English men who are in rebellion and revolt against
your legitimate queen, which cannot be without your entire
ruin and the destruction of the prosperous estate of your kingdom, which by the incomprehensible will of God, after the
course of long years, has returned by lawful succession into the
posterity of the kings of Scotland, from whom the Saxons had
wrested it by violence, as your histories show, even as Elizabeth now wrests it, who being born of an illegitimate marriage
contracted in plain adultery between king Henry and Anne
Boleyn, who was convicted of immorality, and for the same put
to death by the authority of the law, as has been plainly
understood by the considerations set out at length in this discourse; which Elizabeth, without any other title but that of
violence, has seized the kingdom, calling herself the daughter
and legitimate heiress of him of whom the issue could only be
bastard, although she could not even be accepted as his bastard daughter without great suspicion having regard to that
dissolute life of licence—against whom God, first of all, who is
the sovereign protector of justice and of the widow and father-
less in their affliction, and next all men who are lovers of
justice and equity, which is the authority and power of the
Pope and all other Christian princes, that she may be constrained either by force or friendship to right this poor captive
queen, being assured of the assistance of the great God in so
holy and Christian an undertaking.

END.

MEMORIALS

OF THE

State and Progress of Events in Scotland during the Reign of Mary Stewart.

. . . As for themselves, as they had begun the business they must needs finish it. Even if all persons would not risk their lives, they at least had gone too far to recede ; and indeed the mischief could not be undone. As for him—Darnley—they reminded him that everything had been done for his advancement, and therefore he must now take the lead so as to give confidence to the others. But be this as it might, they were determined, one and all, that if he were so cowardly and fainthearted as to refuse to carry out the affair, they would support each other without regard to any one, and they would spare no man in this matter.

Finding himself thus singlehanded in the midst of so many murderers the king was much terrified, for naturally he was none of the most determined in time of need or danger. He sent for his father, who came along with some others ; and they deliberated what had best be done. But the conspirators took the upper hand, and themselves proposed two measures. The first affirmed the absolute necessity, before all else, of breaking up the Parliament and sending home all the lords who had a vote in it. This was proclaimed on the next day, being Sunday, and done so effectually that not one of the said lords remained in Edinburgh. The next proposal was that the queen should be sent to Stirling under safe keeping, there to give birth to her child. Lord Lindsay remarked that she would have plenty of pastime there in nursing her baby and singing it to sleep ; shooting with her

A

bow in the garden, and doing such fancy work; for such things delighted her much, as he happened to know. In the meantime the king could manage the affairs of state, along with the nobles. Some persons present remarked that there were certain lords who had been imprisoned who might oppose it by force, to which Ruthven had his answer, "Is there no other remedy? If they raise the least difficulty or cause any uproar by attempting to release her, we will throw her to them piece-meal from the top of the terrace." Another person having reminded them that she was near her childbearing, "I feel certain," said Ruthven, " and I will stake my life on it, that the baby is only a girl, and there will be no danger. But on this matter we will take counsel with Lords Moray and Rothes, and some others, for without them we will do nothing."

These two noblemen had returned from Newcastle on the very day of the murder, being Saturday, about six o'clock in the evening, and remained in hiding in different parts of the town.

At last they thus addressed the king : " If you wish to obtain what we have promised you, you must needs follow our advice, as well for your own safety as for ours. If you do otherwise, we will take care of ourselves, cost what it may." Hereupon they spoke aside with each other, and whispered together, which put the king and his father into great terror, for they did not think their lives safe ; and all the more so when, as they were breaking up, they told him that now he must not talk with the queen save in their presence. They removed his own attendants and left a guard near his chamber.

Moved by these considerations and terrors, the king came

up that night by a private stair to the queen's bedroom.
Finding the door locked, he most urgently entreated her
to open it, for he had something to tell her which much
concerned their mutual safety. But he was not permitted to enter until the next morning. The queen passed
the night in tears and lamentations, in the company only
of the elder Lady Huntley, and some other of her female
attendants, who did their best to comfort her.

Next morning the Earl of Moray came to visit the
queen. He excused himself to her very earnestly from
the charge of having been the bellwether and chief promoter of such atrocities. He promised her in the end to
discuss the matter with the Lords; whom he also advised
her to admit next day into her presence. But petition
as he might the queen still refused.

The king passed that night in great perplexity. He
did not know how to escape out of the labyrinth into
which he had so imprudently allowed himself to be
drawn, urged thereto and tempted by his vanity and
ambition. He saw, on the one hand, how great was the
injury which he had inflicted on the queen his wife;
and, on the other, the great obligations which she had
conferred upon himself. He was in terror for his own
life; for certainly he would be ruined if necessity compelled him to follow the party with which he had identified himself, and from which he could find no safe
means of escape. That party was the stronger of the
two. Moray and his followers were his enemies of old;
they had not forgotten the past, and at the present time
they wanted to make use of him only that they might
involve him in the disgrace and infamy of an act of such
atrocity. This, indeed, they did shortly afterwards,
when they took their revenge by ascribing the whole

crime to him.   In like manner they were eloquent upon the unkind treatment which the queen had received from this young prince, when they wished to throw a false colouring over his murder, a murder which they themselves had committed.   All this while they had been doing all they could to hinder the reconciliation of the queen and her husband.   But he was far too simple to contend with such crafty foxes, whose chief design was the elevation of Moray to the throne, and the deposition of himself and the queen.   This will appear obvious by the whole course of the present history.   Shortly afterwards the Lords, perceiving that they could not effect this so speedily as they had imagined by the violent death of both, fomented discord between the king and queen by underhand dealings, and then recommended a divorce in order to deprive them of all lawful succession.

Thus unable of himself to dispel the various conflicting doubts and fears in which he saw himself involved, the king proceeded to balance matters on either side. He came to the conclusion that it would be wisest for him to have recourse to the queen, his wife.   Remembering her natural kindness and the great affection which she had always shown towards him, he hoped that by owning his fault, and by offering to atone for it, he would set himself right with her.   He believed also that at least he might induce her to provide for their common safety, and deliver them both from the ruin into which they had fallen.   That she should do so had become a necessity.

Before daybreak, then, on the Sunday morning, he came into the queen's bedroom.   Throwing himself on his knees at his first entrance before her—which she was unwilling that he should do—he said, through his tears, "Ah, my Mary" (for so he used to call her familiarly), "I am bound to confess at this time, though now it is too late, that I have failed in my duty towards you. The only atonement which I can make for this, is to acknowledge my fault and sue for pardon, by pleading my youth and great indiscretion. Let these intercede with you for me. I have been most miserably deluded and deceived by the persuasions of these wicked traitors, who have led me to confirm and support all their plots against you, myself, and all our family. I see it all now, and I see clearly that they aim at our ruin. I take God to witness I never could have thought nor expected that they would have gone to such lengths. If I have shared in their sin, it is more through imprudence than from any illwill towards yourself. I confess that ambition has blinded me. But since the grace of God has stopped me from going further, and has led me to repent before it is too late, as I hope, I ask you, my Mary, to have pity on me, have pity on our child, have pity on yourself. Unless you take some means to prevent it, we are all ruined, and that speedily."

Here he handed to her the Articles drawn up and signed between himself and the conspirators, telling her that he was sure that if it were ever known that he had done so, he would be a dead man. Nevertheless, he wished to free his conscience from this burden.

The queen, still troubled with the agitation and weakness arising from the emotions of the previous night, answered him frankly, for she had never been trained to dissemble, nor was it her custom to do so. "Sire," said she, "within the last twenty-four hours you have done me such a wrong that neither the recollection of our early friendship, nor all the hope you can give me of the future can ever make me forget it. As I do not wish to hide from you the impression which it has made on me, I may tell you that I think you will never be able to undo what you have done. You have committed a very grave error. What did you hope to possess in safety without me? You are aware that, contrary to the advice of those very persons whom you now court, I have made earnest suit to obtain for you of them the very thing which you think you can obtain through their means and wicked devices. I have been more careful about your elevation than you yourself have been. Have I ever refused you anything that was reasonable, and which was for your advantage, by placing you above those persons who to-day are trying to get both you and me into their power, that they may tread us under their feet? Examine your own conscience, sire, and see the blot of ingratitude with which you have stained it. You say you are sorry for what you have done, and this gives me some comfort; yet I cannot but think that you are driven to it rather by necessity than led by any sentiment of true and sincere affection. Had I offended you as deeply as can be imagined, you could not have discovered how to avenge yourself upon me with greater disgrace or cruelty. I thank God that neither you nor any one in the world can charge me with ever having done or said aught justly to displease you, were it not for your own personal good. Your life is dear to me, and God and my duty oblige me to be as careful of it as of my own. But since you have placed us both on the brink of the precipice, you must now deliberate how we shall escape the peril."

"Have pity upon me, my Mary!" said this poor prince; "I assure you that this misfortune will make me cautious for the future ; nor will I rest until I have avenged you upon those wretched traitors, provided we can escape out of their hands."

Having read the Articles already mentioned, the queen promised to do all she could for their mutual escape, but said that the king too must exert himself. The first thing that he ought to do, should be to procure the removal of some soldiers who had been appointed as a guard. Hereupon he advised her Majesty to pardon the conspirators, if she should be solicited by them to do so, in order to mollify them, and that in the meantime he would try to bring about a reconciliation. To this, however, she would in no wise consent, remarking, " Sire, my conscience will never allow me to promise what I do not mean to perform, nor can I bring myself to tell a falsehood even to those men who have betrayed me so villanously. You, however, have already gone as far as I have ; if you think it good, you can promise them whatever you please in my name. But as for me, I will never pledge them my faith." To this the king consented, and he and the queen quietly separated without the interview being discovered.

Her majesty was guarded very strictly. She did not taste anything until four o'clock in the afternoon, when her food was examined very narrowly by Lord Lindsay, who remained close by her. Next morning, as I have already mentioned, proclamation was made through the town that all the lords who had a vote in Parliament should leave Edinburgh. After they had gone, on the Monday following, the Earl of Moray and some other rebels came through the town to the Tolbooth, and there protested that they were ready to answer the Parliament, well knowing that no one could be found who would then venture to accuse them.

During this period the old Lady Huntley (right glad to have her revenge upon Moray), having permission to visit the queen, gave her a message from the Earl of Huntley, her son, and some other noblemen who had escaped, to the effect that they had raised some troops, and that if she could manage to descend from a window, which they would point out to her, by means of a rope ladder, they all would be in waiting to receive her. Lady Huntley undertook to bring this ladder to the queen, between two dishes, as if it had been some meat. As she was talking with the queen (who was seated upon her *chaise percée*), Lord Lindsay suspected what was going on, and coming into the room, ordered Lady Huntley to leave it, and not to return. However, she carried away with her, between her body and her chemise (though she was searched from the outside of her dress), a letter from her majesty to those noblemen. In it she told them that their plan was impracticable, for the guard was placed above her chamber, and opposite the window proposed by them. She asked them, however, to wait for her in a village near Seton, where she would not fail to keep tryst with them the following night; and in the meantime to warn the Earl of Mar, who was in Edinburgh Castle, to hold it for her, and to assure him of her speedy deliverance.

The plan of the escape is due to the queen's ingenuity. She sent for the Laird of Traquair, surnamed Stewart, captain of her Guard. When he came he spoke with her through the king's chamber, and she explained to him the details of her plan. She meant to go down next night into the king's bedroom, and thence to the office of her butlers and cupbearers, all of whom were French. A door was there, which opened into the burial-ground; it was insecurely fastened, and was broken, being only sufficiently wide for a man to pass his head through. Arthur Erskine, an esquire of the queen's stables, was warned by the laird of Traquard to wait near this door about midnight. He was told to bring with him a strong and tall gelding, on which the queen was to be mounted on a pillion behind him, and two or three other horses for the king and his attendants. All this Erskine did with the greatest accuracy.

The king had spoken to his wife about the state of terror in which his father, Lennox, was, and observing that when they were deliberating upon their escape, she made no reference to what he had said, he again entreated her to arrange so that they might carry off Lennox along with them. In this he showed more than ever before his affection towards his father. But the queen would by no means consent, and answered that Lennox had been too often a traitor to her and her's to be trusted on an occasion so hazardous as the present, which if he should happen to reveal, would cost the life of everyone connected with it. Since their marriage, out of regard to him, her husband, she had always honoured his father and paid him respect, and sometimes more than he, Darnley, liked. She had invited him to dine with them at their own table; she had consulted him on all matters of importance; she had even frequently checked and admonished him, her husband, to conduct himself towards his father with greater respect than he had been in the habit of doing. In short, had he been of higher rank than he is; had he been no subject of her's, she had forgotten nothing which could be done to satisfy him. Instead of any want of respect, she had treated him as her equal. Since he had forgotten himself, and had joined her personal enemies, nothing could happen to him but what he deserved. In short, she was not disposed to admit him to a share in their plans. As to the king, he was her husband, therefore in her conscience she could not abandon him, even in a danger so imminent.

The plan of their escape being thus settled, as above is mentioned, nothing remained but to make the noblemen who were in the castle acquainted with their intention.

Here, in passing, I must not forget to mention that the queen having gone to the window of her room, as soon as she was noticed by the townspeople and some of her own officers, they all began to weep and murmur rather loudly. Hereupon Lord Lindsay came in and dragged her away from the window, threatening her that if by her presence or in any other way, she excited any tumult, it would be as much as her life was worth. He said that in the meantime the doors and windows should be closed.

On the following Monday the king brought his father, singly, to visit her Majesty, who spoke very coldly to him, for she knew that he possessed little of either worth or fidelity. He had fully proved this through the whole of his life, especially upon that occasion when, having received the money of France to aid Scotland, he took up his abode in England and sided with the enemy.

All the other lords of the same faction having met together, came to the queen in her antechamber, and being on their knees before her (excepting the Earl of Moray, who speedily arose), they asked her to pardon them. Their spokesman, the Earl of Morton, knelt on the very spot on which the late David had been murdered, and which was yet all bestained with his blood. The said earl alleged, in their excuse, that their intention had not been directly hostile to her Majesty; although hurried on by the straits in which they perceived they would be placed if the Parliament should be held, they had been forced almost in despair to do what they owned to be a violation of their duty as subjects, in order to preserve life and estate for themselves and their children. But they begged her Majesty to consider that the same thing had happened pretty frequently before now. The loss of one mean man, and he a foreigner, was of less consequence than the ruin of so many lords and gentlemen, her subjects, who one day might do her many a good, great and signal service. They promised, upon their honour, that their future conduct would be loyal if she would be pleased to forgive them all the past.

These men acted as the Laird of Drumlanrig had done, he whom Lord Herries took with them into England. He soon owned his fault and returned to the queen; he made a thousand protestations that never should these fools and traitors (for so he styled my Lord of Moray and his accomplices) again draw his foot into the snare, and that he would always march under the royal standard. Yet he speedily changed his mind, and was one of the foremost in this later conspiracy.

Close and cunning in all his dealings, my Lord of Moray was among the earliest to excuse himself of the murder of the late David. He swore by his God that he knew nothing of it before his return; and very humbly did he entreat the queen not to be offended that he had come back without her leave and order. He was ready, he said, to answer any charge which could be brought against him. Next, he recommended to the queen the case of those noblemen then in her presence. As far as the general good was concerned, they were the most important individuals in the whole realm; indeed, every single subject of her's had an interest in the present question. Here he discoursed at great length in praise of clemency, a virtue which he affirmed to be both advantageous and very necessary to kings for their own safety and the preservation of the state. He concluded by advising her Majesty to recall the whole of these noblemen to the court, so as to profit by the great affection which they bore to the king and herself.

This language was very different from that in which they had addressed her two days previously; but they had been persuaded to use it after a conference held with the others who had escaped. They had already collected large forces by the king's obvious want of decision, under whose protection they could no longer shelter themselves.

In answer to these remonstrances, her Majesty gave them to understand, in the first place, that they had offended her in several kinds of ways; by the aforesaid attack upon her honour, by casting off her authority, by plotting against her state, and by weakening the wedded love which ought to exist between the king and herself, if they had not ruined it entirely. She could not forget her indignation so speedily. There was no one more guilty than another in the crime of treason, of which they did not hold themselves guilty. She put them in mind of the strict obligation by which each individual was bound to her, not only as a natural subject to a direct and lawful sovereign, but still further by the benefits which they had received from herself. If she might use the expression, she had shared her crown with them; nor had she ever undervalued their goodwill whenever it had been exhibited towards her.

Speaking of individuals; she reminded the Earl of Morton of his former acts of rebellion against the late queen, her mother, the late King of France, her lord and husband, and now, more recently, against herself. When it was known that he, Morton, had identified himself with the party of the Earl of Moray, the king and the Earl of Lennox, his father, had urged her to behead him, but she had prevented it. She had given him the earldom of Morton, and had entrusted him with the seals on the forfeiture of the late Earl of Huntley.

"I owe justice," continued she, "to every one, nor can I deny it to those persons who ask it in the name of one who has been murdered. Whatever his rank may have been, the honour to which he had attained as my servant should have protected him from every outrage, especially in my own presence. Do not hope, therefore, that I can promise you full pardon for your crime so speedily as you ask me to do; but if on your part you earnestly endeavour to blot out the past by the services which you now promise, I give you my word that on my part I will endeavour to forget what you have done."

As to the lesson which the Earl of Moray wished to teach her on the subject of clemency, ever since her earliest youth, her nobility, and others of her people, had given her frequent opportunities of practising that virtue and becoming familiar with it. She was naturally inclined towards the exercise of clemency; every one had blamed her for being too easy in this respect rather than too harsh or too severe. Possibly many had been encouraged by past impunity to continue in their present evil ways, perhaps even to advance still further, hoping that they would escape as cheaply now as they had done on former occasions.

Hereupon the queen, fearing that she might be compelled to go further than she intended, made as though she had been suddenly taken ill and was in great pain, as if childbirth was at hand. She ordered the midwife to be summoned, who had been in attendance from the previous day ; and, retiring into her bedchamber in great haste, she asked the king to tell the nobles what her intentions were, as had been arranged between them. Darnley then entered more fully into the particulars of the pardon which he and the queen had agreed upon. Some of the nobility, however, were not satisfied with this ; they thought it nothing but a trick, and, in a conference among themselves, they ruled that it did not guarantee their safety. But having consulted the midwife, whom they themselves had appointed, as to the queen's condition, and having been assured that she was extremely ill and in danger of her life — which the woman firmly believed, for in consequence of the agitation through which she had passed, the infant was very near the birth,—they postponed the farther prosecution of the matter until the following day.

Next morning, however, was too late ; for during the night the queen and king had escaped, as they had arranged. They were accompanied only by the Laird of Traquair, Captain of the Guard ; Arthur Erskin, behind whom the queen rode upon a pillion ; one servant of the king's bedchamber, and two or three soldiers. They crossed the cemetery in which lay buried the body of the late David, and almost over the grave itself. Oppressed by a sudden fear, the king began to sigh. The queen, who knew nothing about the grave, asked what troubled him. He answered, " Madame, we have just passed by the grave of poor David. In him I have lost a good and faithful servant, the like of whom I shall never find again. Every day of my life I shall regret him. I have been miserably cheated." He was interrupted in his talk, for it was feared that he might be overheard.

As soon as he had cleared the town the king began to gallop, and Arthur Erskin after him, until they reached

the outskirts of Seton.   Here some soldiers had been
posted on guard by the nobles of the queen's party to let
them know when she had passed.   When the king saw
them he took it into his head that they belonged to the
enemy, and, goaded on by the dread which he felt that
he might fall into their hands, he spurred on his horse
with increased energy.   At the same time he tried to
make the queen's horse go faster, by flogging it on the
hind quarters, crying out, "Come on! come on!   By
God's Blood, they will murder both you and me if they
can catch us."

Worn out by the fatigue which she had already
endured and in great suffering, the queen dreaded a miscarriage, and entreated him to have some regard to her
condition.   She said she would rather expose herself to
any danger than deliberately imperil the life of their
child.   Hereupon the king put himself into a fury.
"Come on!" said he, "In God's name, come on!   If
this baby dies we can have more."   At the last, however,
the queen could bear the galloping of the horse no longer.
She asked him to push on and take care of himself. And
this he did, very thoughtlessly; he, the occasion of all
her miseries, abandoned this poor princess in the midst
of the open country, near her confinement and in danger
of her life by reason of her exertions.   Nevertheless she
reached Dunbar Castle in safety, in company with the
Earls of Huntley and Bothwel, the lords Fleming, Seton,
Livingstone, and some others who joined her on the
road.   They found the king was a man without any
constancy, and all complained of him.   Some would not
speak to him or associate with him; others (especially
Lord Fleming), openly found fault with his conduct towards the queen, his wife, and all of them whom he had
consigned to death.

When the king saw how the lords resented the insult which he had passed upon them, and when he noticed how strong was the force which they had raised to fight against the rebels, he came to the queen, his wife, and having told her of his distrust towards these lords, who, he feared would revenge themselves upon him, he asked her to bring about a reconciliation with them. He offered to promise, upon his oath, to enter into a close and perfect friendship with them for the future, and never to abandon them. The queen exerted herself to the utmost to accomplish this, but she found it very difficult, and for these reasons : They had risked their lives, they said, in his quarrel, and in return he had betrayed them to their personal and greatest enemies. Not only had he undervalued their own individual services, but he had made light of the obligations which he owed to their true and lawful sovereign. Although she had permitted him to share her bed (the earls in their language called him her 'Bethfallow'), yet their obedience was due to her alone, and to no other person. For the future, neither his promises nor his orders should move them. The only obedience which he could expect to exercise over them must spring from their respect to the queen, his wife. They were no more bound to him by a solemn oath than he was bound to them ; for neither they, nor any of the nobility had accepted him or admitted him as their king.

In the meanwhile, on Tuesday morning, the Earl of Lennox, who was in the palace of Holyrood, was informed that the queen and his son had escaped. Against the latter he forthwith launched many wicked imprecations, giving him his curse and calling him traitor for having abandoned his father in such danger. Secretary Lethington was also told of it by the ladies in waiting of the queen's chamber, who went to ask him as to the truth of the report which was rife, namely, that the palace would be sacked. Here let it be remarked that Lethington was secretly of Moray's party—not so openly however that he could be charged therewith. Thus, he did not sue for his pardon, along with the others; but upon the queen's flight he went to reside with the Earl of Athol, with whom he remained for some time, until recalled by the earl's intercession.

Tidings of the escape of the queen and the king spread through the city, whereupon all the lords who had been in the plot, either on the one side or the other, absented themselves. All the soldiers did the like, each one trying to clear himself and get his own pardon. They did this all the more eagerly when they understood that a proclamation had been made in several parts of the realm to the effect that within the six days next following, all persons who were of an age capable of bearing arms should present themselves at Dunbar. Many letters to the same purport were sent to various lords and gentlemen, who came to meet the queen in all haste. She reached the abbey of Haddington on the night of the 18th of March, well attended.

On the 19th, the Bishop of St Andrews, bastard brother to the Duke of Châtelherault, and the Hamiltons, met the queen near the village of Musselburgh, and accompanied her into Edinburgh, where she stayed for some time in the house of the Bishop of Dunkeld. With her were the Earls of Huntley, Athol, Bothwel, Crawford, Marischal, Sutherland, and Caithnes; the Bishops of St Andrews, Ross, and Su . . . ; the Lords Livingstone, Fleming, Seton, Hume, Borthwick, and others. By their counsel the affairs of the realm were quieted, and for a time all was at peace. And in this

state of calm they might have remained but for the tur-
bulence of the king, who could not long continue on
good terms with any one.

When the council met in the house of the Bishop of
Dunkeld, the king foresaw that the Earl of Moray, and
certain others of his personal enemies, now that they
had got back to the court, would never again trust him,
and would have their revenge upon him as soon as they
could. He was still further pushed on to do this by
the Earls of Huntley and Bothwel, who had their own
private feuds with the lords, more particularly with
Lethington, the secretary. So the king proposed that
the office of secretary should be given to the Bishop of
Ross in the place of Lethington, whom he especially
charged with having been a principal in the late conspiracy ; and in the queen's absence he signed the resolution passed thereupon in council. The queen, however, would not consent to this measure, for she was
persuaded that the king had brought this charge against
Lethington, in order to put into his office a man at his
own devotion. Darnley's object was now to play off,
by every means in his power, the one party against the
other, so that he himself should become stronger than
either of them. The queen had reason to dread this,
knowing, as she did, the inconstancy and treachery
which (it must be admitted) she had found in his character. She refused therefore to dismiss Lethington,
although advised to do so by the king and the said lords;
for he was a man of understanding, experienced in the
affairs of the country, and of whom — if the truth
must be told—she stood in need in the midst of this
turmoil of tempers and disputes. And further, as there
was no proof of the charge against Lethington, she caused
him to be recalled shortly afterwards, trusting more

than he deserved to his good qualities and his loyalty to herself.

When the king understood that the queen had refused to confirm and sign this resolution in favour of the Bishop of Ross—whom, however, she valued and willingly employed in other matters—he became exceedingly angry. On the following night he sent to her one of the grooms of his chamber, who told her Majesty how much he was displeased with her, and that he had primed and made ready his two pistols, which she would find hanging at the back of the bed. The queen went directly, and after having stayed with him for some time she quietly carried off the pistols. Next day she told the members of the council what had occurred, hoping thus to remove from her husband's mind the prejudice which he had conceived against Lethington, and to let the councillors understand the decision at which she had arrived, and which they followed, as you will hear presently. She forbade the Bishop of Ross to accept this office, even if it were offered to him.

As for the others, each of them sued out his own pardon. It has been already mentioned that at the beginning the king was openly hostile to the Earl of Moray and his adherents, but in the end the Laird of Traquair, surnamed Stewart, made him understand the true position of affairs. The queen was unwilling that Moray should lay all the blame upon herself, who really had no illwill against him save on the king's account, and he was now mollified; so the earl's pardon was granted to him when he was at Linlithgow. The like she did for the Earl of Argyll and Lord Boyd, who were ordered to betake themselves into Argyll, there to remain during her pleasure, which they did. The Earl of Rothes also had his pardon; so had the Earl of Lennox, at the request of his son, the king ; as likewise had the Earl of Glencairn and the Laird of Cunninghamhead, who came to her Majesty when she was at Dunbar. The king had a high regard for the Lords Ruthven and Lindsay, Douglas L'Apostolat, and some others, of whom however he did not venture to speak openly to her Majesty. From the outset she had vowed that she would never pardon these persons, whom she regarded as the originators and executors of this conspiracy. When they and the Earl of Morton saw that they could not obtain their pardon they fled into England, where Ruthven died, a maniac, in the town of Newcastle.

When the queen heard of the arrival of these lords in England, she sent James Thornton, chanter of the bishoprick of Moray, to the queen, her good sister. Thornton also went to the queen's relations in France, the king and the princes of Lorraine, to let them know the state of her affairs, and the rebellions and insurrections of her subjects against her, and to ask help. The Queen of England having been requested neither to receive these rebels nor permit them to remain within her kingdom, sent into Scotland a gentleman named Henry Killigrew. He brought with him very civil letters, in which Elizabeth promised that these rebels should soon be expelled. But she did not keep her word; for the Earl of Morton and the son of the late Lord Ruthven resided in the town of Alnwick and the neighbourhood, until they had their pardon and were restored, which was after the birth of the Prince.

Before his death Lord Ruthven showed great repentance for his wicked life. He thanked God for having given him the opportunity and the inclination before He called him to Himself, to pray for mercy and the pardon of his sins. Others say that he died like a madman, exclaiming that he saw paradise opened, and a great company of angels coming to take him. It is probable that these were diabolical illusions, wrought by evil spirits, who wished to delude him as he was passing away, that he might not escape them, for during his life they had possessed him with the art of magic.

Conscious that the time for her delivery was at hand, the queen took up her abode in the Castle of Edinburgh. She was anxious not only to prepare for her confinement, but also to guard against what she had been warned would occur, namely, that the lords were resolved to take possession of the infant from the moment of its birth. Regarding it as the heir to the crown, they determined to have it baptized in their religion, and educated and guarded by some of themselves, without any interference on the part of the king, her husband, or herself. She saw, moreover, that many parties and serious differences already existed among the nobles, and she was aware that, in the event of her death during her confinement, these dissensions would widen day by day, so as to make the position of her child most insecure. She felt, too, that she could not entirely trust that child to the keeping of her husband. She determined, therefore, that she would reconcile all the feuds already existing among the lords and bring them together, especially those of her council, so as to effect some good reconciliation.

About the end of April, therefore, she sent for the Earls of Argyll and Moray, and settled all such disputes as remained between them and the Earls of Athol, Huntley, and Bothwell, as far as these disputes had been referred to her. This having been done, these nobles remained with her Majesty during the remainder of the following summer.

The pardon of the Earl of Moray and his adherents has already been mentioned, to which we may now append the following remarks. These persons told her Majesty that they had taken up arms in consequence of the king only, against whom alone they had acted in their own defence—not against her. She had no cause, they said, to complain against them, except for this reason only, that they had not appeared in a court of law in obedience to her simple orders—orders which had been obtained from her by their enemies, by whom she was surrounded, and who aimed at nothing less than the entire destruction of themselves, their properties, and their families. "We always listen with attention," continued they, "to the excuse of the man who is fighting for his life, or his possessions, or his honour, and who does his best to repel the attack of those who seek to injure him in matters of such vital importance." These considerations joined with the necessity in which they found themselves, compelled them to take the last expedient which presented itself for their recovery. They could do nothing less than break up a Parliament which was assembled for their trial and condemnation. They had no share in the insults and indignities offered to the person of the queen in her own palace, nor with the murder of the late David; for these Lord Ruthven and his accomplices were entirely responsible.

When the queen heard such explanations as these, they had their weight with her. She admitted to herself that in truth at the outset she had no patent cause of hostility, no private quarrel with the Earl of Moray and his followers. All had come through the king, her husband. She had grounds for believing that even he was now satisfied with the lords, for he had recalled them to the Court even against her wishes. She knew, moreover, the credit in which these lords stood with the English, a power, the support of which might keep her, she feared, in perpetual trouble, and in the end lead to a fatal issue. Seeing, also, that the king was resolved to pardon Moray, despite all the difficulties which he had urged until now, she was easily induced to yield her consent. The rigour with which she had hitherto acted towards the earl, was chiefly to please the king, her husband, by whom it had been feebly seconded. To some extent here was the primary cause of all the evil which Moray and the conspirators subsequently attempted. Aware, then, that she could not trust either the one party or the other, it seemed to be the wisest course, therefore, to fortify her own position by firmly reconciling these rivals, and keeping them as united as possible.

Having retired into Edinburgh Castle, while the greater part of the nobility remained in the town, according to her orders, the queen prepared herself for the birth of her child. She made her will and received her sacrament, like one who is in proximate danger of death.

About this time there came from the King of France, a gentleman named Le Croc, sent as ambassador, resident with her Majesty. He was gentleman in waiting to her Majesty even during his embassy, while at the same time he depended entirely upon the queen mother, whose creature he was.

We must not forget to mention a trick which was set forward by the Queen of England. She sent an old gentleman named Ruxby, to the queen, who came under the assumed name of the Earl of Northumberland and Sir Henry Percy, his brother. He proposed to the queen that they would join with her in any insurrection

which she might wish to raise against the Queen of
England, and used all the arguments he could devise to
lead her into the plot.   He urged chiefly that Elizabeth
was offended because Mary had married Darnley without
her knowledge and consent.   Elizabeth could not but see
that by the birth of a child, Mary's claim to the throne
of England was greatly strengthened ; she did not cease,
therefore, from trying to work the ruin of her and the
king, her husband, whom she hated most bitterly.
Ruxby suggested that the queen should secure the
adhesion of every Catholic who would join her party,
the names of some of whom he specified.

From Ruxby's mode of procedure, the queen suspected
that the whole affair was a fraud.   She told him that she
thanked the said lords for their good will and kind intentions ; but that instead of being induced to undertake
any movement prejudicial to her good sister, Queen
Elizabeth, she had never been more anxious to please her,
and to maintain a good understanding with her.   She
was going to ask the Queen to be godmother to her child.
As to his request that she would give him her letters to
these lords, she would not write aught to them without
having previously heard from them, or at least received
a more distinct message of credence.

With this answer Ruxby returned to England ; and
having fraudulently obtained documents from Sir Henry
Percy and some others, who were well affected towards her Majesty, he made his way back to Scotland.   In the meantime her Majesty's doubts about
him had been cleared up.   No sooner was she informed
that he had returned than she caused all his papers to
be seized.   Among them was found a document signed
by the hand of William Cecil, Secretary of State for
England, in which the Queen of England promised to

grant Ruxby and his heirs in perpetuity an annual rent of one hundred pounds in land, provided he would bring back letters signed by Queen Mary, and addressed to the Earl of Northumberland and his brother, in answer to the offers made to her by them.

This having been clearly established, Ruxby was sent as a prisoner to the northern district, in the house of the Bishop of Moray, where he remained for nearly eighteen months, without any application having been made for his release. In order more successfully to play the Catholic, he gave the queen a tablet of ivory, in which was engraved the entire Passion of our Lord.

On Tuesday, the 19th of June, between ten and eleven o'clock in the morning, her Majesty gave birth to a son, with great labour and suffering, in the presence of many of the ladies; who, seeing her danger, and telling her of the peril in which she and the child were, she prayed that the infant might be saved, without any regard to herself. The prince came into the world with a large and thin caul, which covered the whole of his face. On June the 15th a report had gone through the whole town of Edinburgh that her Majesty had given birth to a son, whereupon bonfires were lighted. Immediately upon the birth of the Prince, all the artillery of the castle was discharged, and the lords, the nobles, and the people gathered in St Giles' Church to thank God for the honour of having an heir to their kingdom. After the birth, certain gentlemen were despatched to the King of France, the Queen of England, and the Duke of Savoy, to ask them to be godfathers and godmother to the Prince, to which they very gladly consented. The King of France sent the Count de Brienne, of the house of Luxemburg, shortly before whom M. de Mauvissière had been despatched into Scotland by the family of Guise, to threaten the King of Scotland, and to ask him to behave himself better towards his wife. The Queen of England sent the Earl of Bedford, with a large retinue; but Henry Killigrew had arrived previously to express the joy and congratulations of his mistress at the queen's happy delivery. The Duke of Savoy sent M. de Morette, who arrived too late, not until after the celebration of the baptism. M. du Croc filled his place. As the Earl of Bedford would not enter the church, the Countess of Argyll was his proxy, and assisted at the ceremonies of the baptism in the name of the Queen of England. As long as the queen remained in Edinburgh Castle, she caused her son to sleep in her room, and often watched by him herself.

While the queen was a resident in the Castle, and during the period of her confinement, the king, her husband, led a very disorderly life. He vagabondised every night; sometimes he went to bathe in the sea, sometimes in other out-of-the-way places. When the queen heard of this, she became apprehensive of the danger which might follow because of the ill-will which the greater number of the Lords bore towards him. As he even caused the gates of the castle to be opened at every hour of the night, there was no safety for either herself or her son. She entreated him, therefore, to be careful, and not to put himself so indiscreetly into the power of his enemies.

To all these remonstrances Darnley paid very little attention. Naturally of a very insolent disposition, he began to threaten all the lords, especially the Earl of Moray, whom he told that the laird of Balfour had promised him that he would kill him (Moray) as soon as the latter had retired to his castle.

The queen saw the great danger of such an enterprise, which was calculated to lead to serious troubles in the kingdom, and a sudden insurrection in the town ; she contrived, therefore, to be always busy near the king, so as to thwart his project. But in private he did not abandon the idea.

In the midst of these difficulties the king was much offended also because, contrary to his advice, the Queen of England had been invited to become godmother, whom he said, he would no more own to be the lawful Queen of England than she would own him to be King of Scotland. The council, however, endeavoured to keep this princess well affected towards them for their good and prosperity, so they kept to their resolution.

With all this Darnley was much annoyed, and took daily opportunities of showing his rebellion. By the persuasion of some dissipated youths, who were his chief companions, he resolved to go secretly into France, and there to support himself upon the queen's dowry. When she heard of this, she spoke to him about it with great frankness. But do what she might, she could not prevent him from leaving Edinburgh upon a day fixed for receiving the sacrament, to the great scandal of the Catholics.

About the beginning of August the queen crossed the sea and went to Alloa, a house belonging to the Earl of Mar, where she remained for some days in the company of the ladies of her court and the said earl. While she was on this excursion the king visited her, making, as it were, a passing call. He spent only a few hours with her, although it had been arranged that they should go back to Edinburgh Castle together.

Towards the end of the same month, her Majesty, attended by the king, the Earls of Moray, Huntley, Bothwell, and Athol, and several other persons, went into Meggotland, on the borders of England and Scotland, to amuse herself by hunting the stag. As she was on her way back to Edinburgh, she decided upon removing the prince, her son, to Stirling. For this purpose she raised four or five hundred harquebusiers, who, on the journey, surrounded the prince's litter, and accompanied him to Stirling, along with the queen. The care of the Prince was in the first instance assigned to Lord Erskine, and afterwards to the Earl of Mar and his wife.

During this excursion into Meggotland, the queen paid a visit to the house of the Laird of Traquair. While the party was at supper, the king, her husband, asked the queen to attend a stag hunt. Knowing that if she did so, she would be required to gallop her horse at a great pace, she whispered in his ear that she suspected she was *enceinte.* The king answered aloud, " Never mind, if we lose this one, we will make another," whereupon the laird of Traquair rebuked him sharply, and told him that he did not speak like a Christian. He answered, " What! ought not we to work a mare well when she is with foal ? "

On returning from Stirling the queen made a progress to Glen Arknay, and thence to Edinburgh, where she remained for some time. She wished to be present at the passing of the public accounts, which would then be presented ; and further, to cause new inquiries to be made about the rebels who still were in England, and to arrange the preparations for the baptism.

From thence she went to Jedburgh to keep the Law Days, which are wont to be held there every year, with the intention of bringing the Borders into order, and punishing the thieves who live in the neighbouring mountains. The Earl of Bothwell, who had been sent there to keep them in order, as he was pursuing them, was wounded so dangerously in the hand that everyone thought he would die. He thought so himself. Such being the case, her Majesty was both solicited and advised to pay him a visit at his house, called The Hermitage, in order that she might learn from him the state of affairs in these districts, of which the said lord was the hereditary governor. With this object in view, she went very speedily, in the company of the Earl of Moray and some other lords, in whose presence she conversed with Bothwell for some hours, and on the same day she returned to Jedburgh.

On the following day she was seized by a pain in the side which confined her to bed. It proved to be a severe attack of the spleen, which had troubled her during the previous week, and to which pain in the side she had been more or less subject ever since her confinement. Some thought she was dead. She vomited more than sixty times, and on the third day of the attack she lost her sight.

About this time a person named John Shaw came to tell the queen that Andrew Carr of Fawdonside had returned into Scotland from England, to which he had been banished, for having presented his dagger at the queen, and having killed the late David. Some people having refused to admit him into their houses, because he had been put to the horn (and therefore could not well be admitted), he boasted that within fifteen days there would be a great change in the Court; that he would soon be in greater credit than ever, and then he would boldly enquire how their queen was.

From the frequency and the violence of the vomiting within the period of a single day, it was suspected that she had been poisoned, particularly as among the matter ejected from the stomach was found a lump of a green substance, very thick and hard.

On the Thursday news came that the prince was so ill that his life was despaired of; but after having been made to vomit he recovered.

On the Friday, her Majesty lost the power of speech, and had a very severe fit of convulsions. About ten or eleven o'clock at night, all her limbs became so contracted, her face was distorted, and her whole body became so cold that all present, especially her domestic servants, thought she was dead, and they caused the windows to be opened. The Earl of Moray began to lay hands on the most precious articles, such as her silver plate and rings. The mourning dresses were ordered and arrangements were made for the funeral. But Arnault, her surgeon, having observed that there were still some tokens of life in one of her arms, which as yet had not entirely stiffened, used an extreme remedy in an extreme case. He bandaged, very tightly, her great toes, her legs, from the ankle upwards, and her arms; then he poured some wine into her mouth, which he caused to be opened by force. When she had recovered a little, he administered a clyster, the evacuations produced by which were considered by the physicians to be very suspicious. From that time she gradually recovered until she returned to Edinburgh, where she vomited a great quantity of corrupt blood, and then the cure was complete.

On the day before this convulsive fit, the queen, feeling that her strength was decaying and believing that she was in danger of her life (for she had now lost her sight), called together the lords who were of her Court. She reminded them at great length of the importance of their union and agreement for the good of the country and the safety of her son. She especially recommended him to their care; not doubting that the king his father would wrong him as to the succession to the

Crown, to which he laid claim in his own right, and might probably take a second wife.

She also asked M. du Croc, the Ambassador of France, to recommend her son, his country and affairs, to the most Christian king, his master. Then she caused the prayers to be read by the Bishop of Ross, and disposed herself as one at the point of death, requesting those who were near her to take care of her, for she felt confident that if she could get over that Friday she would not die of this illness.

The queen returned to Edinburgh to make the necessary arrangements for the baptism, which was celebrated about the Feast of the Kings, with great splendour; and gifts were bestowed upon the ambassadors. The king was not present at the baptism, for he refused to associate with the English, unless they would acknowledge his title of king, and to do this they had been forbidden by the Queen of England, their mistress.

Shortly afterwards he went to Glasgow, where he was seized with the smallpox. He sent several times for the queen, who was very ill, having been injured by a fall from her horse at Seton. At last she went, stayed with him, and attended him on his return to Edinburgh.

During the journey a raven continually accompanied them from Glasgow to Edinburgh, where it frequently remained perched on the late king's lodging, and sometimes on the Castle. But on the day before his death, it croaked for a very long time upon the house.

On his return to Edinburgh, the king lodged in a small house outside the town, which he had chosen on the report of James Balfour and some others. This was against the queen's wishes, who was anxious to take him to Craigmillar, for he could not stay in Holyrood Palace lest he should give the infection to the prince. On his own account, too, he did not wish anyone to see him in his present condition, nor until he had gone through a course of baths in private: He always wore a piece of taffeta drawn down over his face, and the windows of his room were always closed.

While he was in this house the king was often visited by the queen, with whom he was now perfectly reconciled. He promised to give her much information of the utmost importance to the life and quiet of both of them. He warned her of the necessity of cultivating a good understanding with each other, and of guarding against those persons who meddled between them (whose names he said he would reveal), and who had advised him to make an attempt upon her life. The designs of these persons tended to the ruin of both of them. He warned her more particularly to be on her guard against Lethington, who, he said, was planning the ruin of the one by the means of the other, and meant in the end to ruin both of them, as he could perceive more clearly than ever by their conduct and counsel.

That very night, as her Majesty was about to leave the king, she met Paris, Lord Bothwell's *valet-de-chambre*, and noticing that his face was all blackened with gunpowder, she exclaimed in the hearing of many of the lords, just as she was mounting her horse, "Jesu, Paris, how begrimed you are!" At this he turned very red.

On the 10th of February 1567, about three or four o'clock in the morning, a match was put to the train of gunpowder which had been placed under the king's house. It was afterwards made public that this had been done by the command and device of the Earls of Bothwell and Morton, James Balfour, and some others, who always afterwards pretended to be most diligent in searching out the murder which they themselves had committed. Morton had secretly returned from England, to which he had been banished.

This crime was the result of a bond into which they had entered. It was written by Alexander Hay, at that time one of the clerks of the council, and signed by the Earls of Moray, Huntley, Bothwell, and Morton, by Lethington, James Balfour, and others, who had combined for this purpose. They protested that they were acting for the public good of the realm, pretending that they were freeing the queen from the bondage and misery into which she had been reduced by the king's behaviour. They promised to support each other, and to avouch that the act was done justly, licitly, and lawfully by the leading men of the council. They had done it in defence of their lives, which would be in danger, they said, if the king should get the upper hand and secure the government of the realm, at which he was aiming. He was but deceiving the queen, whom they often blamed for so faithfully having come to a good understanding with her husband; and they told her that he was putting a knife not only to their throats but to her own.

The king's body was blown into the garden by the violence of the explosion, and a poor English varlet of his, who slept in his room, was there killed. The news spread quickly through the town. When the queen was told what had occurred, she was in great grief and kept her chamber all that day. The corpse was brought into full council and there examined, to discover the mode of his death. Diligent inquiries were made about it on all sides, especially by those who were its authors, among others by the Earl of Moray. He had absented himself on the day of the murder, on the pretext that he was going to visit his wife, who, he said, was very dangerously ill. This same earl, after having matured all his plans necessary for his success in seizing the crown and ruining the queen, asked her permission to go to France, which she granted, giving him also letters of introduction to her relations, with power to draw money on her dowry. Moray chiefly trusted the Laird of Grange with the execution of these designs, and Grange was the tool of Moray and Lethington, the latter of whom was the chief conductor of all the plots and rebellions of the former. Moray had told several Englishmen that it was necessary to get rid of the king, not only because he was a Catholic, but also because he was an enemy to the Queen of England. But there had been private feuds of an old standing between them, both before and after the marriage. The king never forgot the ambuscade at Lochleven before he married the queen ; and wanted to kill him after he had got rid of the others.

Earl Bothwell was much suspected of this villainous and detestable murder, and the impression was strengthened by the many evil reports circulated about him. He replied, by many placards of defiance and challenges, that he was ready to answer these charges and justify himself; which he ultimately did in full parliament. If we may judge by the plots, deeds, and contrivances of his associates, it would seem that after having used him to rid themselves of the king, they designed to make Bothwell their instrument to ruin the queen, their true and lawful sovereign.

Their plan was this, to persuade her to marry the Earl of Bothwell, so that they might charge her with being in the plot against her late husband, and a consenting party to his death. This they did shortly after, appealing to the fact that she had married the murderer.

This poor young princess, unexperienced in such devices, was circumvented on all sides by persuasions, requests, and importunities ; both by general memorials signed by their hands and presented to her in full council, and by private letters.

It happened one day, that all these lords and the chief of the counsel of the nobility, having held a meeting in the Earl of Bothwell's house, in Edinburgh, sent Lethington, the Justice Clerk, and a third, to the queen as their delegates. It had become absolutely necessary that some remedy should be provided for the disorder into which the public affairs of the realm had fallen from the want of a head ; and they had now come to tell her of the course which they had agreed upon recommending for the purpose. They had unanimously resolved to press her to take Bothwell for her husband. They knew that he was a man of resolution, well adapted to rule, the very character needed to give weight to the decisions and actions of the council. All of them, therefore, pleaded in his favour.

To these representations and others of the same kind, the queen gave a refusal, pure and simple. When the deputies repeated their request, she made a second answer to the same effect. She reminded them of the reports which were current about the death of the late king, her husband. Lethington and the other deputies replied that Lord Bothwell had been legally acquitted by the council. They who made this request to her did so for the public good of the realm, and as they were the highest of the nobility, it would be for them to vindicate a marriage brought about by their advice and authority. In the end her Majesty asked them to assemble the Estates, in order that the question might be considered ; and then they, one and all, signed the request which they had presented, thereby to authenticate it and to take on themselves the responsibility of its contents.

Thus vehemently urged in this matter, and perceiving that the said Earl of Bothwell was entirely cleared from the crime laid to his charge, suspecting, moreover, nothing more than what appeared on the surface, she began to give ear to their overtures, without letting it be openly seen, however, what would be her ultimate decision, in such a way as to found a judgment upon it. She remained in this state of hesitation partly because of the conflicting reports which were current at the time when this marriage was proposed, partly because she had no force sufficiently strong to punish the rebels, by whom (if the truth must be told) she was rather commanded than consulted, and ruled rather than obeyed. Their malice became apparent at a later date, when, under the plea of punishing the Earl of Bothwell, they took up arms in the open field against herself.

You shall hear presently how they acted when, in good faith, and in reliance upon the public honour, she surrendered herself into their hands. She did so upon the understanding that she was to join with them in discovering and prosecuting the murderers of the late king, as they themselves had demanded. She ordered that no one should interfere in this matter by favour, or indeed in any way whatsoever, to impede justice ; for the rebels had complained (but without a direct accusation of her Majesty) that until now she had been under the influence of the very persons whom they wished to accuse. They also required that she should give sanction to the Parliament which they determined to hold. As for Bothwell, while full Parliament was sitting, they let him escape in safety, without taking any effective measures against him.

With reference to the queen, they took a different course. Without regard to the forms and precedents used in Parliament, they attacked her directly. They imprisoned her in Lochleven [under the custody of the] natural brother of the Earl of Moray, without even telling her their reasons for so doing. Of a truth, their one object was the usurpation of the crown by means of the disastrous and abominable proceedings which had been planned before the departure of the Earl of Moray out of the kingdom.

It must not be forgotten that Bothwell had gained over and drawn to his side all the lords of the council, with a view to this special object. Some helped him honestly, from friendship; others from fear, being in dread of their lives; others dissembled, meaning through him to carry out their own secret ends and private designs. Having thus secured their help and advice, and seeing the difficulties which would arise from the delay to which he was subjected, Bothwell resolved, by some means or other, to seize the person of the queen, and then (having already gained the consent of all the lords) to compel her to give hers, in order to bring the negociation to a conclusion. Different plans were proposed, varying according to the varying intentions of the proposers; but in the end, it was carried out in the following way.

As the queen was on the road from Stirling (where she had been to visit her son, the prince) to Linlithgow, she was met by the Earl of Bothwell at the head of fifteen hundred horsemen, armed according to the custom of the country. The Earl of Huntley was in attendance upon her, but at that time he was a warm partizan of Bothwell. Bothwell carried her to Dunbar Castle, which belongs to ·her Majesty, of which the keeper was Whit-law. In answer to complaints which she made, she was reminded that she was in one of her own houses, that all her domestics were around her, that she could remain there in perfect liberty and freely exercise her lawful authority. Practically, however, all happened very differently, for the greater part of her train was removed, nor had she full liberty until she had consented to the marriage which had been proposed by the said lords of the council. Shortly afterwards, it was publicly celebrated in Holyrood Palace in Edinburgh, by the Bishop of Orkney. All the people were admitted, and the chief of the nobility were present, who gave proof that they looked on the union with great satisfaction, as greatly tending to the advantage of the kingdom.

Shortly afterwards, however, a conspiracy was formed against the Earl of Bothwell, under the pretext of avenging the late king's death. It may have originated in some secret feuds among the lords of recent date, or possibly from grievances of a remoter origin, which though long hidden, at last came to scatter their poison on the surface. It was settled that Bothwell should be accused of Darnley's murder. All this was done by the advice of Secretary Lethington, with whom Bothwell was on bad terms. Lethington induced the Laird of Grange to join this party, a very brave gentleman, and a man of great reputation. The conspirators never let him know the depth of their nefarious designs, but wiled him on under the pretexts mentioned above. They worked also upon his regard for the Earl of Moray, upon whom he entirely depended, and whom he had followed in the rebellion which had been got up under the name of religion, against the late queen mother. Some others joined this party out of jealousy of Bothwell's rapid promotion. They were the more easily led to do so, because they found him to be a man whose natural disposition ʃmade him anything but agreeable, or inclined to put himself to much trouble or inconvenience to gain the good-will of those with whom he associated. This party consisted entirely of men who had formerly been rebels on the subject of religion.

The first who joined this league were Lord Hume and the Laird of Tuliberne, the latter of whom introduced the Earl of Mar, who had lately received that title from her Majesty, and to whose care she had entrusted her son, the prince. She had also made him keeper of Stirling Castle, confirming it in heritage to him and his heirs. In doing this she had removed him from the office of keeper of Edinburgh Castle, by the advice of her Council, who considered these trusts too important to be both in the hands of one single individual. To a certain extent the Countess of Mar was the cause, a malevolent woman, and full of the spirit of revenge. The Laird of Tulliberne was her brother. Many of the lords were told that the queen hindered justice being done for the late king's death ; consequently the greater number were in part engaged against Bothwell himself.

With many . . . the truth of the queen's defence against my lord of Huntley was made plain, for he had entered into this quarrel in consequence of having been refused, by advice of the Council, of a priory which he asked for, and which was one of the most beautiful and celebrated of the domains of the Crown. The Earl of Morton, who held the first rank among them, was also one of these plotters (as he was in every deadly treason), and held out before them the marriage of his nephew, the Earl of Angus. The wardship of this young nobleman had been entrusted to him

[Morton], and he proposed to marry him to one of the daughters of the Earl of Athol, hoping thereby to induce him to enter into this league. He managed to do so by the help of the Laird of Lethington, who had married the sister of the said Earl's wife. He showed his trickery afterwards, for no sooner was her Majesty a prisoner, than he married him to the daughter of the said Earl of Mar, thereby to bind him more closely to his devotion. So he employed this poor young nobleman as a fisherman uses a hook, thereby to catch the careless fish.

These conspirators agreed that their place of meeting should be Liberton Church, about two miles from Edinburgh, on Tuesday, 10th June 1567. On the night of that day, the Earl of Morton and Lord Hume arrived there, and on the following day, Wednesday, they were joined by the Earl of Mar. As the others did not appear they decided that they would attempt to surprise the queen and Bothwell in Borthwick. (From thence her Majesty went to Dunbar, after having been besieged in Borthwick for nearly three or four days by seven hundred light horsemen.) The said lords Hume and Morton came, as had been agreed upon, with seven or eight hundred horsemen to besiege Borthwick, against which they discharged several volleys of musketry. They also railed at Bothwell, making use of many insulting terms to provoke him to issue from the Castle, which he would have done more than once, had not he been held back by his own people, who saw that the danger was too great. But at the last he could stand these insults no longer, so, followed by forty or fifty good men-at-arms, he sallied out bravely. Passing in front of the besiegers he gained the open country, and began to collect his forces. On the same day he got the queen from Borthwick Castle and took her to Dunbar, where she was met by the Lords Seton, Yester, and Borthwick, together with the Lairds of Walkton, Bass, Ormeston, Wedderburn, Blakader, and Langton. Their united forces amounted to about four thousand men. There were also two hundred harquebusiers of the Queen's Body Guard. A messenger was sent to hasten the arrival of Lord Fleming, the Hamiltons, and the Earl of Huntley, who had been summoned by Baron Brokar, but who did not arrive until it was too late.

At length the said lords retired to Edinburgh, and there began to gather themselves together and to collect all who were of their party along with their forces. These were the Earls of Morton, Athol, Mar, and Glencairn ; the Lords Hume, Lindsay, Ruthven, Semple, and Sanquar ; the Lairds of Dumblane, Tulibardine, Grange, and the young Cessford. Their company amounted to four thousand men, good soldiers and well drilled.

The evil design of the Earl of Moray sufficiently showed itself in this way that, having ruined the Earl of Huntley, and then overthrown the House of Lennox by the death of the late king, and having next accomplished the resignation of the queen,—no sooner was he Regent and had the government of the realm, than he set about to persecute the Hamiltons (by whom he had been previously assisted), under the pretence of a false friendship. He was especially hostile to the said Lord Lennox, remembering the ancient hostility between the two houses.

When the queen was yet in Dunbar she was advised by James Balfour (who had been appointed keeper of Edinburgh Castle), to take the open field and to march direct to Edinburgh, so as to meet the insurgents on the road. He assured her that they would not keep their ground for a moment, especially when they knew that he had declared against them, and would open fire upon

D

their troops. If she did not do so, he would be compelled, he said, to come to terms with them. But he had been won over by the rebels to give this counsel.

Following the advice of this traitor, who offered himself first to the one party and then to the other, on Saturday, June 14, her Majesty marched to Haddington, whence, passing by Gladismore, she reached Seton where she spent the night. Next morning she marched to Carberry Hill in order of battle, where her troops posted themselves advantageously on a slight eminence. The leaders ordered the cavalry to dismount, not only because they saw that they were outnumbered by the cavalry of the enemy, but because they feared their light-armed troopers would take to flight, it being their custom to fall back after making a few insignificant charges. They were for the most part borderers, men never drilled to keep the line in action, and who make light of all military discipline ; but who do good service only as skirmishers, or scouts, when prompt measures are needed, if you want to employ them to advantage. The disorder into which they fell was partly occasioned by this habit of theirs. For when the two armies were about to come to blows, M. du Croc, Ambassador from the King of France, who had left Edinburgh in company with the rebels, came to the queen and proposed various suggestions for an agreement, during which negotiations he passed several times from one camp to the other. Pending these conferences the soldiers, who were tired and exhausted with the great heat of the day, began to disband, and dispersed themselves through the villages in quest of drink and other refreshments. And it must not be forgotten that they had made a very long march on the day previous.

Du Croc thus contrived so to protract matters that the

queen's troops were prevented from charging the enemy, which they were ready to have done. Her artillery had already killed some of the enemy's horses. It was now growing late; and just as these Borderers were advancing, certain deputies came for the fourth time from the enemy and demanded a conference.

Hitherto her Majesty had received from them no intimation of what their intentions were; least of all, was she aware that they meant to charge the Earl of Bothwell with the death of the late king. Of this they had given no indication whatever, and it was by them that Bothwell had been promoted. A meeting was held between the two camps; and the first question proposed on the queen's part to the insurgents was this;—They had there risen against her and appeared in arms, Had they done so as subjects or as enemies? And what object had they in view in coming? They answered that they had come there as most faithful and obedient subjects, and that they required nothing but justice for the murder of the late king. They demanded that the queen should be restored to perfect liberty; for they asserted that at the present time she was under the authority and control of those very persons against whom proceedings ought to be taken. In order that this might be done, they petitioned that she would deliver up such persons as they would specify, with whom at that very time she had associated herself. And here they named Bothwell. Further, they required that she would accompany the lords there assembled, who would reinstate her in her due position. She would thus be rescued out of the power of men who had estranged her from them, in order that they might shroud themselves under her authority, and hinder the course of justice.

Her Majesty replied that it seemed very strange to

her that they had waited so long before proceeding
against the earl. They had not charged him with this
crime until he had become her husband. Long before
now there were many occasions when they could have
seized him ; and they could have done this without the
large force which they now employed for the purpose.
Hence it appeared that she alone was the object of
their attack, in order to deprive her of her crown. It
was also, she said, at the instance, and by the common
consent of the chief nobility, even of many who were
here assembled against her, that she had married the
Earl of Bothwell, which she would not have done, if
sooner and more clearly the said accusation had been
made known to her ; and consequently she ought to
help him until the charge of which he was accused was
proved against him.

But, on the other hand, she owed a duty to the
memory of the late king, her husband, a duty which she
would not neglect. Most willingly, therefore, would she
authorise every one to exercise the fullest liberty of inquiry into the circumstances of his death ; she intended
to do so herself, and to punish with all severity such as
should be convicted thereof. She herself claimed that
justice should be done upon certain persons of their party
now present, who were guilty of said murder, who were
much astonished to find themselves discovered. In order
to attain this, she was willing to entrust herself to the
good faith of the nobles here assembled, thereby to give
an authority to whatever they might do or advise. She
would aid them, as was her duty, in all prosecutions
such as these.

She then asked to speak privately with Lethington,
who caused her to be informed that he was not with the

rebels. Next she applied to the Earl of Athol, who excused himself in like manner. At last the laird of Grange came to her, and, after having discussed with him these matters at considerable length, she decided that she would return with the lords, thinking thereby to remove all doubts and suspicions as to her wish either to shelter or support the persons guilty of the crime. This she did relying upon Grange's word and assurance, which the lords in full council, as he said, had solemnly warranted him to do.

Before doing so, however, she desired the laird of Grange to provide for the safety of Lord Bothwell, namely, that no harm should be done to him whilst he was awaiting the meeting of Parliament, in which such matters as these would be settled. Grange answered that he had received no authority from the noblemen of his party to discuss any such question ; and that they all were already angry with him for having exceeded the powers which they had prescribed to him. Grange thereupon took Bothwell's hand, and advised him to depart, promising that, as he was an honest man, he would do his utmost to prevent him from being pursued.

At the first, Bothwell would by no means submit to this arrangement, but was determined to fight. At the end, however, he was overcome by the queen's entreaties, who persuaded him to absent himself for a time till the issue of the coming Parliament should be known. She promised that if he were found innocent of the crime with which he was charged, as he said he was, nothing would prevent her from rendering to him all that a true and lawful wife ought to do. If he failed to do this, it would be to her an endless source of regret that by their marriage she had ruined her good reputation, and from this she would endeavour to free herself by every possible means.

At parting from the queen, Bothwell wished to ease his conscience by making known to her the wicked design of her enemies. He told her Majesty that the Earl of Morton, secretary Lethington, James Balfour, and some others, who at that moment were on the opposite side, were guilty of the death of the late king, the whole having been executed by their direction and counsel. He showed her their signatures to the bond agreed upon among themselves, and told her to take good care of that paper.

Lord Bothwell went first of all to Dunbar, then to Orkney, where he remained for some time, and at last retired to Denmark, where he was thrown into prison. He survived until the year 1578, in which he died, having drawn up a testament, in which he gives an account of the death of the late king; a copy of which testament here follows.

Her Majesty came into the enemy's camp, along with her domestics, where she was welcomed by the great acclamations of the soldiers, who rejoiced at having recovered their queen. Meeting the Earl of Morton, she said to him, openly, and quite aloud, " How is this, my Lord Morton? I am told that all this is done in order to get justice against the king's murderers. I am told also that you are one of the chief of them." He replied, " Come, come; this is not the place where we ought to discuss such matters," and then slunk behind her back, as not one of the nobility ever did, and never presented himself before her Majesty.

Two very wicked men were appointed to have the queen in charge—young Drumlanrig and young Cessford —both of them most cruel murderers, and men of very scandalous life. The former had murdered his own cousin, when he was in bed and in his wife's arms. Of this cousin he was the next heir ; and because Drumlanrig could not get from this cousin a certain inheritance at the price he wished he killed him. The other, Cessford, had most cruelly slaughtered his own uncle, the Abbot of Kelso, who was also his godfather, because the abbot would not give him in fief some land which was dependent upon the said abbey. The queen happened to see near her the elder Laird of Drumlanrig, the father, and said, " Laird of Drumlanrig, this is not the promise you made me, upon your knees, when out in the fields you assured me, after your first rebellion, that you would follow none but the royal standard ? " He answered, " In God's name, why have not you granted my son a pardon ? It would only be just," meaning for the murder of his cousin already mentioned, whose wife became an idiot after having seen her husband butchered before her eyes.

Her Majesty's capture happened upon 20th June 1567.

During the journey into Edinburgh the lords separated all her domestics from her Majesty, and caused the troops from Edinburgh to keep so close to her that none of her own party could say a word to her. She now began to understand that she was a prisoner. In this wise she was taken to Edinburgh, and placed in the house where the Laird of Craigmillar lodged, near the town. He was a man of very wicked life and of no religion, who had been induced to join this faction by reason of a disappointment. The custody of Dunbar Castle had been taken from him, in exchange for which, however, he had a grant of the provostship [of Edinburgh.] This, joined to the persuasion of the Laird of Lethington—

whose first wife was sister of Craigmillar's second wife—induced him to change sides. He was a man of little feeling ; at the end of his life however (he died in Paris, of the " grosse verole," or leprosy) he gave tokens of being very penitent for his rebellion against her Majesty, considering not only the allegiance which he owed her as a sovereign, but the gratitude which was due to her as a benefactress.

On her arrival at the said house, she there found the lords ready to sit down to the supper table, who asked her whether she would not sup in their company. Her Majesty replied that they had already provided her with supper enough, considering the condition to which she saw herself reduced, and that she needed repose more than food. She was then shut up in a chamber, and guards were posted on the stairs and at each door in the house. Some of the soldiers were so shameless as even to refuse to leave the room, so that the queen passed the whole night lying on a bed, without undressing. The utmost liberty which she could obtain was to be allowed to write a letter to the lords, more particularly to the Laird of Grange (in reliance upon whose word she had come among them), and to Secretary Lethington. With the latter she wished to discuss the troubles which confronted her, and to understand from him the particulars of the intentions of these lords. She offered to assist personally in the Parliament in furtherance of the justice which they demanded for the murder of the late king. She also demanded to know the grounds upon which she had been so disrespectfully treated by them, and detained as prisoner by them, so that none of her servants could come near her, and why she had not been lodged in her own castle, as hitherto she had been. She told them that where she was she had neither bed nor furniture befitting her rank; and that they did not conduct themselves towards her as the good and faithful subjects they professed to be.

The only answer which she received was this :—That fearing she might do herself a mischief in her despair they had placed guards over her, even in her bedroom. As they refused to give her the key of that room, she lay down upon the bed fully dressed as she was, for about an hour and a half.

About eight or nine o'clock next morning, as the queen was looking out of the window of her chamber, she saw Lethington pass, on his way to the council of the lords. She called him several times by his name, in a piteous voice and through her tears. She reminded him of the obligations under which he lay to her, and of the many favours and kindnesses she had conferred upon him; in return for which she asked him for nothing more than that he would come and speak with her. Lethington drew down his hat and made as though he had neither seen nor heard her Majesty. Hereupon several of the queen's soldiers and others of the common people becoming riotous, the guards over her Majesty came to remove her from the window, telling her that possibly some one might fire at her, for which the lords would be very sorry; and they consequently forbade her to go near the window.

Her Majesty had no dinner that day, but ate only a morsel of bread and drank a glass of water. In the meantime she was much threatened and most unbecomingly addressed by Drumlanrick and Cessford.

No answer having yet arrived to the letter which the queen had addressed on the previous evening to the lords of the council, she sent them a second. She demanded to know the reason why she was thus detained in prison, and why thus treated as she had been. She demanded to speak with them, or some one of them, and to be taken to her castle, or to the Palace of Holyrood, in which she could be kept with quite as much safety, but much more honourably than at present, until they had decided what they meant to do with her. The only reply which she received, was this :—that she could have no answer that day.

Lethington came in the course of the evening to pay her Majesty a visit, led partly by the advice of his friends, and partly because the report of his great ingratitude had been circulated through the whole town. Such was his internal shame and fear, that so long as he was speaking to her, he did not once dare to raise his eyes and look her in the face.

At the beginning of the conversation, she asked him to explain the cause of all the present ill-treatment to which she was exposed, and to let her know what was yet in store for her. She reminded him of what she had done for him ; how she had favoured and supported him, how she had even saved his life, all of which he admitted. At length he told her that it was suspected and feared that she meant to thwart the execution of the justice demanded upon the death of the late king ; and that she was held in custody until everything had been done to authorise this investigation, and put all other matters into good order. He told her also that the council would never permit her to return to the Earl of Bothwell, who, he said, ought to be hanged, and until this were done, there could be no peace in the kingdom, nor trust in her Majesty towards the nobility. Here he discoursed with something more than freedom upon Bothwell's habits, against whom he manifested an intensity of hatred.

The queen was fully alive to Lethington's insolence and false pretences; she knew that he knew better and more than he had said. She knew the false pretexts which the lords were employing to carry out their evil designs against her, by charging her with wishing to hinder justice being done for the murder which they themselves had committed. She knew that nothing terrified them so much as the prospect of an investigation. So she answered Lethington with great calmness to the following effect. She was ready, she said, to refute these accusations, by joining with the lords in the enquiry which was about to be made into the murder. As to Earl Bothwell, Lethington knew — no one better — how everything had been arranged; he, more than any other person, having been the adviser.

The conversation between them now glided from one point to another. The queen saw that Lethington's object was to play the part of one who is misunderstood, and to support the actions of the nobility; she felt herself compelled, therefore, to speak to him plainly. She told him that she feared that he, Morton, and Balfour, more than any others, hindered the inquiry into the murder, to which they were the consenting and guilty parties. The Earl of Bothwell had told her so, who swore, when he was leaving her, that he had acted entirely by their persuasion and advice; and showed her their signatures. If she, a queen, was treated as she had been, merely as one suspected of wishing to prevent the punishment of the criminals, with how much greater certainty could they proceed against him—Lethington— the Earl of Morton, James Balfour, and others of the council, who were the actual murderers? They knew the sincerity of her intention in this matter. They all were miserable wretches, if they made her bear the punishment of their crimes. She threatened Lethington that if he continued to act in conjuncticn with these noblemen, and plot along with them, she, who until now had supported and preserved him, would publish in the end what Bothwell had told her about his doings.

Seeing himself thus detected Lethington became exceedingly angry. He went so far as to say that if she did so, she would drive him to greater lengths than he yet had gone, in order to save his own life, which (as he remarked frequently, but like a very coward) he held dearer than all else in the world. On the other hand, if she let matters tone down little by little, the day would yet come when he might do her some good service. For the present, as it was necessary that he should go to confer with the lords, he begged she would give him permission to depart, and would not ask him to return to talk any more with her. It caused him to be suspected, and did herself no good. If his credit with the nobility were shaken, her life would be in great peril. It had already been frequently proposed that she should be put out of the way ; and this he could prevent.

About nine o'clock in the evening, the Earl of Morton came to her Majesty with a message from the council to the effect that they had decided that Holyrood Palace (which is outside the town) should be her place of residence. They meant, however, speedily to remove her elsewhere, and they were afraid that if her departure should be in the sight of the people, some insurrection would follow. With this intention they waited until the night.

When she reached her Palace of Holyrood supper was ready, and the greater part of her female attendants and domestic servants were there. All were very sad to see their poor mistress in such a miserable plight, in the midst of her own subjects, men whom she had exceedingly advanced and favoured.

In the middle of the supper the Earl of Morton, who all the time had been standing behind the queen's chair, asked an esquire of the stable whether the horses were ready. He ordered the dishes to be removed from the table, and told the queen to prepare to mount on horseback. Partly from distress of mind, partly from the fear of being poisoned, the queen had eaten nothing the whole day. She inquired where they were going to take her in such haste, and asked that some of her female attendants and domestic servants might go with her. This request was absolutely refused; two *femmes-de-chambre* only were appointed to attend upon her, all the rest crying and entreating that they might follow their mistress. The hardest heart among the most cruel barbarians would have been moved to pity at the departure of this poor princess.

Morton gave her to understand, indirectly, that she was going to visit the prince her son; but she was taken, with great haste, direct to Lochleven, the house of the Earl of Moray's natural brother. Moray in the meantime was in France, and a frequent visitor with the Admiral Gaspar de Coligny.

The queen was permitted to take no other clothes than her nightdress, nor any linen. She passed Leith, which was filled with soldiers, ready to put down any insurrection among the people. Lords Lindsay and Ruthven took charge of her to Lochleven. Many persons imagined that the Hamiltons and the Earl of Rothes had got together some forces for her rescue, and so her Majesty was informed by the way, and advised therefore to linger on the road as long as possible. But this was not permitted her, for some one was always near her who whipped her hackney to urge it on.

At the edge of the lake she was met by the laird and his brothers, who conducted her into a room on the ground floor, furnished only with the laird's furniture. The queen's bed was not there, nor were there any other articles proper for one of her rank. In this prison, and in the midst of such desolation, her Majesty remained for fifteen days and more, without eating, drinking, or conversing with the inmates of the house, so that many thought she would have died.

In the meantime a house-steward of her Majesty, an Italian, seduced by the rebels, handed over to them her silver plate and the other furniture which he had in charge. The same persons laid hands on all the remainder of her most valuable moveables, as well from her cabinet as her chambers, as also her entire wardrobe, from which she could never obtain one single garment, or even a chemise, until the return of the Earl of Moray, who caused his wife's tailor to make the queen a dress of violet cloth, which he sent to her, along with some beggarly old clothes, for which he could find no other use.

This good gentleman, the Earl of Moray, who at that time was in France, so soon as he heard of the queen's imprisonment, went to the king and the princes of Lorraine, her relations, and pledged himself to them by endless promises, protestations, and perjuries, to set out forthwith for Scotland, and there to strain every nerve to free her from prison, to re-establish her authority, and to put everything into its former good order. Making good profit out of his treachery, he received many good and great presents. But he had already planned out all the acts of this tragedy, which he meant to have brought to a different conclusion. Not satisfied with the accursed wickedness and treason already executed (from which he imagined his absence was a discharge sufficiently clear in the eyes of the world), he intended that the game should be played out before his return, so that he might take possession of his new kingdom with the less trouble. As he did not wish it to be said that he had lawlessly usurped it during the life-time of its sovereign, it was proposed in a meeting of his own party that the queen should be put to death, one way or other, after which there would be no great difficulty in disposing of her son the prince. This project, however, was opposed by some of the party, who were horrified at the idea of such a detestable crime, which would disgrace their memory and their country to all posterity. The plan therefore was changed. At first they had said that after what they had already done there was no safety for them except in the queen's death (since she might on some future occasion have it in her power to punish them); but they now decided that they would compel her to resign the crown and transmit it, as of her own free will, in favour of her son, the prince. Thus they began to use his name against his poor mother, just as they had already employed the memory of his father and some others against her, meaning to benefit themselves by the common ruin of the whole family. But be that as it may, I have heard it asserted that the intention of this monster of ingratitude was first to deprive her Majesty of her crown, and then of her life. He did not dare openly to propose the queen's death in the Parliament, which had assembled—for at that time Lethington, Grange, and many others had acknowledged their past faults, and were endeavouring to amend them —but with the same design he asked the Parliament that the question of her custody should be referred to him, so that he might make such arrangements as to him should seem fitting.   This, however, was absolutely refused.

On his return from France, Moray went to visit her Majesty at Lochleven, where he found her in a lamentable plight.   As she was now nearly twenty-five years old, she still had it in her power to revoke the gifts of many parcels of the best domains of the crown which had been made to a large number of the conspirators. Here was an additional reason for hurrying on the resignation already mentioned.   A resolution on the subject was arrived at in a council of the nobles, and the letters were prepared by Lethington, a man who always liked to have two strings to his bow.   He drew them up in a form which was to the queen's advantage, and they contained such conditions as made them worthless whenever she pleased.

The lords having come to this decision, the Earl of Athol, Lethington, and the Laird of Tulibardine dispatched an esquire of the stable, called Robert Melvil, to tell the queen that ere long these instruments of resignation would be sent to her for signature.   They entreated her not to refuse, since, if she did not sign them, her life would be in danger, and that her enemies would seek her death by every means in their power, dreading that she would take vengeance on their misdeeds.   As for themselves, they were unable, they said, to hinder such doings.   Nothing could be done until the return of Moray, with whom, however, they might find some way of cancelling the resignation.   The only effect of this document would be to protract the time, and thereby give the opportunity of bringing all things back into good order.

In token of all this, and in accordance with the custom of the country, the Earl of Athol sent her Majesty a turquoise which he had received from her. Lethington sent a small oval ornament of gold, on which was enamelled Æsop's fable of the lion enclosed in the net, which is being gnawed by a mouse, with these words in Italian written round it, "A chi basta l'animo, non mancano le forze." The queen's cipher was engraven within the lid, which had a cord of violet silk and gold. Some Italian verses on a paper were enclosed. Tullibarne reminded her of a certain password, which had been agreed upon between her Majesty and himself.

The Lords Lindsay and Ruthven were the queen's guards within Lochleven. One morning about four o'clock, Ruthven came to her Majesty, and throwing himself on his knees near her bed, promised that he would free her if she would love him. (Her Majesty concealed her women behind the tapestry to serve as witnesses.) The queen felt the deepest indignation at Ruthven's insolence; she still continued to be his sovereign, whatever might be her present condition. She reminded him that she had given him no occasion to use any such infamous language towards her; and protested that she would rather remain in perpetual prison as an innocent woman than leave it as a guilty one. In fact, she informed the elder lady of Lochleven of Ruthven's villanous attempt, and afterwards showed her a letter which the said Ruthven had written. Hereupon he was recalled at the instance of the Laird of Lochleven. Ruthven was exceedingly irritated, and this induced him to calumniate her; yet afterwards he joined her party, as also did Lindsay.

On the afternoon of the . . . day of . . . 1567, the Lords Lindsay and Ruthven, accompanied by two

E

notaries and the said Melvil, came into the queen's chamber. She was lying on her bed, in a state of very great weakness, partly by reason of her extreme trouble (partly in consequence of a great flux, the result of a miscarriage of twins, her issue by Bothwell), so that she could move only with great difficulty. With extreme audacity and anger Lindsay gave her to understand of the commission with which he was charged by the nobility, namely, to make her sign certain letters for the resignation of the crown ; which he required her to be pleased to read. Although she had already been assured by Melvil, in the name of the nobles mentioned above, that she need make no difficulty, she plainly refused to do so ; she could not in conscience (her heart telling her that she was innocent) prejudice her honour by sanctioning such an unjust statement. At the same time she knew that her life was in great and immediate danger. And of a truth it was the intention of the rebels, if she did not sign these letters, to take her from Lochleven, and as they were crossing the lake to throw her into it, or secretly to convey her to some island in the middle of the sea, there to be kept unknown to the whole world, in close custody for the remainder of her life. Lindsay confirmed this ; for, as soon as he saw that her Majesty resolutely refused to sign these letters, he told her to rise from bed, and that he had charge to carry her to a place where he would give a good account of her to the lords of the country. Several times he advised her to sign, for if she did not, she would compel them to cut her throat, however unwilling they might be.

This poor princess, seeing herself thus treated by her own subjects, and being without any of her domestics (for the two *femmes-de-chambre*, whom only she had with her, had been turned out), asked where she was to be taken. She demanded very earnestly to be admitted before the estates of the country and the parliament to answer to the points mentioned in these letters. Lindsay replied that he had no instructions on these heads, and could say nothing more. Thus, without any form of legal proceeding or knowledge of the cause, they compelled her Majesty by threats and present violence to sign these instruments, which they caused to be read by the said notaries. When they asked her what she thought of the matter, she answered several times that she did not consent to the contents of these instruments, that she had signed them in direct opposition to her intention and will, and that they had been extorted from her by force and constraint. She protested, therefore, that she would observe and keep them no longer than during her imprisonment, and she frequently asked those who were present to be her witnesses.

The queen's steady firmness of purpose angered Lindsay exceedingly. He replied (very rudely) that whereas she was obliged to do as she had done, she had better affirm boldly that what she had done she had done with her free will. For the efficacy of these instruments did not depend upon herself, and they would take good care that she should never have the power to revoke them; but they saw well that this act of resignation would never be approved and legalised by the estates of the country, who even then contradicted these instruments when published, as you will hear presently.

I have forgotten to say that the queen, influenced as well by her malady as by the information which she had received about the plot for her death, refused to leave the house. She declared aloud that she would rather be dragged out of it by the hairs of her head. Melvil upon this told her that George Douglas was not such an enemy to her as she imagined, he having seen him in tears in the garden. She sent a message to him, asking him to intercede with his brother and the rest of his house, telling them that they would be disgraced if some day it could be said of them that their queen had been carried off from them by force in order to be taken, as it was said, to the shambles. Melvil brought George Douglas to speak with the queen, who having read an instrument and promise of pardon for Monsigneur de Moray and the members of his house, George promised that he would do his best to prevent her removal. This he did very skilfully, causing all his relations and the servants of the house, by whom he was much respected, to rise in rebellion. Ruthven had cautioned her Majesty against George Douglas, assuring her that he was a very great enemy of hers, and that she would do well to beware of him. And this she had believed.

After the queen had signed these said letters, contrary to the promises made to her, she was taken (with great altercation on both sides) into a great gloomy tower in Lochleven. She was there shut up, within an iron gate, in such a miserable condition, that no poor criminal could be treated worse. They deprived her of all her ink, paper, and books, and all her attendants, save her two *femmes-de-chambre* and one cook. Her surgeon was left because she was ill, who afterwards was of great service to her. This poor queen, despoiled of sceptre, crown, and all the goods of this world, and to whom nothing remained but the bare life itself, was now attempted to be poisoned, as appeared plainly by the swelling of one half of her body, and chiefly of one arm and one leg, which came upon her. A deep yellow tint spread over her whole body, and many pustules appeared which discharged a humour, clear and very venomous ; which caused a swelling wherever it touched. The vigour of her youth contributed much to expel this poison and hinder its effects. She was much helped by a liquor which strengthens the heart, the action of which grew weaker day by day, and she felt a very violent pain through her whole body until she was bled.

Seeing the treatment to which she had been exposed, and that she was urgent to remain in his house, the laird caused a deed to be drawn up by notaries, to the effect that she was not detained by force, and that she remained where she was of her own free will. Furthermore, he declared that he was no party to compel her Majesty to sign her resignation to the crown, of which she discharged him, and, moreover, protested again that this was done by the Lords Lindsay and Ruthven.

By virtue of these letters of resignation on 19th July, the prince was crowned in the Church of Stirling, and in his stead the oath was taken by the Earl of Morton and Lord Hume. The latter nobleman before long owned his error and fought on the queen's side against the prince's authority. These two lords had been appointed to superintend the coronation in the place of the Bishop of Argyll. The letters of commission and attorney, signed by the queen and sealed with the Privy Seal, were read. The first contained the resignation of the crown and the government of the kingdom in favour of My Lord the Prince. The second established a regency in the name of the Earl of Moray, during the king's minority; the third was for the appointment of a council to act along with the said earl, on which were placed many

persons who served as shadows and ciphers. For they
were never either seen nor heard.

The said letters here follow.

Throgmorton ?

The said Robert Melvil also carried to her Majesty,
in the scabbard of his sword, a billet written by the
hand of Frokmartin, at that time ambassador to the
queen, from the Queen of England. By the express
order of his mistress, the said ambassador advised Queen
Mary to sign the instruments mentioned above, for they
could do her no harm, she being in prison and detained
there by force.

On the same day on which the prince was crowned,
the Laird of Lochleven without informing her Majesty of the reason, caused all the artillery of his
house to be discharged and bonfires to be lighted everywhere, while he himself began to sing and dance in his
garden.   At last the queen having made many inquiries
as to the cause of these rejoicings, the laird came into her
chamber and asked whether she would not make merry
with them upon the coronation of her son, who now was
their king. As for her, it might well be said, " *Deposuit potentes.*"   The bystanders made game of her
Majesty, some in one fashion, some in another, telling
her in their bravadoes that her authority was abolished,
and that she no longer had the power to avenge herself
upon them. Hereupon her Majesty answered, that they
had a king who would avenge her, and she prayed
God to preserve and defend him from their wicked and
damnable treasons. If they could prevent it, they would
never allow him to come to the age when he could make
his authority felt.

Here the queen being extremely annoyed, threw
herself upon her knees in the middle of the chamber,

near the table, she wept long and very bitterly, and with hands stretched out and raised up she uttered her prayer to God. The import of it was this—that He would be pleased, (seeing the indignities which had been heaped upon her most unjustly, even by those persons to whom she had done the greatest kindnesses, always having had pity upon the innocent in their affliction); to grant her the favour before her death, to see her enemies and rebellious subjects brought into the same trouble, sorrow, and desolation to which they had now reduced her; and especially that, before the end of the year, she might see the laird as wretched as she then was; and then she laid her curse upon him and his house. Hearing this, the laird was seized with terror, and full of thought he left the queen's chamber. Her prayer was not without its effect; for before the end of that same year, when she escaped from the castle, the laird would have committed suicide had not he been hindered by his servants, and for a very long time he was in as desperate a state of frenzy as man ever was.

Shortly after the coronation the Earl of Moray, seeing that all matters had now come to a head, and were well prepared for the execution of his purpose, hastened to return from France. As soon as he reached Scotland, he was met by several of the queen's friends, partly because they trusted his promises, and partly because he had expressed himself in kindly terms towards her advantage. He protested that he would bring about her release, and he seemed to feel much regret at the present state of affairs, and at the lengths to which things had been carried. But the intentions of this good gentleman were directly opposite, as he speedily showed to his natural brother, George Douglas, whom the queen had sent to meet him, to discover his real sentiments towards assist-

ing her, and how far he would provide for her in her
necessity. Douglas reminded Moray, on the part of the
queen, that he had frequently and publicly confessed
that he was " her creature ;" he spoke also of the honours and benefits which she had already heaped upon
him, as of others which he might earn from her in her
present extremity. ·He told Moray how the queen,
against her will, had signed the letters by which he afterwards became regent, and that accordingly the regency
would be offered to him. But he advised him to beware
of accepting it, if he wished to keep well with her
Majesty, and had any regard for their early friendship.
To all these observations Moray replied very coldly, and
remained three or four days with the queen's enemies
before coming to visit her.

The queen's furniture, dresses, tapestries, beds, silver
plate, horses, mules, and all the other equipage of the
stables, had been distributed, some to one person some to
another ; for these miserable wretches always pillage the
unfortunate. Even when Moray came to visit the queen
he was mounted on one of her hackneys, which she was in
the habit of riding, wherewith she was much displeased.
By this she saw for herself, besides what had already been
told her, namely, that when he had taken possession of
her furniture it was not with the intention of restoring
the articles to herself. She prayed that the hackney
might break his neck ; and in fact it did throw him
into a lake, in which he thought he would have been
drowned.

This bastard [Murray] arrived at Lochleven about
supper-time, just as the queen was going to sit down to
table. The Earl of Morton, the Laird of Tullibarne,
and some other people came with him. From the
moment that he came into her presence he never spoke

but in a loud voice, always turning towards the persons of his own company, as if his visit were to them an object of suspicion. At length this traitor even asked their permission to have a private conference with her Majesty, assuring them with a smile that he would not betray them. They all paid him much honour and respect, calling him "Grace" when they spoke to him, a title usually given only to kings, or their children, or their very near relations. All these circumstances confirmed the queen still more in the mistrust in which she already held him.

Moray refused to sup with her, nor did he offer to give her the napkin, until she had reminded him of it, telling him that in former days he had not thought it beneath him to do so.

After supper, the queen and Moray went into the garden, where they walked for a considerable time. Crafty as ever, he told the queen that the people of Scotland were much dissatisfied with her conduct during his absence, and that even though innocent before God, she should have had regard to her reputation in the eyes of the world, which judges by the outward appearance and not by the inward sentiment. Here he particularly discoursed upon her marriage with the Earl of Bothwell, which, he said, was the cause why many persons suspect that she, along with him, had been a consenting party to the murder of the king, her late husband; that it is not enough to avoid a fault, but also the occasions of being suspected of it; that reports are frequently more significant than the truth itself; along with many other remarks worthy of a real hypocrite, which he was in all his actions, his only anxiety being to make them appear outwardly good, without any respect to his conscience.

The queen in reply said that she felt herself innocent in all that could be laid to her charge; that she was always ready to justify herself before her own subjects, although she was not bound to do so ; that she did not fear all the frauds and calumnies of her enemies, feeling assured that God, before whom she had never voluntarily, as she said, worn a mask, would in the end manifest her innocence and the false treasons of her enemies. In short, she would rather hear of the evil which she had not done, than do the evil of which nothing was heard ; for she had a greater respect for God, whom no one could deceive, than for man.   As to himself, personally, since he had so much of the honourable blood of this world, she cautioned him against being led under this pretext to forget his duty towards God and her. Not only was she his queen, but she had been more than a sister towards him both by affection and liberality. The opportunity now presented itself for him to show his gratitude towards her.   Let him pay her back in kind ; let him show by his actions, and without disguise, how much he valued what she had done for him, as he well might do towards others who could not see as clearly as she had the means of doing.

Passing from this subject the conversation turned upon many others.   Moray asked the queen to give him her advice upon the regency, which had been offered to him, and which he had been urged to accept.   He assured her that he would never take it of his own free will, nor to further his own personal aggrandisement ; for his own private tastes led him to shun such like grandeur and ambition, as she well knew.   But it seemed to him that were he to do so he might be of service to her Majesty.   Some one or other must, of necessity, fill the post.   He would be very glad to avail himself of it for a time, to put her affairs into better order.   Another person might aim at her total ruin.

As was her custom, the queen spoke to him without reserve, and told him briefly that it was not a position becoming him, either as regarded his own private interests or his duty towards herself. She begged therefore that he would not take such a charge upon himself. Besides this, it was not in her power to bring herself to look with favour upon the man who should usurp her authority, whatever might be his motive, though successful. Moreover let him also reflect upon this ;—if those persons who, from their birth, were bound to pay her entire obedience, and under the law of God were obliged to honour and respect her as their sovereign, if they were so unfortunate as to forget her (who had never oppressed them nor extorted from them a single penny by extraordinary taxes, but rather had enriched them by her own property), he could not expect, said she, that they would long be faithful to him, to whom the just authority had never been given, beyond the fear that they would be punished for rebelling against lawful authority. It was this very authority which they were now attempting to abolish and extinguish. Let this fear be removed from before their eyes, and as soon as they needed no more of his protection they would not be long in casting off the respect which they now professed towards him. Upon the least discontent (which, as he knew, they were not slow to take) they would cast him off with the same licence that they had used towards her, aye, and with even less scruple, since he was a bastard by birth and origin, and to him they had never been under any obligation. For this is a true maxim, " He who does not keep faith where it is due, will hardly keep it where it is not due."

After some talk full of dissimulation, Moray began to

discuss with the queen who was the fittest person to be made regent. He named those whom he knew to have been the most riotous and most obstinate in their rebellion, such as the Earl of Morton, thinking thereby to induce the queen to propose himself, the very person whom of all others she had the greatest cause to dread. When he found that he could not wring from her any decision tending to his own advantage, he ventured to tell her that he had already promised to accept the regency, and that he could not go against his promise. However, he would do every kindness for her that lay in his power. In the meantime, he advised her to be patient, and to comfort herself with the thought that her neighbour, the King of France, would speedily be in a worse condition than herself. He admitted that he had heard this from the Admiral Coligny, whom he had visited, and found to be very hostile to her Majesty. But the matter would soon be a certainty in consequence of the hostility and intrigue between him and the house of Lorraine, from which she was descended.

In the last place, the queen asked him to remain at Lochleven for a day or two, to talk over her affairs more fully with her. This he refused to do, upon the plea that he was already suspected. She took advantage of this occasion to recommend the payment of the wages and board of her poor officers, chiefly the French, who were dispersed here and there, and who were in great distress through the great misfortunes of their good mistress. Very little attention was paid to this, and the queen was compelled to allow them even their board out of the proceeds of her own dowry, from the time of her arrival in England. I believe that the fidelity which these good servants preserved towards their mistress made them the partakers of her sorrows.

Her Majesty also spoke to Moray about her rings, which were both very numerous and many exceedingly precious. She asked him to secure them for the prince, her son, to whom she would willingly give them, that they might be united with the crown jewels of Scotland in such a manner that it would be unlawful for the council to alienate them. They had not come to her, she said, by descent from the earlier kings of Scotland, but had been bought by herself, or had been given to her by the late King Henry the Second, her father-in-law, or the late Francis, her lord and husband. Moray answered that her request was not reasonable, for the lords might find it necessary to interfere in this matter for the good of the kingdom; as if, for instance, said he, some one should attempt to rescue her Majesty out of their hands. Here you may notice the impudence of this miserable creature, who did not hesitate to turn the queen's private property against herself.

On 15th December next following, the Parliament met at Edinburgh, where it was held by the orders of the Earl of Moray. Being informed of this, and wishing to vindicate her innocence in this public assembly, the queen addressed a long letter to the earl. She reminded him of the obligations which he owed to her, as he had admitted in his letters written to her from Berwick, in which he called himself " her creature ;" the great crimes and rebellions against her of which he had been guilty, and which she had pardoned ; how she had treated him, not as a bastard, but as her lawful brother ; how, in fact, she had entrusted him with the entire government of the realm since it had come under her authority. She referred to the promises which he had made to the King of France and the members of the house of Lorraine, her relatives, and to the protestations which he had made at his last visit to Lochleven.   Lastly, she demanded permission to be heard in this Parliament, either in person or by deputy, thereby to answer the false calumnies which had been published about her since her imprisonment. She also wished to enlighten the minds of the members of the Estates on all matters connected with herself bearing on public interests.

For this purpose she offered to lay down, of her own free will, her authority as queen, and to interfere only as a private individual; likewise she would submit herself to all the rigour of the laws, according to which she earnestly desired that proceedings should be taken for the punishment of all persons who might be found guilty of the murder of the late king. She even went so far as to offer that if, after she had been heard, it should be decided by the said Estates that for the good of the realm she should resign the authority which God had given her over them until now, she would do so. Should they refuse these offers, she protested that this Parliament, and everything resulting from it, grounded upon the letters which she had been compelled to grant and sign, would be null and void. There was extant no law which permitted anyone to be condemned without his cause having been heard, if it touched but the welfare of the least of her subjects. It was much more reasonable, then, that justice should be done to her, their queen, in a matter which touched her honour, which was dearer to her than her life. She had never shut her ear against the complaint of the humblest of her subjects; she had never refused justice to any one of them; which facts proved to her the gentleness and clemency with which she had governed them. None of them could complain, with justice, that she had ever wronged them of a single penny; for she had been contented

with her own ordinary revenues ; she had not burdened
them with any exceptional loan, charge, or impost ; but
rather she had kept herself poor in order that they might
be enriched. She concluded again by demanding that
she should either be acquitted, or condemned under the
accusation which they wished to bring against her.

The only answer which Moray sent to this letter consisted of three or four lines, expressed in general terms,
to the effect that the queen's demands could not be
granted her, but he did not specify what these demands
were. He had still enough shame left to·be unwilling
to have it known that he had rejected anything so
just and reasonable. He caused to be chosen as Lords of
the Articles in this Parliament such persons as were at
his devotion, except two or three, who were added as a
cloak for the rest, and who were not so much dependents
as adherents. He also caused it to be proposed secretly
that he should be invested by the Parliament with full
authority to dispose of the queen's person ; ostensibly
out of regard to the safety of those who had taken up
arms against her, but, as has already been said, his real
intention was to procure her death. No sooner was this
design known than it was vehemently opposed, even by
some who suspected what his real intentions were. They
knew that many of his party were now earnest with
him to declare himself king. Others, more prudent
(considering it less odious to advance step by step),
thought it better for him to proclaim himself heir to the
kingdom after the person of the prince, of whom he
could presently rid himself.

With these views Moray had employed various persons to discover how he might establish his legitimacy
by proving the marriage which he was now advised to
assert as having been secretly contracted between King

James the Fifth and his (Moray's) mother, although she was then married to another man, with whom she had lived for a long time after the king's death, without any mention having ever been made of any divorce or separation between them. This proposition then was abandoned, for Moray saw there was but faint hope of the success which he had expected. An Act, however, was passed for the indemnity and security of all those persons who had taken arms against the queen, who had been at Carberry Hill, and who had agreed to her imprisonment at Lochleven Castle. The queen's abdication, and the resignation of the crown in favour of the prince, her son, were ratified in like manner, and the regency of the Earl of Moray was affirmed, or rather confirmed, since he had assumed it from the beginning of the previous August.

But when these letters of the said demission, resignation, and regency came to be read in this Parliament, many lords and barons there present requested to be more clearly informed as to the queen's intention on these subjects. Among the rest, Lord Herries stood up and spoke. Having showed the importance of the question as affecting not only themselves, but all their successors, he requested that he and two or three others, whom the Parliament should appoint, might be permitted to visit her Majesty in order to ascertain her intention, and whether, of her own good and free will, and without any constraint, she had granted these letters. These letters were insufficient for the purpose for which they were intended. It might be alleged that, taking into consideration the place where she was detained, and the treatment to which she had already been exposed, she had been forced to consent to these acts, or that they had been falsified, and her signature counterfeited. Upon the faith of such documents as these it was impossible to ratify the proposed measures. Hereupon he demanded an act or instrument, and, according to the custom of the country, he publicly offered a piece of money to the clerk of the Parliament. Following his example, many lords refused to sign the Acts of this Parliament, nor were they pressed to do so, for it was feared that the opposition among them would become too notorious. Thus it happened that the larger and the worse party overcame the better.

At this Parliament were passed forty-one ordinances, intended to abrogate not only the Pope's authority, but also to annul certain acts previously made in Parliament as well by the assent of the Lords as by the queen on her arrival in Scotland, and which were meant to put an end to all searches after the Catholics, and all persecutions of them ; measures tending to the quiet and peace of the country. A Confession of the Faith and Doctrine held by the Protestants of Scotland was also prepared and confirmed in this Parliament.

It must not be forgotten that though the Queen of England made it seem as if she were interposing with the lords in favour of the queen, and although for the re-establishment of her affairs, her ambassador had frequently been charged to recommend in her name the cause of her Majesty, which he actually did in public;—yet in secret she had made use of the lords as a means whereby to weaken the power and strength of Scotland at the points which had served in the olden time to bridle all the kings of England. Remembering the advantages which the French had recently gained over the English by means of the insight afforded by the fortresses which they held in Scotland, she contrived to induce this Parliament to order that the Castle of Dunbar, which had

F

long been held in the interests of France, and the fortress of Inchkeith (called by the French, l'Isle aux Chevaux) should be demolished and levelled with the ground. This was done by the Scotch, who thereby violated their duty as true Scottish subjects, and the fidelity which they owed to their country, for this castle of Dunbar was a very important safeguard to the kingdom against the English.

Shortly after this Parliament the Earl of Moray, in company with the Earl of Morton and several others of the nobility, came to visit her Majesty in Lochleven with very great pomp, but with such contempt and disdain that the breach ever afterwards grew wider. For Moray, after having frequently spoken with the queen about his mother's earnest wish that some good agreement might be brought about, spoke to her Majesty very discourteously and with great audacity; having no regard to the proposals which she had made to him, though they were much to his safety and advantage. Especially he could never bear her to insist (as she did earnestly and continually) that she ought to be discharged of the crimes imputed to her, about which she was much more solicitous than for her liberty and the re-establishment of her authority. When her Majesty had fully understood his hateful determination, and seen that he was resolute to listen to no pacification, but to go on to the end as her mortal and sworn enemy, she could no longer tolerate his prodigious ingratitude. She told him openly that since he had dealt with her so unjustly and basely in every particular which she had required of him, however just and reasonable, she would never apply to him on any occasion whatever. She would rather wear out her life in perpetual prison than have freedom by means of him. She hoped that the just God, the avenger of the oppressed, would free her, to his disgrace, damage, and ruin. Then, taking him by the hand, she protested, in the presence of the lords, that cost what it might, sooner or later he should repent. And then she left him.

It is not out of place here to remark that, during this visit, James Balfour came with the lords. He it was who had sold Edinburgh Castle, which had been committed to his keeping, together with all the queen's furniture and jewels. At the very moment when Balfour came into the queen's chamber, although the weather had been very calm till then, there arose a gust of wind which forced open all the windows in the room with a great noise. When the queen saw Balfour enter, she said aloud that this sudden and violent commotion must of necessity be for some arch traitor. Balfour hereupon took himself off behind backs among the company who were there along with the lords, reddening excessively. The Earl of Morton spoke very courteously to her Majesty, and said he would do everything in his power for her freedom, which, however, he hindered, more than any other person.

Before leaving Lochleven Moray ordered that his maternal brother, George Douglas, the youngest son of the Laird of Lochleven, should never again enter that house ; and after much brave talk he threatened that if he did so, he would have him hanged. George, who was a gentleman, well born, and of a high spirit, took this in very evil part, and conceived a great hatred against Moray, whom, till that time, he had always respected as his own father. Seeing that he was no longer trusted, he resolved to try by every means in his power to set her Majesty at liberty. Until now he could not bring himself to do so ; for although on the one hand he was her subject, and, as such, was thereto bound, yet on the other he was an inmate of his brother's house. So long as he was trusted by his brother, he had some scruples about deceiving him, as he said ; but now the case was altered. It is true that he had already been employed to effect some arrangement between the queen and the arrogant lords. But now finding himself driven away from the home of his family, and deprived of the confidence of his nearest relatives, he became one of the queen's most active agents for the re-establishment of her fortunes.

This George Douglas, having had some communication with Moray about the queen's business, was permitted by the earl to carry his answer back to her Majesty. But Moray immediately despatched one of his own servants to Lochleven, forbidding the laird to receive his brother into his house. George having discovered this secret message, got the start of the earl's messenger, and having reached Lochleven, bade her Majesty a last farewell after having made her acquainted with the means she must employ in order to carry out the plan which he had formed for her escape. She must especially endeavour to win and gain over the person who had charge of the boats upon the lake, who was also of the same name as the laird. This individual was of greater importance than any of the others for the execution of the design ; for by means of him the queen could always learn what he, Douglas, and the other lords of her side were doing on her behalf. The chief of these was Lord Seton. He and the other noblemen of her party agreed, out of respect to the queen, to forget whatever private feuds they might have among themselves. George swore that he would faithfully render her all the loyalty and fidelity of a good subject, protesting that he would continue to be such until death. He carried a short letter to Lord Seton, which the queen had written with her own hand,

though she was so closely watched that she was compelled to make her ink with the coal which was in the
chimney, for neither paper nor ink were allowed to her.

As George was leaving the queen, his brother, the
laird, met him, and having told him of the prohibition
which Moray had sent by his servant, commanded him
at the same time to take his departure and never again
to enter the house, or come near it. George was much
offended herewith, and told his brother, more than once,
that sooner or later he would be revenged, and that for
the future he had better keep clear of him. Their
mother was in great trouble about all this, for she was
very fond of George; but, on the other hand, she dreaded
the ruin of her elder son and of the house.

Shortly after this occurrence George made as if he
would cross near Lochleven alone, and had gone into the
loch as far as his horse would carry him, in order to make
a certain signal to the queen. Hereupon his brother
ordered a cannon-shot to be fired at him, which was done
promptly. Then followed some conversation between the
brothers, very angry and threatening. Irritated more
than before, George worked with increased energy; and
having pressed the nobles of the queen's party, one by
one, to see that her affairs were in good order when she
should be set at liberty by him, his next attempt was
upon the boatman. He tried persuasions of all kinds to
induce him to carry a box into Lochleven, and to bring
it back again to him; giving him to understand that it
contained many papers on matters of business which the
queen needed. The lad, who had already carried some
packages, quickly suspected the object at which they
were aiming, and spoke out frankly, for he had some
time previously been won over to George's service. He
could clearly see, he said, what George was driving at;

but he warned him that not only would such a plan never succeed, but that it was fraught with great danger. Let George therefore tell him, without reserve, what he wanted him to do and it should be done, even at the risk of his life. Seeing that the lad was so very earnest of his own free will, George let him into the very depths of his plan, and admitted that his design was to carry her Majesty off in this box. He and the boatman discussed the matter, and at the end they decided upon getting her away under the disguise of a borrowed dress, under the eyes of every one. All other plans were very difficult of execution and easy of discovery. Hereupon George went without delay to the noblemen, asking them to fix a certain day on which to meet near Lochleven, with all their forces under arms, there to receive the queen. She was informed of the whole plan by letters which the boatman carried to her.

The Laird of Markyston, who had the reputation of being a great wizard, made bets with several persons to the amount of five hundred crowns, that by the 5th of May her Majesty would be out of Lochleven. From this circumstance, and in consequence of some other private notices said to have been given by some of the queen's party, the Laird of Lochleven received a warning to be on the watch and to take all precautions to defeat any such design. He was more particularly put on his guard against William Douglas.

Nor must I forget to say that the Earl of Moray now began to suspect Lethington, having ascertained that he was making advances to her Majesty. To discover on what terms he stood with her, Moray caused a false alarm to be made in the town in which they were staying, where the cry was raised that the queen had escaped from Lochleven. Hereupon Lethington and many others mounted their horses and prepared to escape, dreading the just punishment of their rebellion. Even while Lethington was making advances towards the queen, he never ceased to hold his ground with Moray, whom he saw to be the stronger of the two. Having as yet received no assurance from her Majesty (whom he continued to amuse with fair words), he was afraid of being paid the wages which were due to him.

The nobles frequently reproached each other with the treasons and misdeeds which they had committed against the queen, and by way of joke the one threatened, in her name, to have the other punished; an event which they considered impossible, for that they had made ample provision against it. But God, who always confounds the wicked, had arranged otherwise than they had intended.

It happened very conveniently that the laird's wife (whose business it was to be the constant companion of her Majesty, and to act as spy and keeper) had just given birth to a child; consequently the queen had more liberty to prepare for the business she had on hand. She pressed it on with the utmost possible speed, for she saw that the opportunity was very favourable, and that should the laird's wife be astir again before the enterprise was ended, it would become doubly difficult. The Laird and the Lady of Lochleven made sport of the queen, even before her face, upon occasion of her reported escape, which had got abroad, and they boasted that they would take good care of her. William Douglas, too, became much suspected at last; partly because when he gambled—to which he was much addicted—he made show of a large number of pieces of gold which the queen had given him; partly because once, as he was delivering a number of letters to the queen, which had been badly packed up, they fell to the ground in the sight of a daughter and a niece of the laird, who generally slept with the queen, and were always in her company.

These two young girls, of about fourteen or fifteen years of age, had conceived a very great affection and respect for the queen ; more especially the laird's daughter. A day or two after the receipt of the letters mentioned above, and apparently in consequence of the reports then current about the queen's escape, the laird's daughter had a dream. She dreamt that William Douglas brought a black raven into the house, which flew away with the queen, she being at that time on the edge of the loch. When she heard of this dream, her Majesty feared that if it were talked about it might tend to confirm the suspicion about her escape, and also—what was of greater moment—strengthen the distrust already conceived against Douglas. She was so earnest, therefore, with this young girl (who especially dreaded such a removal as the cause of her separation from her Majesty), that she promised not to speak about the dream, nor about the letters which she had seen, upon the understanding that the queen would take her with her when she went away. Her Majesty promised that she would do so ; adding, however, that she had no hope nor means of escape.

Besides, one of these young girls having noticed William Douglas speak to the queen, she mentioned this circumstance to the laird. Being questioned about it, William immediately admitted, through fear, that he had been solicited to carry off her Majesty ; but as he did not know the time nor the means, he could disclose nothing but in general terms, and thereupon he was expelled.

Matters, however, could not be kept so secret but that some hint of them reached the laird's ears. Hereupon he drove William Douglas from his house, and wrote also to his brother George, forbidding him henceforth, as he valued his life, to come near either the castle or the village on the shore of the loch. Taking advantage of this, George now pretended that he had resolved to go to France, and he came to the said village for two reasons ; one was to let his mother and brother know of this decision of his; the other was to ask the queen to give him letters of recommendation and some assistance. Both the laird and his mother were much annoyed at this resolution, for they did not wish to lose George entirely. They advised him to go to live with Moray, but this he absolutely refused to do. Hereupon the lady of Lochleven asked the queen to write a letter commanding George to obey them in this matter, which letter she offered to send. The queen did so, and added several particulars of news, expressed in covert terms, urging him especially to hasten on the business before his sister-in-law should be astir again. George Douglas sent an answer, and then worked so successfully that by the intercession of one of his sisters William Douglas was recalled into the house on the last day of April. As soon as he was reinstated in his former charge, he began to make every preparation for the day which had been fixed, namely, the 2d of May. Taking advantage of the opportunity afforded by the expulsion of William, George came very often to the village to talk and discuss matters with his brother; so that this misfortune contributed greatly to the renewal of the prospect of the success of the enterprise in all that was necessary, for it could not have been done so easily if William had remained in the house. His return was brought about

chiefly by the tears which he was continually shedding
for having been the cause of George being detected, but
which were attributed to his repentance for having consented to these practices, and his regret for having lost
the service of his master, which greatly helped his
return.

In the meantime the queen went one day along with
the laird to amuse herself upon the lake. On their return the servants of the house made a joke of the queen's
reported escape, at that time current. They pretended
to storm the castle, and to attack some persons who were
on the side of the loch in company with the old lady of
Lochleven. These latter, standing on the land, threw
things at the people in the boats. But the sport ended
badly to two of the chief keepers, spies and enemies,
whom the queen had in the house. The person who
had the principal charge in the establishment, and who
bore her as much ill-will as either of the two others,
took up a long harquebus, which he thought to be charged
only with paper, and fired it right at the crowd—somewhat large,—then, standing on the edge of the loch. Just
as if he had picked them out, he wounded these very
two persons, putting seven or eight pellets into the hip of
the one, and a large ball into the thigh of the other. On
this he became so frantic that he was going to kill himself. Hereupon the queen's surgeon was sent for, a man
very excellent in his profession, who ordered that his
patients should be put to bed, where he kept them as
long as was necessary. When George Douglas heard of
this accident, which in no small degree made his success
the easier, he and all the rest of his party exerted themselves to be ready at the day appointed, and provided
with all the necessary equipment.

According to their first plan it was intended that the

queen should leap from a wall which was in the garden,
of seven or eight feet in height, but she was afraid to
incur the risk. Three or four days beforehand she and
her two *femmes-de-chambre* pretended, as if in play, to
chase each other, all going wherever the first had gone,
and in this way they came to a wall in another quarter
of the house, equal in height to that which had to be
passed. Here one of her attendants (who already had
leapt) when the queen was on the top of the wall to leap
after her, became afraid of being hurt, but yet compelled
herself to leap, for she thought it a matter of duty, and
leapt accordingly. Although she was caught when half
over by one of the gentlemen of the household, yet she
seriously injured one of the joints of her foot, which were
very weak. The queen, fearing what might happen to herself if she leapt this wall (which had to be done), namely,
that she might injure herself so seriously that she would
be unable to escape from the castle, gave notice to those
of her party who were to be in waiting for her on the
other side of the loch, to the effect that if she should
happen thus suddenly to injure herself, in that case one
of her women who would remain in her chamber would
let them know by a signal, of fire, in order that
they should withdraw. This was intended more particularly for George and Lord Seton, who had a vessel
ready in which they might embark and find safety in
France.

When William Douglas saw how much the queen
feared this plan of leaping from the wall, he set
himself about finding some other way, at once easier
and less dangerous; and he proposed that she should go
out by the great gate of the gate-tower. With this
view (having received money for the purpose), he
invited the entire household to partake of a de-

jeuner on the second of May, to be given in that
part of the house which was furthest from that gate.
The queen and the laird both attended, in the presence
of whom, and of the whole company, William presented a
branch to her Majesty and to each person of the party,
calling himself "The Abbot of Unreason." He made
the queen swear and promise that for the remainder of
the day she would follow him wherever he went, and
then, having puzzled her Majesty, every one laughed at
him, as if he were drunk, or a very simpleton.

The queen remained in this part of the house during
the rest of the day, as well to detain the laird and
his wife there, as to avoid the suspicion which they
might have had if she had retired.

In the afternoon, she threw herself upon a bed,
letting it be known that she wished to rest, of which,
however, at that time, she had no great desire, although
she had not slept during the whole of the previous night.
While she was lying on the bed, the laird's wife was
close at hand, chatting with a woman who kept an
inn in the village, and who was telling her how on that
very day a great troop of men on horseback had passed
through the said village. Lord Seton was among them.
They said they were going to an Assise, which in the
language of that county, they call a Law Day, to
accompany James Hamilton of Ormiston. Also that
George Douglas, her brother-in-law, was staying in the
village, who was reputed to have come to take leave of
his mother before going into France. And, of a truth,
the lady of Lochleven had been to visit her son, and
had persuaded him, instead of going to France, to return
openly to the Earl of Moray. She had given him a
sum of money, and in order to confirm him in this
resolution, she had brought him letters from the queen,

which expressly commanded him to go to Glasgow with
the greatest expedition, this being the road agreed upon
between them.

Not only was the laird's wife astir that day, but the
two soldiers who had been wounded had now recovered
also.   One Draysdel also, who served within the house as
a second spy, came back on the same day from Edinburgh,
where he had been expressly sent by the queen to
receive a certain sum of money of which she had made
him a gift.   Before he set out she had asked him to
buy for her a piece of lawn, with a pattern of which
she had provided him, and on this pattern she had
written to her officers requesting them to detain Draysdel
as long as possible.   And this they did very successfully.

I must not forget two very remarkable circumstances.
The laird's mother began to talk with the queen about
the report of her escape, which was rife.   She assured
her Majesty that such an event would be the ruin of
her and her family, whereas in time some good understanding might be brought about between her Majesty
and Lord Moray, for the security of all.   The queen
answered frankly, that since she was detained there,
against her will and unjustly, she would do her best by
every means in her power, to escape from prison.   Yet
the more freely she spoke about it, the less did they
trust what she said, for they supposed that if there were
any truth in it she would have kept her own counsel.

The second incident was this.   When this lady was
walking in the garden with the queen, she saw a great
troop of men on horseback riding along the opposite side
of the loch, about whom she raised an outcry, and said
she would send off a messenger to ascertain who
e.   To divert her from this intention, her
pretended to be very angry with the Earl of

Moray, so that by passing from one subject to another, she kept the lady in conversation until supper-time, which was intentionally delayed until everything should be ready.

Shortly after the laird had conducted the queen into her own room, as he was looking from the window, he noticed that William Douglas was putting little pegs of wood into the chains and fixings by which the boats were fastened, one boat being excepted. This he did to prevent the queen from being followed. Seeing this, the laird spoke roughly to William, and called him a fool. The queen became alarmed as to what might follow, and pretending that she felt very unwell, she asked for some wine. No other person being in the room, the laird himself had to bring it, and in so doing, forgot what he had seen. And again, when he was at supper, he ordered the window to be shut, which according to custom was left open, in order that from time to time he might look out upon the loch and notice what might be coming from the village.

As George Douglas was taking leave of his mother, he sent to the queen by a maid of the household, who had accompanied his mother, a pearl in the shape of a pear, which her Majesty was in the habit of wearing in one of her ears. This was understood as a signal that all was ready. Along with it he sent a message to the effect that a boatman, who had found the pearl, wished to sell it to him, but that he having recognised it as her property, had sent it to her. At the same time he promised the queen that without fail he would set out for Glasgow that very evening, and would never return.

An hour before suppertime the queen retired into her own chamber. She put on a red kirtle belonging to one of her women, and over it she covered herself with

one of her own mantles. Then she went into the garden
to talk with the old lady, whence she could see the
people who were walking on the other side of the loch. *No, she couldn't.*

Everything being now ready the queen, who of set
purpose had caused the supper to be delayed until that
time, now ordered it to be served. When the supper
was finished, the laird (whose ordinary custom it was to
wait upon her at table) went to sup along with his wife
and the rest of his household, in a hall on the ground
storey. A person called Draisdel, who had the chief
charge in the establishment, and who generally remained
in the queen's room to keep her safe, went out along
with the laird, and amused himself by playing at hand-
ball.

In order to free herself from the two young girls,
who remained with her, her Majesty in the meantime
went into an upper room, above her own, occupied by
her surgeon, on the plea that she wished to say her
prayers ; and, indeed, she did pray very devoutly, recommending herself to God, who then showed His pity
and care for her. In this room she left her mantle,
and having put on a hood such as is worn by the
countrywomen of the district, she made one of her
domestics, who was to accompany her, dress herself in
the same fashion. The other *femme-de-chambre* remained with the two young girls to amuse them, for
they had become very inquisitive as to the cause of
the queen's lengthened absence.

While the laird was at supper, William Douglas, as he
was handing him his drink, secretly removed the key of
the great gate, which lay on the table before him. He
ntly gave notice of this to the queen, in order that
d come downstairs instantaneously ; and im-
y afterwards as he came out of the door he gave

the sign to the young woman who was to accompany her
Majesty, as she was looking towards the window.   This
being understood, the queen came down forthwith; but
as she was at the bottom of the steps she noticed that
several of the servants of the household were passing backwards and forwards in the court, which induced her to
stand for some time near the door of the stairs.   At last,
however, in the sight of the whole of them, she crossed
the courtyard, and having gone out by the great gate,
William Douglas locked it with the key and threw it
into a cannon planted near at hand.   The queen and her
femme-de-chambre had stood for some time close to the
wall, fearing that they would be seen from the windows
of the house ; but at length they got into the vessel, and
the queen laid herself down under the boatman's seat.
She had been advised to do this, partly to escape notice,
partly to escape being hit, if a cannon shot should be
sent after her.   Several washerwomen and other domestics were amusing themselves in a garden near the loch
when her Majesty got into the boat.   One of the washerwomen even recognised her, and made a sign to William
Douglas that she was aware of it, but William called out
to her aloud, by name, telling her to hold her tongue.

As the boat was nearing the other side William saw
one of George's servants, but failed to recognise him, as
he was armed.   Apprehending some fraud, he hesitated
to come nearer the shore ; at length, however, the servant
having spoken, he landed, and then her Majesty
was met and welcomed by George Douglas and John
Beton, who had broken into the laird's stables and seized
his best horses.

Being mounted as best she might, the queen would not
set off until she had seen William Douglas on horseback

also—he who had hazarded so much for her release. She left her *femme-de-chambre* behind her, but with directions that she should follow her as soon as she could have an outfit.

Two miles off she met Lord Seton and the Laird of Riccarton, with their followers, accompanied by whom she crossed an arm of the sea called Queensferry, where every arrangement for the purpose had been made by Lord Seton. About midnight she reached Niddry, one of the houses belonging to the same Lord Seton, where she was very honourably received and feasted, as well as provided with dresses and all other necessaries befitting her sex and dignity. Thence she took the road to Hamilton, where she remained until the 13th of May 1568, collecting all the forces she could muster.

When the whole of the inhabitants of the village of Lochleven saw the queen ride past, they all blessed her and prayed for her safety. No one attempted to raise any hindrance; even the laird's uncle, who recognised her. A countryman promptly got into the boat by which the queen had crossed, and rowed back to Lochleven Castle, to let them know, by the same means, that she had escaped. But the discovery had already been made by the report of the girls already mentioned, who were left in the queen's chamber. Having gone up into the room above, and there finding her mantle, after having searched for her, they imagined that she had hidden herself for some purpose; so not finding her, went downstairs to tell the laird. But first they met Drysdel, of whom I have spoken above, and they told him that they could not find the queen and that they supposed she had escaped. Drysdel was amused at this, and said he would soon find her; he would give her leave to escape if she could. At one

moment he whistled, at another he cut capers.   But in
the midst of these scoffs arrived the countryman with the
boat, who battered at the gate and cried out that he had
seen the queen pass through the village.

When the laird was told of this he fell into such a
transport of frenzy that he drew his dagger to stab himself, but was prevented by the attendants.   As he had no
hope of being able to recapture the queen, who at that
time was more than six miles distant, he sent off a messenger to the Earl of Moray to let him know of this
misadventure.

The Earl of Moray at that time was at Glasgow.
When he heard of the queen's escape he was marvellously
astonished.   His first intention was to fall back upon
Stirling; but when he considered that if he retreated
ever so little he would discourage all his party and would
encourage his enemies, he resolved to remain at Glasgow.
Glasgow is only eight miles distant from Hamilton.

During the queen's stay at Hamilton, many difficulties
arose among the lords and the other leading men of her
Court.   In the opinion of many it was inexpedient that
she should remain in the hands of the Hamiltons.   Not
only was the personal safety of her Majesty compromised
hereby, but further, many persons who were at enmity
with that house refused to join her.   Hereupon it was
decided that she should retire to Dumbarton, where
everyone could have free access to her.   Thus it came to
pass that on the 13th May the queen set out for Dumbarton, accompanied by the Earls of Argyll, Casselis,
Eglinton, and Rothes, by Claud Hamilton, son of the
Duke of Chastelherault, who commanded the vanguard;
the Lords Seton, Fleming, Somerville,.Yester, Borthwick,
Levingston, Herries, Maxwell, Sanquhar, Boyd, and Ross;
the Lairds of Lochinvar, Bas, Wartiton, Dalhousey,

Roslin, Sir James Hamilton, and many others. It was expected that shortly afterwards they would have been joined by the troops assembled in the north, by the Earl of Huntley and Lord Oliphant, whose march however was somewhat interrupted by an armed body of the Forbes men, enemies of the house of Huntley, who had risen on the side of the Regent. Of his party were the Earls of Morton, Mar, Glencarne, Monteith, the Master of Graham ; the Lords of Hume, Lyndsay, Ruthven, Semple, Ogiltree, and Cathcart ; the Lairds of Bargony, Blacquham, Drumlanrig, Sesford, Lus, Buchannan, Tullibardin, Pitcur, Grange, Lochlevin, Ledington, and Sir James Balfour.

The two armies marched the one against the other. Some troops were detached from the Regent's army, and were placed in ambush in certain old houses by the side of the narrow road along which the queen's troops had to pass. In the meantime she had halted, along with some cavalry, upon a hill close at hand, rather to muster her forces than for any other reason. The battle began with a skirmish between some harquebusiers, who conducted themselves remarkably well on both sides ; although among the Regent's soldiers were a few Frenchmen, who had promised to come over to the queen's side as soon as the battle began. But as ill luck would have it, her soldiers advanced much further ahead than they were aware and charged them, and thus compelled them to act on the defensive. Lord Claud Hamilton now showed his courage and fidelity towards his princess, for he sustained the attack of his enemies until he found himself surrounded on all sides, and assailed on the rear by the Laird of Grange. The queen's main body of troops could not help them in time, either by the want of courage of its commanders or some other secret dealing on the part of the enemy. And so it came to pass that this poor young nobleman, seeing the whole force of his enemies made to bear upon him, was at last compelled to retreat; and falling back upon the main line he was so hotly pursued that in the end the rest of the army was put to flight. Of the surname of Hamilton fourteen were killed; and Lords Seton and Ross and Sir James Hamilton were taken prisoners. On the Regent's side Lord Hume was wounded in the face and in one of his legs, and Lord Ogilvy was wounded on the neck by Lord Herries.

It should not be forgotten that, at the time when the queen was leaving Hamilton the Regent's party had decided to retreat; in fact, many of them had already booted themselves for that purpose. Then the old Lord Semple, eighty years of age or thereabouts, a Catholic in religion, but very turbulent, came to point out to them how seriously they would injure their own interests if they fled before the queen instead of showing themselves on the field; that instead of fortifying themselves in ruinous old hovels, they might meet and brave their enemies, without being compelled to come to a battle; and that they still had the city of Glasgow as a place of refuge, in which they would be perfectly safe. Again, if the queen's forces did not pass along the road on which these old huts were situated, but took the direct route to Dumbarton, then they could attack them in the rear, or at the least escape the disgrace of having failed to show themselves on the field. Thus it was that they gained this signal victory over the queen's party.

On the regent's side was a gentleman from the Highlands, named Macfarlane, at the head of two hundred men, of his own friends and relations, who was wild to fight. When the battle was over, in memory of this piece of service, his life was saved by the Earl of Moray at the request of his wife, this Macfarlane having been charged with many crimes.

The road which the queen took after the loss of this battle to reach England.

How she drank some sour milk in the house of a poor man.

How she borrowed some linen.

How she caused her head to be shaved.

How she was twenty-four hours without eating or drinking.

How the Laird of Lochinvar gave her some clothes and a hood.

When the queen had crossed the sea and was getting out of the boat she fell to the ground, which many persons accepted as an augury of good success, interpreting it according to the common form, to mean that she had taken possession of England, to which she laid claim as of right. She arrived at a small hamlet where supper was being prepared. Lord Herries sent a message to the Laird of Curwen, who was a friend of his, to the effect that he had arrived in England, and had brought with him a young heiress, whom he had carried off in the hope of causing her to marry Curwen's son; Lord Herries asked therefore that he might be received in the laird's house. The answer which was returned stated that the laird was in London; but the house was offered by one of the laird's principal servants, amongst whom was a Frenchman, who recognised her Majesty as soon as she had crossed the threshold, and remarked to Lord Fleming that he had formerly seen the queen in better plight than now. In consequence, the report hereupon got abroad, and well nigh four hundred horsemen arrived next morning. Seeing that she was discovered her Majesty thought it prudent to let it be known that she had come in reliance upon the promise of the Queen of England, who was immediately apprised of her arrival. She was conducted from that place by the gentlemen of the neighbourhood. A dress of black cloth was made for her there, which she got on credit, along with certain other stuffs for some of her people at Carlisle, where she was well received by the inhabitants of the town, and by Mr Lauder, the deputy of the same for Lord Scrope, who was very urgent with her Majesty to lodge in the Castle, which she did. Lord Claude visited her there, and many others of her subjects. The Earl of Northumberland arrived there, bringing with him a commission by which the council at York ordered Lauder to deliver over the queen to the earl. Hearing of this, and having been warned not to leave the castle lest she should be carried off by force, her Majesty induced Lauder to go to the Queen of England with all possible diligence, in order to ascertain her intention, whereupon Lord Scrope and Mr Knolles were despatched with all speed. To a certain extent the Earl of Northumberland was the queen's enemy, not only by reason of the Countess of Lennox, with whom he was on very intimate terms, but on account also of fifteen thousand ducats sent by the Pope to her Majesty, of which the earl kept possession under the pretext that the ship had come to land a wreck in the port of Tynemouth, which the earl had in his keeping.

Before fighting her last battle, her Majesty, in order to provide against the disasters which might arise, sent one of her gentleman servants, John Beton, to the queen of England. He carried with him a ring having in it a diamond in the shape of a rock, which the queen had

formerly received from Queen Elizabeth in return for a
diamond heart. Beton was to inform the Queen of England that his mistress had escaped from Lochleven, and
that if she found herself hard pressed by her subjects,
her determination was to take refuge in England and to
ask her aid. Mary reminded her of the promise formerly made when the ring was sent, which was to the
express effect that whenever, and as often as, her Majesty
had need of her help she would send this ring back to
her as "a token" that she should either come in person to
help her, or else send it. Elizabeth herself gave the confirmation of this to Beton, assuring him that the queen
should be heartily welcome, and that she should have
the best possible reception and treatment.

Upon this assurance her Majesty came into England,
as we have said already, and sent the Lords Fleming and
Herries to inform Queen Elizabeth that she had arrived
in her realm, and that her chief reason for doing so was
that she might receive that support against her rebels
which had been promised. She asked permission in the
meantime to come to London to visit the queen, her
good sister, which, however, was not thought good.

Her Majesty was still detained at Carlisle, and Mr
Middlemore was sent there to her on his way to Scotland. The letters of credit which he brought with him
requested her to bring about some good pacification, by
means of which her friends, who at that time were
the stronger of the two in the field, should lay down
their arms. If she would do this, the Queen of England
undertook to compel the rebels to do the same. But
her Majesty, who never neglected any proposal which
tended to the quiet of her kingdom, having satisfied this
article, was duped. For, instead of this threatened
prohibition being put into force, it came about that all

those persons who had befriended her and done their duty towards her as faithful subjects during her flight, were ruined and persecuted to the death. Some were executed, irregularly, as was a poor man (drunk), who was cut into four quarters because he had served as a guide to her Majesty, an act of humanity due to one's enemies. Another, named Moor, who one night permitted the queen to sit at his hearth in his poor cottage (he could not do otherwise, for her party was the stronger) was hanged and his house burnt down; an act of execrable and unprecedented cruelty.

After the queen had remained at Carlisle for about three weeks or a month, a company of one hundred and fifty soldiers, who had been serving at Berwick, were sent over to her ("old soldiers," as we say in France), under the command of Captain Read. They came under the pretext of guarding her against her own subjects, and to this effect they quoted the promise of the Queen of England.

About this time Queen Elizabeth sent a little box a foot and a half square, which contained seven yards of taffeta, and as many of satin, some lawn, and a few shoes of black velvet, to set her up, having heard that she had brought nothing with her from Scotland. Her Majesty lived there for a long time at her own personal expenses, and also paid those of the English nobles, especially Mr Knooles, who had been sent to her.

At length, when it was determined that the Queen of Scotland should be retained, her removal was decided on by the Queen of England, by whose orders she was transferred from Carlisle to Bowton, which was further inland. This change was against her will, and she declared publicly that it was done by force, and against the promise of the Queen of England, before whom she desired to appear, so that the matters might be more fully sifted. And hereupon she demanded an Act, and made protestations before the bailiffs and the chief officers of the town. All this notwithstanding, about the end of July she was taken to Bowton, where she remained for five months, or thereabouts. This period was spent in negotiations, as well to pacify affairs in Scotland, and for the same purpose in England, between the commissioners and deputies of the two queens and the deputies of the Scottish rebels.

[Here should be inserted the discourse of the Bishop of Ross upon what passed with the said commissioners, and of the marriage of the Duke of Norfolk, and of his trial and death, which the book was about.]

Upon the proposal of her Majesty's marriage with the said duke, she sent certain separate articles to the chief members of the council of England, which was held partly that greater security might be given to the negotiation. She also specially protested that she had no desire to listen to this proposal unless the Queen of England would sanction it as agreeable to them. This was promised in the said conferences by the persons most intimate with the queen, as appears by the letters written and signed by their hands.

The letters may be here inserted.

Lethington being in Scotland, saw that the scales had turned from the side to which he had trusted the most, and that it was no longer in his power to hold the middle course, as he had intended, so as always to keep matters in the balance. He now began to traffic for the queen's return into Scotland, and was one of the

most active in the advancement of the duke's marriage.
On the other side, this bastard Earl of Moray (who, in
speaking of Lethington, called him "the necessary evil"),
presuming that his chief drift was always to have everything in his own hands, looked out for some means of
getting rid of him. To effect this he one day caused one
of the retainers of the Earl of Lennox to accuse Lethington in full council of the murder of the late king, and
caused him to be confined to his house, under the form
of obeying the law. Lethington could not refuse to do
this, and thus his design of getting quit of him was
skilfully . . . mischief. Hereupon things began to grow
very bitter between them on both sides, and Lethington,
seeing that his life was in immediate danger, began, with
increased activity, to organise a party for his own security. Thinking that he could not do this more effectually
than under the authority of the queen, he planned her
restoration. He began to negotiate with every member
of her party. He secured as allies the laird of Grange
and others, his friends, and being a man of skill and cunning, and having gained the Castle of Edinburgh, which
was held by Grange, he advanced himself thereby.

The siege of the castle.

The abode of the English.

Du Croc and Verac sent by the King of France.

Service of silver for M. de Fleming.

M. de Seton and the brother of the laird of Grange.

The surrender of those who were in the said castle and
their adherents outside.

The Earl of Moray, who, along with Lethington, had
pretended to approve of the duke's marriage, began to
play a double game, and afterwards discovered it to the
Queen of England.

AFTER THE DUKE'S DEATH.

The Earl of Shrewsbury, on the part of the Queen of England, informed the Queen of Scotland that his mistress had been put to some trouble on her account by reason of many addresses and remonstrances which had been sent to her, he said, by various princes from several quarters of Christendom, especially from France, urging the queen to put the Queen of Scotland to death, mainly upon the ground that she was the pillar and chief hope for the re-establishment of the Papistical religion in this island. Consequently, the queen was greatly indebted to the Queen of England for the act of grace which she had thus done her.

Her Majesty asked to see this address, which was refused. Hereupon she declared that, so far from wishing to reject this title which had been given to her of being the hope and defender of the Catholic religion, on the contrary, she accepted it most joyfully and willingly. As to the remainder, she, Mary, was a sovereign queen, and as such could neither receive nor acknowledge any act of grace from any living person whomsoever. She therefore begged the Earl not to use any such terms, for what she had done she could do lawfully. As for the Duke, since the treatment which he had received had been on her account, she was bound to do what she had done for his deliverance, and could she have done more, she would have done it to deliver him, for she had always continued to regard him as betrothed to her, and, as it were, her assured husband.

The journey of M. de Burghley to Chatsworth.

APPENDIX I.

REPORT upon the State of Scotland during the reign of
Queen Mary, written in A.D. 1594, and sent to
Pope Clement the Eighth by the Jesuit Priests in
Scotland.[1]

IN the year 1560 heresy for the first time took public
possession of the realm of Scotland, in which, however,
it had been making secret progress for some years previously. It was introduced by the Scottish merchants,
who traded with the Germans, among whom the Lutheran
heresy was rife. It was greatly forwarded in its progress at the beginning by the help of George Wichard, a
Scotchman, who for long had been trained in Luther's
school. He was a man of considerable intelligence and
of good family, who, by the pretence of a holy life, contrived in a very short time to poison the minds not only
of many of the common people, but even of the nobles
also. When this was discovered (although it was then
too late), he was apprehended; and as he clung obsti-
nately to his heresy, he was condemned to be burnt.
From this time his followers began to be punished; for
so zealous was James the Fifth, at that time King of
Scotland, in the cause of religion, that he would not
permit heretics to remain anywhere within his realm.
As long as he lived it was impossible, therefore, for
heresy to strike its roots deep into the soil of Scotland;
and for this reason these heretics used every effort to

[1] Translated from the early Latin copy in the Barberini MS.,
xxxii. 210 (1197).

bring about the death of this most worthy prince. At length they accomplished their design by poison, as is very currently reported.

King James left a daughter named Mary, who afterwards was put to death in England in consequence of her adherence to the Catholic faith. The child was scarce seven days old at the time of her father's decease in 1542. He left the government of the realm to his wife, Mary of Lorraine. Cardinal Beton, Archbishop of St Andrews, the Primate of Scotland, had the care of the child in conjunction with the principal members of the nobility, by whose advice he was to regulate his own conduct. But upon the king's death James Hamilton, Earl of Arran (the next heir to the kingdom after the queen), took possession of its government as due to himself by right of inheritance, in which claim he was supported by all the heretics, and not a few of the other members of the realm. A certain monk, brother William by name, craftily contrived to ingratiate himself in Arran's favour; who, even when he was wearing his habit, had imbibed all Luther's heresies, which he gradually instilled into Arran's mind. Thus matters went on, until this William publicly spoke to the people from the pulpit against indulgences. At that time the whole realm might very easily have been overrun with heresy had not the most illustrious Cardinal Beton, a man of great talent and prudence, raised himself up as a bulwark in defence of the house of God.

Thus Scotland became divided into two factions; one was supported by the English and the heretics, whose design it was that a marriage should take place in due time between Edward, King Henry's son, and Mary, the heiress of the Scottish crown—an arrangement which would unite these two realms into one kingdom under

one head. The other party, which consisted of the
French and the Catholics, aimed at a marriage between
the young queen and Francis, the son of Henry, King
of France.

In the meantime the most illustrious Cardinal Grimani[1] was sent into Scotland by Pope Paul the Third
to prevent the formation of a treaty between the Scots
and the English heretics, which he effected by his
prudence and influence, in doing which he received no
little help from Cardinal Beton. Under the same influence the Earl of Arran, who seemed to be the leader
of the opposite faction, joined the French party; to
confirm him in which the king made a grant to him of
the duchy of Châtelherault, near Poitiers.

Although the Earl of Arran was the governor of the
realm, everything was really done by the direction of
Cardinal Beton. The heretics considered this to be
intolerable. Their number was considerable, but they
kept themselves secret. The politicals, who wished to
see the queen married to King Edward, made common
cause with them. Both these parties strained every
nerve that the individual whom they well knew to be
the author of this better line of policy should be removed out of the way either by secret treachery or open
violence. They first tried the latter plan; but when
this did not succeed, they had recourse to fraud and
treachery. They corrupted one of his servants, a man
who was already a heretic (a fact, however, of which the
cardinal was ignorant), who admitted the conspirators
into the castle of St Andrews, which is the archbishop's
see and a place of very considerable strength. In 1546
these cruel murderers slaughtered this excellent prelate,

[1] Marino Grimani, Patriarch of Aquilea, and Cardinal S. Vitalis tit.
Vestinæ. He died in 1546. See Ciaconius, ii. 1464.

H

a man who deserved well of his country. They then began to proclaim as a victory an event whence sprang wars and other calamities, which have no immediate connection with religion.

We ought not to forget to remark that out of the large number of those persons who either laid their sacrilegious hands upon the cardinal, or planned his death, only one is said to have escaped the punishment due to this terrible crime. One man alone is said to have been an exception, and to have survived for many years. This statement, however, appears doubtful when we consider that he showed no tokens of repentance sufficient to warrant the belief that he died a better death than the others.

On the death of Cardinal Beton religion appears to have declined rapidly; but inasmuch as James Hamilton, Earl of Arran, was at this time on the French side, the Catholics kept their ground. On the death of Henry the Eighth in 1547, the king's uncle, the Duke of Somerset, assumed the government of the realm. Cruel wars broke out between the Scots and the English, embittered by the fact that a marriage between the Dauphin Francis and Queen Mary, to the exclusion of Edward, was planned between the King of France and the chief of the Scottish nobility. Although the latter had as yet scarcely reached her fifth year, she was conveyed into France.

Since war is always a period of license, so it came to pass that heresy now made daily inroads; nor did religion prosper so long as James Hamilton, Earl of Arran, could act as governor of Scotland. But his administration came to an end in A.D. 1553 when Queen Mary attained her majority, and her mother, Mary of Lorraine, was appointed to the regency of Scotland. Cer-

tainly she was a prudent woman, but she did not
exercise sufficient caution so as to be on the watch
against the politicians, who were in great numbers in
that kingdom. These persons managed their affairs so
well that they contrived to gain such a footing in her
court as gave them the management of almost all her
affairs. One of the devices which they especially employed was this :—they urged the queen to adopt such
plans as were apparently for her good, but which, at
the same time, were sure to earn for her no small share
of the ill-will and hatred not only of the common
people, but also of the nobility. Thus it came to pass
that the heretics had it in their power to do almost anything they pleased without being questioned for it.
There were also many persons who were seduced by the
love of novelty to abandon the religion of their ancestors,
and of these the number was daily on the increase, while
many others were greedy after the possessions of the
Church. Meetings were held by night everywhere in
the towns.

When these disorders came to the knowledge as well
of the prelates of the realm as of the queen herself, they
attempted to apply the necessary remedies, which, however, did not meet the urgency of the case. It came to
pass, therefore, that, as no fitting attempt had been made
to crush it, within a very short space of time the heresy
which had formerly glided along in secret now stalked
forth in public, and penetrated into every province of
the kingdom. At this time, as Henry, King of France,
was alive, and Mary, Queen of Scotland, was the wife of
the Dauphin of France, the insurgents did not venture
to make any open outbreak. In the year 1560, however,
a certain Scottish priest named John Knox, who some
considerable time before had been outlawed upon the

charge of incest and other very grievous accusations, returned home from Geneva at the request of the heretics. He had a cunning and crafty wit, and was admirably fitted for exciting the mob to sedition.

But before these heretics broke out into open warfare, they decided among themselves that certain persons of their faction should visit the chief of the Scottish nobility in order to ascertain their feelings and dispositions. For this purpose they selected the most prudent and the most influential. This was partly for the sake of civility and courtesy, partly for other reasons. Finding, as they did, that there were many of their way of thinking, in the month of May, A.D. 1560, this party took up arms openly under the leadership of James Stuart, base-born son of James the Fifth, and the Earl of Argyll. A very large body of men assembled with great speed, which took the name of "The Congregation," since it had congregated together for the purpose of wrecking the Catholic churches. Like crazy men, these persons went over the whole realm, conducting themselves as if possessed by furies ; and they began to tear down the monasteries (of which there were many in the realm), and to level them with the ground. Scarce any one opposed them. The church of the Carthusians at Perth was the first building on which they laid their sacrilegious hands. It had been founded by King James the First, and was remarkable for its costly and magnificent architecture. They took John Knox along with them, a great snare of the devil, who could easily persuade the ignorant crowd to do anything he pleased. He was always repeating to the mob his advice to pull the monasteries down to the ground, "for (said he) if you leave the nests standing the old birds are sure to come back to them."

While this sudden outbreak was in progress the queen
dowager summoned the Scottish nobility to come to her.
But they did not supply her with the aid which they
might have done; for the more powerful of their number
either felt very cold towards her or were much estranged
from her. Yet she had about three thousand excellent
French soldiers, the chief of whom was the Sieur de
Martigues. Before long she had raised about seven or
eight thousand Scottish troops. She was also daily
joined by several of the barons, so that her army by
degrees became more numerous and more powerful than
that of the heretics. All parties now anxiously awaited
the issue of a battle. But while the result hung in the
balance, and the two armies were within a few miles of
each other at Cupar in Fife, certain politicians dissuaded
them from coming to blows. The prospect of a battle
having thus been entirely removed the queen's troops
began to drop off little by little, until she was at last
constrained to betake herself into Edinburgh Castle,
which she did with very great sorrow and regret. These
feelings were considerably increased when she saw with
what contempt and violence the churches, and indeed
whatever was sacred, were treated by the heretics. But
the French troops together with some of the Scottish
nobility threw themselves into the town of Leith, which
is about one mile distant from Edinburgh. Its position
is naturally strong, and as it is a seaport it could supply
its garrison with fish. From Leith several of the neighbouring towns received a stock of provisions.

In the meantime the army of the heretics committed
whatever havoc it pleased without interruption, and
profaned not only churches but whatever was sacred.
As yet, however, none of them had ventured into the
northern parts of Scotland, for they were restrained by

fear of the Earl of Huntley. This nobleman was a Catholic, and so powerful was he that if he had pleased he might have curbed any hostile attempt on the part of the heretics. But he was by no means on friendly terms with the queen dowager, from whom not long before he had received some slight, of the nature of which I am ignorant. From him, therefore, she received neither advice nor assistance. The barons and the rest of the nobility in the other districts of Scotland would willingly have risked their lives in defence of their religion; but among the principal men there was not one who would stand forward as their leader in the warfare. Thus it came to pass that whereas the Catholics were scattered up and down over the entire realm, and the heretics were collected into one body, the latter possessed the greater freedom of action.

The Catholic cause was still further weakened by the return into Scotland of James Hamilton, the eldest son of the Duke of Châtelherault. He had been induced to leave France, where he had been treated with the greatest honour, by the wiles of the Queen of England, who had promised to marry him. This gave considerable confidence to the heretics of Scotland, for they believed that just as their matrimonial alliance would lead to the union of the two kingdoms, so it would lead to the severance of Scotland from France, along with which would perish all hope for the Scottish Catholics, whose existence depended upon the assistance of France. James Hamilton joined the Earl of Moray, so these two persons were at the head of the entire movement.

Although literature is generally silent during the clash of arms, yet upon the present occasion it was not so. Catholic preachers came forward who not only refuted the errors of the heretics with great spirit from the pulpit, but also kept the people to their duty when they were dropping away ; and this they did by the publication of many works in the Scottish language. Among them was the Abbot of Crossraguel,[1] who wrote an admirable treatise upon the authority of General Councils and the duty of retaining the ancient faith. Ninian Winzett[2] produced a volume of questions, touching upon every religious subject, which all but silenced the ringleaders of the heretics. Sir David "Sewrotius"[3] has left behind him a most accurate work upon the Sacrifice of the Mass. There were also Sir John Watson,[4] Sir John Black,[5] and others.

At this time there was in Scotland a considerable number of scholars, well versed not only in scholastic theology but in the works of the Fathers, and indeed in every department of antiquity. These men held frequent public disputations with the heretical ministers, especially in the celebrated University of Aberdeen, and in Edinburgh, which is the abode of royalty. By this means many persons were kept safe in the Catholic faith ; for, even in the opinion of persons who were only moderately versed in such matters, the heretics were always defeated in discussions of this nature. It was impossible that a better mode of proceeding could be followed at a time when everything was done by violence and arms. But there is one thing which ought not to be passed

[1] This was Quintin Kennedy. See Knox, Hist., ii. 352; Keith, iii. 405.

[2] Concerning Ninian Wyngate and his controversial writings, see Keith, iii. 33, 412.

[3] Such is the reading of the manuscript, apparently incorrect.

[4] I do not find any trace of this theologian in Tanner, nor in any of the biographical works which I have consulted.

[5] John Black, a Dominican, concerning whose disputation with Willock, see Keith iii. 32.

over unnoticed, and it is this. There was not a single Scottish bishop, nor indeed any one individual of any reputation either for prudence or learning, who fell away from the Catholic religion ; whereas the men who sowed the seeds of heresy within this realm were almost all of them persons of no weight and unlearned monks. These latter, in order to have carnal liberty (one of the chief considerations in Calvin's gospel), thought it was one of the most delightful things possible to cast off the yoke of religion. They contrived to gain great popularity with the mob by assuring them (as they did most assiduously) that henceforth no tithes were to be paid ; by which single argument they drew over more persons into their way of thinking than by all the others.

In the meantime the Earl of Moray, who was carrying on his design upon the crown by means of this outbreak, invested the Calvinistic ministers with all the authority which he possibly could give them, a procedure in which he was followed by all the other nobles of the kingdom ; so that at length this class of men who were mean and vile in themselves began to be in some honour. Churchmen were seized and were compelled to redeem themselves by money. Others everywhere betook themselves to places of safety ; while there were some who went to France, Flanders, and such other Catholic states as were near at hand, and gladly endured banishment for the sake of God.

As soon as intelligence of the distracted state of affairs in Scotland had reached France a very powerful fleet was forthwith fitted out, the commander of which was M. D'Aumale, which was to sail as soon as possible. The French and Scots who were in the town of Leith, in the meantime strengthened their fortifications day by day. The Bishop of Amiens was within the garrison

Pellevé, now a cardinal of the Holy Roman Church,[1] as was also the most Reverend Archbishop of Glasgow, who at the present time is living in exile;[2] a man who from his early years has gone through much suffering in his defence of the Catholic religion. They prepared to endure the siege, and were resolved to hold out until reinforcements should arrive from France. The Earls of Moray and Arran having decided upon besieging the town, began to collect troops from all sides. But it soon became clear to many persons that under the pretext of religion open war was being waged against the King of France, whose subjects these men really were. The exhortations of the two earls were therefore disregarded. The rest took refuge with the Queen of England; who being well aware of the agreement into which the Prince of Condé, the Admiral [Coligny], and the other French heretics had entered at the beginning with the Scottish rebels, and having received hostages from them, sent them a reinforcement of six thousand soldiers.

When the siege had actually begun the Catholics had no difficulty in defending the town, and they occasioned no small loss to the besiegers by the sallies which they made among them. But when it had lasted for about nine months they received intelligence of the death of Francis, King of France and Scotland; whereupon they surrendered upon honourable conditions. About the same time Mary of Lorraine, queen [dowager] of Scotland, worn out with sorrow and sickness, died in Edinburgh Castle. The Catholics, having now lost all hope of the arrival of a fleet from France, began to centre

---

[1] As he died in 1594 this portion of the narrative must have been written before that year, or in it at the latest. See Ciaconius, ii. 1708.

[2] He survived until 24th April 1603. See Keith, Scot. Bishops, p. 260.

their whole trust in Queen Mary, for they thought that if this young woman (for she had scarce reached her twentieth year) were to marry some powerful sovereign she could easily reduce these heretics to obedience. It had become an impossibility for the Catholics to contend any longer upon fair terms with the heretics, by whom they were far outnumbered. Learned men, indeed, were not wanting who could easily refute the false superstitions of Calvin, yet the minds of the nobles were so fully preoccupied with these delusions that no place was left for an appeal to reason or argument. This was the case especially with these persons who had the chief management of affairs, and who traded upon the introduction of the new creed as the best means of forwarding their own interests.

In the meantime new disturbances were daily breaking out in France. The Princes of Lorraine, of which family was the Queen of Scotland, and upon whom she depended, after having carefully discussed the question on all sides, at length came to the decision that it was best that she should return home. The Earl of Moray, who was the author of all the ills of Scotland, as soon as he had been informed of this decision by the French heretics, thought that it was for his interest to go into France in order that he might there establish his innocence. Taking the road through England with a large retinue of Scots, he was received by the queen mother [of France] with great honour, as if he had deserved well of that kingdom. The princes of the house [of Lorraine thought it was expedient to dissemble. After many conferences Moray also approved of the decision which ruled that it would be best for the queen to return into Scotland, which, as he perceived, was much the same as giving the sheep over to the wolf.

It has already been remarked that the queen was not yet twenty years old. She took no troops with her into Scotland; she had neither money nor any other way of making head against the fury of the Scots. The Princes of Lorraine, being very apprehensive that she might possibly be driven out of her own realm, at last came to the following arrangement. The Earls of Arran and Huntley were the two most powerful of the nobility in the kingdom; they were united by kindred and friendship, and to their families the realm of Scotland descended by hereditary right after the queen. It might be apprehended, therefore, that these two families would coalesce, and either make the queen prisoner or expel her from her throne. The wisest plan, therefore, in the opinion of the Princes of Lorraine, would be for the queen to follow the advice of the Earl of Moray, who was not only her brother, but was also a man of considerable influence among the nobility of the realm, and (what was the principal consideration) they thought him to be a person who would make no pretension of succeeding to the kingdom. Hence it was that the power of the Earls of Arran and Huntley gave no cause of anxiety to the queen, for the thoughts of these noblemen were directed rather to the protection of the State (to which, however, they rendered no great service) than to the interests of religion.

Her Majesty returned into Scotland in the year 1561, accompanied by the Dukes of Aumale, Elbeuf, the Great Prior of France, D'Anville, and many other noblemen. Nothing further was settled about religion than that it should be allowed to remain just as it was at the date of her return home until the meeting of Parliament, at which period the queen and the Princes of Lorraine imagined that the Catholic faith would be restored to its former condition. The Earl of Moray, however, and the other heretics contrived by their craft to prevent any such meeting from being held. The public services of religion were allowed only in the queen's chapel in Edinburgh, although the public exercise of the Catholic creed was retained in many parts of the north of Scotland.

Having by this time won the queen over to his own plans, the Earl of Moray continued to secure the highest honours for his own relations and the leading heretics in the kingdom, while he secretly persecuted the Catholics, but without doing it under the plea of religion. He weakened their influence, and drove them from the court, so that scarce any but heretics had any position near the queen. The Earl of Arran (who in the meantime had arrived in Scotland from France) having discovered that his marriage with the Queen of England was a complete failure, and that he had been cheated by her, being a man of no mental power, lost his reason, and continues to the present day in a state of madness, a lamentable spectacle to the world. Moray alone remained in the ascendant, and daily planned the steps by which he hoped to mount to greatness. The number of the Catholics declined in the same proportion, for the priests (who were the only persons who retained the people in the old faith) had now grown aged, and were broken down by their many calamities, and when they died there were no others to succeed them.

One thing alone troubled Moray, and seemed seriously to interrupt his success. The Catholic Earl of Huntley was of such considerable power and influence that as long as he survived Moray could not make any progress either towards obtaining the crown to which he aspired, or in establishing the Calvinistic heresy in Scotland. He therefore used every effort to rouse the queen's suspicions against Huntley's over-grown power, and he did this so effectually that upon the slightest possible grounds Huntley was declared to be a traitor and a rebel, and troops were marched against him as if he had been found guilty of such like crimes. Having received no reply [to his explanation] Huntley resolved upon leaving Scotland for a time, and had collected about five or six thousand men. But before he could bring together all his available force, Moray (who never permitted any favourable opportunity to escape him) unexpectedly attacked the earl with a very powerful body of men which he had mustered. Huntley's troops were dispersed, and he himself was killed in the battle. All his goods were forfeited, his eldest son was imprisoned in Dumbarton Castle, his second son was beheaded, and thus at length the entire family with its retainers was ruined. No greater wound could have been inflicted upon the realm. The queen scarcely knew what she ought to do; nor did she understand the full extent of the mischief until it was too late to apply a remedy. The power of the Catholics was hereby much weakened and reduced, so much so that heresy now made wide inroads even in the northern districts of Scotland. The only remedy which seemed to remain for all these evils was the marriage of the queen with some powerful Catholic prince, who could restore the exhausted energies of the Church in that realm. The effort was made to do this by all possible ways and means ; nor had the Earl of Moray any pretext for hindering such an arrangement. As yet it did not seem safe to put her Majesty to death, for the Duke of Châtelherault had four or five children, to whom belonged the right of succession to the throne in the event of the death of Queen Mary.

The watchful care of the Apostolic See did not cease

to occupy itself in regard to the interests of Scotland, for Pope Pius the Fourth sent a nuncio [1] thither to treat with the queen in such matters as related to the confirmation of the Catholic faith; but as at this time everything was arranged by the Earl of Moray, the nuncio could effect nothing. But Moray could not hinder the queen from deciding upon a second marriage, nor did she think it inexpedient to resolve upon selecting a foreign prince as her husband, and it was said that the choice might possibly fall upon her cousin, the Duke of Guise. Moray being thus forced to adopt some middle course, consented that she should marry, but that her husband should be a native of this island; for the earl saw that he would thus easily be able to retain the upper hand through the assistance of the Queen of England. There was no one, either in England nor Scotland, who seemed better adapted in every way to allure Queen Mary than Henry Stuart, son of the Earl of Lennox. He was descended from the royal families of both Scotland and England; he was remarkably handsome, and he was almost the tallest man in the isle of Britain. The queen was beset with reports about him; a correspondence was carried on between them on both sides; although he pretended to escape from England, yet in reality the whole affair was planned by the heretics. As soon as he arrived in Scotland the question of the marriage was discussed. Pope Pius the Fourth was requested to give a dispensation on account of their nearness of blood, which his Holiness willingly granted, and encouraged them to restore the Catholic religion in that realm. On the completion of the marriage, Darnley made open profession of that faith,

---

[1] This was Gaudanus, whose interesting report upon his mission has recently been discovered and printed.

in which he had been brought up from his childhood. In a short time he made himself an object of fear to the heretics, and drove from the realm certain persons of high rank who had begun to plot some new devices.

When Moray saw that Mary's marriage had been more prosperous than he had intended, his plans took a different direction. He had wit enough to perceive (for he was a man of considerable penetration) that if these leading men were constant in their designs and resolutions it would follow naturally enough that he himself would lose all his authority, that the Calvinistic heresy would come to naught, and that the Catholic religion would recover its former dignity. He exerted himself to the uttermost therefore to sow the seeds of discord between the queen and her husband, meaning thereby to alienate them from each other, and to bring the queen to trust herself (as she used to do formerly) to the guidance of him, the Earl of Moray, and his adherents. If they could not do this they decided upon murdering the king.

The queen at this time had become the mother of James the Sixth, who is now King of Scotland. They therefore waited upon Darnley, and explained to him at great length that nothing would be more acceptable to the nobles of the realm than that the Parliament of the kingdom should be assembled, and that he should be inaugurated as King of Scotland; that at the present time the queen strenuously hindered this plan, because she wished to keep him in subjection under her, and to reign alone; but that if he would follow their guidance they undertook that they would do what they proposed, whether the queen liked it or not. Darnley, who as yet knew nothing of the tricks of the heretics, lent a willing ear to their advice. The queen was made a prisoner, and placed under the keeping of armed soldiers, even in her own palace; a secretary of hers was murdered before her eyes, and she was treated with the greatest disrespect by these villains. Since all this was done by the authority of her husband, it might reasonably be thought that things had gone to such a length that the quarrel between the couple was irreconcilable. Nor were there wanting persons on the queen's side who accused her husband of having broken his faith and even been guilty of treason. In the meantime the rebels who had gone into England returned into Scotland. Although the queen speedily recovered her liberty by means of her husband, who bitterly regretted what he had done, yet there were not wanting those who again fanned the embers into a flame, and heaped their reproaches upon Darnley. Some of them attempted to persuade her that it was in her power to punish him as one of her subjects.

By reason of these sudden changes and domestic broils, the leading nobles were somewhat hindered in their plans for the restoration of religion. In the year 1565, Pius the Fourth, careful for the Apostolic See, sent into Scotland the Bishop of Montreale, afterwards a Cardinal of the Holy Roman Church, a man of great prudence and probity. His instructions directed him earnestly to treat with the queen about the restoration of the Catholic religion in Scotland and England, the more especially since both of these realms belonged to her by hereditary right, and Catholics were living in each of them. The Apostolic See offered to contribute a certain sum of money until the heretics should be driven out of both of them, and she should recover the inheritance, of which she was the rightful heir.

The Bishop of Montreale remained in Paris, while the

most reverend the Bishop of Dunblane[1] came into Scotland to convey to the queen the pope's message, along with the expression of his highest regard for her; which he did with singular prudence and good faith. The outline of what he said was this : that it would be an easy matter for her to purge both Scotland and England from heresy, and to restore the Catholic religion to its earlier dignity and splendour. There were Catholics, he said, who would willingly give all their resources and all their energies for such an object, and there were also foreign troops who would help as long as their help was needed. And when the war had begun, in order to avoid the necessity of referring to a locality so far distant as Rome was from the scene of action, he would see that a sum of money sufficient for carrying it on should be placed in the hands of the merchants at Antwerp or Paris. His concluding remark was to the effect that if the queen should neglect such an opportunity as the present, which had been thus offered to her from above, no similar opportunity would ever occur to her as long as she lived.

The queen's answer was to the following effect: that she could not stain her hands with the blood of her subjects; that as for the Queen of England, her sister, she, Elizabeth, regarded her as her lawful heir, and had already sent her some tokens of her love and goodwill. The queen of Scotland was, however, anxious that the apostolic nuncio should come into Scotland for certain political reasons, and had already prepared some ships to convey him thither; but the nuncio having been informed of the queen's sentiments by such persons as he had employed for the purpose, returned into Italy.

---

[1] "This bishop abandoned his diocese and the cares of the world in order to secure for himself greater mental repose, and joined the most holy order of the Carthusians." Note in the original.

I

At the same time, Henry Stuart, the queen's husband, was killed in Edinburgh during the night time, whereupon the Earl of Moray once more began to hold up his head; yet she had a son, one year old, in whose name the kingdom would be governed according to Moray's pleasure, in the event of the queen's death or imprisonment. Moray therefore armed everyone against her Majesty; he accused her (but falsely) of many crimes, for the purpose of making it appear that she was unfitted to govern a state. The chief accusation was this, that she had married the Earl of Bothwell not long after her husband's death. On this point, however, we may remark in passing, that the heretics themselves were the originators of this marriage, so much so, indeed, that they employed a certain amount of force to bring it about for the purpose of making her hateful to the whole realm, and to discredit her in the opinion of foreign nations. Earl Bothwell, who was a soldier, was one of the chief nobles of the realm, and who, although he was not a Catholic, yet permitted himself to be led as the queen pleased. The followers of the Earl of Moray collected their forces, and the queen began to do the like.

As the two parties seemed to be nearly balanced, Bothwell, who was a soldier and always prompt in action and experienced in military affairs, would willingly have crossed swords with his enemies; but the queen (who was unwilling to shed blood) sent a herald to the opposite party, proposing that some sort of a peace should be made upon just conditions, rather than that the best blood of the kingdom should be shed in a single day. Her opponents made oath, in their reply, that they had no evil design against the queen's person, but that they were seriously offended that she had valued her good name so lightly as to marry the Earl of Bothwell, and that a reconciliation could not be effected upon any other basis than the separation of Bothwell from her for a time until the recent wound should have been healed. To this proposal the queen would not in any way consent, and persuaded Bothwell to take refuge in some one of his castles. But as soon as the queen's troops were dispersed, the rebels forgot the oaths which they had taken, and having attacked her with their united forces, they carried her first into Edinburgh with the greatest disgrace and mockery, and then to Lochleven, where they imprisoned her in a very strong fortress.

The heretical ministers now attacked her with unusual bitterness; and after her marriage with Bothwell many even of the Catholics became estranged from her, so that not only heretics but even Catholics conspired against her. In the meantime Moray, who originated all these disturbances, left Scotland while they were in preparation, and went to Geneva under pretence of a feigned religion. He was afraid of the issue of the affair; and he dreaded Earl Bothwell so much that very seldom would he venture to trust himself with him in the same house. It had been predicted by witches (whom he frequently employed) that a Bothwell would kill him, which he understood to mean the earl. And this prophecy came true in the end; for he was actually murdered, not by the earl, but by one of the name of Bothwell.

Charles the Ninth, King of France, was much attached to Queen Mary. When he heard of her imprisonment he was exceedingly indignant, and having summoned the princes of the house of Lorraine, who were the queen's uncles, he ordered that every effort should be made for her speedy liberation. The Earl of Arran

was at this time in France, having left Scotland about
two years previously, being apprehensive that the old
feuds between him and the Earl of Lennox might revive
upon the queen's marriage with Lennox's son.   The Earl
of Moray was also in France at the same time, having
returned thither from Geneva, for he wished to profit by
his absence [from Scotland], whatever turn things might
then happen to take.   King Charles sent to Orleans,
where Moray was, to inform him of the state of affairs
in Scotland.   The earl pretended that he knew nothing
of what was going on there, and feigned great astonishment.   The king, having asked the opinion of many
persons who were well acquainted with Scottish affairs,
was by them answered plainly and honestly that no
easier way suggested itself to them than that the Earls
of Moray and Arran should be detained in France until
the liberation of the queen ; for it was certain that one
of them, or both of them, was at the bottom of all that
had been done in Scotland against the queen.   The king
highly approved of the advice, and gave instructions to
M. d'Aumale to invite the Earl of Arran to accompany
him to the chase, but at the same time to take very good
care that he should not escape out of his hands.   Other
persons, however, who thought themselves wiser, persuaded the king to consult Condé and the Admiral (to
whom Moray had already explained all his plans), and
ascertain their opinion.   When they were summoned by
the king they both began earnestly to oppose the project,
and to swear by all that was holy that as soon as Moray
should arrive in Scotland he would do his best to cause
the queen to be restored to liberty.   Of this the queen
mother and the princes of Lorraine were easily persuaded.

When the earls returned home many of the nobles of

the realm were assembled. The Earl of Arran, who wished to keep his word, was seized and thrown into the castle of Edinburgh ; Moray declared himself regent of the kingdom, and took upon himself to be protector of the baby James the Sixth. He wrote to France that he desired nothing more than that the queen should be set at liberty, but that to do so was impossible, so entirely were the hearts of everyone alienated from her. He was compelled, he said, by the nobles to take upon himself the administration of the realm. He was entirely under the influence of Condé and the Admiral, and was by them fully made acquainted with everything that the King of France attempted to do in Scotland ; and France itself was so disturbed that the king could not send the assistance which he wished to have done.

More diligent search was now made [in Scotland] after Catholics, especially priests, than had been done at any previous time. As there was now no barrier to arrest the fury of the ministers, they and their leader Knox (the calamity of Scotland) began to preach publicly from their pulpits that the election to the throne depended upon the people, and that they ought to elect the person who should seem the best adapted for the preservation and extension of religion. Then began Moray to proclaim far and wide what he had long been premeditating in his heart, namely, that he was the heir to the throne, and that he was born in lawful marriage. To prove this he attempted to produce witnesses who should affirm that in their presence King James the Fifth had married Moray's mother. But since as long as the queen was alive there could be no safety in such a project as this, the question of her death was now seriously debated, and it was decided by the earl and his privy council that she should be put out of the way. Circumstances arose from time to time which, by God's good providence, caused its postponement.

For long Moray had hidden his ambition under the disguise of religion, but now when his plans became visible to every one, many began to be estranged from him. The parties to whom belonged the right of succession to the crown after the queen's death, openly declared their enmity against him; and although they were heretics, they began to hate the Calvinistic ministers, because they encouraged Moray in his ambition. The queen's sad position excited the compassion of many. Various opinions were proposed by various persons; but at last, when the matter had been fully discussed on all sides, it was thought best that the queen should be restored to her former liberty. But this was no easy matter. The place in which she was imprisoned was not only fortified, but also surrounded by a loch of two miles in breadth on every side, and it was situated in the midst of the enemies' country. All this, notwithstanding, the matter was conducted with such prudence and courage, that it was brought to a successful issue, for the queen was restored to liberty to the astonishment of everyone, and almost within the sight of the enemies themselves.

Before the queen had collected all her troops she unfortunately encountered Moray. A part only of her army was defeated, and yet, as a whole, it was stronger than that to which it was opposed. As to her Majesty herself, she was in no danger. Yet for some unknown cause she determined to retire into England, and held to her decision so firmly that she could not be moved from it by any advice or argument. John Hamilton, Archbishop of Saint Andrews and Primate of Scotland, was among the party which was with her, and did not scruple to speak of this plan as an act of madness, since she could never expect to receive from the Queen of England aught that would be for the benefit either of herself or her kingdom. He told her that close at hand were large bodies of men which were hurrying to join her by forced marches. Lord Herries also (a brave and prudent soldier, who thoroughly knew the power of both Scotland and England) assured her that he could undertake to warrant her safety for forty days against all the troops which could be brought against her by both kingdoms. Matters, he added, were not yet by any means hopeless, for nearly the entire strength of the realm was on her side. Nor need she take it much to heart even if a few of her troops were killed in such an insignificant engagement as that which had just been fought, for the number really was not considerable, nor had the more efficient of her soldiers as yet joined the army. But as neither his arguments nor his exhortations availed anything, they summoned a notary, and caused a protest to be drawn up to the effect that the queen had surrendered herself into the hands of the Queen of England contrary to their wish and advice; and this they did for the information of posterity. The Queen of Scotland had possibly been cheated into this act by the receipt of letters full of kindness sent to her from time to time by the Queen of England when she was in Lochleven: trusting to which too confidingly she placed herself in a position of assured danger of her life, contrary to the strongest entreaties of all who loved her.

Civil wars now sprang up in Scotland, but the queen's party was the stronger; for the men who had been estranged from her by reason of her marriage with the Earl of Bothwell now returned to her side. Bothwell had by this time gone into Denmark, nor was there any possibility of the renewal of that ill-fated alliance.

The queen's party received no little accession of strength from the fact that Lord George Gordon, the eldest son of the Earl of Huntley, was now restored to his original dignity. Forgetting entirely all past injuries which he had experienced at the hands of her Majesty, he assured himself that they had proceeded from the craft of Moray rather than from any settled purpose on her part, and that the ruin of his family was due to her brother, and not to herself. He kept steadily, therefore, on her side.

Moreover, an event had happened which told to the advantage of the queen, if such an expression may be permitted. It was this. This Lord George Gordon had formerly been prisoner in a certain strong fortress. Moray noticed that the queen had a kindly feeling towards Gordon; and being apprehensive that she might give him his liberty at some time or other (a step which Moray saw would be very injurious to his projects), the traitor sent a letter sealed with the queen's seal to the keeper of the castle, ordering him to cut off the head of the Earl of Huntley without any delay, without assigning any cause. At the time when the letter was delivered Huntley was playing at dice with the keeper of the castle. When he read the letter the keeper grew pale, whereupon Huntley, seeing how matters stood, told him to keep a good heart, and that as no blame was due to him, he would willingly pardon him. The other, however, being a prudent man—although he had no doubt either as to the queen's seal or the signature, and well knew that he would put his own life into danger by delay—thought it the safest course to make some enquiries. Having let Huntley know what he had been ordered to do, and how urgent and imperative were the letters which he had received, he then decided upon

visiting the queen at his own risk. He therefore posted
off to the Court with all speed, and asked her Majesty
to pardon him for not having at once obeyed her letters.
When the queen heard reference made to "her letters,"
she was much surprised, and told him that she had not
sent any to him on the subject, nor had any intention of
so doing. She admitted that she had been to blame for
using the family of the Gordons with such excessive
severity. As soon as he produced the letters she saw
Moray's fraud; and in order to protect Huntley from
the recurrence of any such danger, she ordered that he
should at once be set at liberty. When Parliament met,
the entire family was restored to its former dignity and
honour. This transaction bound Huntley closely to
Queen Mary; and not only while she was in prison was
he always of her party, but further, after her departure
into England, he acted, along with the other nobles, in
collecting troops for her.

As many as thirty thousand men were got together on
the queen's side—a force which could easily have crushed
all her enemies in Scotland, but for the interference of
the Queen of England, who persuaded Mary to write to
her adherents, exhorting them not to make any new
effort at that time, for another course was about to be
adopted, which would speedily settle every dispute.
They obeyed the queen's letters; but this they did in
such a way that they could reassemble in the course of
a few days should matters so require it.

During these civil discords the Catholics were permitted to remain unmolested; and many of them were
able to profess their religion with greater freedom than
hitherto had been the case. But since the state of religion seemed to depend upon the state of the realm and
the queen's return into Scotland, nothing was attempted

by the Catholics at this time. Their plans, in the first place, extended no further than for the return of the queen into her realm. But the Queen of England, who had her in her power, took very good care that this should not be done; and herein she was seconded by the advice and power of the Earl of Moray, who now aimed undisguisedly at securing the royal crown. But this was effectually prevented by certain leading members of the family of Bothwell, who shot the earl as he was riding through the town of Lithgow, surrounded by fifteen hundred mounted soldiers. He did not die upon the spot, but survived for some hours after he had received the wound. Some of the persons who were present when he died have given us an account of his death, which was exceedingly horrible. As soon as he was carried into a neighbouring house, he could speak of nothing but of the cruel vengeance which he would take upon the person by whom the wound had been inflicted. When he was made aware of his danger by some of his friends, he seemed like a man who awakes from a deep sleep, and began to cry out with a horrible and miserable voice that he saw himself surrounded by troops of devils; and thus the man who had inflicted upon Scotland such an amount of misery breathed out his unhappy soul among the demons who were waiting for it.

Moray having thus met with his deserts, the party which was opposed to the queen requested the Queen of England to send into Scotland the Earl of Lennox, whom they undertook to appoint regent of that kingdom. This Lennox was of Scottish birth, but he had spent many years in England as a banished man. He was the King of Scotland's grandfather. The queen sent him into Scotland along with some of her own troops. Coming unexpectedly he burnt the castles of a few of the Scottish

nobility; and after some delay was accepted as regent by
the party which was hostile to Queen Mary. This person put to a cruel death the Archbishop of Saint Andrews, Primate of Scotland, a man who was at once very
prudent and most constant in his adherence to the
Catholic religion. But the regent speedily met with the
punishment of his crime; for, although he had the support not only of the Scots, but of the English also, he
was killed by the queen's party during the time when
Parliament was sitting, and in the town in which it was
being held. He was succeeded by the Earl of Mar, who
had the care of the young King of Scotland in Stirling
Castle. Although he also enjoyed the favour of the
Queen of England, yet he was so harassed by the adverse
party that he could have peace nowhere, and died in a
short time worn out by trouble and vexation.

Religion, in the meantime, remained much in the same
condition as heretofore. On the side of the Reformers
the Earl of Morton still survived, who steadily refused
the title of regent, although everything was done according to his direction. At last, however, he was elected
regent by his party. He was a man of prudence, and
exceedingly anxious that everything should be done for
the public good of the kingdom. He did not persecute
the Catholics; and if any of them came into the realm,
not only did he permit them to remain there unmolested,
but even showed them a certain amount of favour. As
for the ministers of his own religion, he treated them as
men of no character or consideration. He was in the
habit of continually repeating that there was no room
for comparing the most wealthy of the ministers with the
poorest among the priests whom he had ever seen; that
in the priests there was more fidelity, more politeness,
more gravity, and more hospitality than in the whole

herd of the others ; and this he illustrated by a cunning piece of generalship. In Scotland the parish churches are near each other. Application had been made to the Earl of Morton, while he was regent, that four parish churches should be assigned to each minister, an arrangement to which he gave a hearty approval, for he was anxious that these useless beings should be reduced to the fewest number possible. They, on their side, demanded the stipends of four churches, to which claim of theirs he answered that to him it seemed to be unjust; and by this indirect mode of procedure he escaped from the attempt made by the ministers for the increase of their salaries.

During the time of Morton's regency nothing was done to excite a sharper persecution of the Catholics ; but rather on the other hand their cause was strengthened by means of the books which were written and published on their side by the Scots who at that time resided in Paris. Many noblemen, who had come into France as well for intellectual society as to escape from civil discords at home, through their intercourse with Catholics, bid farewell to the heresy of Calvin. Many further efforts would have been made by the Catholic party had they not been prevented by the queen, who was then a prisoner in England. It was afterwards discovered that she had acted according to the advice which will presently be mentioned.

Pope Gregory the Thirteenth, of happy memory,[1] had formed a fixed resolve to free every kingdom from heresy; in furtherance of which design he considered it a matter of importance that the King of Scotland should be brought up in the Catholic faith. His Holiness was aware of the claim of this king to the whole of Britain.

---

[1] He died in 1585.

Various plans were formed with the object of removing him from Scotland into Italy or Lorraine, that in his youth he might be educated in the true religion. For this end the pope grudged no outlay. But while the affair had proceeded so far as to seem to be all but complete, it failed in being successful, as a punishment for our sins. It was the queen's opinion that no Catholic priests ought to be sent into Scotland. They were willing indeed to shed their blood for the restoration of the faith, but their presence disturbed the tranquillity of the realm and hindered the success of the business then in progress. When this theory succeeded but badly, the Catholics and the party of the Queen of Scotland began to consider how they could remove the youthful king from the Castle of Stirling, in which he was being educated, and how to deprive the Earl of Morton of his authority. Each project was very difficult, but in the party there were some who were gifted with remarkable prudence, while there were others well skilled in warfare; they united themselves together and thus accomplished their purpose. Lord D'Aubigné was brought over from France, a relative of the king, by whose directions everything was henceforth managed in that realm. He was received with the greatest pomp by the king, who was still a youth, and by the nobility; and in the parliament which was held shortly afterwards he had a gift from the king of the Dukedom of Lennox.

Then, for the first time, it seemed as if all Catholics, as well those at home as abroad, were able to draw their breath in peace. At this period the king was entirely guided by the Duke of Lennox, whose directions regulated everything that was done within Scotland. He laid hands on the Earl of Morton, whose authority had now come to an end, and imprisoned him in Dumbarton

Castle. Many accusations were brought against him; among them was one from which he could not free himself, and from the disgrace of which nothing short of his death could vindicate Scotland. This was the betrayal of the Earl of Northumberland, whom Morton was accused of having sold to the Queen of England after he had fled into Scotland. This was the cause of the earl's death.

Morton was the last of the Scottish regents, all of whom came to a miserable end. In many respects Lennox distinguished himself at the outset; but as soon as the heretics began to discover that he was a man who was somewhat defective in judgment, they adopted measures for driving him out of the kingdom. The Calvinistic ministers took the lead in denouncing him from their pulpits as being a very unfit person to have any influence with the king by reason of the religion which he professed; and of this they attempted to persuade the people. The heretical nobility perceived at a glance that their heresy would speedily come to an end if Lennox had the opportunity of exercising, at his pleasure, the authority which he had acquired in Scotland. In that case all the Catholics, of whom the number was considerable, would side with him, and he would become a terror to the heretics, since he had the king in his power, by whom he was much beloved. They strained every nerve, therefore, to weaken his influence with his own party. To do so they requested Lennox to sign the profession of their Calvinistic heresy, while the Catholics advanced sound arguments why he should curb the insolence of the ministers. As Lennox depended upon certain politicians, he was afraid that he might thus involve not only himself in danger but the king also, and considered it best to yield to the pressure

of circumstances.   At length he gave way to certain evil
counsellors, deceived by whom he subscribed with his
hand to this Calvinistic heresy, while at the same time
it was reported that he kept the Catholic faith in his
heart.   The ministers then began to enjoy their triumph,
and had no difficulty in completing it by driving him
out of the kingdom.   For some of the heretical barons
having got together a few troops, seized the king while
he was hunting.   They brought many charges against
the Duke of Lennox, and assured the king that both he
personally and the whole realm would be in danger
unless the duke should leave the kingdom.   Lennox at
this time was resident in Edinburgh.   Having none to
advise him he sent for the Catholics, who (being acquainted with the state of affairs) told him that nothing
more now remained to be done than that all of them
should take up arms; and they promised that within a
few days they could muster a considerable body of
troops.   The king, in the meantime, sent his letters to
Lennox, by which he ordered him to keep quiet, for his
Majesty did not venture to oppose the wishes of his
captors in any way, dreading that it would fare the
worse with himself were he to do so.

These orders threw Lennox into renewed agitation.
The Catholics, the most of whom by this time had
assembled, declared that the king's letters were of no
value from the fact of his being in the hands of his
enemies.   Once more new letters were despatched, to
the effect that the king was at this time in great peril of
his life from the party into whose hands he had fallen,
and that he might possibly be sacrificed if Lennox persevered in his designs.   Even this appeal did not move
the Catholics.   The following story was told to Lennox
as having happened a few years previously.   When King

James the Fifth, the father of Queen Mary, who died in England, was still a boy, he was detained against his will in Stirling Castle by the Earl of Angus and several others of the Scottish nobility. The Duke of Albany, who was the king's uncle, laid siege to the castle. The nobles who held it threatened that they would expose the king to the fire of the cannon of the besiegers. The duke told them to do so, for he was determined that he would have the king, alive or dead. But Lennox could not be induced by this history, nor by any other argument, to make the attempt. Hence it was that a few days afterwards there came other letters from the king ordering him to leave the realm under pain of treason. He yielded to the advice of many Catholics, and returned into France, not without great disgrace to himself and no less danger to the Catholic religion. He died there a few months afterwards, worn out with sorrow, which was considerably intensified by the recollection that he had subscribed the heresy of Calvin.

At the time while Lennox was resident in Scotland along with the king, a golden opportunity presented itself for the return thither of the Scottish priests who were then resident in Paris. Their number was considerable, they were men of high character and admirable learning; and they would most gladly have undertaken the mission. But the persons who measured everything by the dictates of human prudence, fearing that the king might possibly incur some danger hereby, decided that the attempt should be postponed until some other opportunity. But when it became obvious that the daily loss of souls in Scotland was great, and that the plans of these politicians had proved a failure, certain priests of the Society of Jesus, along with a few

inmates of the College of Pont-à-Mousson,[1] set out on
the mission in the year 1584. Its success was very
remarkable, although it had not the approval either of
the Queen of Scotland nor of the more prudent ones.
From that time the face of the country was entirely
changed, and so great was the visible increase among
the Catholics that they could easily have shaken off the
yoke of the heretics, and their English brethren might
have neutralised the power of their enemies in that
realm.

Among the other causes which contributed in no small
degree to the growth of Catholicism in Scotland this was
one. Father Gordon, uncle to the Earl of Huntley, and
a kinsman to the king, not only touched the hearts of
many persons by his holiness of life, but, further, being
a man of great learning, he openly defeated the ministers
of the heretics in the public discussions which were held.
It happened also, most opportunely, that as the king
was expostulating with the young Earl of Huntley for
not embracing Calvinism, Huntley replied that there
was an uncle of his own in Scotland whom he would
much more willingly entrust with the salvation of his
soul than any of that heretical ministry. When his
Majesty heard this remark, he asked the earl to send his
uncle to him at Edinburgh, in which is the king's palace,
and where the more learned of the ministers generally
reside. The king having given his promise that no harm
should come to Gordon, that father accepted the invitation, and in about two or three months he publicly refuted
the teaching of these heretics with so much acuteness
and with such a crushing weight of arguments that the
sting of them rankled ever afterwards in the minds of

[1] In the department of the Meurthe, not very far from Nancy.
Here was a large Jesuit seminary.

K

not a few. His Majesty was present, and as many also of the nobles as chose to attend. The ministers were so enraged with this that they gave the king no rest until he ordered Father Gordon to leave Scotland. Overcome by their importunity, he ordered the Earl of Huntley, under the penalty of ten thousand pieces of gold, to cause Father Gordon to leave the realm within a month. Huntley obeyed the king. Father Gordon embarked at Aberdeen in a ship bound for France, and caused an attestation to that effect to be drawn up by a notary public. Next day a boat left the ship in which Father Gordon returned to Scotland, where he and three other fathers of the Society of Jesus, along with certain other students of the Papal Seminary, there employ themselves with the greatest success.

At this present time the condition of the kingdom is as follows.

A considerable number of the nobles who, according to the usage of that country reside, not in towns, but each in his own castle, are Catholics, and upon them depends almost entirely the strength of the country. This comes about because almost from their childhood they are in the habit of being exercised in arms, and have under them many subjects, who obey the slightest hint of their pleasure. This they do so entirely that within a very brief period of time they can bring together a great number of men, and upon occasion they can hold in subjection even the king himself. But within the greater towns the tyranny of the Calvinistic ministers is the more powerful, nor is it an easy thing for priests to find an entrance into them.

The entire question may be summed up in these words: the larger part of this realm is either Catholic or favourable to Catholics; and although they would

willingly free themselves from the yoke of the heretics
—which they have attempted to do once and again—
they would find it difficult to do so unless they were
aided by troops from abroad. This arises from the fact
that not only are they kept down by the King of Scotland and his heretical subjects, but also by the Queen of
England. It might indeed be otherwise if the English
would unite in attacking their queen; in which case it
is very probable that the Catholics in Scotland would in
a short time gain the upper hand. At present the Queen
of England gives the worst possible advice to the King
of Scotland in regard to the Catholics; for she can easily
understand that considerable danger may come to her
from Scotland if they should unite their forces to attack
her, especially if they were joined by foreign troops.
Hence it is that she keeps upon the most intimate
terms with all the Calvinistic ministers, whose safety
is chiefly endangered, and that she bribes every one of
the Scottish king's friends whom she can reach with her
money, in order to prevent him from joining the Catholic
party.

When the Catholics observed this, they sent a messenger to the King of Spain in the month of December
1593, by whom they promised that they would give him
all the help in their power if he would make an attempt
upon the Queen of England of some kind or other. If
he would not do this, they undertook to make war upon
her themselves with their own forces, provided he would
send them some little assistance. It happened, most unfortunately, that Lord George Kar,[1] who was the bearer
of these letters, was seized; and although nearly everything had been intrusted to his fidelity, yet, under the

[1] These incidents are told at some length by Tytler in his History,
iv. 187.

fear of torture, he made large revelations, and thus placed many of the leading nobles of the realm in the greatest danger. The Earl of Angus and the Baron of Fintry were immediately apprehended and sentence of capital punishment was pronounced upon both of them. The Earl of Angus escaped from Edinburgh Castle by bribing his guards, but the Baron of Fintry was executed. He was held in the highest esteem through the whole of that realm on account of the purity of his life and his wonderful prudence and learning. He might have saved his head if he had accepted the proposal which was made to him of embracing Calvin's heresy. But he answered very resolutely that it would be a bad bargain for him if he were to prefer earth to heaven. The Earls of Errol, Huntley, and many others, who also had been discovered, all ran the same danger; but because their power was considerable, they still remain in safety within the limits of that kingdom, although sentence of outlawry has been pronounced against them. Nor (in my opinion) would they easily be induced to leave it, since the welfare and safety of all the Catholics seems chiefly to depend upon their presence. In the meantime, however, their cause is somewhat bettered by the fact that the whole of Scotland is divided into two parties, not so much on religious grounds as political, which proceeded from the following considerations.

The King of Scotland had married a daughter of the King of Denmark some few years previously, by whom (according to the opinion of certain medical men) it was improbable that he would have any issue.[1] Hence there arose a feud about the succession to the kingdom. Lord Hamilton, son of the Earl of Arran, affirmed that it

[1] This must have been written before the birth of Prince Henry, which happened 19th February 1594.

belonged to him. In consequence, however, of the civil broils which had taken place some months before, several thousand men had been brought together, and the two parties were nearly coming to blows. Not only had the party of the Hamiltons the better title, but they were the stronger, although the king favoured that of Lennox. It was exceedingly doubtful, however, which side would be successful, for it seems probable that the Queen of England supported both the one and the other, for she was apprehensive that if either of them were crushed the whole power of Scotland would become united, an event which, as her long experience told her, would not be for her own advantage. However, there is great ground for hope that as long as this struggle for the succession to the kingdom shall continue, the savage persecution which has been raised against the Catholics may be somewhat modified. The priests who are at work in Scotland are most anxious that they may be reinforced by other labourers.

There is one matter more which ought to excite our especial commiseration. Although every field is white for the harvest, yet from the time when the revenues of Pont-à-Mousson were withdrawn from Pope Sixtus the Fifth, there has been a failure in the number of reapers necessary for the labour. We betake ourselves therefore to the feet of your Holiness, not as the Britons formerly appealed to Aetius[1] the Consul, not as the Irish formerly appealed to Saint Patrick (who used to hear their entreaties even in his sleep),[2] and to whom he was sent by Pope Celestine,[3] not as that Macedonian, who is men-

---

[1] See the Epistle of Gildas in Petrie's Monumenta, p. 11.

[2] Patricii Confessio, cap. iii., in the Acta Sanctorum, 17 March, p. 531.

[3] See the volume last quoted, p. 542.

tioned in the Acts of the Apostles,[1] appealed to Saint
Paul, but as to him whom we acknowledge to be the
Vicar of Christ. Hungry and thirsty we appeal to you;
hungering not for bread, as says the prophet Amos,[2] not
thirsting after water, but hungering and thirsting with
the desire of supplying them with that spiritual food
which shall sustain them in their heavenward journey.
We entreat that the fatherly affection which embraces
the world may be extended also to Scotland, which for
thirteen centuries has been constant in its obedience to
the Holy See. The danger for Scotland is not now from
the barbarians, as it was formerly. What is to be
dreaded at the present is this, that they should perish
from want of the Word of God, and so be exposed to
external misery; which may God avert! These, Holy
Father, are the cries which Scotland in her affliction
addresses to your mercy.

[1] Ch. xvi. 9.   [2] Ch. viii. 11.

APPENDIX II.

1568.

"As to the state of affairs in Scotland, we have received
the following information, partly from letters sent
to the Bishop of Glasgow, partly from the report of
a certain nobleman named William Lesley, brother
to the wife of the Laird of Lochleven, in whose
castle the queen is imprisoned."[1]

THE queen is still kept in as strict ward as ever she
was. During the last quarter of a year a remarkable
change has been observed in her conduct. In addition
to the prayers in which she is often engaged in her bedchamber, when she is in the garden (into which she goes
for the sake of exercise) she often breaks in upon that
period of relaxation by throwing herself upon her knees,
and raising her eyes and hands to God. Those who
have had the opportunity of observing her have noticed
the warmth and earnestness of her devotion. They
report also, that when she rises from her knees she is
always in much better spirits.

She has gained such an influence over the baron in
whose castle she is imprisoned, that although he and the
Earl of Moray are children of the same mother, her
keeper became so moved by her misfortunes as to promise that he would procure her freedom, which he
actually would have done, had he not been betrayed by

[1] Transcribed from the original Report in the Secret Archives of
the Society of Jesus.

a certain person whom he had acquainted with his intention. Hereupon he fell into such suspicion among the Confederates, that he was obliged to explain his conduct before one of their meetings, and to vindicate himself as best he might.

Although the Earls of Huntly and Argyll, and many others of the chief of the nobility, have steadily kept aloof from associating with the conspirators from the time when the queen was thrown into prison, yet these two earls attended the parliament, as indeed did all the nobility, with the exception of the Earls of Errol, Montrose, Eglinton, Cassells, and Rothes. The Lords Seton, Fleming, Livingston, and Oliphant, who hitherto have kept firm in their duty to their sovereign, did the like. Lord Fleming has the custody of Dumbarton Castle, which is the strongest of all the Scottish fortresses. It is situated on the Irish Sea.

When the parliament met at Edinburgh in the beginning of November, the Earl of Moray removed from their seats in it every Catholic, they being the only people in the whole assembly who would either have passed a just law, or would have taken care that just laws were put into force. He introduced in their place some persons of bad character, who were ignorant heretics.

On the 22nd of November the Bishop of Dumblane was summoned, and his cause was tried. His relations and friends mustered in large numbers, and advanced such solid reasons in his defence, that every one imagined that he would have been acquitted. But Moray's hatred was of more weight than the justice of the bishop's cause, or any arguments founded upon it which his friends could bring forward. The bishop was found guilty of treason; he was deposed from his see, and all his goods were forfeited to the State.

On the 16th of December the parliament of all the Estates of the realm began to be held. Out of each Estate were chosen ten men, who, according to the custom of that country, were styled the "Lords of the Articles." They get this name because it is their duty to examine each of the articles which are to form the subject of discussion.

In making the selection above referred to, Moray wished to introduce the novelty of preventing the order of ecclesiastics from being admitted; nor did he pay any regard to the fact, that from the time of the introduction of Christianity into Scotland, it had been the invariable custom for bishops, abbots, and prelates to have the highest place, and the first vote immediately after the sovereign. In this matter the Earl of Moray acted not only very rudely, but also with exceeding insolence and tyranny, yet exactly in keeping with the business in which he was engaged. In order, however, to prevent the idea that the entire order had perished, which would have made the whole of the proceedings of parliament invalid, and at the same time to curb the ambitious insolence of the men thus unduly elevated to such unexpected honour, a few persons elected and named by the ministers were admitted into the place of the churchmen.

The first act of this parliament was to confirm this new heretical superstition of Calvinism. This was done by the consent of all the orders, and disguised under the name of religion. It was decreed, under the severest penalties, that this religion should be conducted under one fixed form in every church within the realm. Whosoever should object to accept it should, for the first offence, forfeit all their goods, and for the second lose their life. In the same act provision was made that no

Catholic should in future be eligible for any public office, magistracy, or dignity.

In the second place a law was passed for the punishment of the king's murderers, and for dealing with all severity against all such as had been either cognizant of it, or assisting in that crime, and this without any respect to persons. This latter clause was added, as we know, so as to include the queen, whom it was their intention to remove out of the road, by this pretext. For they examined her cause, and sentenced her to death, according to their own fashion; and they would long ago have put this sentence into execution, unless some grave dispute had arisen among the conspirators themselves.

Amongst these conspirators there were some, and possibly some of the chiefest, who were dissatisfied with the delay which had taken place in this action, and their dissatisfaction was proportionate to the anxiety with which they wished for its execution. They now violated all the precedents of former times, and added to the subjects sanctioned by the Lords of the Articles certain others, which were to be discussed as the occasion might serve. Of these the first was the demand made by the people for the avenging of the king's murder. As they had pretended that, out of regard for the public good, the complaints of the people should be heard, so now they bribed some of them to demand those things only which they themselves desired to see carried out. They demanded the very things which the confederates themselves could not venture to ask without incurring the suspicion of evil designs.

The first complaint of these popularity hunters was that nothing had been done to avenge the atrocious murder of the king. Next, they demanded that the Earl of Bothwell should be adjudged to be the enemy of the

State, and that all his property should be confiscated. In the third place, that such of his servants as had been seized in Orkney should be executed. Fourthly, that whatever had been done at the king's inauguration should be confirmed. And lastly, that the dignity and authority of the Earl of Moray in the government of the realm should be declared to be good during the king's minority. As to the first of these articles, it clearly shows what was the intention of the queen's enemies, and how unwillingly they waited any longer for her death.

The subject of the Earl of Bothwell's retainers is worth a somewhat fuller notice, as illustrative of God's justice, and as such it demands our consideration and wonder.

The success which Bothwell had experienced in Scotland had been far from prosperous, and he did not better it by the course which he now adopted. Accompanied by a few ships he put to sea, with which at last he reached Denmark, where he was well received by the king, and where he still remains in great honour.

Certain of his followers, leaving the earl in Denmark, again set sail, why I know not. After having been driven hither and thither by the wind at last they landed in the Orkneys, where at that time happened to be the brother of the Earl of Moray, named Robert Stuart, formerly Abbot of Holyrood. He seized the vessel, and he threw into chains all whom he found on board, and with all speed he made his brother acquainted with what he had done, sending for the purpose an express messenger. Having discussed the matter with his councillors, Moray sent back letters to his brother to the effect that he should set at liberty the ship and the sailors, but should take all Bothwell's servants into close custody. Such of them as were of low rank he should hang, and

then send home the others to him, the writer, where
they would be dealt with in a more official manner.

Without reckoning the men whom Robert Stuart
hanged in Orkney, he sent six back to Edinburgh, whom
Moray determined to put to death with greater solemnity,
especially one of the number, a namesake of Bothwell,
and a close friend of his as well as a relation. When
this man knew that he would assuredly be executed he
made a confession, moved thereto, as is believed, by a
divine instinct. He told Moray, in the presence of a
few witnesses, that he was one of those who was present
at the murder, or rather that he was the man who had
executed the crime with his own hands. He admitted
that he knew he well deserved his sentence, even the
severest punishment; and that since such was his own
judgment in his own case, he would not sue for pardon,
even though he knew he would obtain it. One thing,
however, he asked with all earnestness, namely, that he
should not be deprived of the opportunity of speaking
to the public just before his execution. He would then
explain the whole facts of the case, and would warn
those who heard him from embarking in such like
criminal enterprises.

Secretary Lethington was one of the persons who was
present at this conference between Moray and the
prisoner. He was a crafty man, and being very far-
sighted, he feared that if the criminal were permitted
to make this confession he would name him, or some of
his accomplices; for Lethington's conscience accused him
of many crimes. He was anxious, therefore, that a stop
should be put to this speech on the scaffold. But as
many difficulties came in the way he fell upon another
plan to hinder the culprit from accusing either himself or
others. In the meantime a day had been fixed on which

the criminal was to be accused and punished. The secretary prepared an address, in which he exhorted the accused to think only upon God's judgments and his own salvation ; and of all things to be careful not to blacken the reputation of others. This advice was given, how-ever, covertly and indirectly ; and to it he added much more, full of mingled threats and flattery.

Having prepared this address at home, the secretary recited it to the criminal, at the time when he was accused, and in the presence of many of the nobility, Moray himself sitting as the judge. The prisoner, how-ever, boldly answered the secretary, assuring him that his speech was useless, for that he who was now before them had reached that frame of mind when threats and compliments are equally worthless, and that nothing should hinder him from saying what his conscience told him he ought to say. He would do no harm to any one who was innocent.

Turning then to Moray, he said, "Since you, my lord regent, occupy the position in which I now find you, of you I will say nothing ; and I spare you because of your dignity. As for those two persons who are seated by you" (these were the Earl of Glencairn and Lord Sempill), "about them I have nothing to say, for I know that they are innocent of the crime about which I am accused." Turning then to the secretary and others of the same stamp, he said, "Who is there among you who either can or dare accuse me of this crime ?—a crime of which you are quite as guilty as I am. For you planned what these hands of mine put into execution, as is attested by the signatures of all of you, which would establish the truth of all my words if they could be pro-duced." At these words all were so struck that for some time there was silence. The accused was removed back to his prison, where he was detained for a short period, and then executed without any further trial ; nor had he any subsequent opportunity of addressing the people. Whatever charges he brought openly against the secretary, the Earls of Morton and Bothwell, and James Balfour (whom he affirmed to be the first inventors of this crime), the very same he insinuated sufficiently plainly against Moray when he said that he would spare him out of respect to the dignity which he occupied. Besides this, every one who knows anything about this affair knows how true is the statement above made about him and the others there mentioned.

Along with this criminal five other persons were executed, all of whom with one consent bore witness, not only that the queen was guiltless of this crime, but that the individuals mentioned above were the authors of the king's murder.[1] It is held to be certain that the Archbishop of St Andrews is to be cited as having a share in the king's murder. Moray has publicly threatened to charge Lord Oliphant with the same crime, by which threats his lordship is so much alarmed that, although in the opinion of every one he is entirely guiltless, and in his own conscience is perfectly innocent, yet he has been compelled to withdraw himself, and to run the risk of losing all his property. It is unnecessary to say more. The avarice of Moray is like a bottomless pit. He is something more than hostile to all good men, more especially Catholics. When he takes a fancy to the property of any one, or conceives a dislike against him, he soon accomplishes his object by using this accusation of the king's murder as a two-edged sword.

We have ascertained beyond a doubt that a certain

---

[1] Here in the margin of the original occurs the following note, written in a different hand :—" Many doubt whether this is true."

Englishman, named Henry Kyligrew, who last year was employed in Scotland by the queen, his mistress, has brought letters to Moray and his associates in the conspiracy, advising them to continue their work, and not to permit themselves to be frightened from their purpose by the threats of any foreign princes. They shall find the Queen of England most ready to help them in every way, and of this they may assure themselves. It is most certain that Kyligrew has written this much by the directions of his queen. Much light has thus been thrown on several matters which till now have been shrouded in obscurity. Among others, it reveals to us the true meaning of the efforts made by Nicolas Throgmortyn, the English ambassador, who apparently was trying to induce the Confederates to set the captive queen at liberty. Now, however, it is obvious that his intention was exactly the opposite to this. Many suspected as much, but there were few who ventured to affirm it.

The way in which the queen is treated is wretched in the extreme, as well in regard to food as attendance and personal clothing. One single male domestic is left; he cannot be styled a cook, but a scullion, or one of the meanest of the kitchen boys. She has only one woman servant to wait upon her in her bed-chamber. When winter was close at hand, she had great difficulty in obtaining a long dress such as was fitted to keep out the cold, and she got this only after many prayers. The dresses which she wore up to that time were utterly unworthy a woman of her rank.[1]

It was also decided in the same parliament that whoever had any dealings with the Roman pontiff should be held to be guilty of treason. Also, the parliament ab-

---

[1] Here the writing changes, and is continued in another hand to the end.

solved all such persons as had either taken the queen a prisoner, or kept her in prison.   And not only this, but they further left it free to the same persons to make any regulations they pleased.   Assuredly we have here a novelty in legislation, when we find the criminals absolving themselves, and not only pardoning the crimes with which they are charged, but even giving themselves permission to commit others for the future.

For such as refuse to profess the superstition of Calvin, the first penalty is the loss of property; the second is banishment; if they return into this country, the third penalty is death.[1]

[1] This document is addressed, in Italian, "To the Very Reverend Father in Christ, Father Francesco di Borgia, Provost General of the Society of Jesus, at Rome."   The body of the paper is in Latin.

APPENDIX III.

1568.

AN [1]HISTORICAL ACCOUNT OF THE DELIVERANCE OF THE QUEEN OF SCOTLAND FROM CAPTIVITY.

THERE is in Scotland, in the district of Fife, a well-known loch called Lochleven, which apparently derives its name from a river which, rising from that same loch, falls into the sea after a course of about ten miles. There are other lakes in the same district. This of which we are now speaking is three miles broad, and is one mile longer than it is at its extremest breadth. There are several islands in it, but the most remarkable of them are two—one at the east, and above one mile from the mainland, on which formerly stood a church dedicated to St Fillan; the other, situated on the west, is only[2] . . . . distant from the shore. On it stands a castle, strong rather by its natural position than by art, of which the master is a baron of the noble family of Douglas, as far at least as relates to his descent by the father's side; on the mother's side he is connected with the Earl of Moray. In consequence of the natural strength of this fortress, and also because the baron (as we have just mentioned) was a connexion of Moray, the

---

[1] Translated from the Latin manuscript preserved in the Secret Archives of the Vatican at Rome; Politica Varia, vol. lxvi. p. 313. It is a contemporaneous copy.

[2] By an oversight of the scribe this island is said to be *only* five hundred miles distant from the mainland.

Confederate Lords considered it the safest place in which to imprison the queen, whom they had seized during the course of last year. Having conveyed her thither, they treated her with such severity, and kept her in such strict custody, that they seemed to have forgotten not only her former dignity, but also every feeling of humanity. For, whereas formerly she had a large retinue of servants, consistent with her queenly rank, and for her attendants a crowd of nobles of both sexes;—whereas formerly she had a multitude of men and women servants to wait upon her,—now only two maids were allowed for the service of the captive queen (and they of a very low condition), together with a single cook. Nor was she permitted to speak to any one, or any one to her, except in the presence of the master of the castle, or of some other person deputed by him for that purpose.

The queen so conducted herself as to give the impression that she submitted both her fortunes and herself entirely to their pleasure. She bore this calamity indeed with marvellous patience. Nothing, however, that she could either say or do softened the cruelty of these bitter enemies; nothing moved them to pity. Although they had already wrung from her, by their threats, all that she had to give, still they threatened, and did not cease to plan her death. All this she bore patiently, and with a great and lofty spirit; but she was too far-sighted to abandon the thought of how she might at some time or other free herself from these miseries. She trusted that the goodness and mercy of God would never entirely abandon her in the midst of such calamities. She endeavoured, therefore, to deliberate about her deliverance with certain of her subjects whom she knew to be trustworthy and well affected towards her. Her first attempt was through the lady of the castle, by whose assistance she sent letters to some of her friends ; but as this woman acted with considerable fear, dreading her husband's severity, this effort was a failure. The queen therefore looked elsewhere, and began to deal with the servants of the household, by whose agency she contrived (though with difficulty) to send letters to such persons as she pleased, from whom she also received letters in reply.

In the first place, she wrote to that illustrious nobleman the Lord Seton, by means of John Beton, a very dear friend, the brother of the Archbishop of Glasgow, a man not only of high family, but also endowed with remarkable gifts of mind and body, among others, with singular prudence, as indeed was proved in the present instance. Earnestly intent on this business, Beton, having first received the queen's letters, delivered them, and then conveyed to her the answer. Knowing that among all the loyal nobility there was no man more devoted or more attached to her Majesty than Seton (whose devotion to her equalled his own), Beton made him acquainted with the position of affairs. In the family of Seton the reputation of devoted loyalty to their sovereign descended as a traditional inheritance ; for with them nothing was dearer or nearer than their piety to God, and their faith to their prince. Among them have been many who were ready to sacrifice life, and all that men value most highly in this world, in defence of their country and the public good. Nor did the nobleman of whom we are now speaking degenerate in this respect from his ancestors ; for, according to the testimony of Beton himself, in the execution of this remarkable exploit, to Seton (after God) is due the chief praise. And yet, if respect be paid to steadiness of purpose, hard work, and long watchings, Beton also is worthy of very high praise, higher, indeed, than his modesty will permit him to accept. But let us return to the sequence of our narrative.

These two, then, Seton and Beton, after careful deliberation upon the circumstances, came to the conclusion that the best plan would be to assault the castle. They had ascertained, as well from the queen's letters as from the reports of the persons with whom they had conferred, that close by the castle lay a vessel capable of holding about eighty armed men. This vessel was used on certain fixed days to bring coals and other household necessaries into the fortress. Their plan, then, was either to bribe the captain or to seize the boat, as soon as it should touch the shore, and having filled it with armed men to make an assault upon the castle. God's goodness, however, made this plan impossible; for it happened that one of the household of the castle having been questioned by a servant of the queen (who brought her such things as she needed from time to time) as to how many armed men that boat would carry, the man, being no fool, told his master what had occurred, and advised that the boat should be drawn up on land, and secured by a chain. There was danger, he said, that the vessel might afford the means of carrying off the queen, if indeed there were any persons who entertained such a project. Hereupon the lord of the castle, who dreaded nothing so much as to lose such a prisoner as her Majesty was, caught at the advice as soon as it was uttered, and caused the vessel to be hauled up on to the land, and secured by an iron chain so firmly that it could not be unfastened save by very great violence.

When Seton heard of this misadventure, he stormed and was exceedingly angry; but he and Beton speedily busied themselves in forming new plans. Shortly after-

wards it came about that George Douglas, youngest
brother of the laird of Lochleven (for that was the name
by which the keeper of the castle was called), was expelled from his home in his brother's house, because it
had been discovered that he was inclined to favour the
queen and her party. When driven from the fortress, he
lingered in a village near the loch, called Kinross. Beton,
who never permitted any opportunity to escape him,
went there one day, and meeting this Douglas, fell into
conversation with him in a friendly way; for he had
been informed by one of the queen's letters that he might
safely discuss the whole subject with him. Here Beton
soon discovered a difficulty. On the one hand he was
aware that the fidelity and assistance of Douglas would
contribute largely to the success of the undertaking, as
was really the case; yet, on the other hand, he knew
that there existed a deadly feud between the two families
of Douglas and Seton, and this presented a formidable
obstacle. To persuade Douglas to believe in the fidelity
of a Seton, and Seton to trust the constancy of a Douglas,
was no easy task, yet Beton's good management brought
even this to pass. The two met together for a private
conference, and from that time old feuds were forgotten,
and a firm friendship sprung up between them.

In this conference Douglas remembered that one boat
still remained near the castle, smaller indeed than that
already mentioned, but still capable of carrying thirty
soldiers, more or less; whereupon it was decided that the
attempt which had formerly been decided upon should
now be made by means of this smaller vessel. Douglas
contrived so to deal with the master of this boat that he
was won over, and agreed to come to the shore of the
mainland for the purpose of conveying to the castle a
chest filled with the queen's commodities. But Seton and

Beton had planned that the boat should receive on board not only this chest, but also a number of armed men, who, favoured by the darkness, should be in waiting close at hand, and that this should be done by force if necessary. They decided that if the whole force could not be carried across to the island at one voyage, as many at least should be taken as could sustain the first assault of the garrison on the island, until the boat could return with the remainder of the assailants. They had ascertained from the queen's letters that the number of fighting men within the walls did not exceed fifteen or sixteen. But neither did this device succeed. For the boy who steered the boat was accused to the laird of having deserted his post and gone to sleep during the night, whereupon he was dismissed from his office, and expelled from the castle. We may believe that all these occurrences happened by the singular providence and goodness of God, in order that (as the result afterwards proved) the final success should be attained without bloodshed and slaughter, and without emperilling the safety of the queen, to all which dangers this second project was open.

It happened not long after this, that the person who had succeeded the boy in steering the boat was severely wounded in the arm by a soldier, who fired off a musket at random, in consequence of which the boy was reinstated in his former post, for so necessity demanded. In the meantime, however, so suspicious had the laird become, that he caused this small boat to be chained to the larger one. Of this difficulty the queen took the earliest opportunity of acquainting her friends by letter, and, at the same time, she let them know that one little boat was all that now was left, which could carry only very few persons, seven at the most. This indifferent success was the occasion of the queen opening her mind to the boy, which she did by the advice of her friends on the outside; for she had been told by Douglas that he had already gained the lad over to her side, and this had been done so effectually, that not only did the youth promise his assistance, but he gave it most faithfully, as will presently appear.

When the queen knew that she could depend upon the boy she made her friends acquainted with the fact, and directed them to be in the neighbourhood on the second of May, accompanied by such a number of horsemen as in their opinion might be necessary. She resolved that upon that day she would hazard the attempt when the keeper of the castle was at supper.

There were two ways of escape from the castle. One was by getting possession of the key of the greater gate; the other was through a certain little window, which was about the height of two cubits from the ground. It was decided that it would be better to try the gate in the first instance; for the second plan was attended by this difficulty, namely, that if the queen in leaping from such a height should injure a limb, so as to be unable to walk any further, then the whole design would be an utter failure. In this case, should it so happen, the queen had provided Beton with special letters to the effect that if the boy should return in the boat without her, they should carry him off with them, and that one of the two should keep him in his own household, or should send him into France to her uncle the Cardinal of Lorraine. The queen was fully aware that by his fidelity to her the lad was hazarding his own life. Such care did this good princess take of the youth, of whose firm fidelity to her in the midst of such difficulties she had this proof. And he, on his side, was no less earnest of purpose in regard to her Majesty, for he assured those persons with whom he had occasion to converse, that he would hazard the experiment, even although he knew that he would be hanged for it the day after.

When Beton had assured himself that all these arrangements were complete, he made a very careful survey of the whole of the surrounding neighbourhood; and having discovered a locality which was admirably adapted for placing men in hiding, he went to Seton and explained to him the plan of the whole action. They both came to the decision that three days before the attempt should be made, they would write to such of the nobles as still stood firm in their allegiance to the queen, taking care, however, that the letters should not contain a full statement of what they meant to do, on which point they considered that secrecy was of vital importance. And this plan they carried out. What Seton wrote was simply to the effect that he had an idea that an attempt to liberate the queen would be made by certain persons; therefore that it would be well that on a fixed day each of them should attend at a place which he specified, accompanied by a body of horsemen.

Matters being thus settled, on the morning of the day which the queen herself had appointed, Beton, at the head of certain mounted troopers, crossed the Forth. (This is the name of a broad river which separates Lothian from Fifeshire, in the former of which districts Seton has large possessions.) The party rode quietly to Kinross, a village near the loch, where they arrived about five o'clock in the afternoon. Douglas was awaiting them at the inn in which he was staying, to the landlord of which they pretended that they were on their way to Glasgow, there to meet the Earl of Moray, who was then residing in that city. And this happened very fortunately for them, for had he been nearer at hand the difficulty would have been all the greater. When Douglas heard Beton give this account of himself to the landlord, he said, "I too am on my road to Glasgow, having been summoned thither by my brother, the Lord Regent,"—for it was the pleasure of Moray that he should be so styled. Thus it was arranged that these two persons, Seton and Beton, being about to be fellow-travellers on the same journey, were afterwards able to talk familiarly together without raising any suspicion.

Seton in the meantime, having dined in one of his country houses, sent on before him a body of his retainers, thus avoiding the suspicion which might have been occasioned by the appearance of a larger troop. He himself followed with the remainder, and about four o'clock in the afternoon he arrived at the spot which had been fixed upon for the ambuscade, to which he was conducted by a guide familiar with the district, whom Beton had left with him for this purpose. This locality was a hill rising towards the south of the loch, and distant about two miles from the point at which the queen landed. It was exceedingly well suited for the present purpose, for it afforded an excellent view of what was passing on the loch and in the castle, and at the same time the whole body of troops had a perfect hiding place in a certain hollow space and valley in the top of the hill.

In the castle the queen, according to her custom, supped about six o'clock. Supper being ended, she went into her bed-chamber, as her keepers thought for the purpose of praying (for this was her daily custom, immediately after dinner and supper); where she really meant to wait until the laird of the castle should sit down at table along with the warders and his own family. The queen then put off the dress which she generally wore in the castle (which did not become her rank), and put on that of one of her maids. The boy had placed two oars by the little window, of which mention has already been made, and by their aid the queen could easily have slid down to the ground. But not satisfied with this, and anxious to provide for every possible contingency, he determined to steal the laird's key; and this he did with such skill that although the laird was generally most watchful and marvellously on the alert, he saw nothing of what was going on. It was the laird's custom to place the key on the table before him while he was at supper. According to his wont, the boy brought in a dish from the kitchen. Placing it on the table with one hand, with the other, which was hidden by the dish, he contrived to secrete the key, leaving the dish in its place. He then hurried off to the gate with all speed. He was noticed by the maid-servant who was to accompany the queen, who was upon the watch, and she in turn informed her Majesty. The queen, attended by the maid, followed the boy to the gate, going along a passage not far from the spot where the laird was at supper. They were noticed by some of the domestics of the household, but, as the queen had changed her dress, they suspected nothing amiss.

Having now reached the gate, they opened it with the least possible noise, and having gained the outside, they carefully locked it with the key, which the boy then placed inside the mouth of a cannon which happened to be lying in the court-yard. When they had got into the boat, he pulled away lustily at the oars, and having made some little way from the island, the queen held up a kerchief in her hand, thereby giving the token to those who were awaiting her on the mainland, as had been agreed upon beforehand. Having done this, she and her attendant laid themselves down on the bottom of the boat, so as to be entirely out of sight, no object being visible on board save the boy at the oars. This she did in order to be safe from such shots as might be fired from the cannon or muskets in the castle.

Beton, in the meantime, complained of headache, and getting up from table in the middle of supper said that he would take a walk along the margin of the loch. Douglas followed him, as he said, out of kindness. They had scarcely gone a few steps, when they noticed the boat pushing off from the island, and presently they observed the queen's signal. Seton, too, saw all this from the hill, and mounting his horse dashed down to the shore as fast as it would carry him.

Although they who had been left in the village in charge of the horses had noticed the signal, yet there was some delay on their part in getting them ready. Nor could Seton come from the distant spot at which he was posted with the speed that was desired. But Beton and his companion broke open the doors of a stable situated near the shore of the loch, and saddled one of the horses which they found in it with a side saddle, which was kept there. Having placed the queen on horseback, they went on the road to meet Seton. While the retainers whom Beton had left in the village to get the horses ready were hurriedly doing this, the inhabitants of the place, having a suspicion of what was going on, came down upon them and began to rise, as if they would hinder the success of the whole undertaking; but when they saw how great a number of mounted men was there, they soon gave up that idea.

When Seton had received the queen, he mounted her on a horse which he had got ready for the purpose, and carried her off with him.   He sent Beton on before them to the point at which the Forth was to be crossed, in order to prevent the departure of any ship before the queen should have passed over.

The inmates in the castle remained at supper in such perfect ignorance of all that was passing, that they knew nothing of the queen's escape until some of the villagers where she had landed had rowed back in the boat in which she had been carried from the fortress, and had given intimation of her escape.   It would seem as if the sluggishness and torpor which had been sent upon their spirits was of the same kind as that which fell upon the soldiers of King Saul (1 Sam. xxvi. 12), of whom we read that they had not observed David either when he came nor when he went.   When they understood what had occurred, they attempted to follow the fugitive and to bring her back ; but all in vain.   For not only was the queen by this time several miles on her journey, but it cost them the work of some hours to break open the gate, the key of which the boy had hidden ; for there was no way of exit from the castle save by that gate.

Seton having now got possession of the quarry for which he so long had been lying in wait, pushed rapidly along on the road, and conducted her Majesty to that spot where the Forth is crossed, of which mention has already been made, and which is named Queensferry.   It has got this name, I believe, for this reason.   At this point the river is pent in so closely by the hills, that it is only one mile broad, or at least not much broader ; thus presenting a convenient place of transit for delicate women, and such others as cannot endure sea sickness. Here ships were waiting, as had previously been arranged, in which the party was speedily carried across, the sailors who conveyed them offering their warm congratulations to Beton, who had spent a considerable sum of money among them during the previous months ; the end and fruit of which heavy outlay they now easily understood. The queen, and all who were with her, had a hearty laugh at this remark of theirs.

The party then reached Seton's residence, Niddry by name, not more than three miles distant from the river. As the queen now considered herself safe from further peril, while the others were taking some bodily refreshment, she withdrew herself to pray in private, thanking God for His goodness in restoring her to liberty. In the meantime arrived Lord Claud Hamilton, the youngest son of the Duke of Châtelherault, who, warned by the archbishop of St Andrews, had been in waiting at no great distance with some horsemen. Having left Seton's residence they proceeded to Hamilton, in which place is a tolerably strong castle and also a palace, the magnificent buildings of which fit it for a royal residence. On the road thither, the queen met Lord Herries, attended by a large body of cavalry. Her Majesty reached Hamilton about six o'clock in the morning, where the archbishop was waiting to receive her. Between that hour and the evening of the previous day she had ridden thirty miles, such being the distance between Hamilton Castle and Lochleven, the place of her imprisonment. Although Hamilton is only eight miles distant from the city of Glasgow (in which, as has already been stated, Moray was at that time resident), he had no information of what had occurred until two hours after the queen had reached Hamilton. On the first intelligence he and all his followers were so thoroughly disconcerted, that they did not know what course it would be best to follow ; nor indeed was it an easy matter to decide whether they should stay where they were or abandon it.

In the meantime the men who were in office flocked to the queen from all sides; nay, many of those who were of the hostile faction began to write to her, and to use the intercession of their friends, entreating forgiveness of past misconduct, and admission into her favour. She determined to do nothing in the matter without due deliberation.

While she remained in Hamilton Castle, waiting for the arrival of the rest of her nobility, some of the "sectarian" lords who were on her side tried to persuade her that since the external profession and worship of the Catholic religion was not permitted to her, she should chose one of the ministers of "the sect" (as the expression is), and should be present at the sermons and prayers which he recited, according to the custom. They assured her that this would be good policy; for not only would it show that she followed some definite form of religion, but would also draw to her side many from the opposite faction, who were opposed to her on no other grounds than religion.

The queen's answer was to this effect :—She neither would nor could in any way do aught which she judged to be contrary to God's will, especially in matters of religion. She was well aware that He punished, and punished severely, such as seemed to play with Him in an affair so serious and of such moment. She even believed that it was for this very reason that the troubles to which she had formerly been exposed had happened to her; because she had made certain concessions in this direction, in which no such licence was permissible. Were she again to stumble at the same rock of offence she would be acting impiously and

unwisely. By so doing she would prove that the ills
through which she had passed had not made her more
careful, and would once more draw down upon herself
God's anger. So then, as far as she herself was concerned, she would gladly do anything, and suffer anything, rather than make such a concession, which was
unbecoming a Christian and Catholic prince.

We entreat all persons who hear this to join with us
in our prayers to the goodness of God that of His mercy
He would preserve her Majesty in this resolution, to the
glory of His name, and the restoration of the Catholic
religion in that sadly afflicted kingdom.

PRAISE BE TO GOD.

APPENDIX IV.

1568.

A TRUE ACCOUNT of what the Queen of Scotland has been doing from the time when she escaped from her imprisonment and had arrived at the castle of Hamilton, until the 20th day of June. Drawn partly from her own letters to her Ambassador in France, and partly from those of the Ambassador resident in the English court.[1]

WHILE the queen was resident in Hamilton Castle, many persons flocked to her from various quarters, and so confident grew her partizans that they longed for nothing so much as to come to blows with the enemy. That they might do this the more conveniently, they thought it would be well that her Majesty should be placed in some stronghold where she would be safe from her enemies, to which side soever the victory might ultimately fall. The question was therefore debated in council, and it was unanimously decided that the queen should be lodged in Dumbarton Castle, under convoy of the troops which at that time were at her disposal. This is by far the strongest fortress in all Scotland, and (thanks to the fidelity of its custodian, Lord Fleming)

---

[1] Translated from the Latin manuscript preserved in the Secret Archives of the Vatican at Rome; Politica Varia, vol. lxvi., p. 309. It is a contemporaneous copy. This paper contains information which extends to 7th July, instead of 20th June, as stated in the title given above.

remains still constant to her Majesty. It is sixteen miles distant from Hamilton; but as they were anxious that this arrangement should be carried out before there was any need of a conflict with the enemy, it was of great importance to them that the opposing force should remain ignorant of their plans. But by God's permission (whose every judgment is just, although for the most part hidden from us) among the many who attended this council there was one who secretly conveyed the intelligence to the enemy, and fully instructed them of all that had therein been decided.

Moray and the Confederate Lords, whom he had summoned to join him with all possible expedition, at this time was resident in Glasgow. Aware of how much depended upon the issue of the struggle before him, he felt that his difficulties would increase if the opportunity were afforded to his adversaries of placing the queen where she should be safe; because then they would be able to give their undivided attention to the fighting which would be going on. It was decided, therefore, by him and his adherents that they would risk the hazard of a battle, and attack their opponents while they were hampered in considering the safety of the queen. He thought—and truly —that the care of her Majesty would prove a very great hindrance to the efficiency of the entire army, and would cause it to be distracted by a double anxiety. Moray, therefore, when he knew from the traitors who revealed the queen's plans that the royal troops were going to march towards Dumbarton very early in the morning of the 16th of May, put his forces into order, and led them out of Glasgow by dawn of day, and placed them in a kind of ambush in the road by which the queen had to pass with her troops. Nothing could be easier than to do this. These three places, namely, Hamilton Castle,

M

the town of Glasgow, and Dumbarton, are all of them situated on the banks of the same river. Hamilton is the furthest inland ; Dumbarton is near the Irish Sea, where the Clyde (for that is the name of the river) falls into the ocean ; and Glasgow is situated midway between these two strongholds. It stands on the further bank of the stream, over which there is a bridge of admirable construction.

The queen and her army set out upon their march. When they had gone a few miles, they were told by the advanced guard that the road was held by Moray and his followers. The party in attendance upon the queen held a conference as they best might, and came to the decision that, since they were more numerous than the enemy, they would continue their march, but that they would do their best to avoid a battle, unless forced thereto by absolute necessity. The royal troops were therefore separated into two parts, one of which, with a considerable body of cavalry, was left with the queen, while the other, in three divisions, continued its march on the road they had already taken. The command of the whole army was entrusted to the Earl of Argyll.

When Argyll perceived that an action was unavoidable, he caused himself to be removed by his friends from his place in the ranks, and being lifted on horseback, he rode off. Perhaps he was really unwell; perhaps fear, or some other ignoble reason, caused him to pretend sickness. Some of the men lost heart on the flight of their leader ; but others, who thought it better to die with honour than to live in a condition of base thraldom, began the fight with a good courage. Among these was Seton, who a few days before had freed the queen from her captivity, and his followers. With him was Lord Claud, the youngest son of the Duke of Hamilton, who headed the first line, which was composed of the family of the Hamiltons. These men, then, were the foremost in the fight, and gave the enemy no little trouble, many of whom they slew ; but at length they were so harassed by the musketeers (who occupied a hill not far from the scene of action), and so many of them were killed, that at last the survivors retreated. In their flight many were taken prisoners by the Confederates, and among the rest, Seton. When he was brought into the presence of Moray, he was bitterly rebuked by him as having been the prime author and the chief performer in this tragedy ; whereas, according to Moray, it was his duty to have been one of the first to protect the infant king. Seton answered that he had given his fidelity to one prince, and that he would keep it as long as he lived, or until the queen should have laid down her right of government of her own free will. Irritated by the reply, Moray asked him to say what he himself thought his own punishment ought to be, and threatened that he should undergo the extreme severity of the law. " Let others decide," said Seton, " what I deserve ; on that point my conscience gives me no trouble, and I am well aware that I have been brought within your power, and am subject to your will. But I would have you know that even if you cut off my head, as soon as I die, there will be another Lord Seton." The meaning of this is that he had legally transferred all his inheritance to his eldest son some years previously, in consequence of which, according to the laws of Scotland, none of his property could be forfeited, not even though he should be found guilty of high treason. But it is time that we should return to the queen.

When her Majesty was informed of the defeat of her troops she fled, accompanied by those attendants, who had been left with her for that special purpose. They were all picked horsemen, and well acquainted with the country through which they had to pass on their road to Dundrenan, which is a town in Galloway. Her friends took her into that district because many of her adherents had very extensive estates there, and chiefly Lord Herries, the leader of the party to whose care she had been entrusted. There a second conference was held as to the best course to be adopted. While some said one thing, some another, her Majesty announced her intention of going into England to the queen, her sister and cousin. All earnestly objected to this plan, and did what they could to dissuade her from such a journey, which they thought to be full of danger. Lord Herries assured her that she could remain in these districts perfectly free from every incursion of the enemy; and if her residence in this country did not meet with her approval, he undertook to convey her by sea either into France or into Dumbarton Castle. The queen, however, remained firm in her decision, maintaining that her journey into England was a course which she well knew was not only safe, but would also be for her advantage and honour; that she had full confidence in the affection of her sister and cousin towards her, and that she had not forgotten the many and great promises which Elizabeth had formerly made to her. This she said, influenced not so much by her own judgment as by the recent defeat which she had sustained; for she dreaded to fall once more into the power of her enemies. Nor had she entire confidence in many of the persons by whom she was surrounded.

When the nobles who were present saw that they were unable, by any arguments, to move the queen from the resolution which she had taken, they began to discuss the route by which the party should continue their journey. There are two roads into England. Of these one goes across an arm of the sea, the other is entirely by land; and as the former appeared to be at once the safer and the shorter, they gave it the preference. They got ready one of the vessels which they found on the spot, on board of which the queen embarked with her attendants, and crossed over in safety. In the course of a few hours she reached Carlisle, a town on the borders between England and Scotland, and tolerably wealthy, according to the ideas of the locality. The queen and her suite having been there lodged, the deputy of the Queen of England, who ruled over that county in her name, wrote to his mistress, informing her of the arrival of her cousin. How her Majesty of England was affected by this intelligence will appear in the progress of our narrative.

It is beyond a question that at the beginning Elizabeth showed the appearance of great kindness to her guest and cousin, and does so still. But after she had heard what Moray's secretary had to say, this kindness seemed somewhat to relax from what it had been at first. This secretary was John Wood, a crafty and cunning fellow, whom Moray sent to London when he heard that his sister had taken refuge in England. The object of Wood's journey was to damage the cause of Mary with Queen Elizabeth and the English nobility. Hearing this, Mary sent two of the lords who at the time were with her on a mission with the same object, Lords Herries and Fleming; the management of the embassy being entrusted to the former, as well on account of his eloquence as of his prudence.

Their object was to give the Queen of England some information upon three points.

1. To show her the reasons which induced the Queen of Scotland to have such hopeful confidence in the Queen of England as not only to flee to her for assistance in the midst of her difficulties, but further, to place herself in her hands. The audacious disloyalty of her subjects, which had now gained such strength as to become overwhelming, made it seem necessary for her to invoke the help of some foreign power. Of these the first in her estimation was Elizabeth, from whom there was nothing which she might not expect, as seemed to her clear from many arguments.

In the first place, because while she, Mary, was still a prisoner, she had experienced a remarkable instance of Elizabeth's fidelity and assistance in the despatch of two ambassadors into Scotland. The object of their mission was to deliver her, Mary, out of the hands of the Scottish conspirators. And in addition to this, there existed between these two queens such a close bond of relationship as of itself became the pledge of the kindest good feeling. Nor had Mary forgotten how many and how great were the promises made to her in former days by her cousin ; the performance of which, at the present emergency, would not only redound to the honour of such a great sovereign, but was such as might be expected from her out of regard for her cousin. It would make her name yet more illustrious among foreign princes, and would transmit it to future ages.

From these considerations Mary was anxious that Elizabeth should undertake the defence of her cause against this most audacious treason of the Confederates, who, neglectful of all right and law, had attempted, with unheard cruelty, and by means of false accusations, to deprive her first of her crown and then of her life. She entreated Elizabeth not to suffer herself to be so far beguiled by these hateful reports which the conspirators had put into circulation against her, as to be induced to act with too great hesitation, as if she feared that she might be giving her aid to a cause which was unjust and dishonourable.

2. In the second place, Lord Herries was required to explain to Queen Elizabeth the innocence of her cousin in regard to the death of her husband. Here he should show, and most solemnly affirm, that the persons who, under the pretext of this crime, wished to deprive their sovereign of her life and dignity, are the very men by whose most wicked plots and devices this crime was perpetrated, a crime of which she was wholly ignorant. She would presently make this plain to the princes of Christendom. Already it was well understood by the larger portion of her nobility, some of whom had continued in office, others had not joined her enemies. Strong in this conviction, they had risked their lives and all that they possessed in defending the innocence of their sovereign.

3. Should Queen Elizabeth remain unmoved by such arguments as these, and hesitate about extending her protection to her cousin, then Lord Herries is to state his third proposal; but not until he has tried and carefully tested every other resource. In this case he shall ask the Queen of England to grant to her cousin a favour which is never denied to any one, be he French or Scot, not even to the lowest of the commonalty, namely, a free passage into France. For this purpose Mary had sent Lord Fleming to London on his way to France, in order to prepare the Christian king and his mother, the Cardinal of Lorraine, and her other friends for her arrival.

Provided with these instructions, the two lords set out

on their journey to London.   On their arrival there they
were admitted into the queen's presence.   Lord Herries,
being the chief of the mission, brought forward the first
and second articles.   When he had spoken upon them
he was told that within three days' time he would receive his answer from the council.   Seeing, however,
that the matter was being purposely delayed, he requested a second conference with the queen in private,
which being granted him on the 17th of June, he then
expressed himself to the following effect :—[1]

He had received letters, he said, from his sovereign,
which seemed to imply that he had not been sufficiently
earnest in obeying her instructions.   Here Elizabeth
said, "I am now waiting for an answer to the letters
which I sent to your mistress respecting the business
about which I have already spoken to you."[2] (This
business referred to the king's murder).   "In this
matter," said Lord Herries, "your Majesty need expect
no other reply from my mistress than that which you
have already heard from myself.   She is entirely guiltless of that crime, and will prove her innocence very
clearly, not only to your Majesty but also to the other
sovereigns of Christendom, to the emperor, and to the
kings of France and Spain."   In these words he referred
chiefly to the Pope, whom, however, he did not name,
for very good reasons.   But Queen Mary had written to
the Archbishop of Glasgow, her ambassador in France,
desiring him, among other things, to acquaint the Most
Rev. the Bishop of Ceneda, the apostolic nuncio, that as
soon as she could find the opportunity she would send
an envoy to the holy father, to prove to him her inno-

[1] See the letter of Lord Heries to Queen Mary, printed in Teulet,
ii. 380.
[2] This letter may be seen in Labanoff, vii. 139.

cence, and to treat with him upon other matters touching the welfare of the realm and church of Scotland.

Lord Herries then continued his address as follows :— "If there be any one of the queen's base subjects who is pleased to hold the opposite opinion, let it be known to him that there are very many others who continue in their allegiance to her, and are ready to maintain her innocence to the utmost, both by law and arms. For albeit these cruel thieves have privately and fraudulently pillaged the castles, palaces, and treasures of my mistress, leaving her entirely destitute, there still remain—thanks be to God's grace—the hearts of many of her faithful subjects, of which she cannot be deprived by the acts of such robbers as these men are.

"Nor did Queen Mary come into this realm against her own free will, nor was she driven hither by stress of weather ;"—for Lord Herries had been given to understand that some persons had been trying to persuade Elizabeth that such was the case. "She came here under no pressure. She came because she trusted you more than any other living creature, and because she expected everything from your good faith and kindness. We who were along with her opposed the step, but she insisted upon throwing herself upon you with entire confidence. It is for your Majesty to show that in this hopeful reliance my sovereign has not been mistaken. She builds this assurance partly upon the nearness of blood by which you two are united ; partly upon those promises which you made to her, and of which the recollection is vividly impressed upon her memory. I say nothing upon the consideration which all ought to bear in mind, namely, that every one of us is subject to the laws of one common humanity, and that nothing happens to any single individual which may not happen to another.

My mistress, and we with her, ask God from the bottom of our hearts that this evil spread not wider, and extend not to other princes.

"As to the accusation," said the Scottish ambassador, "which these rebels bring against their sovereign, it is the duty of every one, and most especially the duty of all crowned heads, to be careful how far credit is to be given to such charges. For if—which God forbid—the King of France were to yield himself to the will of these persons who assailed him with such fury on the 30th of September[1] (as my sovereign entrusted herself into the hands of the men who are now planning how to deprive her of her kingdom and her life), although it is the universal opinion that his Christian Majesty is entirely guiltless, yet, according to the theory of our Scottish lords, it would have been easy to have found proof that he should lose both his realm and his head. And if your Majesty is pleased to undertake the protection of your cousin's cause, as your duty requires, she, for her part, will accept your advice as a command. She wishes that as well her conscience as her crown should be regarded thus highly. In such matters as these she can admit no judge, for she is the supreme authority within her own realm, the sovereigns of which have worn a crown for many centuries, a realm which never was subject to any other person. And she is well aware that in matters which relate to God it is her duty to act according to the judgment of the Church, and of none other."

"Far be it from me," said Elizabeth, "to form any

---

[1] This passage is somewhat obscure. Its meaning is that if the King of France had been dealt with as the Queen of Scotland had been dealt with, he would have been a prisoner from 29th September 1567, when the Huguenots attempted to capture him at Meaux. See Hist. de France par H. Martin, ix. 217.

other opinion in respect to the cause of your queen than that at which I can arrive from the case itself, and as I should wish men to judge of me were it mine. But since Moray has submitted the whole dispute to my decision, I will summon him to come before me, in order to ascertain from himself what has induced him and his associates thus to treat their sovereign, contrary to all law and justice. When I shall have heard his reasons, if it still appears to me that the statements are true which you have made in the name of your mistress, and which you wish me to believe, in that case I will defend her cause just as I would defend my own ; if it be otherwise, I will do my best to bring about a reconciliation between her and her subjects. But I will not take on myself to act in the character of a judge."

Lord Herries now saw that all this was said simply to prolong time, and that his mistress had little to hope for in that quarter ; he therefore brought forward the third article of his instructions. He requested that if Elizabeth and her council thought it unsafe to take in hand the cause of the Scottish queen, then at least she would not refuse to grant her a safe conduct and free passage into France, a privilege generally conceded to every applicant. This having been obtained—and he could not suppose it would be withheld—then other Christian sovereigns would in such sort embrace and defend her cause, "that unless your Majesty," said he, "be pleased to stand forward as the patron and open defender of the other party, it is incredible that any person will venture, out of the whole number of these rebels, to support such a dishonourable cause. And even if there be any of your Majesty's councillors," continued he, "who would try to persuade you to favour Moray's side, it should be considered, aye, carefully considered, whether they are not herein giving your Majesty a piece of advice which is not only far less honourable than that which my mistress would have you accept, but at the same time less safe, and assuredly much more difficult. For you cannot but see (I know how far-sighted your Majesty is), you cannot but see at how much less cost and charge you can replace my sovereign in her realm than you must needs incur if you favour the action of these disobedient subjects who are in rebellion against the laws of God and man, and of Nature herself. But if it be supposed—which God forbid—that you incline to their side in such wise that new feuds arise between you and certain powerful monarchs, will not you find yourself and your prosperous realm involved in a matter at once grave and dangerous? For you cannot suppose that all these princes will quietly submit to see a sovereign thus crushed and trampled on by these evil men who are her own subjects.

" As far as the present condition of my sovereign is concerned, you have dealt with her with such liberality and munificence that for these she cannot but offer your Majesty her most ample thanks. She needs nothing more, even for the state of a queen. She cannot but observe, however, that, in the first place, she is debarred from your presence. In the second place, she notices how severely her cause has suffered from delay, for in her case success depends upon expedition. In the third place, she remarks how great is the loss inflicted in the meantime upon those in Scotland who hold firm in their fidelity and fury towards her. Under these circumstances all that she can receive, not only from England, but even from the wide world, in the way of succour, so far from being a relief is a misery. Nor in this respect would you satisfy her Majesty if she were to receive from you a daily allowance of thousands of gold for her expenses. Much rather would she prefer to commit her cause to God, and return whence she came in the same vessel which brought her into England." This is the import of what Lord Herries said.

From his lordship's own letters we learn that the queen's answer was exceedingly benevolent. "She wished," she said, "to undertake the cause of her cousin and sister, and desired him to write to her to that effect;" but in the meantime he had been ordered by another secretary to attend at the council on the 21st and 22nd of June, when he should receive a final answer to all the matters which he had brought forward in the name of his mistress.

On June the 22nd the queen made her final reply. She understood the bearing, she said, of all the demands made by her sister, whose cause she would promote, defend, and protect in every way in which a sister's honour and reputation could be advanced. But in so doing she must have due regard to her own good name and dignity. She had not forgotten the promises which she had formerly made to her cousin, nor would she herein disappoint her expectations, as far as the present state of affairs permitted. "And since," said she, "Mary's subjects have publicly brought against her certain charges, which have found their way even into foreign courts, I cannot possibly do less to the two conflicting parties than inquire, with all possible diligence, into the truth of these accusations, as I have already stated. Therefore I intend to summon Moray and his friends into my presence, and I will entrust the investigation of the matter to certain of my councillors, who shall hear the accusations and replies of each party. If it shall appear that there is no truth in the charges which are brought against the Queen of Scotland, then I will defend her cause just as I would my own. If the matter turn out otherwise, I will do all I can to place the queen on a good footing with her subjects.

"As to her journey into France, were I to grant this request as readily as is expected, then foreign sovereigns would form a mean estimate of my prudence ; and this would annoy me much. For I have not yet forgotten that the King of France, Queen Mary's husband, together with his council, assigned to the queen, his wife, the title and arms of this my kingdom, and that he did so during my life-time. Were I to grant to this same queen the power of returning into a position in which she could the second time entail upon me the same danger and annoyance,—although I am ready to bear everything consistent with the equity of my cause and my power,—I might well be charged with a lack of prudence." The queen then added several remarks, which were apparently intended to modify the harshness of the above answer.

To all this Lord Herries made reply as follows :— " My mistress," said he, " as I have already observed, places herself personally in your Majesty's hands with entire confidence, having the fullest trust in your near relationship to her and your promises. You have it in your power to deal with her simply according to your discretion and pleasure. We, for our part, cannot pretend to influence your decision in one way or the other. Yet posterity will speak, and will sit in judgment upon the question, whether your behaviour towards her has been kind or unkind." Lord Herries then asked on what day Queen Elizabeth wished the conference to be held, and was told that these rebel Scots proposed to hold this meeting on the 1st of August, either personally or by their deputies. His lordship next mentioned that a certain lawyer, named James Macgill, a very shrewd man, would make his appearance there, with the object of persuading the queen and the Privy Council of England, that Queen Mary had of her own free will resigned her sovereignty, and consented to the inauguration of her son and to the Regency of Moray. That these assertions were totally false and worthless was easily proved by his lordship, who showed how wickedly they had laid their hands upon Queen Mary, how closely they had kept her in custody, and how cruelly they had threatened her, not only with perpetual imprisonment but with death itself. All this he did so thoroughly, that Elizabeth could not fail to see that the entire suit legally was utterly worthless. And his lordship then continued his address in the following terms :—

"Since the Earl of Morton made Moray Regent of Scotland, and Moray created Morton Chancellor, and these two personages raised their associates in crime to other dignities, how is it possible that the proceedings of such men as these in their parliament can have any force, either in law or equity? If they induced certain of the barons of the realm to subscribe these acts of parliament, when some of the number did so they were driven by fear, and some did not understand the meaning of what they were doing. I say nothing of those braver spirits who consented to affix their names only upon the condition that they should presently be assured by the queen herself that all that had been done had been done by her consent and with her approval. The chief of these were the Earls of Huntly and Argyll, men of the first rank among the nobility of the land, as appears by our public records. And if any weight is to be given to the number of the nobles of the queen's party, far greater authority is due to the act passed at Hamilton Castle by the larger and better part of the Scottish nobility, after her deliverance from Lochleven. Besides these, there are many of the leading barons who opposed these acts of the conspirators in the parliament itself."

Here some of the English Privy Councillors who were present asked Lord Herries to name the Scottish nobles to whom he here referred. "I for one, and among the first," was the reply. "We have been told," continued they, "that you yourself approved Moray's regency by your signature." "I should like to see the man among them who would venture to say so in my presence; that is, provided he were of a rank which would entitle him to try the question with me. But as for these petty lawyers, such as Wood is, I know that they are knaves who owe their present position to their lies and fraud. So accustomed have they become to this mode of life, that they do not know how to abandon it, even were they anxious to do so."

According to the same account, when Lord Herries was preparing to return to Queen Mary with this reply, he was told by the Queen of England that Lord Fleming might depart from the court, but that he was to remain where he was for some time longer. Notwithstanding all the efforts he could make to obtain his own dismissal, he could not succeed in being allowed to depart; nor was Fleming permitted to go into France. Herries writes, among other news, that he hopes soon to be allowed to set out on his journey. There are many persons, however, who look with great suspicion at this treatment; and, indeed, at the whole transaction. In Scotland a new Reformation is now going on, which they call the second. The first destroyed the monasteries, nearly all the cathedral churches, and whatever belonged to God's worship in the parish churches. This second Reformation will root up the castles and palaces of the nobility ; so that, apparently, when the third comes it will find nothing on which to busy itself except men's bodies.

When Mary had been informed by Lord Herries's letters of the turn which her affairs had taken, she caused M. de Montmorin[1] to return back to France. That emissary had been sent over by the French king to obtain from Elizabeth permission for the Scottish Queen to pass through England into France, and to comfort her in her troubles. He carried with him letters by which the King of France was given to understand that Mary was now no longer treated as a guest and friend, but was detained as a captive; and that there was no hope that she would escape from this captivity unless she were liberated by the power and authority of the princes of Christendom. For whatever the Queen of England might pretend, however different might appear to be the language she employed, her real intentions towards her cousin were clearly proclaimed by her actions. She has been boasting in private of the great captive she had made without having incurred the expenses of a war.

That these were her real sentiments was clearly proved shortly afterwards. For by God's providence it came to pass that a packet of letters, sent by John Wood (who, as we have already mentioned, was at this time resident in London) to the Earl of Moray, happened to fall into the queen's hands. In this packet, besides

[1] M. de Montmorin arrived in London from France on 3rd June 1568, and had permission to visit Queen Mary. Concerning the progress of his mission, see Teulet, ii. 372, 375, 378.

many other letters which private sectaries, both in France and England, had addressed to the earl (and which brought to light many evil plans for the queen's ruin), were found certain epistles from Wood written to Moray himself, by command of the Queen of England and her chief secretary. Wood stated what the queen had promised to him, and what she thought had best be done. He further mentioned what was the answer he had received from Secretary Cecil (for that is his name), and from the other English sectaries. The whole of them were of such a character that nothing more hostile to Queen Mary herself, nothing more ruinous to her cause, could be either expressed or imagined.

When the Queen of Scotland had read these letters she forthwith sent them to London to Lord Herries, with orders that he should should show them, in her name, to Elizabeth and her councillors, and take care that they were read. When he had done this, and the letters had been read before the council, in the presence of Herries, both the queen and the secretary made answer that the whole was a forgery. Wood, they said, had invented them out of his own head for the purpose of comforting his master, the Earl of Moray, and to prevent him from losing heart under his difficulties. Afterwards, when Wood was questioned in the council about the matter, in the presence of Lord Herries, he made the same assertions, just as he had been instructed by Cecil. For in England Cecil is a man of the highest authority, and such an expert in inventions and lies, that it almost might seem as if he had acquired these qualifications not so much by practice as by birthright. You may recognise in him the true evangelical and the genuine Calvinist.

Being thus made aware of the manner in which the

letters had been dealt with in the English Privy Council, and observing that after the departure of Montmorin she was kept more closely, and that her Scottish friends and her other followers had much greater difficulty than hitherto in obtaining access to her, and further, that all her dealings, either with Scots or English, were most carefully pried into, she thought she had only one remedy left. She secretly drew up a statement or instruction, which she sent to her ambassador in France, and of which the bearer was George Douglas, the brother of the laird of Lochleven, who had proved himself so true-hearted, and had rendered her such valuable help at the time of her escape.

Douglas set out on the 17th of June, and reached Paris on the 7th of July. The queen directed her ambassador to deliver this writing, in her name, in the first instance to the papal nuncio, to be by him forwarded as speedily as possible to his Holiness; in the next place to the King of France; then to the ambassador of the King of Spain, and lastly, to her uncles, the cardinal and his brothers.

In this writing Queen Mary affirms, in the first place, her constancy in the Catholic religion and faith.

Secondly, she shows her innocence in regard to her husband.

Thirdly, she intreats the Pope, in the first instance, and after him the other princes, to undertake the defence of her person and her cause against the daring violence of such rebels and godless assailants.

APPENDIX V.

Misssion of William Chisholm, Bishop of Dumblane, to the Pope.

Letters Patent of Mary Queen of Scotland and King Henry Darnley, by which they appoint William Chisholm, Bishop of Dumblane, to be their Orator at the Holy See.[1]   Dated 30th January 1566.

Be it known to all men by these presents that we, Mary, by the grace of God Queen of the Scots, and King Henry, have appointed, and by the tenor of these present letters do appoint, the reverend father in Christ, William Bishop of Dumblane, to be our orator and proctor to offer our obedience for us and in our names to our most holy lord the Pope, in like manner as our predecessors the kings and princes of Scotland, who have always been Catholic, have hitherto been in the habit of doing ; and further, to do, say, and transact everything and all things which in this matter are requisite and necessary, even should a special and express command be required. Holding as firm and acceptable whatever our said orator and proctor shall think fit to do, or shall do, rightfully and lawfully in the premises.

From our Palace of Holyrood, on the last of January, A.D. 1565.

MARY R.   HENRY R.

[1] From the original letter, signed and sealed, in Latin, which is preserved in the Secret Archives of the Vatican at Rome.   Miscell. Arm. XV. cap. xiii., No. 210.

LETTER from Queen Mary to Pope Pius the Fifth, dated 30th January 1566.[1]

Your predecessor, Pope Pius, of happy and eternal memory, out of that fervent zeal which, like a good and watchful pastor, he felt for the general welfare of the flock over which he was placed, was moved by a special regard towards those poor scattered sheep of our realm of Scotland, which have become a prey to the ravening wolves. In order to recover them to the unity of the one fold and the one Shepherd, he thought fit to send more than once to us his letters and his messengers. And although we believe that he was fully aware of the constancy of our faith (of which we are by no means ashamed), yet we have never yet been able to put into execution these most pious and holy requests which he urged us to fulfil.[2] Every one knows how great have been the troubles to which our realm has been exposed, and how cruel the agitations which have befallen us personally. The enemies of our religion are many. They are confident in their power, and therefore they are all the more to be dreaded. They have hitherto thwarted every effort which, but for them, should have been made to carry into force the suggestions to which we have referred.

When Pope Pius the Fourth was called out of this mortal life, your Holiness succeeded him in the government of the Apostolic See. Hence, in the midst of our troubles, we have the assurance that what he so happily

[1] Translated from the original in Latin, preserved in the Barberini Library at Rome, MS. xliii. 181, fol. 1. Before coming into the hands of Cardinal Barberini, this letter formed a part of the collections of Giacomo Laderchi.

[2] See Labanoff, i. 177.

began your Holiness will yet more happily complete. For this purpose we have sent to your Holiness our beloved and faithful father in Christ, William Bishop of Dumblane, as our ambassador, orator, and proctor. We have commanded him not only to congratulate your Holiness on your elevation to the high dignity of the Apostolic See, but further to present to you our due and ready obedience. We also most earnestly entreat you that in your holy sacrifices and prayers, and in your deliberations and your contributions, as well spiritual as temporal, you would assist our miserable and unhappy kingdom. Things have not yet reached that extremity of ill which forbids us to hope for a recovery by relying upon your advice and assistance, as we are able to do and bound to do. Your predecessor of holy memory, Pope Pius the Fourth, encouraged us in this confidence, and we are persuaded that your Holiness will complete and fulfil it. Already some of our enemies are in exile, and some of them are in our hands; but their fury, and the great necessity in which they are placed, urges them on to attempt extreme measures. But if God and your Holiness be with us (whose cause we are fighting), by your help we will leap over the wall.[1]

Other matters will be explained to you by our beloved and faithful ambassador, to whose statements your Holiness may give the same credit as if they were spoken by our own lips. By granting what he asks (or rather what we ask by him) we shall have cause to be more attached than ever to the Holy See, to which, however, we have always been most attached. May God long preserve your Holiness to ourselves and to the whole Christian world!

[1] A reference to Psalm xvii. 30.

Given at Edinburgh, in our Palace of Holyrood, on the last day of January, in A.D. 1565.

Mary [1] the Queen,

The most devoted daughter of your Holiness.

Addressed—To the most holy lord, the Lord Pope Pius the Fifth.

The SPEECH of the Most Reverend Father the Bishop of Dumblane addressed to our Most Holy Father Pope Pius the Fifth.[2]

Most Holy Father,—In the midst of those extreme calamities with which the most serene and most Christian sovereigns of Scotland, Mary and Henry, have been afflicted, they have been most wonderfully supported by the conviction that they have obtained from God the Father and our Lord Jesus Christ the blessing for which they have so long been suppliants. That you have been able, by your prudence and example, to sustain the Christian commonwealth at a time when it was hastening to ruin, has been accomplished not by chance or by human wisdom, but by the wonderful providence of God alone. In the first place, they thank God, the Author of all that is good, for the great gift of your succession to the Papal See; and then they congratulate you upon your elevation to the dignity of being His

[1] This and the following line are in the queen's autograph in the original letter.

[2] Translated from a contemporary copy of the original Latin in the MS. xxxiv. 66 number 9, preserved in the Barberini Library in Rome. It is injured in the margin in a few places, by which, however, the sense is not affected. Several passages of a declamatory character have been slightly compressed in this translation.

representative upon earth. To that Apostolic See they profess their entire obedience. Every one knows how faithful the kings of Scotland have always been to the See of Rome, and how firm has been the bond which has bound them together. If we survey the long history of past ages, we shall find many princes who exceeded them in wealth, glory, and power, but we shall find not one who surpassed them in their constancy to the faith.

It is now more than thirteen hundred and sixty years since Donald, at that time King of the Scots, despatched ambassadors to Pope Victor the First, the fifteenth in succession from Saint Peter, requesting him to send some good men into Scotland who would instruct him, his wife, his children, and his entire kingdom in the Christian religion. The Pope did so, and the whole realm was converted.[1] Thus was laid the foundation of that firm friendship and undying unity which has since then existed between that kingdom and the Holy See, every occupant of which, from that day to the present, has done something to perpetuate and increase the strength of the bond. Celestine the First sent Palladius into Scotland to preserve it from the Pelagian heresy; and not only did he do so, but, as Prosper tells us, he brought the Orkney Islands within the unity of the faith.[2] Others were equally successful. Of the many ambassadors who have been sent to us, I may mention Eneas Sylvius,[3] a man of eminent learning, who afterwards became Pope. There was also Marcus . . . . , a Venetian and Patriarch of

[1] A tradition which has no support from sufficient evidence.

[2] The writings of Prosper contain no such statement. See Contra Collatorem, cap. xxi. (Migne, vol. li., col. 271, 595.)

[3] Æneas Sylvius Piccolomini, afterwards Pope Pius the Second, visited Scotland, of which he has left an interesting description. On the frequency of the intercourse between Rome and Scotland, see Tytler, ii. 176.

Aquilea,[1] who made himself exceedingly beloved among us, as well from his many excellent qualities, and especially for his liberality towards the poor. Last of all, I will name Petrus Lippomannus, who would have equalled, or even surpassed the others, if a longer life had been granted to him.

Bound to Rome by so many and such great obligations, the kings of Scotland have remained firm in their allegiance to the religion for which they were indebted to that Church. As they, in their generation, never wavered in any single point, so is it now with their most serene Majesties, Queen Mary and King Henry. Had they consented to have gone over to the enemies of the Christian faith, or even to have come to a compromise with them, they might have lived among them in peace and prosperity. Yet this most illustrious queen, who is a young woman, has had the courage to hold firm to the faith ever since her return from France into that remote land where she is now placed, unbefriended and without one adviser, in the midst of enemies both domestic and foreign. During the year which has elapsed since her marriage, both she and her husband have been kept in perpetual agitation, for no cause whatever save this, that they would not deviate one single hair's-breadth from their obedience to the See of Rome.

For these reasons, most holy father, you are required to receive all the more willingly the obedience which their Majesties now offer to you by me. They offer it, and can keep it only at the greatest personal peril to themselves and their fortunes. Such is the state of affairs at this present moment in Scotland, that unless you help them no hope of the preservation of religion remains for that kingdom. When Pius the Fourth of

---

[1] Marco Grimani, Patriarch of Aquilea.

blessed memory was informed of this, he promised that
he would use every effort for the defence of that realm;
and he would assuredly have done so had he lived. It
remains for your Holiness to complete the work, and to
rescue Scotland from that danger in which she stands.
Nor does this danger threaten Scotland only, for England,
Ireland, and the Orkneys are equally imperilled. They
will all rise or fall together. Especially is this the case
with England, which, as all the world knows, belongs by
the right of inheritance to Scotland. Thus, then, these
most Christian sovereigns ask your assistance not only for
themselves (for, were it possible, they would rather live
a private life than continue to exist in the midst of so
many dangers), they ask it for their subjects, they ask it
for the salvation of souls, for the Church, and the honour
and glory of God Himself. In doing this, your Holiness
will do for Scotland no less a benefit than was done by
your predecessors, Victor and Celestine.

LETTER from Hippolytus of Este, Cardinal of Ferrara, to
Queen Mary.[1]

Most serene and honoured queen, to whom all respect
is deservedly due.

The letters which your Majesty has condescended to
address to me by the Reverend the Bishop of Dumblane
have occasioned me the greatest joy and the greatest

[1] From the original corrected draft in the Barberini MS., xxxi. 43.
It is in Latin. Hippolytus of Este, Cardinal of Ferrara (born in
1509), was sent on official business to the court of Francis the First,
with whom his family was connected. He was a frequent resident at
Paris during the reign of Henry the Second, where he became
acquainted with the young Queen of Scotland. He was present at
the Colloquy of Poissy in 1561, and died at Rome in 1572. See
Ciaconius, ii. 1530.

sorrow. I grieve to be informed of what you tell me concerning the state of misery and peril into which your kingdom is reduced ; but at the same time I rejoice to learn that you still retain a kindly recollection of me, for although I never doubted the continuance of this feeling on your part, still it is a very great pleasure to find such proofs of your good will as are expressed in these your letters. I cannot but think, however, that the evils which you mention will be of no long continuance ; for I trust, in the first instance, to the goodness of God, and in the next place, to your Majesty's wonderful prudence. My conviction, then, is that if not totally removed they will assuredly be mitigated.

In reference to my own wish and good will to help your Majesty, I beg you to be assured that it shall always be my most earnest endeavour to do everything in my power which, as far as I either know or can imagine, will be for the furtherance of your wishes. I will permit no opportunity to escape me of doing what will give you pleasure. It has always been my wish to do this, and your recent letters have increased a desire which I had imagined to admit of no increase.

In regard to other matters the Bishop of Dumblane will supply your Majesty with fuller information. Although he could not accomplish a greater success than what he himself will recount to your Majesty, yet I can confirm his information in one important matter. It is this. His Holiness has the kindest feelings towards your Majesty, nor will he ever fail you in whatever concerns either your own personal dignity or the preservation of the faith in the noble kingdom of Scotland.

I cannot conclude without asking your Majesty to be assured that as long as I live I will be no less entirely devoted to your service than if you still were Queen of

France, as once you were. I cannot say anything more than this in order to express the sincerity of my regard. May our Lord Jesus Christ long preserve your Majesty in health and safety.

Dated at Trevi, ...

Your Majesty's most humble servant,   H.

LETTER from Queen Mary to the Bishop of Dumblane.[1]

Since my last letters sent to my uncle the Cardinal of Lorraine, I have returned to my royal residence in Edinburgh ; and for greater security I have taken up my abode in the castle. We believe that these rebellious conspirators (all of whom have now fled into England), are so evilly disposed toward us that the two parties are about to collect men and money against us, so that if we be not aided by the holy father we fear that we shall be driven to accept whatever terms and conditions they may please to offer, or to sacrifice our kingdom and life.

Moved by these reasons, and in order to avert the destruction of this our Church, a matter which so much concerns ourselves and our subjects (for we are all worn out by our past efforts), we command you to inform our said holy father that without his assistance, on which we rely next after God, it is impossible for us by any means to save the Catholic religion from an entire overthrow. And therefore we take God to witness of this our diligence in the present matter, hereby imploring the pope's help for this kingdom, which is in such straits that (as I have already said) we shall be compelled to take whatever

[1] Translated from a contemporary Italian version of Queen Mary's letter of 1st April 1566, addressed to the Bishop of Dumblane, which occurs in the Vatican Library, MS. Urbin. 1040, fol. 203. At the same time she wrote to the Archbishop of Glasgow, her ambassador in Paris, and to the Cardinal of Lorraine. See Labanoff i., 342.

conditions our rebels and heretics may please to propose. But know this for certain that much more willingly would we lose our kingdom, and life itself, rather than accept such conditions as these; and thus much you shall tell our holy father, namely, that we hereby exonerate ourselves, and throw the entire responsibility upon his Holiness.[1]

LETTER from Pope Pius the Fifth to Philip the Second, King of Spain.[2]

To my very dear Son in Christ, Philip the King Catholic of Spain, Pope Pius the Fifth.

Very dear Son in Christ, etc.—When we were informed of the wicked plots which have of late been planned against our very dear daughter in Christ, Mary Queen of Scotland, by the heretics of that realm who are banished from it, we were overpowered with the deepest sorrow and horror. Our heart was oppressed by the thought of the extreme peril through which that excellent and pious queen had passed, and not only she herself, but also the unborn infant. But out of this danger she has been snatched and delivered by the hand of the Omnipotent. When we reflect upon the nature of this crime it appears to us to be so atrocious that, in our opinion,

[1] At fol. 229 b in the same Vatican MS. occurs the following note :—Rome, 18th May.—His Holiness sends a messenger into Scotland with a good sum of money for the aid of this queen, in order that she may be able to resist the designs of her rival of England and preserve the kingdom in its Catholicity. He has also written such a letter as will be most satisfactory to her.

[2] Translated from the original Latin draft preserved in the Secret Archives of the Vatican, Arm. xliv., tom. 7, fol. 47. In connection with this correspondence see Lab., i. 355, and Con, ap. Jebb., ii. 49, 50, 51. The present letter, (which is dated 2d May 1566,) does not occur in the Epistolæ Pii V., Antv. 1640, quarto.

the heart of every Christian prince cannot but be moved with one consent to avenge her cause; and to act with the same earnestness as if the life of each of them singly had been assailed by the treachery and violence of these heretics. Your Majesty has doubtless heard from the letters of other princes how this tragedy has been attempted, nay, all but completed.

Now since the author and promoter of this detestable crime is supposed to be the person who passes herself off as the Queen of England, and who has offered a place of refuge within her realm for those heretical Scots who are the queen's enemies; since, further, she seeks the destruction of this excellent queen by every means within her power, we cannot but appeal to your Majesty on her behalf.

We are aware, my dear Son, that your authority is of the greatest weight with the so-styled Queen of England. We therefore advise and entreat you in the Lord sharply to rebuke her, as well by your ambassador as by your own letters on this subject, drawn up with all precision, in order that she may be deterred from again attempting anything, either directly or indirectly, against the Queen of Scotland. Give her also to understand that you are displeased with the attempts which have already been made against that queen; and that you will not fail to befriend her if any of the subjects of England supply any assistance, either openly or secretly, to the Scottish rebels, or give them counsel or favour.

Furthermore, it would be a Christian action, and one becoming your devotion and humanity, as well as most grateful to God and ourselves, if you would encourage the Queen of Scotland by your letters, and promise that you would not fail to assist her. If our finances permitted us to do so, we would be the first to set an example to other princes, showing them what help ought to be afforded to such a devout princess as she has proved herself to be against her rebellious heretics. But not only are we placed at such a great distance from that kingdom that we cannot conveniently render her such assistance, but we are compelled to afford all the help we can from hence not only to the Knights of Malta and to your brother Charles in the war which is about to break out with the Turks, but further to protect our own sea-board against the fleets of the enemies of the holy Roman Church. Various other expenses press upon us, and we found the Apostolic See burdened with a very heavy debt.

Hence, then, it is that we flee to you, our very dear son, and that we recommend to you the Queen of Scotland and her affairs with all possible earnestness. Whatsoever kindness you can do her in this her present emergency will be valued by us as done to ourselves. It will afford us the greatest pleasure if we find that these our letters shall have been of use to her, as we hope they will.

Dated at St Peter's at Rome, under the Fisher's ring, 2d May 1566, in the first year of our pontificate.

ANTONIUS FLOREBELLUS LAVELLINUS.

SPEECH addressed to His Holiness, Pope Pius the Fifth, by the Bishop of Dumblane, on the part of Mary Stuart, Queen of Scotland.[1]

To the praise of Almighty God.

During my residence in Paris, when nothing was further from my thoughts than the important business on which I am now engaged, I most unexpectedly re-

[1] From the MS. xxx. 170, in the Barberini Library, Rome. It is fairly written by a clerk, and corrected (chiefly in diction) by the bishop himself. It has sustained much injury by damp, and is in many places scarcely legible.

ceived a command from the most serene Queen of Scotland, my mistress, and from the most serene king, by which I was ordered to take upon myself the office of legate to your Holiness. Although I was not ignorant of my own deficiency, yet I considered that I should be guilty of a crime were I to refuse to obey my rulers, or to fail in a cause which was at once excellent in itself and closely connected with the interests of religion. Having, therefore, taken upon myself this mission I set out as fast as my horse would carry me to visit the Cardinal of Lorraine, with whom, for many reasons, I thought it advisable to have a conference. At that time he was at Varennes.[1] When we met, he informed me that an event had occurred which cannot but give pain to every well-disposed person ; namely, that an insurrection had broken out against our queen, which had originated with certain wicked heretics. Yet, as there was some doubt as to the truth of the report, arising partly from the improbability of the event in itself, partly from regard to the source whence it had reached him, which induced most men to be suspicious as to its accuracy, I decided that I would leave Varennes and remain at Lyons until some distinct and trustworthy evidence upon the subject should reach us. And so I did.

During a stay of a few days at Lyons, I became acquainted with the full particulars of the case. It is not easy to say whether one ought to rejoice or mourn about it. There is cause for joy when we reflect that this innocent queen has escaped alive out of the hands of those most cruel murderers ; on the other hand, our sorrow is excited by the rebellion of those wicked insurgents, by the depth of the misery into which we have

---

[1] A small town in Champagne (Meuse), not far from Verdun, where the cardinal had a considerable property.

fallen, and by the calamities which have overtaken the realm of Scotland. What these are, your Holiness will easily discover.

At a time when, by the queen's directions, the usual solemn conferences were being held in the royal city of Edinburgh, for the purpose of passing a law for the punishment of rebels, and for the revival of the primitive Catholic religion, which had all but faded out of the minds of the inhabitants of that realm, the enemies of the faith (who at the same time were the queen's enemies) obtained from the new king certain concessions, which her Majesty in her wisdom had refused to grant. Although they were aware that they were acting contrary to the usages of the realm, these men promised the king that they would gratify his desire of wearing the crown; and that the way to obtain it lay through the parliament. Of all this the queen was ignorant. Having thus obtained the means of returning home, these men reached Edinburgh on the day previous to that on which the last meeting would be held; and on the same day they entered the royal palace where the king and queen had supped together shortly before, and there, about the eighteenth[1] hour of the day, they cruelly murdered David Riccioli, the queen's secretary, a most excellent and worthy man. Seeing this the queen fled into her bedchamber, which, from having been a place for rest, had now become a prison, for eighty musketeers were immediately told off by the rebels to keep her in ward; and this they did with such strictness that not only could none of the men of the household visit their young queen, but not even her women servants were permitted to come near her. Whatever food was brought was carefully examined.

[1] That is, according to the Roman mode of reckoning time.

o

At this time there were in the palace three[1] of the principal earls of the realm, men of piety, and faithful to the poor queen. Perceiving that they were unable to help her, and were themselves prevented from leaving the palace, they escaped by the windows. When this was known to the heretics, they gave the earls to understand that if they raised troops with the intention of delivering the queen from prison, they would assuredly put her to death.

The rebels in the meantime carried on their work with the king, whom they so fascinated with their promises that he refused to take any part in the meeting of the Estates unless the crown were granted to him. This they undertook to do, in order to retain him in their

---

[1] Originally "two," but corrected by the bishop, by whom the following passage was added (in Latin) in the bottom margin, but afterwards cancelled so effectually as to be in some places beyond recovery.

"One of these three was named the Earl of Huntley, who was the first who brought the queen help against the heretics. After escaping from the hands of the enemy, he could not refrain from coming beneath the window of the bedroom in which the queen was imprisoned, and having called her, which he did as well as circumstances then permitted him to do, he attempted to give her comfort and courage, and offered to help her. The queen on her part began to exhort him to be of good heart, to be constant in his faith, and on no account to swerve from the Catholic religion. She said that as for herself, she had a firm hope in the Lord that, although she had been overthrown by these turbulent gatherings of the heretics, yet that He would deliver her out of their hands. 'And should it happen,' added she, 'that I were to die for the Catholic religion (which would be the happiest event that could befall me), I would be an intercessor with God for the Catholic religion, and thus would be able to help it.'"

The latter portion of this passage has undergone so many alterations, that in several places the reading is very doubtful. As all passages have alike been cancelled, it is impossible to say which of the readings are to be preferred.

party. When the persons who were going to hold the parliament understood this, they fled in various directions, for they were unwilling to be governed by him, or to give their consent to such unusual proceedings. When he noticed that he was not obeyed even by the persons whom he had recalled from banishment, he betook himself to the queen. He confessed that he had sinned against her, he humbly begged her pardon, and promised that he would provide a remedy for all the mischief that he had done. He himself told her Majesty, what she had already discovered by her own acute observation, that the rebels longed for her death more than anything else, and that there were certain other persons whom they meant to hang on a gallows in front of the royal palace. He also told her that if she did not make some speedy arrangement for her escape, her life was not worth a rush.

In the midst of such difficulties as these, what could the queen do? She was a woman, and not a strong woman, she was in the sixth month of her pregnancy, and (the most serious matter of all) she was closely guarded. Yet, being a person of wonderful strength of will, she decided upon a mode of escape, the like of which would seldom occur to any woman, least of all to a woman near her confinement. Her plan was this :—she determined that she would let herself down by ropes from a very lofty tower, and that she would take refuge in some strong castle, and thus save her life.

While this innocent queen was thus detained in prison (it might almost be said in fetters) she endured with the greatest patience two very severe trials. In the presence of her husband she bore with wonderful meekness the most cruel threats, and the most atrocious insults ; strengthened, I presume, by the memory of

One Who, for her sake and not for His own, endured not only reproaches but also torments. This was the first, and the second was as stern. For two days and three nights she was exposed to this persecution, during which period she heard a proclamation made in the king's name, commanding that all Papists (the favourite name for Catholics) and all their belongings should depart from the city, and that a new parliament would be summoned, in which the queen would be deprived of the government of the realm.[1] This was all the more distressing to her Majesty, since the rebels intended to shut her up in some castle, and that they themselves should manage the affairs of the kingdom. I have an additional fact to add, which I do with great pain, for I do not know how the ears of your Holiness will bear it. The rebels had determined that, if the castle in which the queen was imprisoned should be attacked by her faithful subjects, they would tear her limb from limb, cut her into morsels, and throw them over the walls.[2]

Terrified and trembling to find himself associated with such cruel monsters, the king went to the queen, asked her to form some plan how they might preserve their lives, and promised that he would not desert her. They discussed the plan of escape to which I have already referred ; but God arranged a better one for them. The rebels had decided that the queen should not be removed from the palace in which she then was resident to the castle (that is, the prison) in which they had resolved that she should be confined until she had signed the wicked decrees which they had drawn up. The king, following the advice of the queen, now urged that she

[1] Here the original is much injured in the margin.
[2] Two lines of declamatory matter are here cancelled in the MS.

should have her liberty, thereby to prevent the possibility of her retracting her promise. He undertook to make her do whatever the lords pleased and to keep her in safe custody. Believing the king, the confederates entrusted him with the charge of the queen, and permitted the captain of the royal guard to come to him. In the middle of the night, the king, the queen, the captain, and a servant set off at full speed; and about daybreak they reached a strong fortress. Thus they were delivered from the snare of the fowler, and from the hands of those who sought their life. May the name of the Lord be blessed.[1]

Hence you may perceive, holy father, the extent of the difficulties and dangers in which not only is our queen involved, but also the entire Church of Scotland. Of a truth it would have become extinct but for the wonderful, nay, almost incredible courage of her Majesty. Her conduct bears abundant tokens of the divine assistance, to which it is unnecessary for me to add any testimony. Your Holiness may easily conjecture the extent of her Majesty's devotion to the Catholic Church and the Apostolic See from the fact that, before the occurrence of the incidents which I have just recorded, I had already been sent on a mission to your Holiness in the joint names of the king and queen. They acknowledge you to be the most holy pastor of the Church Catholic, and the true successor of the blessed Peter, the chief of the Apostles. They congratulate you on the honour which comes to you through this burdensome dignity. The principal duty then with which I am charged is to express to your Holiness how much they rejoice and how thankful they are to God for having placed such a steersman as yourself to guide the bark of

---

[1] Some declamatory matter is here cancelled.

course, and on this point I shall be brief. Since these personages by whom I am sent to your Holiness profess themselves to be the children of the Church, they most earnestly ask of you, as the common father of all Christians, that they may continue to retain all the privileges which they have hitherto enjoyed by the liberality of your predecessors. They ask your blessing, and they implore your aid, advice, and protection. Especially they request . . . .[1] supported and encouraged by which they may be enabled to protect and preserve the Catholic faith within their realm. They ask this for many reasons, for these especially : because they are your own children, because of old . . . .,[2] and because the early kings of Scotland have always been most devoted to the Holy See. In this respect they who now wield the sceptre are no whit behind their predecessors, perhaps, indeed, they surpass them. If I did not recognise in your Holiness one who is not only a most loving father, but also a most watchful pastor, I would do what every one who is invested with the office of an emissary would do under similar circumstances ; I would venture to advise and entreat you to grant their petition. But every one knows what love you bear towards the weakly ones of the flock, of whom the number among us is far from small. I doubt not that your Holiness will do everything which Christian affection would prompt for the confirmation of the faith. But I will detain your Holiness no longer than to express the hope that, like a loving father, you will not only preserv but will revive the faith which Pope Victor,[3] of bless 1 memory, the

[1] At this point a few words are illegible in the original, but the general drift of the sentence can be followed.

[2] Again the manuscript is defaced.

[3] This tradition is unsupported by history.

the great expense which I have incurred in the queen's service, as well in Scotland as elsewhere, and the sums of ready money which I have expended by her orders ; added to which, I have received nothing from my benefice, which is the poorest see in Scotland as to its revenue, and this in consequence as well of the troubles there as of the great hate which all of the queen's enemies there bear me :—

Therefore I beg you, Monseigneur, to do me the favour to order the treasurer to pay me as well the balance of the said five hundred crowns, as also the other hundred crowns which you granted me last year, as you yourself have lately written from Nancy and Compiègne to the said treasurer.

Monseigneur, if you do not help me to escape from this great annoyance to which I am exposed by the banker and merchant of this town, I shall be compelled to leave it, in order to escape from their observation and the other inconveniences which may happen to me.

NAU'S NARRATIVE,

IN THE ORIGINAL FRENCH.

. . . . foys [1] ils avoient mis la main à l'œuvre, il falloit parachever si tous ne vouloient se mectre au hazard de leur vies d'autant qu'ils estoient trop avant pour reculer, et que l'offense ne se pouvoit réparer. Alléguoient que le tout avoit esté faict pour sa grandeur, et pour ce qu'il debvoit y marcher le premier, affin de donner courage aux aultres. En tout cas que s'il estoit si couard et défailly de ne vouloir poursuivre l'enterprise, ilz estoient tous résoluz de se maintenir l'ung l'aultre sans aultre respect, et qu'ilz n'y espargneroient personne.

Le roy se trouva tout effrayé, se voyant ainsi seul entre telz meurtriers ; car de son naturel il n'estoit des plus résoluz en la nécessité et au danger. Il envoya quérir son père, lequel veint avec quelques aultres. Ils entrèrent en conseil pour délibérer de ce qu'estoit à faire. Mais lesditz conjurateurs se meirent sus de plus beau, et proposèrent [2] premièrement qu'il estoit nécessaire avant toute aultre chose de rompre le Parlement et renvoyer tous les seigneurs que y avoit voix en leur maison, ce que fust le lendemain, jour de Dimanche, proclamé ; de façon qu'il ne demeure aucun desdits seigneurs en la ville. Secondement, qu'il falloit envoyer Sa Majesté à Striveling, [3] et avoir bonne garde pour là fere ses couches. Et disoit ledit seigneur Lindsey qu'elle passeroit assez son temps à berser son

---

[1] Nau's orginal narrative here begins. The following text is printed from the Cottonian MS. (Cal. B. iv. 94.)

[2] Originally . . . en fin próposerent.

[3] Et là la fere garder, cancelled.

enfant et luy chanter Baleliou [1] en l'endormant, tirer de l'arc dans le jardin, et fere des ouvrages tant que bon luy sembleroit, d'autant qu'il scavoit qu'elle s'y plaisoit fort ; cependant que le Roy gouverneroit les afferes avec la noblesse. Lors quelques remonstrant le faict des seigneurs que avoient esté enfermez et qui se pourroient mectre en contrager avec forces, ledict Ruthven respondist, " N'y a il point aultre remède ? s'ilz font la moindre instance et [2] font aucun remuëment pour la ravoir, il fault leur jecter par pièces du hault de la terrasse." Et sur ce qu'un aultre répliqua qu'elle estoit grosse. " Je m'asseur," dist il, " et le prendray sur ma vie, qu'elle n'est grosse que d'une fille, il n'y a point de danger. Mais de ce nous prendrons conseil avec les seigneurs de Murray, comte Rothes et quelques aultres" (revenuz de Neufcastel le mesme jour du meurtre Sabmedy sur les six heures du soir, et estoient demeuréz secrettement cachéz dans la ville) "car nous ne voulons rien faire sans eulx."

Or sus luy dirent à la fin ; " Si vous voulez [3] parvenir à ce que nous vous avons promis, il fault que vous suivez nostre conseil, affin de vous conserver avec nous. Si vous faictes aultrement, nous pourvoirons, à quelque prix que ce soit, pour nous mesmes." Et sur ce murmurans les ungs avec les aultres, parlans à l'aureille, meirent le Roy et son père en grande deffiance. Et ne tenoient entre eulx leur vies bien asseurées ; principallement lors qu'au départir il luy fust dit qu'il ne debvoit parler à Sa Majesté pour ce temps qu'en leur présence ; et luy ayans osté ses serviteurs, luy laissèrent garde auprès de sa chambre.

[1] In this word, which preserves the memory of the dreaded wolf, we recognise the original of the old Scottish " Balow," now obsolete, but well-known from its use in " Lady Bothwell's Lament," the first stanza of which reads thus :—

> " Balow, my babe, lye still and sleep,
> It grieves me sair to see thee weep.
> If thou'lt be silent I'll be glad,
> Thy maining makes my heart full sad ;
> Balow, my boy, thy mither's joy,
> Thy father breids me great annoy."
> From a copy written in 1781.

[2] Et veulent remuer, cancelled.

[3] Voulez . . . à la fin, cancelled.

Toutes ces consideracions et appréhensions furent cause que le Roy la nuit monta par ung degré secret veres la chambre de Sa Majesté, et ayant trouvé la porte fermée pria[1] très instamment qu'elle luy fust ouvrerte pour dire à Sa Majesté ce qu'importoit grandement à leur commune sauveté. Toutes foys[2] il ne luy fust permis d'entrer jusques au lendemain matin,[3] Sa Majesté ayant passé la nuit en larmes et plaintes, accompagnée seulement de la viele[4] Dame de Huntly et quelques aultres de ses dames, qui mectoient toute la peine qu'elles pouvoient de la consoler.

Le lendemain matin le comte de Murray vint voir Sa Majesté, et luy ayant fait ses excuses de ce qu'il estoit tenu sonnailler estre grand arriere sur tels désordres, luy promist en fin s'en parler aux seigneurs ; et de mesme advisa Sa Majesté de les faire venir le lendemain en sa présence. Mais elle n'y voulust condescendre, quelque requeste que luy en fust faicte. Le roy passa ceste nuit en grand perplexité[5] pour sortir du labyrinthe où inconsidérément il s'estoit laissé conduire, poussé et alléché de vaine ambition ; se remectant tantost devant les yeux la griefve offense qu'il avoit commise à l'endroict de la Royne sa femme, les grandes obligations qu'il luy avoit,[6] et tantost la crainte de sa vie et de sa ruine, s'il, contraint par la nécessité,[7] suivoit le party où il s'estoit engaigé, dont il ne pouvoit trouver moyen de se retirer avec sa seureté, d'autant que les aultres estoient les plus fortz, et ledit seigneur de Murray avec ses partisans, ses anciens enemys, qui n'avoient oublié le passé, ains[8] s'estoient seulement voulu servir de luy pour porter la honte et infamie d'un si meschant acte, comme de fait peu après ils luy imputèrent le tout, affin de se vanger soubz ce prétexte de luy; de mesme façon qu'ils voulurent colorer le meurtre par eux commis de ce jeune

[1] Originally, supplia.
[2] Pour ceste nuit, cancelled.
[3] Jusques au lendemain matin, an interlineation.
[4] Viele, added above the line.
[5] Originally, le roy . . . sur le matin ayant.
[6] Les grandes obligations qu'il luy avoit, an interlineation.
[7] Contrainte par la nécessité, above the line.
[8] N'avoient oublie le passé, ains, an interlineation.

prince, trop facile pour si fins renards,[1] du mauvais traictment [2] que Sa Majesté avoit receu de luy, empeschans par tous
moyens leur réconciliation.   Car à la vérité leur principal
desseing estoit, et principallement dudict de Murray, comme il
se congnoistra par tout le cours de ceste histoire, de dépossèder
du royaume tous les deux, affin de s'en approprier.   Et à
ceste intention, voyant peu après qu'ils [3] n'y pouvoient si tost
parvenir par la mort violente de l'une et l'autre, les nouris-
sans soubz main en continuelle malcontantement, ils leur con-
seillerent de fere divorce pour leur oster toute légitime succession.

Ne se pouvant donc ledict seigneur Roy depeler des pas-
sions et diverses considéracions où il se trouvoit envelopper,
après avoir balancé toutes choses d'une part et d'aultre,
s'arresta d'avoir recours à la royne sa femme, et congnoissant
son bon naturel[4] et l'extresme affection qu'elle luy avoit
tousjours .portée [5] espéra qu'il pourroit en recongnoissant sa
fault et luy offrant d'ý satisfaire, se remectre bien avec elle, et
pour le moins,[6] la persuader de pourvoir, comme la nécessité
le requéroit,[7] à leur commune seureté et le délivrer du
danger où il se trouvoit.   Donc le Dimanche matin avant
jour la vint trouver en sa chambre, et de prime abordée se
jetant à genoux devant elle (ce que Sa Majesté ne voulut
souffrir)[8] luy dist en pleurant[9] " Ha, ma Marie " (ainsi
l'appelloit il familièrement) il fault maintenant que je confesse,
mais trop tard, la faulte que j'ay faicte contre vous : et ne la
pouvant amander que par vous, en requérrir pardon et la
recongnoistre.   Ma jeunesse et trop peu de jugement me
servent d'excuse en vostre endroict, me trouvant malheureuse-

---

[1] In continuing the narrative from the bottom of one page to the top
of the following, the transition is so abrupt, that possibly some few words
may be wanting.

[2] Originally, du malcontentement.

[3] A ceste intention voyant peu après qu'ils, an interlineation.

[4] Originally, et recongnoissant sa faulte et trouva plus expedient.

[5] Se remectre bien avec elle et pour le moins, an interlineation.

[6] Demonstrée, cancelled.

[7] Comme la nécessité la requéroit, an interlineation.

[8] Ce que sa Majesté ne voulut souffrir, an interlineation.

[9] En pleurant, above the line.

ment abusé et deceu par les persuasions de[1] ces meschans traistres, qui m'ont faict tesmoing[2] fauteur de leur conspiracions contre vous, moy, et toute nostre race. Je le congnoy[3] maintenant, et voy bien que toute leur intention est de nous ruiner. Je n'eusse par mon Dieu jamais pensé ny préveu qu'ils fussent venus à telle extremité; et si j'en suis coulpable, c'est plus par imprudence que par aucune mauvaise volonté que j'eusse vers vous. L'ambition m'a aveuglé, je le confesse. Mais puisque Dieu m'a faict ceste grâce de ne me laisser transporter plus oultre et qu'il m'advise à bonne heure (comme j'espère) de m'en repentir, je vous supplie, ma Marie, d'avoir pitié de moy, de nostre enfant, de vous mesmes, qui sommes tous perduz si vous n'y donnez promptement ordre."

Et sur ce il luy bailla les Articles signéz entre luy et les conspirateurs; disant qu'il scavoit bien que si cela estait jamais descouvert ce seroit sa mort. Ce néantmoins, il s'en vouloit descharger.

La royne, troublée encores et foible de l'esmotion où elle avoit passé le nuict, luy respondist franchement, n'estant nourrie ny accoustumée à dissimuler.[4] "Monseigneur, vous m'avez faict ung tel tort depuis 24 heures que la souvenaunce de nostre ancienne amitié, ny toute l'espérance que vous me scauriez donner pour l'advenir, ne me le scauroient faire oublier. Et affin que je ne vous céle le resentement que j'en ay, je pense qu'il ne sera jamais en vostre puissance de le réparer. Vous vous estes par trop mescongnu.[5] Qu'espériez-vous[6] d'avoir seurement sans moy? Qui ay, comme vous scavez, contre l'advis de ceulx que vous affectez maintenant,[7] poursuivist pour vous et instamment requis d'eulx ce que vous[8] avez prétendu d'emporter par leur

---

[1] Les persuasions de, added above the line.
[2] Ou quasi, cancelled.
[3] Originally, m'en appercoy.
[4] Comme elle ne dissimuloit jamais, cancelled.
[5] Originally, oublié.
[6] Originally, de posseder.
[7] Mon conseil, cancelled; ceulx qui vous affectez maintenant, added above.
[8] Originally, vous aujourdhuy.

P

moyens et meschans pratiques. J'ay esté plus songneuse de vostre grandeur que vous mesmes. Vous ay-je jamais desnié chose raisonnable que vous peust advantager par dessus ceulx qui aujourd'huy vous veulent tenir soubz leur pouvoir, et quasi mectre avec moy[1] soubz le pied ? Pensez, Monseigneur, à vous mesmes[2] en vostre propre conscience, remarquez la tasche d'ingratitude dont vous l'avez souillée. Le regret toutes foys que vous en avez, à quoy je pense que la nécessité vous a plus amené qu'aucun ressentement de vraye et sincère amitié, me donne quelque consolation. Si je vous eusse le plus griefvement, qu'on scauroit imaginer offensée, vous n'eussiez sceu plus honteusement et rigoureusement en prendre vengeance. Et grâces à Dieu, vous ny homme du monde ne me scauroit reprocher que j'aye jamais fait ou dist chose que pour vostre propre bien qui vous peust justement desplaire. Vostre vie m'est chère, et me suis obligée selon Dieu et mon debvoir de vous conserver autant que moy-mesmes. Mais puisque vous nous avez mis tous deux en ce précipice, advisez et travaillez de nous en tirer."

"Ha ma Marie," respondist ce pauvre prince, "ayez pitié de moy ; je t'asseure que ceste infortune me fera sage pour l'advenir, et n'auray jamais repos que je ne te vange de ces malheureux traistres, si nous pouvions eschapper de leur mains."

Sa Majesté en fin ayant leu les Articles dessusdits, luy promeist de pourvoir à leur commune délivrance, mais qu'il falloit que de son costé il y travaillast, et pour le premier qu'il trouvast moyen de faire départir quelques soldats qu' on luy avoit appoinctéz pour sa garde. Sur ce il conseilla[3] Sa Majesté que si elle estoit requis des conjurateurs de leur pardon, elle leur accordast, affin de les adoucir, et cependant il se trouveroit quelque moyen d'appoinctement. Mais Sa Majesté ny voulust aucunement entendre, et luy dist ; " Monseigneur, le cœur ne me bastera jamais de promectre chose que je n'aye intention de tenir ; et ne me puis forcer tant que de mentir

---

[1] Avec moy, above the line.
[2] A vous mesme, above the line.
[3] Originally, luy fust d'advis que.

à ceulx mesmes qui m'ont si vilainement trahie ; mais vous,
qui avez desjà franchys comme moy, si vous le trouvez bon,
vous pouvez leur promectre en mon nom tout ce qu'il vous
plaira, car je ne leur obligeray jamais ma foy." Le roy y
consentist ; et sur ce estans partis secrettement l'un de
l'aultre.

Sa Majesté estoit gardée[1] fort estroictement, et ne mangea
jusques sur les 4 heures du soir, ou sa viande fust visitée fort
curieusement par lord de Lyndsey, qui demeura près d'elle.
Le matin, comme j'ay dist cy dessus, la proclamacion fust
faicte par la ville que tous les seigneures qui avoient voix au
parlement se départissent de la ville. Eux ainsi licentiéz,[2]
le Lundy ensuyvant le comte de Murray passant par la ville
vint au Tolbuth avec quelques aultres qui estoient contumacéz,
et là firent protestacion qu'ils estoient prestz de respondre au
Parlement ; sachans bien qu'il ne se trouveroit personne qui
en ce temps les osast accuser.

Durant ce temps la vielle dame de Huntlay, qui estoit bien
aise d'avoir sa revanche contre Monseigneur de Murray,[3] eust
permission de venir visiter[4] Sa Majesté ; et lui apporta advis,
de la part de son fils et des aultres Seigneurs qui estoient
eschappéz, qu 'ilz avoient assembléz des forces ; et que si Sa
Majesté pouvoit trouver moyen[5] de descendre par une fenestre,
que luy appoinctèrent, avec une chaine de corde, que ladicte
dame luy porteroit entre deux plats comme si c'eust esté de
la viande,[6] ilz se rendroient là tous pour la recevoir. Comme
la dicte dame parloit à Sa Majesté, estant sur sa chaire percée,
Lord Lindsey soubçonnant ce que estoit, y entra et la rappella,
luy défendant d'y rentrer ; ce néantmoins elle remporta entre
sa chair et chemise, d'autant qu 'elle estoit fouillée par dehors,[7]

[1] Originally, estoit secrettement gardée.

[2] Et soudain qu'ls furent, originally.

[3] Qui estoit bien aise d'avoir sa revanche contre Monsieur de Murray,
an interlineation.

[4] Originally, de venir trouver.

[5] Trouver moyen de, above the line.

[6] Avec une chaine de corde que ladite dame porteroit entre deux platz
comme c'eust esté de la viande, an interlineation.

[7] D'autant qu'elle estoit fouillée en dehors, between the lines.

une lettre de Sa Majesté addressante auxdits Seigneurs, par laquelle elle leur mandoit qu'à cause de sa garde qui estoit dessus sa chambre et vis à vis de la fenestre, elle ne pouvoit exécuter leur desseing ; mais les appoincta de se rendre en ung village[1] près de Setoun, où elle ne fauldroit la nuict suivant de les rencontrer, et cependant fault advertir le conte de Mar, qui estoit dans le chasteau de Edimbourg, de tenir bon et l'asseurer de sa déliverance prochaine.

Les moyens estoient de l'invention de Sa Majesté, qui envoya quérir lard de Traquuard du surnom de Steward, cappitaine de ses gardes ; et estant venu parle à elle par la chambre du roy. Luy déclara particulièrement son intention, qui estoit de descendre la nuict prochaine en la chambre du Roy, et de là en l'office de ses sommelliers d'eschansonneries,[2] tous Françoys, où il y avoit une porte respondante sur le cimetière[3] légèrement munie, qui fust rompue, de la largeur suffisante pour y passer[4] la teste d'un homme seulement. Artus Herskin, escuyer d'escurye de Sa Majesté, fust adverty par lord Traqward de se trouver[5] sur la mynuict près de ladicte porte, avec ung grand guilledin fort, pour porter Sa Majesté[6] en crouppe derrière luy, et deux ou troys aultres chevaux tant pour le Roy que pour ceulx qui l'accompagneroient, ce que le dit Seigneur Herskyen exécuta fort songneusement.

Le Roy ayant remonstré la crainte où estoit Monseigneur de Lenox son père, et voyant que sa femme n'en faisoit point mention en ceste delibéracion, l'a supplia de rechef d'y pourvoir et qu 'ilz le peussent emmener avecques eulx ; en quoy il monstra plus que jamais son bon naturel vers ledit Seigneur de Lenox. Sa Majesté n'y voulust aucunement entendre, et luy respondist que sondit père avoit esté trop de foys traistre à elle et aux siens pour s'y fier en une occasion si hazardeuse, laquelle s'il venoit à révéler, cousteroit la vie à tous ceulx[7]

[1] Originally, se rendre près de la ville.
[2] Originally, sommeliers de panneterie.
[3] Respondant sur la cimetière, note added in the margin.
[4] Passer . . . l'ung apres l'autre, cancelled.
[5] Originally, de tenir près.
[6] Originally, ung cheval fort grand . . . pour monter Sadite Majesté.
[7] Tous ceulx, tous above the line.

quy s'en seroient entremeslez.   Que depuis leur mariage,
pour son respect, elle avoit tousjours honoré et estimé le dit
Seigneur Lenox, et quelques foys plus qu'il ne l'avoit trouvé
bon, comme de le faire manger à leur table et requérir son
advis en toutes choses d'importance; mesmes avoit souvent repris
et admonesté le dit Seigneur Roy son mary de se comporter [1]
plus révéremment qu'il ne faisoit l'endroit de sondit père.
Bref qu'elle n'avoit rien oublié de ce que pouvoit [2] suffire
pour obliger ung plus grand, qui ne luy eust point esté subject.   Qu'au lieu de ce elle l'avoit eslevé comme elle-mesmes;
et puis qu'il s'estoit tant oublié que de prendre party avec
ses propres ennemys, il ne luy pourroit mesadvenir que ce
qu'il meritoit.   En fin n'estoit délibérée de le rendre participant
le leur conseilz.   Quant au Seigneur Roy qu'il estoit son
mary, et pourtant ne pouvoit elle en sa conscience l'abandonner,
mesmes en si éminent péril.

La résolution donc prise de leur partement en la façon
qu'il est dict cy dessus, il ne restoit que d'asseurer les seigneures
estans dans le chasteau.

Et en passant je ne veulx oublier que Sa Majesté s'estant
mise à la fenestre de sa chambre, soudain qu'elle fust veue
par le peuple de la ville et quelques uns de ses officiers, qu'ils
se meirent tous à pleurer et murmurer assez hault.   My lord
de Lyndsey survint, qui la retira de la fenestre; et la menaça que
si par sa présence, ou aultrement, elle excitoit aucune tumulte,
il luy cousteroit la vie, et oultre que ce pendant on luy
fermeroit portes et fenestres.

Le jour de Lundy prochain ensuyvant le Roy amena particulièrement le Seigneur de Lenox son père vers Sa Majesté,
qui luy parla fort froidement, congnoissant qu'il estoit de peu
de valeur et fidellité, comme toute sa vie l'a assez tesmoigné [3];
mesmes lors qu'ayant receu l'argent des François pour le
secours d'Escosse, il s'arresta en Angleterre et print le party
des ennemys.

[1] Originally, de luy porter.

[2] De ce elle peuvoit, cancelled.

[3] Originally, de sorte qu'elle ne pouvoit . . . . le rendre, which is cancelled, and, et puis de le rendre, is an addition written between the lines
and continued on the margin, le rendre being erroneously repeated.

Tous les aultres seigneurs de la mesme faction[1] assembléz vindrent trouver Sa Majesté en son antichambre, et se tenans à genoux devant elle (hormis le comte de Murray, qui soudain se releva), la supplièrent de leur pardonner[2] par le comte de Morton, qui en porta la parolle ; estant à genoux au mesme lieu, encores tout ensanglanté, où avoit esté tué feu David.[3] Et pour leur raisons alléguoit ledit Seigneur comte que leur intention n'avoit esté directement mauvaise contre Sa Majesté ; d'autant que presséz de la nécessité où ils se voyoient advenant que le Parlement se teint, ils avoient esté forcéz quasi par désespoir pour la conservation de leur vies et biens, tant pour eulx que pour leur postérité,[4] à entrependre ce qu'ils confessoient contrevenir au debvoir de subjectz. Mais que si Sa Majesté considéroit[5] encores que la perte d'un simple homme estranger, le mesme estant assez souvent jadis adveneu,[6] fust moins considérable que de tant de seigneurs et gentilhommes, ses subjects, qui pouvoient ung jour luy faire plusieurs bons, grands et signales services ; en quoy ilz luy promectoient sur leur honneur de s'employer doresnavant fidellement, s'il luy plaisoit leur remectre tout le passé.

Mais ils feirent comme laird de Dumblanreig, que my lord de Hieries avoit amené avec eulx en Angleterre ; car soudain recongnoissant sa faulte vint retrouver Sa Majesté, et luy ayant faict mille protestacions que jamais ces fols et traistres (ainsi appelloit il Monseigneur de Murray et ses complices) ne le ratraperoient au piége, et qu'il ne marcheroit jamais que soubz la bannière royalle, aussi tost changea il de délibéracion, et estoit des plus avant en ceste dernière conspiracion.

Monseigneur de Murray, couvert et dissimulé en tous ses déportances, s'excusa premièrement du meurtre de feu David,

---

[1] De la mesme faction, above the line.

[2] De les pardonner, above the line.

[3] Encores tout ensanglanté, and feu, occur above the line ; the orginal teinct du sang son sang y paroissoit en, being cancelled.

[4] Pour la conservacion, to posterité, an interlineation.

[5] Mais que si Sa Majesté consideroit, cancelled, but erroneously, and here restored in the text, as necessary to complete the sense.

[6] Le mesme estant assez souvent adveneu, added between the lines.

jurant sur son Dieu qu'il n'en avoit eu avant son retour aucune congnoissance ; et assez[1] doucement supplia qu'elle ne trouvast mauvais qu'il estoit revenu sans son congé et commandement, estant prest de respondre sur tout ce qu'on luy vouldroit imposer. Recommandoit au surplus la cause de ceulx de sa noblesse, qu'ils estoient beaucoup importants au bien public de tout le royaume, de manière qu'il n'y avoit aucun subject qui n'y eust intérest ; et sur ce entrant en ung assez long discours des louanges de la clemence (vertu ce disoit nécessaire et fort advantageuse aux roys pour leur sauveté et conservacion de leur estatz), conclud en fin que Sa Majesté debvroit rappeller tous ces seigneurs près d'elle, affin de s'en servir selon la bonne affection qu'ils avoient vers le Roy et elle ; langage bien contraire à celle qu'ils luy avoient tenu les deux jours précédents. Toutes foys à ce faire estoient-ils persuadéz par l'assemblé des aultres qui estoient eschappéz, lesquels avoient ja de grandes forces, et le peu de résolution qu'ils voyoient au Roy, ne se pouvant plus longuement couvrir de son adveu.

Sur ces remonstrances Sa Majesté leur feist premièrement entendre qu'ils avoient en tant de sortes offensé ; par ung sudit attempté son honneur, enfraint son authorité, entrepris contre son estat,[2] sinon rompu pour le moins altéré l'amitié conjugale d'entre le roy et elle, qu'elle ne pouvoit en perdre si recentement le ressentement ; ne voyant chef en crime de Lèse Majesté, dont ils ne se trouvassent coulpables. Leur remeist devant les yeux l'estroicte obligacion qu'ung chacun d'eux luy avoit, tant pour estre ses subjects naturels par droicte et légitime succession, que par les grands bienfaicts qu'ils avoient receuz d'elle ; ayant par manière de dire party sa couroune entre eulx, tant s'en fault qu'elle jamais mescongnu leur bonne volunté,[3] s'ils en eussent eu aucune à la conservacion d'icelle.

Et particulièrement reprocha audit Seigneur comte de

---

[1] Originally, et seulement.

[2] Entrepris contre son estat, an interlineation.

[3] Originally, eust jamais tasché entendre les priver de la communication des affaires.

Morton ses anciens révoltes contre la feu royne sa mère, le feu Roy de France son seigneur et mary, et contre elle mesmes encores recentement, lors' qu'éstant advertye[1] de l'intelligence qu'il avoit avec le comte de Murray, elle rompist le délibéracion du Roy et du conte de Lenox son père, qui la pressoient de luy faire tranchir la teste.   Oultre ce qu'elle luy avoit donné le comté de Morton et s'etoit fist en luy de ses seaux au défault du feu comte de Hontly. " Je[2] doibs justice à un chacun, et ne la puis desnier à ceulx qui me la demanderont pour celuy qui a esté tué, auquel (de quelques qualités qu'il fust) pour l'honneur qu'il avoit de m'appartenir on ne debvoit faire aucun oultrage, mesmes en ma présence."   Quant à ce que le Seigneur de Murray luy avoit voulu enseigner de la clémence,[3] elle l'avoit eu depuis sa plus grande jeunesse tant d'occasions par eulx et aultres ses subjects[4] de la practiquer[5] et se la rendre familière.   Oultre ce, naturellement elle y estoit assez inclinée qu'il ny avoit personne qui ne la deust plustost blasmer de trop grande facilité en cest endroict[6] que d'aucune sévérité ou rigeur.   Et l'impunité du passé en a paradventure encouragé[7] plusieurs à continuer de mal faire et donner l'audace d'entreprendre davantage, espérans d'en sortir à aussi bon marché une foys que les aultres. " N'espère donc que si soudainement je vous puisse asseurer entièrréz ; mais avec le temps si vous mectez peine de vostre costé d'éffacer le passé par le bon debvoir et services que vous me promectez,[8] il ne m'en demeurera."

[1] Originally, elle ne voulust suivre le conseil du conte de Lenox et du Roy son fils.

[2] Transposed to its present position from a lower part of the same page in the MS. (where it follows the sentence ending with the words, " les aultres ") by direction of Nau himself.

[3] La clemence, il n'estoit besoing, originally.

[4] Par eulx et aultres ses subjects, an interlineation.

[5] La practiquer et oultre l'inclinacion naturelle qui, cancelled.

[6] En cest endroict, added above the line.

[7] Originally, encouragé, et donne l'audace a plusieurs de retenir leur premier audace.

[8] Il ne m'en demeurera. Et le pourra estre eu mon endroict, ledit Seigneur conte et ses adherens ayant respondu que cela ne suffisoit pour leur seureté Sa Majeste, cancelled, the next sentence commencing, il ne m'en demeurera.

Sa Majesté, craignant d'estre contraincte de passer oultre contre son intention, feist semblant de se trouver mal et sentir de grandes tranchées, comme si elle eust esté proche d'acoucher, commandant qu'on luy feist venir la sage femme qui luy avoit esté amenée dès le jour précédent ; et se retirant en sa chambre en grande haste pria le Roy de leur faire entendre son intention, selon qu'ils en avoient résolu ensemble. Le Roy leur déclara lors plus amplement le particularitéz du pardon par eux prétendu, et ce néantmoins quelques ungs ne s'en voulurent contanter, soubz contenance qu'il estoit un feincte,[1] et remonstrèrent en leur conseil que cela ne pouvoit suffire pour leur seureté ; de façon qu'ayans enquis la sage femme (par eulx appoinctée)[2] de l'estat de Sa Majesté, et leur ayant esté respondu qu'elle estoit fort mallade et en danger de sa vie, ce que ladite femme croyoit sincèrement (d'autant que l'enfant par l'esmotion précédente estoit descendu fort bas), ils supercédèrent jusques au lendemain d'en faire plus grande instance.

Mais ce fust trop tard ; car sur la mynuict ensuyvant Sa Majesté eschappa avecques le Roy selon leur desseings, accompagnéz seulement de laird Traquuard, cappitaine des gardes, Artus Herskin, qui avoit Sa Majesté en croupe, et ung varlét de chambre du Roy, avec deux ou troys soldats.[3] Ils passèrent par le cymetière où estoit enterré le corps de[4] feu David, et quasi sur sa fosse, de façon que le Roi entrant quasi en une soudaine peur commença à souspirer. Requis par la Royne de l'occasion qu'il en avoit, d'autant qu'elle ne scavoit rien de ceste sépulture, il luy respondist, "Madame, nous venons de passer près de la fosse de pauvre David. J'y ay perdu ung bon et fidelle serviteur, et n'en recouvreray jamais un tel. Il ne sera jour de ma vie que je n'y aye regret. On m'a malheureusement abusé." Estant interrompu en ces propos, de peur qu'il ne fust entendu.

Soudain qu'il fust hors de la ville il se meist à galloper, et le Seigneur Artus Herkin après lui tante qu'ils arrivèrent aux

---

[1] Soubz contenance que c'estoit une feincte, an interlineation.

[2] Par eulx appoinctée, above the line.

[3] Avec deux ou trois soldatz, between the lines.

[4] Le corps de, above the line.

environs de Seton, où ayans descouvert quelques soldatz, mis en garde par les seigneurs du party de Sa Majesté pour estre par eulx informéz de leur passage, le Roy s'imaginant que c'estoient de leur ennemys, esperonné de la craincte qu'il avoit de tumber entre leur mains, se meist a piquer plus roide que devant,[1] et vouloit haster le cheval de Sa Majesté, frappant sur la croupe et criant, " Allons, allons ! Par le Sang Dieu ils nous tueront, et vous et moy, si nous peuvent attraper."

Sa Majesté desjà lasse du travail qu'elle avoit faict avec grandes douleurs, craignant d'avorter, le supplia d'avoir esgard à l'estat où elle estoit, et luy dist qu'elle aymoit mieux se hazarder à tout danger que de perdre à bon escient leur enfant. Lors le Roy, entrant en cholère, "Venez de par Dieu, venez,[2] dist il ; si cesluylà se perd, nous en aurons d'aultres." En fin[3] Sa Majesté, ne pouvant supporter le gallop du cheval[4] plus longuement, le pria d'aller devant et se mectre en seureté, ce qu'il feist assez inconsidérément, laissant ceste pauvre princesse aussi affligée à son occasion au mylieu des champs preste d'acoucher et de perdre la vie en tel effort. Toutesfoys elle arriva saufve au chasteau de Dunbar, accompagnié des comtes de Huntly et Bothuel, my lords de Flamyng, Seton, Levingston, et quelques aultres, qui la recontrèrent sur les chemins ; et demonstrèrent après avoir trouvé le Roy estre fort malcontant[5] de luy, murmurans les uns avec les aultres. Les uns ne le voulans acoster ny parler à luy ; les aultres luy reprochans (et particulièrement lord de Flamying)[6] tout ouvertement ses déportemens[7] vers la royne sa femme, et eulx tous qu'il avoit destinéz à la mort.

Le roy, voyant le ressentement que les seigneurs avoient de l'injure par eulx receue, et les grandes forces qu'ils avoient prestes pour combattre les rebelles, vint trouver la royne sa femme ; et après luy avoir remonstré la deffiance qu'il avoit

---

[1] Sans regarder derriere de luy, cancelled.

[2] Adure a dure, cancelled. Venez de par Dieux, venez, written above.

[3] Enfin voyant que, cancelled.

[4] Du cheval, above the line.

[5] Originally, telle malcontantement.

[6] Et particulièrement lord de Flemyng, an interlineation.

[7] Originally, vers eulx tous et.

desdits Seigneurs, et qu'ils ne se voulsissent vanger de luy, la pria de moyenner avec eulx son accord, s'offrant de leur promectre jurer et tenir pour l'advenir une estroicte et perfaicte amitié, sans jamais les abandonner. Sa Majesté y travailla en ce qu'elle peust, y trouvant beaucoup de difficulté à cause que lesdits seigneurs, qui avoient (ce disoient-ils) hazardé leur vie pour la querelle du Roy, avoient esté par luy en récompense trahys à ses propres et plus grands ennemys. Et puis qu'il avoit[1] fait si peu de compte[2] de leur services et de l'obligacion qu'il avoit à leur vraye et légitime souveraine,[3] laquelle ils recongnoissent avoir toute puissance de leur commander et nul aultre, ores que Sa Majesté l'eust faict son compagnon de lict (comme il appellent en leur langage Bethfallow) ils n'estoient délibéréz à l'advenir de s'asseurer beaucoup à ses promesses ou commandemens ;[4] tout l'obéissance qu'il debvoit espérer d'eux estant seulement pour le respect de la royne sa femme, d'autant qu'ils ne luy estoient obligéz par serment solennel, non plus que luy envers eulx, qui ne l'avoient jamais (ny aucun de la noblesse) receu ou advoué pour Roy.

Ce pendant le comte de Lenox, qui estoit dans le palais de Sainte Croix à Edimbourgh, fust adverty le Mardy matin du partement de Sa Majesté et du son filz ; auquel soudainement il feist plusieurs imprécations mauvaises, luy donnant sa malédiction et l'appellant traistre, l'ayant délaissé en tel danger. Le Secrétaire Ledinthon en eust aussi advis par les filles damoiselles de la chambre de Sa Majesté, qui allèrent vers luy pour scavoir la vérité du bruit qu'on faisoit courir, que tout le palais debvoit estre pillé.[5] Or fault notter que ledit Ledinthon[6] estoit secrettement de la partie du comte de Murray, sans en faire demonstration que le peust charger, de façon qu'il ne demanda point de pardon avec les aultres, et se retira après la fuytte de Sa Majesté chez le comte d'Athel, où il demeura quelque temps jusques à ce que par l'intercession dudit Seigneur comte il fut rappellé.

---

[1] Originally, avoit, ung foys peu faulser sa foy n'estoient deliberéz.
[2] De sa foy, cancelled.   [3] Reyne, cancelled.
[4] Et ne vouloient, cancelled.   [5] Les aultres, cancelled.
[6] Ledinthon, sans se monstroit estoit demeuré, originally.

Le bruit de ce partement de Sa Majesté et du Roy espandu par la ville, les Seigneurs qui avoient esté de la conspiracion s'absentèrent, quie[1] d'un costé qui d'aultre, et tous les soldats pareillement, chacun taschant de se purger et pourchasser leur pardon ; principallement lorsqu'ils entendirent qu'en plusieurs endroictz du royaume on avoit fait une proclamacion que dans six jours prochains toutes sortes d'hommes en aage qu'ils pouvoient porter armes se rendissent à Dunbar.[2] Plusieurs lettres aussi furent escriptes à mesme effect à diverses seigneurs et gentilzhommes, qui avec grande dilligence vindrent rencontrer Sa Majesté ; laquelle bien accompagnié arriva à l'abbaye d'Hadington vers la nuict le 18 de Mars, et le 19 l'évesque de Saint André (frère bastard du duc de Chastelherault) avec les Hammiltons rencontrèrent Sa Majesté près la bourgadde de Muskelbourgh et l'accompagnèrent à l'Islebourgh, où elle séjourna quelque temps en la maison de l'évesque de Dunquelkdes, ayant avec elle les comtes de Huntley, Athole, Bothuel, Crawfourde, Marshal, Sutherland, Cathnes, l'évesque de Sainte André, l'évesque de Rosse, de Suri de . . . . .[3] lords de Levingstone, Flamyng, Seton, Hume, Borthuaik, et aultres ; par le conseil desquels l'estat du royaume fut remis en repos et toutes choses pour un temps pacifiées. Et fussent demeurées en ce repos sans l'inquiétude du Roy, qui ne pouvoit durer avec personne.

Le conseil estant assemblé en ladite maison de Dunkeldes, le Roy (prévoyant que le comte de Murray et quelques aultres[4] ses particuliers ennemys rentrant en court ne se fyeroient jamais en luy, et qu'ilz s'envangeroient s'ilz pouvoient ; induict aussi à ce par les comtes de Huntley et de Bothwel, qui avoient particulières inimitiéz avec lesdits seigneurs,[5] et particulièrement avec Ledinthon, le Secrétaire)[6] proposa de

---

[1] . . . que . . . que (?)

[2] Pour passer, cancelled.

[3] Et l'evesque de Rosse du Suri de, an interlineation, the last words are indistinct owing to the binding.

[4] Que les conspirateurs cancelled, le comte de Murray et quelques aultres ses particlières ennemys, between the lines.

[5] Conspirateurs, originally.

[6] Le Secretaire, cancelled.

donner[1] l'estat de Secrétaire à l'évesque de Rosse au lieu dudit Ledinthon, lequel il chargoit beaucoup de ladite conspiration, et[2] en signa la résolution prise audit conseil en l'absence de Sa Majesté, laquelle ny voulut condescendre, estant persuadée que le Roy chargoit ledit Ledinthon pour mectre en sa place ung homme à sa dévotion ; taschant en tout ce qu'il pouvoit de practiquer les uns et les aultres pour se faire le plus fort ; ce que Sa Majesté avoit occasion de craindre, pour l'inconstance et perfidie (s'il fault dire) qu'elle avoit trouvé en luy. Partant, contre l'advis du Roy et desdits seigneurs, ne se voulut deffere dudit Ledinthon, homme d'entendement, practiqué aux afferes du pays, et duquel—à vray dire—elle avoit besoing en ceste confusion d'humeurs et dissencions, joinct qu'il ny avoit aucune preuve en ce faict contre luy.[3] Elle le feist donques peu après rappeller, espérant plus qu'il ne meritoit de son bon naturel et debvoir vers elle.

Le Roy ayant entendu le refus qu'elle avoit faict de signer et approuver ceste résolution en faveur du dit évesque de Rosse, (qu'elle estimoit ce néantmoins et s'en servoit volontiers en aultres charges,) entra en extrême cholère ; et la nuict ensuyvant envoya quérir Sa Majéste par un sien varlet de chambre, qui l'advertist du malcontantement que le dict seigneur avoit d'elle, et qu'il avoit faict amorcer et bander ses deux pistolles, qu'elle trouveroit pendues au dossier du lict. Sa Majéste ne laissa de l'aller trouver, et après avoir demeuré quelque temps avecque luy osta doucement lesdites pistolles, dont elle advertist le lendemain ceulx du conseil, affin de luy oster ceste opinion qu'il avoit prise contre Ledinthon ; et leur feist entendre sur ce son intention qu'ilz suivirent comme vous entendrez cy après ; et deffendit au dit seigneur évesque de Rosse d'accepter ceste charge, encores qu'il luy fust offerte.

Pour le regard des aultres chacun d'eux poursuivast son pardon. Le roy (comme dict estoit cy dessus) estoit au commencement[4] directement contraire au comte de Murray et

---

[1] Originally de faire donner.

[2] Lequel il chargoit beaucoup de ladite conspiration, an interlineation.

[3] Joinct qu'il ny avoit aucune preuve en ce faict contre luy, an interlineation.

[4] Au commencement, above the line.

ceulx qui deppendoient de luy. Toutesfoys, en fin laird de Trakward, qui estoit du surnom de Stewart, luy persuada d'y entendre, de sorte que Sa Majéste l'y voyant incliné ne voulant que le dit seigneur de Murray rejectast toute l'offense sur elle, qui n'avoit eu inimitié avec luy que pour le respect du roy,[1] luy accorda son pardon comme il estoit à Lithguo ; et pareillement au conte d'Arghil et my lord de Boyd, qui furent commandés de passer en Arghil et là demeurer tant qu'il plairoit à Sa Majesté, à quoy ilz obéirent. Le comte de Rothes obtint aussi son pardon, et pareillement le comte de Lenox, à la requeste du Roy son filz ; le comte de Glencarn et laird de Cuninghamhead, qui vindrent trouver Sa Majesté à Dumbar. Le roy avoit en extreme recommendacion les lords de Ruthwen et Lyndsey, Douglas l'Apostolat, et quelques aultres ; dont ce néantmoins il n'osoit parler ouvertement à Sa Majesté laquelle dès le commancement avoit juré de ne pardonner jamais à ceulx là, comme ceulx qu'elle tenoit autheurs de ceste conspiracion par eulx commancée et exécutée. Voyans donc lesdits conspirateurs et le conte de Morton, qu'ils ne pouvoient obtenir leur pardon, s'enfuyèrent en Angleterre, où le dit Ruthwen mourut enragé en la ville de Neufcastel.

Soudain que Sa Majesté eust advis de l'arrivé desdits seigneurs en Angleterre dépescha vers la Royne, sa bonne soeur, James Thorneton, chantre de l'évesché de Murray, lequel aussi passa en France vers le roy et Messieurs de Lorraine, parens de Sa Majesté, pour leur faire entendre l'estat de ses affaires, les attentatz et rebellions de ses subjectz contre elle, et requérir leur secours. La Royne d'Angleterre, requise de ne recepvoir lesditz rebelles ny les laisser séjourner en son royaume, envoya en Escosse ung gentilhomme, Henry Killigrewe, avec letteres fort courtoises ;[3] par lesquelles elle promectoit de chasser les dits rebelles en bref. Mais elle ne teint promesse ; car le conte de Morton et le fils de feu my lord de Ruthwen demeurèrent[4] en la ville

---

[1] Originally, voulant le prevenir affin que ledit Seigneur d'Murray luy en demeurast obligé, in the clause rejected . . . . pour le respect du roy, being added between the lines.

[2] Depuis aussi, cancelled.   [3] Originally, favorables.

[4] Originally, car ils demeurent encores.

d'Annwike et es environs jusques à ce qu'ils eurent leur pardon et furent restabliz, qui fut après l'acouchement de Sa Majesté.

My lord Ruthven devant son décèz démonstra grande repentance de sa meschante vie, rendant grâces à Dieu de ce qu'avant l'appeller à soy il lui avoit donné le temps et l'advis de luy requérir mercy et pardon de ses faultes. Les aultres disent qu'il mourut comme tout insensé, criant qu'il voyoit Paradis ouvert et grand nombre d'anges, qui le venoient quérir. Il est à présupposer qu'ils estoient illusions des diables, qui le vouloient décepvoir en ce passage, affin qu'il ne leur eschappast; l'ayans tant possédé avec l'art magique durant sa vie.

Sa Majesté sentant son terme approcher pour sa délivrance, se logea au chasteau d'Edinbourg, pour y faire les préparatifs de ses couches, et oultre pour obvier à ce qu'on l'avoit advertye, qu'incontinent après son acouchement[1] les seigneurs avoient délibéré de se saisir de l'enfant, comme héritier de la coronne, et le faire baptiser selon leur relligion,[2] nourrir et garder par quelsques uns d'eux, sans qu'elle ny le roy son mary y en peussent ordonner leur volonté.

Or Sa Majesté voyant les partialitéz et grandes divisions qui se nourissoient entre les seigneurs, de façon que si elle venoit à mourir en sa délivrance,[3] elles eussent toujours augmenté et en eust esté l'estat moins asseuré pour son enfant, lequel aussi elle ne vouloit fyer totallement au roy, son mary, elle advisa d'appoincter toutes offenses passées entre lesdits seigneurs et les unir ensemble,[4] mesmes ceulx de son conseil, par quelque[5] réconciliation.

Donques sur la fin d'Apuril elle envoya quérir les comtes d'Arghil et de Murray, et les appoincta avec[6] les comtes d'Athel, Hontly et Bothwel, de toutes querelles dont ils s'étoient remis à elle, de façon qu'ils demeurèrent avec Sa Majesté toute le reste de l'esté ensuyvant.

[1] Accouchement, on avoit délibéré de luy oster son enfant, originally.
[2] Baptiser selon leur relligion, an addition above the lines.
[3] Delivrance l'estat devenait, cancelled.
[4] Ensemble, en son conseil.
[5] Bons et seurs moyens.
[6] Avec les . . Bothwell, above the line.

Nous avons parlé cy dessus du pardon du comte de Murray et ceulx qui l'avoient assisté, sur quoy nous dirons davantage que lesdits remonstroient à Sa Majesté qu'ils ne s'estoient mis en armes qu' à l'occasion du roy, contre lequel seul ils s'étoient mis en deffense, et non contre Sa Majesté, laquelle ne pouvoit prétendre offense d'eulx que pour n'avoir pas comparu en justice à son simple commandement practiqué par leurs ennemys, qui estoient autour d'elle [1] et ne cherchoient que leur entière ruine d'eulx, de leur biens et familles.   Que l'éxcuse estoit toujours considerable de celuy qui combat [2] pour la conservation de sa vie, biens,[3] honneur, et tasche a repoulser de soy ce que y peut luy préjudicier en choses de telle importance. Que ces considérations, et la necessité où ils se trouvoient,[4] les avoient contraincts d' accepter le dernier party qui leur avoit esté proposé pour leur restablissement, en rompant le Parlement assemblé pour leur procès et condemnation, sans qu'ilz eussent esté participans des insolences et indignitéz faictes à la personne de Sa Majesté en son palais propre, ny du meurtre de feu David, qu'ils rejectoient entièrement sur my lord de Ruthven et ses complices.

Telles persuasions entrèrent aux aureilles de Sa Majesté, qui recongneust qu'à la vérité elle n'avoit eu du commencement aultre occasion d'inimitié apparente,[5] ou offense particulière, contre les dits Seigneurs de Murray et ses adhérens qu'en conséquence du roy son mary, lequel elle pouvoit penser avoir esté satisfaict d'eux, puisqu'il les avoit rappelléz près de soy contre ellemesmes.   Oultre ce, elle congnoissoit le crédit que lesdits Seigneurs avoient avec l'Anglois, par le moyen et support duquel elle craignoit d'estre tenue en continuels troubles, et d'en avoir avec le temps quelque mauvaise issue.   Aussi voyant le Roy persuadé et resolu de pardonner audit Seigneur de Murray, quelque [6] difficulté qu'il en eust fait auparavant,

---

[1] D'elle, les considerations mises devant les yeux de Sa Majesté, et oultre que le Roy, cancelled.

[2] Qui travaille à repousser tels attemptatz, cancelled.

[3] Riens, above the line.

[4] Et la situation où ils se trouvoient, an interlineation.

[5] Apparente, above the line.

[6] Quelque difficulté qu'il en eust fait auparavant, between the lines.

elle fut induicte facilement a y prester son consentement ;[1] considéré que le rigeur qu'elle leur avoit tenu par le passé, afin de complaire au Roy, son mary, avoit esté si mal recongneu de luy, et en partye cause de ce que les aultres avec luy avoient depuis attempté, de façon qu'elle [2] ne se pouvait n'y osait fyer à ung et aulx aultres à part, elle trouva bon de se fortifier de tous ensembles et les tenir tous absolument unis.

Sa Majesté s'estant retirée au chasteau de l'Islebourgh, et la plus grande part de la noblesse assemblée en la dite ville, suivant son mandement, elle se prépara pour sa délivrance, faisant son testament, et receva son Sacrament comme proche et en danger de la mort.

Vers ce temps vint de la part du Roy de France un gentilhomme nommé le Croc, dépesché pour résider près de Sa Majesté comme ambassadeur. Ledit Seigneur estoit gentilhomme servant de Sa Majesté, et la servoit ordinairement depuis mesmes qu'il fust ambassadeur, deppendant entièrement de la Royne mère, comme sa créature.

N'est à oublier une practique mise en avant par la Royne d'Angleterre, laquelle envoya vers Sa Majesté un vieux gentilhomme, nommé Ruxby, soubz le nom emprunté du comte de Northumberland et Sir Henry Persey, son frère, avec offres á Sa Majesté de se joindre avec elle, si elle le vouloit entreprendre aucune innovation contre la Royne d'Angleterre ; à quoi le dit gentilhomme taschait de la persuader par toutes les remonstrances qu'il pouvoit luy amener. Et particulièrement que la Royne d'Angleterre (se sentant offensée de ce que sans son advis et consentement elle s'estoit mariée, voyant que par la naissance de son enfant son droict en la coronne d'Angleterre seroit davantage confirmé), ne laisseroit de pourchasser par tous moyens sa ruine et du Roy son mary, lequel elle hayssoit en toute extrémité. Luy proposoit la bonne volonté de tous les Catholiques qui se rendroient de son party, et luy en nomma quelques uns en particulier. A quoi Sa Majesté, (soubçonnant par la façon de laquelle il proceddoit que

---

[1] Les parties vouloient se prevaloir des ungs et des aultres, ausquels seule et apart elle ne pouvoit et n'osat fier entièrement. . . . cancelled.

[2] Elle, not in original.

Q

c'estoit une feincte négotiation,) luy respondist qu'elle remercyoit lesdits Seigneurs de leur bonne volonté et inclination ; mais qu'au lieu d'entendre à tels remuëments au préjudice de la royne, sadite bonne soeur, elle n'eust jamais meilleure intention de luy complaire et s'entretenir en bonne intelligence avec elle ; car elle avoit délibéré de la faire sa commère. Et sur l'instance qu'il faisoit d'avoir lettres de sa part aus dits Seigneurs, qu'elle ne leur escripvit point sans avoir premièrement eu de leur lettres, ou créance plus particulière.

Sur ce il s'en retourna en Angleterre, et ayant pris mémoires[1] du dit Sir Henry Persey et de quelques aultres practiquéz soubz main affectionnéz à Sa Majesté, s'en veint en Escosse. Cependant Sa Majesté s'etant esclaircys du soubçon qu'elle avoit pris, et en ayant eu advertissement, soudain que ledit Ryxby fust de retour, fist saysir tous ses papiers ; entre lesquels se trouva ung Brevet signé de la main de William Cecile, secrétaire d'estat d'Angleterre, par lequel la Royne d'Angleterre promectoit audit Ruxby, et aux siens à perpétuité, cent *punt* de rente en terre foncière, moyennant qu'il rapportast lettres signées de Sa Majesté ausdits Seigneurs de Northumberland et son frère sur les offres à elle faictes.

Cela estant bien vériffié ledit Ruxby fust envoyé prisonnier au quartier du north, chez l'évesque de Murray, où il demeura près de dixhuit moys, sans qu'on feist instance pour sa délivrance. Ledit Ruxby donna à Sa Majesté ung tableau d'yvoire, où toute la Passion estoit gravée, affin de contrefaire plus apparemment le Catholique.

Le xixme de Juin, jour de Mercredy,[2] entre les dix et onze heures du matin, Sa Majesté acoucha d'un fils, avec grand travail et douleurs, en présence des plusieurs dames ; lesquelles la voyans en danger et luy remonstrans le hazard où elle estait et son enfant, elle les supplia de sauver l'enfant sans aucun respect d'elle. Le prince vint avec une fort grande coiffe fort deliée, qui lui couvroit tout le visage. Le xv. jour de Juin il estoit couru un bruict par toute la ville d'Edinbourgh que Sa Majesté estoit acouchée d'un fils, et sur ce furent faicts des feus de joye.

---

[1] Originally, lettres.   [2] Jour de Mercredy, an interlineation.

Soudain après la naissance du Prince toute l'artillerie du chasteau tira, et les seigneurs avec la noblesse et le peuple s'assemblèrent au temple St Gilles, pour rendre grâces à Dieu de l'honneur qu'ils estimoient avoir par un héritier à leur royaume. Après l'enfantement furent dépeschés certains gentilshommes vers le Roy de France, la Royne d'Angleterre et le Duc de Savoye, pour les prier d'estre compères et commère ; ce qu'ils acceptèrent en fort bonne part. Le Roy du France envoya le comte de Brienne, de la maison de Luxembourg. Peu avant, y avoit esté dépesché le Seigneur de Mauvissière pour menacer le roy d'Escosse et le prier de se mieux comporter de la part des Messieur de Guyse.[1] La royne d'Angleterre [envoya][2] le comte de Bethfort, fort bien accompagné, mais avant Henry Killegrewe pour se resjouyr et congratuler avec Sa Majesté de son heureuse délivrance. Le duc de Savoye dépescha le Seigneur de Morete, lequel arriva trop tard, et après le baptesme célébré, auquel assista en sa place le Seigneur du Croc. Au nom du comte de Bethfort, d'autant q'il ne vouloit entrer en l'église, fust mise la comtesse d'Arghil, pour assister au nom de la Royne d'Angleterre à la cérémonie du baptesme. Tant que Sa Majesté demeura au chasteau d'Islebourgh elle feist coucher son fils en sa chambre, et le veilloit souvent elle mesme.

Durant le séjour de Sa Majesté audit chasteau, et durant ses couches, le Roy son mary menoit une vie fort desbauchée, et alloit courir toutes les nuicts ; tantost se baigner dans la mer, tantost en divers aultres lieux esgaréz. Donc Sa Majesté estant advertye, et craignant les inconveniens qui en pouvoient sourdre à cause de la malveillance que lui portoient la plus part[3] des seigneurs, mesmes qu'il faisoit ouvrir à toutes heures de nuict le chasteau, elle et son fils n'estoient en seureté, elle le pria de se tenir sur ses gardes et de ne se commectre ainsi indiscretement au danger de ses ennemys.

Il feist fort peu de compte de toutes telles remonstrances, et comme de son naturel il estoit fort insolent, de mesmes au

[Envoya] supplied to complete the sense.

Pour menacer le roy d'Ecosse et le prier de se mieux comporter de la part de Messieur de Guyse, an interlineation in the margin.

[3] Originally tous, instead of la plus part.

lieu de pourvoir à ce désordre, il commença à menasser tous les Seigneurs, et particulièrement le comte de Murray, lequel il dist qu'un laird de Bafour luy avoit promis de tuer lors q'il se retiroit au chasteau.

Sa Majesté trouva ceste entreprinse fort pernicieuse, et pour susciter de grands troubles au royaume, et une soudaine sédition dans la ville. Qui fust cause de s'employer près dudit Seigneur Roy, son mary, affin de rompre ce desseing, où il ne laissa secrettement de persister.

Parmy[1] ces difficultés ledit Seigneur se monstra fort offensé de ce que, contre son advis, ou avoit requis la Royne d'Angleterre pour commère; laquelle il disoit ne vouloir non plus recongnoistre pour légitime Royne d'Angleterre qu'elle luy[2] pour Roy d'Escosse. Le conseil néantmoins, taschans de rendre ceste princesse affectionnée à leur bien et conservation, passèrent oultre.

Dont ledit Seigneur Roy se monstra fort malcontant; et prenant de jour en aultre nouvelles occasions de se mutiner, entra en délibération, (par la persuasion de quelques jeunes hommes débauschéz, qu'il avoit près de luy plus que nuls aultres), de s'en aller secrettement en France, et là s'entretenir du douaire de Sa Majesté; laquelle en estant advertye lui en parla librement. Ce néantmoins, elle ne peust tant faire qu'un jour, ordonné pour recepvoir le Sacrement, il ne s'absentast hors de la ville, avec grand scandale des Catholics.

Sur le commencement du moys d'Aoust Sa Majesté passa la mer pour s'en aller en Alloway, maison appartenant au comte de Mar,[3] ou elle demeura quelques jours, accompagnée seulement des dames de sa court et du dict comte de Mar. Le roy en ce voyage la vint visiter, comme en passant, n'ayant séjourné que quelques heures avec Sa Majesté, ayans ensemble appoincté leur retour au chasteau de l'Islebourgh.

Sur la fin du mesme moys Sa Majesté, accompagnée du Roy, des comtes de Murray, Huntley, Bothweil et Atheil, et divers aultres, alla passer son temps à la chasse du cerf[4] sur les frontières d'Angleterre, en Meggot Lande. Et de là

[1] Originally, tout ces.   [2] Luy, above the line.
[3] Maison appartenant au comte de Mar, an interlineation.
[4] Du cerf, between the lines.

estant de retour à l'Islbourg, se résolut de conduire[1] Monseigneur le Prince, son fils, à Strivelingh. Et à cet effect feist lever quatre ou cinq cens harquebustiers, lesquels marchans autour de la lictière du mondit Seigneur le Prince l'accompagnèrent avec elle audit Strivelingh. La garde en fust premièrement baillée à lord Erskin, depuis au comte de Mar et à sa femme.

Sa Majesté estant au voyage de Meggot Lande, en la maison de lord de Trakward, fust requise, durant le soupper, par le Roy son mary, d'aller en une chasse du cerf; et d'autant qu'il luy falloit galloper avec violence, elle luy remonstre à l'aureille qu'elle craignoit estre grosse. Le Roy luy respondist tout hault, "Hé biens; si celuyla se perd, nous en ferons un aultre;" dont le dit laird de Trakward le réprint fort aigrement, jusqu' à lui dire que ce n'estoit pas une parolle de Chrestien. Il luy respondist; "Quoy fait on pas bien travailler une jument après qu'elle est pleine?"

Sa Majesté au retour de Strivelingh feist un progrès à Glen Arknay, et de là veint à l'Islebourg, où elle séjourna quelque temps, tant pour assister[2] à l'audition des comptes du royaume, qui se rendoient lors, que pour faire nouvelles informations contre ses rebelles qui estoient encores en Angleterre, et pour donner order aux préparatifs du baptesme.

De là Sa Majesté feist un voyage à Gedword, pour tenir les jours de justice, qui ont accoustumé de se tenir annuellement pour pollicer le pays des frontières, et chastier les larrons qui habitent par les montagnes prochaines. A la poursuitte desquels le comte de Bothwel avoit esté envoyé, et y fust blessé en une main si dangereusement que chacun, et luy mesmes, pensant la mort s'en debvoir bien tost ensuyvre, Sa Majesté fust requise et conseillée de l'aller visiter en une maison appellée l'Hermitage, pour entendre de luy l'estat des afferes du pays, duquel ledit Seigneur comte estoit gouverneur héréditairement.[3] Pour ceste occasion elle y alla en dilligence, accompagnée du comte de Murray et quelques aultres seigneurs,

[1] Originally, d'envoyer.
[2] Pour ouyer les, originally.
[3] Héréditairement, above the line.

en présence desquels elle communiqua quelques heures avec le dit Seigneur comte, et s'en retourna le mesme jour a Gedouard, où le lendemain elle tumba mallade, sans bouger du lict, estant fort tourmentée d'une extrême maladie de ratte, duquel quelques huict jours auparavant elle se sentoit travailler, et que l'avoit quasi toujours tenue depuis ses couches. Les[1] uns pensoient que ce fut la mort, avec ung grand vomissement plus de 60 foys, et perdre la veue dans le iij jour de la malladie.

En[2] ce temps un nommé John Shaw vinst advertir Sa Majesté que André Kar of Faydensyd estait revenu en Escosse, ayant esté banny et s'estant retiré en Angleterre, pour avoir tiré le dague sur Sa Majesté et avoir tué feu David ; et s'estoit vanté en présence de ceulx qui refusoient le recepvoir en leurs maisons, d'autant qu'il estoit à la corne, qu'ils le pouvoient bien recepvoir, d'autant que dans 15 jours ils les asseuroit que la court changeroit, et luy seroit plus en crédit que jamais, et lors il s'enquissoit hardiment comment leur Royne se portoit.

De[3] façon qu'il fust subçonné que Sa Majesté estoit empoisonée, veu ses grands vomissemens et si frequens en un mesme jour, et que parmy ce qu'elle jecta se trouva un morceau tout verd et fort espais et dur.

Le Jeudy vindrent nouvelles que Monseigneur le Prince estoit extrêmement mallade, et qu'il n'y avoit plus d'espérance de vie, de façon qu'on le feist vomir dont il guérist.

Le Vendredy ensuyvant Sa Majesté perdist la parolle, et tumba en une forte grande convulsion sur les dix ou onze heures du soir, et tous ses membres se retirèrent tellement, avec telle déformité du visage et froideur de tout le corps que ceulx qui estoient là présens, et principallement ses serviteurs domestiques, la jugèrent pour morte, et feirent les fenestres

---

[1] The passage beginning with the word "Les uns," and ending with "malladie," is an addition to the text as originally written. The original reading was "douleur de ratte," for which "malladie" was substituted, and douleur de costé written above the line.

[2] This paragraph is obviously out of place, but no notice to this effect is given in the MS.

[3] The history of the Queen's illness at Jedburgh is here resumed.

ouvertes, et Mon. de Meura commença à se sayser de tous le
plus precieux meubles, comme de la vaisselle d'argent et
bagues de Sa Majesté. Les robbes de deuil furent com-
mandées, et les préparatifs pour les funérailles. Mais son
chirurgien Arnault, y recongnoissant encores quelques indices
de vie sur[1] un de ses bras, que n'estoit encore tout roide,
usant de l'extrémité en tel désespoir, luy feist lyer fort serré[2]
les orteils des pieds, les jambes au dessus du col du pied, et
les bras ; puis jecter du vin par la bouche, qu'il luy feist
ouvrir par force, de sorte qu'estant un peu revenu à soy on
luy donna un clystère, la dejection duquel fut trouvée par les
medicins fort estrange. Et depuis elle amanda toujours
jusques à ces qu'elle retourna à Lislebourg, où elle vomist
une fort grande quantité de sang meurtry, et fust là entièrement guerye.

Le jour précédent ceste convulsion, Sa Majesté, sentant ses
forces diminuer et ce jugeant en hazard de sa vie, (ayant ja
perdue la veue), feist appeller les Seigneurs que estoient de sa
court, et leur remonstra fort amplement combien leur union
et accord importoit au bien du pays et à la préservation de
son filz, lequel elle leur recommandoit, se doubtant aucunement qu'il ne luy fust faict tort en la succession par son père,
qui y pretendoit droict par luymesme, et eust peu se re-
marier.

Manda aussi le Seigneur du Crocq, ambassadeur de France,
pour recommander sondit fils, son estat et afferes, au Roy très
Chrestien, son maistre. Puis après feist lire les prières par
l'évesque de Rosse, et se disposa comme à la mort prochaine ;
advisant ceulx qui estoient près d'elle de prendre garde à elle
ledict Vendredy ; lequel elle s'asseuroit si elle passoit, ne
mourir de ceste malladie.

Sa Majesté vint de là à Lislebourgh pour donner order aux
préparatifs du baptesme, lequel fut célébré environ les Roys,
avec grande magnificence et dons aux ambassadeurs. Le Roy
ne se trouva point au dit baptesme, d'autant qu'il disoit ne
vouloir se trouver entre les Angloys s'ils ne le recongnoissoi-

---

[1] Sur un de ses bras, qui n'estoit encore tout roide, added between the
lines.   [2] Fort serré, an interlineation.

ent pour Roy, ce que la Royne d'Angleterre leur avoit deffendu.

Et peu après s'en alla à Glasgo, où il tumba mallade de la petite verolle et envoya quérir Sa Majesté par diverses foys. D'autant qu'elle estoit fort mallade d'une blessure de chute de cheval au Seton, à la fin elle le feist visiter, et l'accompagna à son retour à Lislebourgh.

Durant[1] ce voyage un corbeau les accompagna continuellement depuis Glasgo jusques à Islebourgh, et là demeuroit souvent sur le logis du feu Roy, et quelques foys au chasteau. Mais le jour précédent la mort du Roy il cria fort longuemet sur sa maison. [A son retour à Lislebourgh] il se logea en une petite maison hors de la ville,[2] qu'il avoit choisie sur le rapport de James Bafour et quelques aultres, contre[3] la volenté de Sa Majesté, láquelle le vouloit mener à Krecmeller, pour ce qu'il ne vouloit pas loger dans le palais de Sainte Croix pour n'infecter Monsieur le Prince ; et d'aultre part ne desiroit estre visité en l'estat qu'il estoit de personne jusques a ce qu'il eust faict secrettement ses baings ; portant toujours un taffetas abbaissé devant son visage, et les fenestres de sa chambre estoient toujours fermées.

Il fust là visité souventes foys par Sa Majesté, avec laquelle le dit Seigneur Roy s'estoit fort bien remis, et luy promeist de luy dire plusieurs choses importantes grandement à leur vie et repos : l'admonestant de se conserver l'un avec l'aultre en bonne amitié ; se donnant garde de ceulx qui s'entremectoient entre eulx deux (lequels il vouloit luy descouvrir) sur ce qu'on luy avoit conseillé contre la vie de Sa Majesté tendant à leur commune ruine. Et sur tous la pria de se garder de Ledinthon, lequel il disoit tendre à la ruine de l'un par l'aultre et à la fin de tous les deux, comme il s'appercevoit par leur déportemens et conseiléz plus que jamais.

Sa[4] Majesté se retirant la nuict mesme rencontra Paris,

[1] The incident of the raven is a later addition, and it is introduced so abruptly as to render necessary the repetition of five words at the beginning of the following paragraph.

[2] Appartement . . . cancelled.

[3] Contre la volonté de Sa Majesté, laquelle. . . . between the lines.

[4] This passage to the end of the paragraph is an addition.

varlet de chambre dudit Seigneur Bothuel, au quel montant
à cheval elle dist en presence de plusieurs Seigneurs, le voyant
tout gasté par le visage de pouldre-à-canon "Jesus, Paris, tu
es noirci ;" dont il rougist bien fort.

Le xme de Février audit an 1567 sur[1] troys ou quattre
heures du matin, fust mis le feu en une traînée de pouldre,
faicte soubz la maison dudit Seigneur Roy par le commande-
met et instruction (à ce que a depuis esté publié,) [2] des comtes
de Bothuil et de Morton, lequel revenu secrèttement d'Angleterre, où il estoit banny, James Bafour, et quelques aultres, qui
onc se sont monstréz les plus dilligens en la recherche du
meurtre par eulx commis, suivant la conjuracion entre eulx
faicte, [3] escripte par Alexandre Hay, lors l'un des clercs
du conseil, et signée par le comte de Murray, les comtes
de Hontley, Bothuel, Morton, le Seigneur Ledinthon, James
Bafour, et aultres, qui s'estoient liguéz pour cest effect, et pro-
testoient de l'avoir résolu pour le bien public du royaume, et
prenans prétexte d'oster ladite Royne de la servitude et
mauvais estat où elle estoit par le traictment qu'elle recepvoit
dudit seigneur Roy, et se promectoient soustenir l'ung l'aultre,
et en respondre comme chose faicte par justice et ordonnée
licitement et legitimement[4] par eulx qui estoient les principaux du conseil, et pour la deffense de leur vies propres, dont
ils estoient en danger si ledit Seigneur Roy eust esté le
plus fort et eust eu le gouvernement du Royaume, lequel ils
disoient qu'il vouloit occupper, et abuser Sa Majesté. Laquelle
souvent ils reprenoient de ce qu'elle se rappoinctoit si fidellement avec le dit Seigneur Roy, son mary ; et luy remonstroient
qu'il leur mectroit, et à elle mesmes, le couteau sur la gorge.

Le corps du dit Seigneur Roy fust emporté par la violence
de la pouldre dans le jardin, et un sien pauvre varlet de
chambre Angloys, qui couchoit en sa chambre, y fust tué.

La rumeur soudain s'en espandist par la ville, et en fust
advertye Sa Majesté, qui en fust fort attristée, et garda sa
chambre tout le jour. Le corps fut apporté en plein conseil,

[1] Nau, originally intended to have written "minuit," but stopped
before the word was finished.

[2] This parenthesis is an addition.   [3] Et signeé, cancelled.

[4] Legitimement, an interlineation above licitement, neither cancelled.

et là visité pour scavoir la façon de sa mort; et sur ce informacions dilligemment faictes et poursuictes de tous costéz, mesmes par ceulx que estoient autheurs du crime, et entre aultres le comte de Murray, qui s'absenta ce mesme jour du faict, soubz prétexte d'aller visiter sa femme qu'il disoit estre en extrémité de malladie. Et depuis ayant dressé toutes practiques nécessaires pour parachever son desseing d'empreter [1] le royaume et pour ruiner Sa Majesté, luy demanda congé de se retirer en France, où elle luy bailla lettres de recommandation à Messires ses parens, et assignation d'argent sur son douaire. Bailla la principale charge de ces desseings à laird de Grange, qui deppendoit entièrement de luy, et à Ledinthon, principal conducteur de toutes ses enterprinses et rebellions. Avoit [2] dist a plusieurs Angloys qu'il se falloit deffaire dudit seigneur Roy, tant pour ce qu'il estoit Catholique, que pour ce qu'il estoit ennemy de la Royne d'Angleterre; mais de long temps ils avoient inimitiés ensemble, et devant et depuis le marriage. Le Roy, se souvenant de l'embusche qu'il luy avoit faict à Lokleven avant le mariage, le vouloit fere tuer, depuis les aultres.

Le comte de Bothuel fut fort soubçonné de ce villain et détestable meurtre, et s'en semoient plusieurs fort mauvais bruictz, desquels il se déclara, par divers affiches et cartels de deffy, estre prest à respondre et se justiffier, ce qu'il feist à la fin en plain parlement. Mais comme il est vraysemblable, par le jugement, menées et practiques de ses compagnons, lesquels par son moyen s'estans deffaictes du defunct Roy, voulurent aussi se servir de luy pour la ruine de leur vraye et legitime Souveraine, et leur intention tendoit à luy persuader le mariage dudit comte de Bothuel, affin par après de luy imposer, comme ils firent, qu'elle estoit consentant et de la partye dressée contre son feu mary, et qu'elle avoit espousé le meurtrier d'icelluy.

Ceste pauvre jeune princesse, mal exercitée à telles traverses, et circonvenue par les persuasions, requestes et poursuictes des uns et des aultres, tant en general par requestes

[1] Apparently an error for emporter.
[2] The remainder of the paragraph is an addition.

signées de leur main, presentées en plain conseil, qu'en particulier. [1]

Mesmes un jour en la ville de l'Islebourg tous lesdits
Seigneurs et les principaux du conseil de la noblesse, s'estans
assembléz en la maison du dit Seigneur Comte de Bothwell,
envoyèrent de leur part vers Sa Majesté les dits Seigneurs de
Lethinthon et le Justice Clerc, avec un aultre, pour luy fere
entendre la resolution qu'ils avoient prise pour pourvoir à la
nécessité présente des afferes du royaume, délaissés à faulte de
chef, pour y mectre ordre; et que pour ce ils avoient advisé de
la supplier tous unanimement d'accepter ledit Seigneur de
Bothuel pour mary, lequel ils cognoissent estre homme resolu et digne de commander; et ne restoit pour authoriser
ses actions et les resolutions dudit conseil, qu'un tel homme,
duquel en sa faveur ils requéroient tous Sa Majesté.

A telles et semblables remonstrances fust faict refuz par
sadite Majesté purement et simplement, et encores une aultre
foys depuis; leur remectant devant les yeux les bruictz
qui couroient de la mort du feu Roy, son mary. A quoy
luy fust repliqué par ledit Seigneur de Ledinthon et aultres
depputéz, que ledit Seigneur de Bothwel en estoit deuement
deschargé par ledit conseil, et qu'estans entre eulx les principaux de la noblesse qui faisoient ceste requeste pour le
bien public du royaume, ce serait à eulx d'en respondre si
par leur conseil et resolution telle chose se passoit. Mesmes
à la fin estans requis de fere sur ce assembler les Estatz ils
signèrent tous ensemble la requeste qu'ils avoient presentée
pour la valider, et se chargerèrent du contenu d'icelle.

Ainsi Sa Majesté, poursuivie[2] très instamment de ceste
ouverture, voyant ledit Seigneur de Bothwel suffissamment
deschargé de ce qu'on l'avoit accusé, et ne soubçonnant rien
davantage, commença à y prester l'aureille,[3] toutes foys sans
aucune demonstracion ouverte sur laquelle on peut fonder
jugement de l'effect d'icelle, demeurant en irresolution, tant
à cause des bruictz que s'espandoient diversement sur l'ouver-

[1] There is a mark at "particulier," corresponding with one on the opposite page, showing that the long paragraph, (commencing, Mesmes un jour,
nd ending de ceste ouverture,) is to be inserted at this point.

[2] Originally, persuadée.   [3] A ceste ouverture cancelled.

ture dudit mariage, que pour n'avoir aucun moyen ou force
bastante de punir ses rebelles, desquels à la verité elle estoit
lors plus commandée que conseillée, et gouvernée que servie.
Et leur meschanteté appareust lors qu'ayant pris pretexte de
poursuivre ledit Seigneur comte de Bothwel, ils se meirent en
armes et plaine compagne contre Sa Majesté ; laquelle (comme
vous entendrez cy àpres) s'estant rendue de bonne[1] foy, et sur
la foy publique, entre leur mains pour leur assister et tenir
la main à l'execution de la pursuitte et recherche par eux requise contre les meurtriers du feu roy, et donner ordre qu'aucun
n'y meist empeschement par faveur ou aultrement, comme ils
se plaignoient, sans charger, en façon que ce soit, sadite
Majesté, laquelle ils disoient seulement estre entre les mains
de ceulx lesquels ils vouloient accuser, et mesmes pour valider
le parlement qu'ils avoient délibéré fere assembler.   En plain
parlement, qu'ils avoient promis de fere assembler du faict
dont ils accusoient ledit Seigneur Bothwel, il le laissèrent
aller sain et saufve sans faire aucune dilligence contre luy.

Mais sans aucune forme et voye qu'on a accoustume de
tenir audit parlement, s'attaquèrent directement à Sa Majesté, et la meirent en prison à Lokleving, frère[2] naturel de
comte de Murray, sans luy fere seulement entendre les raisons
qu'à ce les mouvoient; n'estans à la verité aultres que l'usurpation de la coronne par telles voyes sinistres et abominables
dressées avant le partement dudit Seigneur de Murray hors
du royaume.

Or est à noter que ledit Seigneur Bothwel avoit gaigné et
tiré à sa devotion pour cest effect tous lesdits seigneurs du
conseil ; les uns luy assistans fidellement comme amys ;[3] les
aultres par contraincte, craignant leur vies ;[4] les aultres par
dissimulation, pour parvenir à leur desseings et intentions
secretes, et avec leur ayde et advis,[5] voyant les difficultés et
longueurs ausquelles on le tenoit ; se resolut de se saysir, par

---

[1] . . . de bonne foy, et sur la foy publique . . . added between the
lines.

[2] A few words are here wanted to complete the sense.

[3] Comme amys, an interlineation.

[4] Craignant leur vies, added above the line.

[5] Se resolut de se . . . cancelled.

quelque moyen que ce fust, de la personne de Sa Majesté ; et puis, ayant desja le consentement de tous lesdits Seigneurs, l'induire à bailler le sien pour l'effect de ceste négociation, que fust diversement manié selon la diversité des intentions de ceulx qui s'entremesloient.

Le projet et l'execution que s'en ensuyvirent furent tels que Sa Majesté, allant de Sterlingh, où elle avoit esté pour visiter Monseigneur le Prince, son fils, vers Lythquho, accompagnée du comte de Huntly, lors intime partizan dudit Seigneur de Bothwel, fust rencontrée sur les chemins par ledit Seigneur de Bothwel, accompagné de 15 cens hommes de cheval, armé à la mode du pays, et de la emmenée au chasteau de Dunbar, appartenant à sadite Majesté,[1] dont Whitlaw avoit la garde ; luy estant remonstrée, sur les plaintes qu'elle faisoit, qu'on ne la menoit que chez elle, et avec tous ses domestiques pour demeurer en toute liberté et puissance telle que luy appartenoit. Mais aultrement en advint ; car la plus part de son train luy fust retranché, et n'eust entière liberté jusques à ce qu'elle eust consenty au mariage que lesdits seigneurs de son conseil luy avoient proposé ; lequel fust peu après celebré publiquement à Edimbourgh au palais[2] de Sainte Croix par l'évesque d'Orknay, tout le peuple y assistant, et en compagnie des principaux de la noblesse, qui demonstroient avoir ce mariage fort agréable et grandement à l'advantage du pays.

Mais tost après, soit par quelques inimitiés secretes qui intervindrent, ou que estans de longue main cachées commancèrent à se descouvrir et jecter leur venin, il se feist une conjuration contre ledit Seigneur de Bothuel soubz prétexte de vanger la mort du feu Roy, duquel on delibera de l'accuser, et tout ce par l'advis et conseil du Seigneur de Ledinthon ; secrétaire, avec lequel ledit Seigneur de Bothuel estoit tumbé en mauvais mesnage. Il tira à sa cordelle laird de Grange, gentilhomme fort[3] vaillant et de grande réputation, auquel les conjureurs ne descouvrirent jamais le fonds de leur meschante intention, ains seulement luy amenèrent soubz le prétexte dessusdit et sur le respect du comte de Murray,

---

[1] . . . appartenant à sadite Majesté . . . an interlineation.

[2] Originally, chasteau.   [3] Originally, fort sage.

duquel il deppendoit entièrement, comme [1] l'ayant suivy en la rebellion dressée pour la cause de la relligion contre la feue Royne mère.　Estoient aussi de ceste partye quelques aultres par jalousie de l'advancement dudit Seigneur de Bothuel, qui y furent facillement attiréz, joinct que ledit Seigneur de Bothuel n'estoit homme qui de son naturel se rendoit fort agréable, ne qui meist beaucoup de travail et peine à gaigner la bonne volonté de ceulx avec lesquels il conversoit.　Tous [2] ceulx de ce party furent les anciens rebelles pour le faict de la relligion.

Les premiers qui y entrèrent furent my Lord Hume, laird Taliberne, qui y attira le comte de Mar, faict nouvellement comte par Sa Majesté, et auquel elle avoit baillé en garde Monseigneur le Prince, son fils, avec le chasteau de Striveling, qu'elle luy confirma en héritage pour luy et les siens.　Et en ce faisant [3] luy avoit osté la garde du chasteau d'Edinbourgh par l'advis du conseil, qui trouvoit que c'estoit trop grandes ferais en une seule main, et de ce la comtesse de Mar, femme fort malicieuse et pleine de vindicacion, fust en partye cause, ledit Tuliberne estant son frère.[4]　On feist entendre à plusieurs d'entre eulx que Sa Majesté empeschoit la justice du meurtre du feu roy ; et ainsi la plupart n'alloient que contre le comte de Bothuel.

Depuis plusieurs,[5] la verité estant descouverte de la deffence du party de Sa Majesté contre my lord de Huntley, qui entra en cette querelle pour avoir esté refusé par l'advis du conseil d'une priuré qu'il demandoit, estant du plus beau et plus clair domaine de la coronne.　Le comte de Morton[6] estant aussi des premiers, comme en toutes trahysons il à toujours

---

[1] The words, from " comme " to "mere," are added between the lines.
This sentence is an interlineation.

[3] Originally, Mais depuis luy . . . . . afterwards cancelled, and En ce faisant, written between the lines.

[4] Originally, son beau frère.

[5] The whole of the narrative, from this point as far as the end of the section, is obscure, and at certain points unintelligible, in consequence of the various interlineations, cancels, and other alterations, to which it has been subjected.

[6] In illustration of the incident here mentioned, see the Letters of La Mothe Fénélon, vi. 427, 481.

tenu ce rang, meist en avant le mariage de son nepveu le
Comte d'Angus, duquel il avoit la garde noble, avec une des
filles du Comte d'Athol, pour fere entrer sur ceste esperance
ledit Seigneur Comte en ceste ligue ; ce qui advint, y aydant la
persuasion du Seigneur de Ledinthon, que avoit espousé la sœur
de la femme dudit Seigneur Comte.[1]   Mais après il monstra sa
dissimulation ; car sitost que[2] Sa Majesté fust prisonnière, il
le maria avec la fille dudit comte de Mar, pour le gaigner
davantage à sa devotion ; et aussi se servoit de ce pauvre
jeune seigneur comme d'un hameçon, pour prendre les moins
adviséz en ses fillets.[3]

Le rendezvous des dits conjuréz fust appoincté en l'eglise
de Liberton, près de deux miles de l'Islebourgh, au jour de
Mardy xme de Juin 1567 ; et là se trouvèrent de nuict
le comte de Morton, et lord de Hume, estans le[4] lendemain
Mercredi, rencontréz là par le comte de Mar.   Mais d'autant
que le reste ne s'y trouva, il fut advisé d'aller surprendre la
Royne et le dit Seigneur Bothuel a Borthwoyk, (d'où Sa
Majesté se retira[5] à Dunbar après[6] avoir esté assiegée audit
Borthwick pres de trois ou quatre jours par sept cens
chevaux legers).[7]   Les dits Seigneurs de Hume et Morton
vindrent, suivant leur déliberation, avec sept ou huit cens
chevaux legers au devant dudit Borthwic, et là tirèrent
plusieurs harquebusades, crians plusieurs pouilles contre ledit
Seigneur Bothuel, lequel ils provoquoient de sortir, dont il
fust souvent empesché par les siens, qui y voyoient un trop
éminent danger.   Mais à la fin ledit Seigneur Bothuel, se

---

[1] Y aydant . . . to dudit Seigneur Conte, added between the lines.

[2] Originally, que Bothuel fust hors du pays.

[3] Originally, embusches.

[4] Two words, here added in the margin, have been so closely bound into
the back of the MS. as to be illegible.

[5] The original text stood thus ; Sa Majesté se retira promptement à
Dunbar, et sur l'advertissement qu'elle receust de la conjuration.

[6] . . . . Après, added above the line. The arrangement again becomes
involved.

[7] . . . près de . . . legers, added above the line in consequence of the
frequency and obscurity of the corrections and additions. Apparently the
clause here placed within brackets should have been cancelled, as it occurs
in the text in a more extended form.

voyant tant oultragé, ne peust estre retenu qu'avec quarante ou cinquante bons hommes d'armes il ne sortist hardiment, et passant à la teste des assiégeans se jecta en la campagne et commença à assembler ses forces, ayant pareillement tiré le mesme jour la Royne hors de ceste forteresse, et la conduict[1] à Dunbar, où les vindrent trouver Lord de Seton, Yester, et Borthwike; lairds de Wakton, Bas, Ormiston, Wedderburn, Blakater, et Langton, faisons tous ensemble environ quattre mil hommes, et[2] y estoient deux cens harquebusiers de la garde de la Royne. Estoient appoinctéz les seigneurs de Flaming, les Hammiltons, avec le comte de Huntley, vers lesquels estoit allé le baron Brokar pour les haster, mais lesdites forces arrivérent trop tard.

Les dits Seigneurs se retirèrent enfin à Edimbourg[3] et là commencèrent à assembler et fere venir tous ceulx de leur party avec leurs forces, qui estoient les comtes de Morton, Athol, Mar, Glencarne; lords de Hume, Lyndsay, Ruthven, Simple et Sanquhar; lairds de Dumblane, Tulibarne, Grange, et le jeune Seaford; et leur compagnie montoit à quattre mil hommes de bons soldats et gens exercitéz.[4]

La meschante intention du comte de Murray se monstra assez en ce que ayant deffaict le comte de Huntley, et depuis la maison de Lenox par la mort du feu Roy, s'en estant ensuyvie la démission de la Royne, sitost qu'il fust Régent et eust le gouvernement, il se meist à poursuivre les Hammiltons, desquels il s'estoit aydé auparavant, soubz un pretexte de faulse amitié, mesmement contre ledit Seigneur de Lenox, sachant l'ancienne inimitié de ces deux maisons.

Sa Majesté estant encore à Dunbar fust advertye par James Bafour, commis à la garde du chasteau de l'Islebourg (et qui avoit esté practiqué à ceste effect par les rebelles du Sa Majesté), de se mectre en la campagne et tirer droict à Edinburgh, pour rencontrer lesdits rebelles; lesquels il s'asseuroit s'en debvoir promptement retirer; mesmement lorsqu'ils

---

[1] Originally, la mena à.
[2] The last clause of this sentence is an addition.
[3] Enfin, an interlineation.
[4] A line is here drawn across the page of the MS. It is obvious that the paragraph immediately following is out of place.

verroient ledit Bafour se declarer ouvertement contre eulx, et tirer sur leurs troupes; sinon, qu'il seroit contrainct de s'appoincter avec eulx.

Sur l'advis de ce traistre, qui tendoit le main d'un costé et d'aultre, Sa Majesté vint le xiiij. Juin, jour de Sabmedy, à Hathinton, et de là passant par Gladesmore[1] arriva pour loger à Seton, d'où elle partit le lendemain, et marcha en ordre de bataille jusques à Carbary Hill; et là, sur une petite montagne choisie à l'advantage, les trouppes descendirent à pied par le commandement des chefz, qui prévoyoient la cavellerie ennemye estre la plus forte. Aussi, pour la doubte qu'ils avoient que leurs chevaux legers ne prinsent la fuytte, leur coustume estant de fere seulement quelques légeres charges, et puis se retirer. C'estoient la plus part gens des frontières, qui ne sont nullement dresséz à tenir ordre de bataille, ny la discipline militaire, ains propres[2] seulement à escarmoucher, ou aller descouvrir, et qu'il est besoing de mectre promptement en besongne si vous en voulez tirer bon service; ce que fust en partye cause de leur désordre. Car comme les deux camps s'approchoient, le Sieur du Croc, ambassadeur pour le Roy Très-Chrétien, qui estoit party d'Edimbourg et venu avecques lesdits rebelles, vint trouver Sa Majesté et proposa diverses ouvertures d'appointemens, faisant plusieurs voyages en l'un et l'aultre camp, de sorte que cependant, les soldats, lassez et rompuz par la chaleur extrême du jour, commencèrent à se desbander pour aller boire et se rafraischir par les villages. Et est a notter qu'ils avoient faict une forte grande journée le jour de devant.

Ainsi par les menées du dit Sieur Du Crok les choses étans tirées en longeur et les soldats de Sa Majesté retenuz de charger, dont ils étoient prestes, ayans ja esté tué quelques[3] chevaulx à coups d'artillerie des rebelles. Etant là sur le tard, et comme les dits soldats s'advancoient, sortirent pour la quatrième foys quelques depputéz des ennemys qui demandèrent à parlamenter.

[1] Originally, "logea ce jour."
[2] . . . propres . . . an interlineation.
[3] . . . quelques advantureurs, originally, chevaulx à coups d'artillerie, added above the line.

R

Sa Majesté, qui jusques alors n'avoit par eulx rien entendue de leur intention, mesmement qu'ils voulussent charger ledit Seigneur de Bothuel de la mort du feu Roy, d'autant qu'ils n'en avoient faict aucune demonstration et que s'estoit par eulx qu'il avoit esté advancé.[1]   On leur envoya au devant entre les deux camps ; et leur fust premièrement demandé s'ils estoient là assembléz et venoient ainsi en armes, ou comme subjectz, ou comme ennemys ?   Et à quelle fin ils venoient ?[2]   Ils respondirent, venant comme très fidelles et obéisans subjectz, qui ne requéroient aultre chose que la justice du meurtre du feu Roy, et la plaine liberté de Sa Majesdée, qu'ilz remonstroient estre possedée et detenue par ceulx à qui ce faict toucher.   Et que pour ce ils supplioient Sa Majesté leur délivrer ceulx qu'ils luy nommeroient, estant lors en sa compagnie, (nommant lors ledit Seigneur de Bothuel)[3] et de s'en venir elle avec lesdits seigneurs estans là assembléz pour estre remise en l'estat qui luy appartenoit, et hors de la puissance de ceulx qui l'avoient jusques à lors retirée d'avec eulx pour se couvrir de son authorité pour empescher la justice.

Sa Majesté à ce feist respondre qu'elle trouvoit bien estrange qu'ils eussent attendu de poursuivre ledit Seigneur de Bothuel, et le charger de ce crime, jusqu'à ce qu'il fust en la compagnie de Sa Majesté, veu qu'avant ils avoient eu moyen se saysir de luy sans si grandes forces.   Par où il apparoit qu'a elle seule on se vouloit attaquer pour luy oster la coronne,[4] qu'à l'instance et du commun consentement des principaux de la noblesse, mesmement de plusieurs qui estoient là assembléz contre elle, elle avoit espousé le comte de Bothuel, ce qu'elle n'eust faict si plustost[5] et plus claire-

---

[1] The greater part of this section is very crowded; the clause commencing Sa Majesté to avoit esté advancé, is entirely written between the lines, its place in the MS. has been retained in order to follow the original as closely as possible.

[2] Et a quelle fin ils venoient, added below the lines.

[3] The clause within brackets is an interlineation.

[4] This clause, Sa Majesté . . . oster la couronne, has been closely written in a blank space in the MS., and continued between the lines.

[5] Et . . . avant le mariage, cancelled.

ment elle eust esté informée et advertye de ladite accusation. Et que partant elle se sentoit obligée de luy assister jusqu'a ce qu'il appareust de ce qu'on le vouloit accuser.[1]

Mais que d'aultre part, ne voulant manquer à la mémoire du feu Roy, son mary, elle estoit tres contante[2] de donner la voye de justice, et la rendre la plus libre que le se pourroit à tous ceulx qui vouldroient, comme c'estoit son intention pour fere rechercher de la mort dudit Seigneur Roy, et punir exemplairement ceulx qui en seroient convaincuz ; requérant[3] elle mesme la justice de quelques aultres qui estoient présent, de leur party coulpables de ladite mort, dont ils furent fort estonnez se voyant descouvertz.[4] Pour à quoi parvenir elle s'accorda de commectre[5] (sa personne) à la foy des dits Seigneurs pour leur authoriser ce que par eulx seroit en ce faict et traicté, et les assister selon son debvoir en toutes telles pursuittes.

Sur quoy elle[6] feist demander de parler elle mesme à Ledinton ; qui feist dire qu'il n'estoit pas[7] avec lesdits rebelles ; et depuis au comte d'Athol, qui pareillement s'excusa.   En fin vint devers elle laird de Grange, avec lequel ayant discouru fort particulièrement des choses dessusdites, elle se resolut, sur sa parolle et asseurance qu'il luy donna de la foy desdits seigneurs, laquelle il disoit avoir eue d'eux solennellement et en plain conseil,[8] de retourner avec eulx pour oster tout doubte et soubçon qu'elle voulust en rien supporter les culpables du dit crime, ny les maintenir.

Mais avant la main elle requist ledit sire de Grange d'adviser à la seureté du dit Seigneur Bothuel, à ce qu'il ne luy fust mesfaict en attendant l'assemblée du Parlement, où

---

[1] Ce qu'elle . . . accusation, added between the lines.

[2] Dont elle protesta ne scavoir aucune chose, cancelled.

[3] Tres contante de rendre en ce qu'elle pouvoit, originally.

[4] . . . requérant . . . descouvertz, an addition.

[5] Originally . . . se commectre.

[6] Originally, elle mesme.

[7] Pas au camp avec, originally.

[8] The text originally stood thus—en plain conseil se rendre entre leur mains, se sentant totalement incoupable de toutes telles accusations, des-quelles par ce moyen elle se aussi declara verytablement en fere fere l'exact et l'exemplaire justice.

telles choses se debvoient déterminer. A quoy luy fust respondu par ledit Seigneur de Grange, qu'il ny avoit aucune lieu d'entrer en ceste ouverture avec les seigneurs de son party ; lesquels estoient ja tous mutinéz de ce qu'il avoit passé plus[1] oultre qu'ils ne luy avoient prescript. Et sur ce touchant la main dudit Seigneur de Bothuel, le conseilla de se retirer, et luy promeist d'homme de bien qu'il empescheroit en ce qu'il pourroit qu'il ne fust suyvy.

Commance le dit Seigneur Bothuel n'y voulust au commancement condescendre, ains estoit résolu de combattre. Mais en fin fust vaincu par les prières de Sa Majesté, qui luy persuada pour un temps de s'absenter jusques à ce qu'on veist l'issue du Parlement que se debvoit tenir, et luy promeist que si il estoit trouvé innocent (comme il pretendoit) du faict dont on l'accusoit, rien ne la pouvoit empescher de luy rendre le debvoir de vray et légitime femme ; sinon qu'elle regretteroit toute sa vie d'avoir[2] apprêté par leur marriage de quoy damner sa reputation ; et qu'elle s'en vouloit descharger par quelque moyen que ce fust.

Au partir[3] du dit seigneur Bothuel d'avec Sa Majesté, voulant descharger sa conscience et descouvrir la meschante intention desdits ennemys, il déclara à Sa Majesté que le comte de Morton, le secrétaire Ledinton, James Bafour et quelques aultres, estant lors du contraire party, estoient coulpables de la mort du feu Roy ; le tout s'estant exécuté par leur advis et conseil. Et luy monstra leur signature[4] . . . en la ligue pour . . . . entre eulx ; disant qu'elle garderoit ce papier.

Aussi ledit Seigneur Bothuel s'en vint à Dunbar, et de là ayant passant[5] en Orknay, où il séjourna quelques temps, se retira en Dannemark, où il fust arresté prisonnier. Il y a vescu jusques en l'an 1578[6] qu'il est décéddé, rendant compte par

[1] . . . plus, added above the line.

[2] . . . . d'avoir esté si imprudentement conjoinct à luy . . . . de quoy souiller sa . . . was the original reading.

[3] This paragraph is written lengthways in the margin of the MS.

[4] At this point a few words are illegible in the original.

[5] . . . ayant sejourné quelques jours en Orkney, is the original text. Ayant ought to have been cancelled.

[6] The last figure is so indistinct that it is not easy to decide whether it is 7 or 8. One numeral has been written over the other.

son testament de la mort du feu Roy, lequel testament s'ensuyt.[1]

Sa Majesté vint au camp des ennemys avec ses domestiques, où elle fust receue avec grande acclamation des soldatz, qui[2] se jouissoient d'avoir rescouvret leur Royne. Laquelle rencontrant le comte de Morton luy dit plainement et tout hault, "Comment, Monseigneur de Morton, on dist que tout cecy se faict pour avoir raison des meurtriers du Roy; et l'on m'a dist que vous estes l'un des premiers." Il luy respondist, "Allons, allons, ce n'est pas icy que telles choses se debvoient debattre;" et se retira derrière Sa Majesté, comme pas un des Seigneurs, ne se presentast jamais à Sa Majesté. Laquelle ils feirent accompagner par deux très meschans hommes; le jeune Dunblanrick et le jeune Sesford, deux très cruels[3] meurtriers et de fort scandaleuse vie. Ledit Dumblanrick avoit tué un sien cousin dedans le lict, entre les bras de sa femme, duquel il debvoit estre heritier; et ce à cause de quelque héritage que ledit Dumblanrick ne pouvoit avoir au prix qu'il désiroit de sondit cousin. L'aultre, Sesford, tua aussi fort cruellement son propre oncle et parrain, l'Abbé de Kylso, d'autant qu'il ne luy vouloit donner en fief certaine terre deppandante de la dite Abbaye. Quand[4] Sa Majesté veist laird de Dumblanrick le père près d'elle, elle luy dist, "Ha, laird de Dumblanrick! ce n'estoit pas la promesse que vous me feistes après votre première rebellion, quand à genoux parmy les champs vous protestiez ne suivre jamais que l'enseigne royalle." Il luy respondist, "Au nom Dieu, pourquoy n'avez-vous pas accordé la rémission à mon filz, qui estoit chose juiste?" Et pour le meurtre cy desjà mentionné d'un sien cousin, la femme duquel estoit devenue folle d'avoir veu tuer son mary en sa présence.

La[5] prise de Sa Majesté fut le xx Juing 1567.[6]

[1] No such document occurs in the MS., nor was it ever entered in this place.

[2] . . . qui pensoient . . cancelled.

[3] . . . tres cruels . . added above the line.

[4] This paragraph, ending with the word "presence," is written lengthways, on the margin of the original.

[5] This memorandum seems to have been added by Nau, but at a later time.　　　　[6] Originally written 1566.

Durant les chemins lesdits Seigneurs esloingèrent de Sa Majesté tous ses domestiques, et approchèrent d'elle les soldatz de Lislebourg, sans permectre qu'aucun de ceulx de son party parlast à elle; par ou elle commença à s'apercevoir qu'elle estoit détenue prisonnière. Et ainsi fust elle amenée à L'Islebourgh, en la maison où logoit[1] lard de Cragmiller, près de ladite ville, homme de fort mauvaise vie et de nulle relligion, lequel avoit esté attiré à ceste faction par son malcontantement pris sur qu'on luy avoit osté la garde du chasteau de Dunbar, en la récompense de la dicte prevosté, et aussi par la persuasion du Seigneur de Ledinthon, la première femme duquel estoit sœur de la seconde femme dudit Cragmillar. Homme de peu de cœur, et lequel à la fin de sa vie dans Paris (où il mourut de la grosse vérole, ou ladrerie), tesmoigna avoir une extrême repentance de sa rebellion contre Sa Majesté, veu l'obligacion qu'il luy avoit, oultre debvoir de subject.

Estant arrivée audit logis elle trouva lesdits Seigneurs prestz de se mectre à table pour le soupper; et luy fust demandé si elle ne vouloit pas soupper en la compagnie. Sur quoy Sa Majesté répliqua qu'ils luy avoient trop apresté de quoy soupper, veu l'estat où elle se voyoit réduicte, et qu'elle avoit plus de besoing de repos que de manger. Ainsi fust elle enfermée en une chambre, avec gardes mises sur le degré et à toutes les saillies dudit logis; mesmement quelques unes furent si impudens que de ne vouloir partir de ladite chambre, de sorte que Sa Majesté demeura toute la nuict[2] couchée sur un lit, sans deshaibiller. La plus grande licence qu'elle eust se fust d'escripre ausdits seigneurs, principallement à laird de Grange, sur l'asseurance duquel elle estoit venue avec eulx, et au secrétaire Ledinthon, auquel elle desiroit parler, pour resouldre avec luy du trouble qui se présentoit, et scavoir particulièrement l'intention desdits Seigneurs; offrant d'assister au parlement pour rechercher la justice qu'ils avoient requise du meurtre du feu Roy. Demandoit de scavoir les occasions de ce qu'elle estoit ainsi indignement par eulx traictée et detenue

---

[1] Où logoit, added above the line.
[2] . . . toute la nuict . . ., an interlineation.

comme prisonnière, d'autant que aucun de ses gens ne pouvoient avoir accéz vers elle, et qu'elle n'estoit logée en son chasteau, comme elle avoit au paravant accoustume ; leur remonstrant que là elle n'avoit ny lict, ny meubles dignes d'elle, et qu'ils ne se comportient envers elle comme bons et fidelles subjects, tels qu'ils se prétendoient. A ce ne luy fust faict aucune response, ains seulement craignans qu'elle ne se mesfeist par désespoir, luy baillèrent gardes, dans sa chambre mesmes ; et ne luy voulurent bailler la clef de ladicte chambre, de sorte qu'elle coucha toute vestue[1] environ une heure et demie sur le lict.[2]

Le lendemain matin sur les huit ou neuf heures, Sa Majesté (estant à la fenestre de sa chambre) veist passer Ledinthon, qui alloit au conseil desdits Seigneurs ; et l'appella par diverses foys par son nom fort lamentablement, et en pleurant luy ramentevant l'obligacion qu'il luy avoit ; et que pour le moins en recompense de tant de biens et faveurs qu'elle luy avoit faict, il vint parler à elle. Ledit Seigneur baissa son chappeau, et ne feist aucune démonstration d'ouyr ou voir Sa Majesté ; sur quoy plusieurs soldatz de Sa Majesté et aultres du commun peuple se mutinans, les gardes de Sadite Majesté la vindrent retirer de la fenestre, et luy remonstrèrent qu'on luy pourroit tirer quelque arquebusade, dont les Seigneurs seroient bien marryz, et pour ce luy deffendirent d'approcher ladite fenestre.

Sa Majesté ne disna[3] pour ce jour là, ains seulement mangea un morceau de pain et beult un verre d'eaue, et durant ce fust fort manassée et très indignement arraisonnée par lesdits Dumblanrik et Sesfort.

Sa Majesté, voyant n'avoir encore aucune response de sa lettre qu'elle avoit escripte le soir précédent ausdits Seigneurs du conseil, elle leur escripvist de rechef pour scavoir l'occasion de la détention de sa personne, et du traictement qu'il luy estoit faict ; demandant de parler à eulx, ou[4] aucun d'eulx, et d'estre menée en son chasteau, ou au pallais de Sainte

[1] . . . toute vestue . . . above the line.
[2] Originally . . . . dans le lict . . . .
[3] " Sa Majesté disna fort peu," was the original reading.
[4] . . . Ou aucun d'eulx . . . between the lines.

Croix, où elle pourroit estre aussi seurement, mais plus honorablement gardée, jusques à ce qu'ils eussent résolu de leur intention. Fust[1] respondu que pour ce jour ne luy pouvoit estre faicte aucune response.

Ledinthon, à ce mené tant par le conseil de ses amys que par la rumeur qui courroit par toute la ville de son extrême ingratitude, vint trouver Sa Majesté sur le soir, mais avec telle honte et crainte intérieure qu'il n'osa jamais lever les yeux pour regarder Sa Majesté, tant qu'il parla à elle.

De prime abordée Sa Majesté s'enquist des occasions de tout le mauvais traitement qu'on luy faisoit, et ce qui en debvoit advenir; luy remectant devant les yeux ce qu'elle avoit faict pour luy, comme elle l'avoit favorisé et maintenu, mesmement lorsqu'elle luy avoit sauvé la vie, ce qu'il advoua et en fin luy declara qu'on vouloit fere justice de la mort du feu Roy, et qu'il y en avoit qui soubconnoient et craignoient qu'elle n'empeschast la justice qu'on en vouloit fere; et pour ce[2] la détenoient jusques à ce que le tout eust esté exécuté pour authoriser ceste pursuitte et remectre toutes choses en bon estat. Luy remonstrant aussi que le conseil ne vouloit aucunement permectre qu'elle retournast avec le conte de Bothuel, lequel il disoit estre besoing de fere exécuter, qu'aultrement il n'y auroit jamais repos au royaume, ny fiance en Sa Majesté pour[3] lesdits seigneurs; discourant sur ce plus que librement des conditions dudit Seigneur de Bothuel, vers lequel il démonstra une extrême hayne.

Sa Majesté, voyant l'impudence dudit Seigneur de Ledinthon, sachant mieux et plus qu'il ne disoit[4] et le faux pretexte que prenoient lesdits seigneurs pour exécuter[5] leur meschant desseing contre elle, la voulans charger d'empescher la justice du meurtre qu'eulx mesmes avoient commis, et duquel ils ne craignoient rien tant que la recherche,—répliqua doucement

---

[1] The whole of this sentence has been added by Nau in a different ink.

[2] Originally . . . pour ce ne voulloient . . .

[3] . . . Pour les dits seigneurs . . . an interlineation.

[4] Dudit seigneur de Ledinthou . . . disoit, an interlineation.

[5] Originally . . . pour s'attaquer à elle . . . This reading having been cancelled, in its place was inserted . . pour luy oster la coulpe, which in its turn was superceded by that which now stands in the text.

Seigneur de Ledinthon qu'elle estoit preste de fere paroistre le contraire, et de se joindre à la poursuitte qui se feroit du dit meurtre. Quand au conte de Bothuel, que luy mesmes scavoit bien comme toutes choses estoient passées, et par son advis plus que de nul aultre.

Sur quoy estants tumbéz de propos en aultres, et voyant que ledit Seigneur de Ledinthon vouloit fere le mescongnoissant et supporter les actions desdits Seigneurs, elle fust contraincte de luy dire lors plainement qu'elle craignoit[1] que luy, Morton et Bafour, plus que nuls aultres, empescheroient la recherche dudit meurtre, veu qu'ils en estoient consentants et coulpables, comme elle avoit sceu[2] du dit Seigneur de Bothuel sur son partement d'ave celle, qui[3] luy jura de n'avoir rien faict qu'à leur persuasion et advis, luy ayant monstré leur signature;[4] et que si elle, qui estoit Royne, estoit traictée de ceste façon sur le soubçon qu'on prenoit, qu'elle voulust obvier à la punition desdits coulpables, on pourroit bien plus seurement procedder à l'encontre de luy et du comte de Morton, James Bafour,[5] et aultres, estans audit conseil, qui estoient les meurtriers mesmes, et qui scavoient la sincérité de l'intention de Sa Majesté en cest endroict. Et qu'ils estoient tous bien malheureux de luy fere porter la peine de leur meschantetéz; menassant ledit Seigneur de Ledinthon que si il continuoit[6] en la compagnie et conjuration desdits seigneurs, elle,—qui l'avoit jusques à présent maintenu et conservé,—déclaroit à la fin ce que ledit Seigneur de Bothuel luy avoit dit de luy.[7]

Lequel, se voyant descouvert et entrant en fort grande cholère, vint jusques à dire que si cela advenoit, elle le forceroit de faire pis que n'avoit encore faict, en ayant esté contrainct pour sauver sa vie; laquelle (comme il disoit

---

[1] . . . Plainement qu'il avoit occasion de craindre . . . cancelled.

[2] Sceu par le serment dudit . . . was the original reading.

[3] . . . Qui luy . . . advis . . . an interlineation.

[4] . . . La signature dudit seigneur de Ledinthou . . . originally.

[5] . . . James Bafour, added above the line.

[6] . . . Continuoit de la mal traicter . . . was first written.

[7] This sentence has undergone several alterations, the following clauses having been cancelled . . . seroit a la fin contrainte . . . ce qu'elle scavoit par la declaration . . . touchant le dit seigneur de Ledinthou.

ordinairement assez peu virilement) il avoit plus chère que chose du monde. Au lieu que les choses s'adoucissant peu à peu, il pourroit luy fere encores quelque jour un bon service. Et que ce pendant il luy estoit besoing s'entretenir avec lesdits seigneurs ; prians pour ceste occasion Sa Majesté de le licencier et ne demander plus de parler à luy, d'autant que cela le mectoit en soubçon et ne profitteroit de rein à elle; et que si elle ne luy laissoit lieu[1] de crédit entre lesdits seigneurs, il y alloit de la vie de Sa Majesté, ce qu'il pourroit empescher, ayant ja esté proposé par plusieurs foys de s'en deffaire.

Environ les neuf heures du soir le comte de Morton vint vers Sa Majesté luy fere entendre, de la part de ceulx du conseil, qu'ils avoient ordonné qu'elle allast loger en son pallais de Sainte Croix, qui est hors de la ville. Mais leur intention estoit de l'enlever soudainement delà, craignans que si son partement eust esté veu par le peuple, quelque[2] sedition ne fust survenue. Et à cest effect ils attendoient jusques à la nuict.

Estant arrivée en son pallais, elle y trouva le soupper préparé, et la plus part de ses filles et de ses serviteurs domestiques, tous fort tristes de voir leur pauvre maistresse en un si misérable estat entre ses propres subjects, et ceulx mesmes qu'elle avoit le plus advancéz et favoriséz.

Au mylieu du soupper le comte de Morton, qui avoit tousjours esté derrière la chaire, demanda à l'escuyer d'escurye si les chevaux estoient prestz ; et faissant desservir, dist à Sa Majesté qu'elle se préparast de monter à cheval. Sa Majesté (oultre sa tristesse, craignant d'estre empoisonnée) n'avoit point[3] mangé de tout le jour, demanda où on la vouloit mener si précipitamment ; et requis qu'on luy baillast quelques unes de ses filles et de ses serviteurs domestiques, ce qui luy fust totallement refusé ; et luy fust seulement accordé de mener deux femmes de chambre ; tout le reste criant et faisant instance de suivre Sa Majesté. Il n'y a cœur si dur entre les plus cruelz barbares que n'eust esté esmeu à compassion voyant le départ de ceste pauvre. . . . .[4]

¹ . . . lieu de . . . an interlineation.
² Possibly the word quelques has been cancelled in the MS.
³ . . . point encores mangé . . . original text.
⁴ A few words are here cut off by the binder at the bottom of the page.

Morton la faisoit entendre indirectement qu'elle alloit avec
Monsieur le prince son filz.[1]   Mais elle fust menée en grande
dilligence droict à Lokleving, chez le frère naturel du comte
de Murray, qui cependant estoit en France, et visitoit souvent
Gaspar de Colligny, admiral.

Il ne luy fust permis de prendre aultre habit que son
manteau de nuict, ny aucun linge.   Elle passa au Petit
Lyth, qui estoit plain de soldatz pour empescher le remeue-
ment du peuple ; et fust accompagner à Lokleving de my
lord Lyndsay et my lord Ruthven.   Plusieurs avoient opinion
que les Hammiltons et le comte de Rothes avoient[2] assemblé
quelques forces, et ainsi Sa Majesté fust advertye par les
chemins de retarder le plus qu'elle pourroit.   Mais il ne luy
fust permis, ayant tousjours quelqu'un près d'elle, qui frappoit
sa hacquenée pour la haster.

Elle fust receu sur le bord du lac par ledit laird et ses
frères, qui la[3] conduirent en une chambre basse, meublée seulement des meubles du dit laird, et non du lict de Sa Majesté
et aultres équipages propres à ceulx de sa qualité.   Sa Majesté
fust quinze jours et plus en ceste prison avec telle désolacion,
sans boire, manger ny converser avec ceulx de la maison, que
plusieurs pensoient qu'elle debvoit finir ses jours.

Ce pendant, un sien Maistre d'hostel, Italien, pratiqué
par les rebelles de Sa Majesté, leur délivrast la vaisselle
d'argent et aultres meubles qui estoient en sa charge, et de
mesmes furent saysis tous les aultres plus precieux meubles
de sadite Majesté, tant de son cabinet que pour les chambres,
mesmement toute sa garderobe, d'ou elle ne peust jamais tirer
une seule robbe, ny avoir une chemise, jusques au retour de
Monseigneur de Murray, qui luy feist fere par le tailleur de
sa femme une robbe de drap violet, et luy envoya[4] avec
quelques meschantes hardes, dont ailleurs il ne se pouvoit servir.

Ce bon seigneur estant en France,[5] si tost qu'il eust

---

[1] At the top of this page is written in the margin of the MS., Le moys
de Juin.

[2] . . . avoient dressé . . . originally.

[3] Nau first wrote, . . . qui la servoient ordinairement . . .

[4] . . . et luy en voya . . . above the line.

[5] . . . estant en France . . . an interlineation.

nouvelles de la prison de Sa Majesté, il s'adressa au Roy et
à messeigneurs de Lorraine, parens de Sa Majesté, et s'obligea
vers eulx par promesses, protestations et perjureures[1] infiniz
de s'acheminer promptement en Escosse, et là fere tous ses
effortz pour retirer Sa Majesté hors de prison, restablir son
authorité et remectre toutes choses en bon estat ; sur quoy il
receust, vendant sa perfidie, beaucoup de bons et de grands
présens.   Mais il avoit tracé tous les actes de la tragédie, et
en desseignoit bien un aultre issue ; et non contant des exé-
crables meschansetéz et trahysons ja exécutéz (dont il pensat
que son absence le dischargoit assez apparemment envers le
monde), il délibera de fere parachever le jeu avant que retourner, affin d'entrer en son nouveau royaume avec[2] moins
d'obstacle, et n'estre dist qu'il usurpast[3] illégitimement la
puissance de sa souveraine vivante.   Et pour ce il fust proposé
au conseil de ceulx de son party de fere mourir, par quelque
moyen que se fust, Sa Majesté, après laquelle l'on trouveroit
assez de moyen de se deffaire de Monseigneur le Prince, son
filz.   Mais la contradiction d'aucuns d'entre eulx, qui eurent
horreur d'un acte si détestable souillant leur mémoire et de
leur patrie envers la postérité, fust cause qu'ils changèrent de
desseing, et au lieu qu'ils disoient au paravant ne pouvoir
trouver asseurance de leur forfaict, sinon par sa mort, d'autant
qu'elle les en pourroit quelque jour punir, ils advisèrent de la
contraindre à la démission de la coronne, et la fere passer
comme voluntairement faicte par elle en faveur de Monseigneur
le Prince, son filz, le nom duquel ils commancèrent à em-
prunte contre sa pauvre mère, ainsi que de la[4] mémoire du
père et des aultres contre luy, mectans gaing de cause en leur
commune ruine.   J'ay ce néantmoins ouy asseurer que l'intention de ce monstre d'ingratitude estoit de fere mourir Sa
Majesté, après l'avoir despouillée de la coronne.   Et pour ce
en un parlement que fust assemblé, n'osant plus proposer
ouvertement la mort de sadicte Majesté, d'autant que dès lors
Ledinthon, Grange, et plusieurs aultres, recongnoissans leurs

[1] The reading of this word is uncertain.
[2] Originally, avec plus de facilité . . .
[3] . . . usurpast le royaume . . .
[4] . . . la mémoire du . . . an interlineation.

faultes passées, taschoient à les réparer, il requist que par le
dict Parlement la disposition de la personne de sa dicte
Majesté luy fust remise, pour en ordonner ainsi que bon luy
sembleroit, ce qui luy fust plainements refusé.

Or le dict Seigneur Murray, estant arrivé de France, alla
visiter à Lokleving Sa Majesté. Laquelle fust partye réduicte
en ce misérable estat, d'autant qu'elle aprochoit de l'aage de
xxv ans, et qu'elle estoit encores en possibilité de revoquer les
dons faicts à la plus grande partye desdits conjuréz de
plusieurs pièces des meilleures du domaine de la coronne.
Qui fust cause aussi de haster la démission cy dessus men-
tionée. Et fust résolu en un conseil tenu entre lesdits
Seigneurs, les lettres en estans dressées par Ledinthon (lequel
estant homme qui vouloit tousjours avoir double corde en son
arc), les feist fort couvertement à l'advantage de la royne, et
avec telles conditions que les pouvoient rendre nulles, quand
bon luy sembleroit.

Or sur ceste résolution prise par lesdits seigneurs, le comte
d'Athol, le dit Lethinthon et lard de Tuliberne, envoyèrent
advertir Sa Majesté (par un escuyer d'escurie de Sa Majesté,
nommé Robert Melwil), qu'on luy envoyroit en bref lesdites
instruments de démission pour les signer, ce qu'ils la supplioient ne refuser, d'autant qu'aultrement sa vie estoit en
danger, et qu'on taschoit par tous moyens de la fere mourir,
craignant la revanche de leux mesfaict. Quant à eulx, qu'ils
ne l'avoient peu empescher, et ne pouvoient y pourvoir encores
jusques au retour de Monseigneur de Murray, avec lequel on
trouveroit quelque expédient pour revoquer ladicte démission;
laquelle ne serviroit que pour prolonger le temps, et attendre
la commodité de restablir toutes choses.

En signe de quoy, à la mode du pays, le dit Seigneur
comte d'Athol envoya à Sa Majesté une turquoise qu'il avoit eue
d'elle, et Ledinthon une petite oualle d'or, sur laquelle estoit
esmaillée la fable d'Esope du lyon enfermé en un fillet et la
sourys qui le rongoit, avec ces mots en Italien escripts à
l'entours; "A chi basta l'animo non mancano le forze." Le
chiffre de Sa Majesté gravé au dedans du couvercle, un cordon
de soye violet et d'or, et des vers Italians en un papier au

dedans.[1]   Tulliberne ramenteust un certain mot du guet, qu'il avoit avec Sadicte Majesté.

My lord de Lyndsey et Ruthven estoient les gardes de Sa Majesté dans ledit Lokleving.   Et ledit Ruthven vint un matin sur les quattre heurs parler à Sa Majesté, se mectant à genoux au près de son lict luy promeist de la délivrer, si elle le vouloit aymer.   (Sa Majesté feist cacher ses femmes derrière la tapisserie pour servir de tesmoignage.)   Sa Majesté receust un très grand mescontantement de l'oultrecuidance du dit Ruthwen, duquel elle demeuroit Royne, en quelque estat qu'elle peust estre ; luy ramentevant le peu d'occasion qu'il avoit de luy tenir un si meschant langage ; protestant qu'elle aymoit mieux demeurer perpetuellement en prison innocente que d'en sortir avec crime ; et de faict elle le descouvrist à la vielle dame de Lokleving, pour luy faire paroistre la meschante intention dudit Ruthwen.   Et depuis luy monstra une lettre que luy escripvoit ledit Ruthwen, sur quoy il fust revoqué, laird de Lokleving en ayant faict instance.   Cela aigrit fort ledit Ruthwen, et l'induisit à mesdire très malheureusement de Sa Majesté.   Toutes foys depuis il est rangé de son party, comme aussi le dit Lyndsay a faict depuis.

Le . . . de . . . 1567 ledit Lindsey et Ruthwen, accompagnéz de deux notaires et dudit Melvil, entrèrent sur l'après disner en la chambre de Sa Majesté, laquelle estoit en son lict extrêmement affoiblie, tant par l'ennuy extrême qu'elle portoit, que par un grand flux de sang (c'estoit son avortement de deux enfans qu'elle avoit du conte de Bothuel), [2] qui luy estoit survenu de sorte qu'à grande peine pouvoit elle bouger. [3] Lindsay fort audacieusement, et [4] ireusement, luy feist entendre sa commission et charge qu'il avoit des Seigneurs, qui estoit de luy fere signer certaines lettres de démission de la coronne ; laquelle il la requist vouloir lire.   Sa Majesté, quoy qu'admonestée auparavant par le dit Melvil de la part des Seigneurs

---

[1] The passage, A chi basta . . . au dedans, commences on the line, but is continued as an interlineation.

[2] The words in this parenthesis are added by Nau, with a different ink, in a blank space a little below the rest of the sentence, with a mark showing where they are to be inserted.

[3] Here occurs a blank space in the MS.

[4] . . . Et tres ireusement . . . an interlineation.

cy dessus mentionnéz, qu'elle n'en feist aucune difficulté,
refusa tout plainement de ce faire; le coeur qui se sentoit
innocent ne luy bastant de passer une si injuste déclaration au
préjudice de son honneur, quoy qu'elle se veist en grand et
présent hazard de sa vie. Car à la vérité, au cas qu'elle
n'eust voulu signer lesdits lettres, le desseing des rebelles
estoit de l'emmener hors de Lokleving, et en passant par le
lac la jecter dedans, ou secrètement la transporter en quelque
isle au mylieu de la mer, pour la tenir enfermée au desceu
d'un chacun le reste de sa vie; ce que le dit Lindsey luy confirma. Car aussitost qu'il veist que Sa Majesté refusa résolu-
mant de signer, il luy dist qu'elle se levast hors du lict, et
qu'il avoit charge de l'emmener au lieu où il rendroit bon
compte d'elle aux Seigneurs du pays; l'admonestant par [1]
diverses foys de signer, qu'aultrement elle les contraindroit, au
despit qu'ils en eussent, de luy coupper la gorge.

Ceste pauvre princesse, se voyant ainsi mener par ses
propres subjects, et sans aucun de ses domestiques (car on
avoit faict sortir les deux femmes de chambre qu'elle avoit
seulement avec elle), demanda où on la vouloit mener, et
requist fort instamment d'estre representée, devant les estats
du pays et au Parlement, pour respondre des poinctz mentionnéz es dites lettres. Ledit Lyndsey luy respondist
n'avoir charge, et ne pouvoir luy en dire rien davantage. Et
ainsi, sans forme de procedder ny congnoissance de cause, con-
traignèrent Sa Majesté par menaces et présent effort de signer
lesdits instruments, lesquels ils feyrent lire par lesdits
notaires. Mais Sa Majesté, enquisit de ce que luy en sembloit,
respondist par diverses foys, et appellant ceulx qui estoient là
prist à tesmoings qu'elle ne consentoit au contenu es dits
instrumens, lesquels elle signoit directement contre son intention et volonté, mais par force et contraincte, de sorte qu'elle
protesta ne les observer ny garder que tant qu'elle seroit en
prison.

Lyndsey, voyant la constance de Sa Majesté, luy répliqua
fort indignement [2] que puisqu'il falloit qu'elle le feist qu'elle

---

[1] Par diverses foys, . . . between the lines.

[2] This abstract of Lindsay's address to the Queen is obscure both in
regard to its expression and writing, and the version is offered with considerable diffidence.

dist hardiment que cestoit de sa bonne volonté, car aussi bien l'effect[1] d'icels ne deppendoit-il pas d'elle, et qu'on empescheroit bien qu'elle n'eust puissance de les révoquer ; mais ils voyoient bien que jamais telle démyssion ne seroit approuvée et moins ordonnée par les estats du pays. Qui y mesmes[2] contredirent sur la publication que fust faict des dits instruments, (comme vous entendrez cy après), aultrement ils n'eussent requis la signature de Sadicte Majesté.

J'oubliois à dire que Sa Majesté, tant pour l'estat où elle estoit de sa malladie que pour l'advertissement qu'elle avoit receu du complot de sa mort, refusa de partir de la maison, et dist tout hault qu'on l'entraineroit plustost par les cheveux ; et sur ce estant advisée par Melvil que Georges Douglas ne luy estoit tant ennemy comme elle se persuadoit, l'ayant veu pleurer dedans le jardin, elle envoya vers luy pour le prier de moyenner envers son frère et ceulx de sa maison que tel déshonneur ne leur fust faict qu'il fust dist quelque jour que leur Royne fust enlevée d'entre eulx par force, pour la mener, comme il se disoit, à la boucherie. Melvil l'amena parler à la royne, à laquelle,[3] ayant lue une instrument et promesse de pardon pour Monseigneur de Murray et ceulx de sa maison, il protesta de s'employer pour empescher le transport, ce qu'il feist fort dextrement, faisant mutiner tous ses parens et serventes de la maison, desquels il estoit fort respecté. Ruthven avoit adverty Sa Majesté que Georges Douglas luy estoit fort grand ennemy, et qu'elle s'en donnast garde ; ce qu'elle croyoit.

Après que Sa Majesté eust signé lesdites lettres, contre la promesse qui luy avoit esté faicte, elle fust emmenée avec grand débat d'un part et d'aultre en une grande tour obscure,[4] qui estoit audit Lokleving, et là fust enfermée soubs une porte de fer si misérablement que n'y a pauvre détestable à qui on sceust fere pis ; luy ostant tout ancre, pappier, livres et serviteurs que ses deux femmes de chambre, un cuisinier et son chirurgien, qui y fust laissé à cause qu'elle estoit mallade, et

[1] . . . L'effect des instruments . . . an interlineation.
[2] Mesmes . . . above the line.
[3] . . . il promist, cancelled. This passage is obscure, and the reading is doubtful.   [4] Obscure, above the line.

depuis il luy servoit bien. Car Sa Majesté, despouillée de sceptre, couronne et tous biens de ce monde, ne luy restant plus que la vie, fust depuis empoisonnée, comme il apparust clairement par l'enfleur de la moictié de son corps, principalement un bras et une jambe, luy estant survenu une extrême jaunisse espandu par tout le corps, et beaucoup de pustulles qui s'eslevèrent et rendoient une humeur claire fort vénémeuse, d'autant[1] que par tout où elle estoit mise elle causast un aultre enleveure. La force de la jeunesse luy servoit grandement à pousser hors ce venin et combattre son effect. Elle s'ayda de licoure pour luy fortiffier le cœur, qui luy affablissoit de jour en jour, et sentoit une extrême et[2] violente douleur par tout le corps, jusques à ce qu'elle fust saignée.

Le dit laird, voyant le traictment faict à Sa Majesté, et qu'elle mesmes faisoit instance pour demeurer en sa maison, prist acte des notaires qu'il ne l'y détenoit par force, et qu'elle y demeuroit de son bon gré. Aussi déclara qu'il n'estoit intervenu pour la contraindre à la signature de sa démission, dont Sa Majesté le deschargea, et protesta derechef que c'estoit les Seigneurs de Lyndesy et Ruthven.

Le xix. de Juillet, en vertu desdites lettres, fust proceddé à la coronation du Prince en l'église de Sterlingh, et fust le serment faict au lieu dudit Prince par le comte de Morton et lord de Humes, qui tost après recongnust sa faulte, et combattist contre l'authorité dudit Seigneur Prince pour celle de la Royne. Lesquels avoient esté establiz superintendens en ladite coronation, et pour l'evesque d'Arghil. Furent leues les lettres de commission et procuration signées par Sa Majesté, seelées du Privé Seel. Lesquelles contenoient, pour premier, pour la résignation de la coronne et du gouvernement du royaume en faveur de mon dit seigneur le Prince; l'aultre établissant de la Régence au nom du comte de Murray durant la minorité du Roy; et le tiers pour l'establissement du conseil auprès dudit comte de Murray, où ils meirent plusieurs pour servir d'umbre et de chiffre. Cars ils n'y furent jamais ny veuz ny trouvèz.

[1] . . . d'autant . . . enleveure, an interlineation.
[2] . . . et violente . . . added above the line.

Lesdites [1] *lettres s'ensuyvent.*

Ledit Robert Melvil porta aussi à Sa Majesté dans le
fourreau de son espée un billet escript de la main de Frokmartin, lors ambassadeur près de Sa Majesté pour la Royne
d'Angleterre; luy donnant advis de la part et par commandement exprès de ladicte Royne, sa maistresse, qu'elle signast
lesdits instrumens, et qu'elles ne luy pourroient préjudicier,
estans en prison et détenue par force.[2]

Le mesme jour de la coronation de mondit Seigneur le
Prince, laird de Lokleving, sans advertir Sa Majesté de l'occasion feist sur le soir lascher toute l'artillerie de sa maison,
allumer par tout des feux de joye, et luy mesmes se meist à
chanter et danser en son jardin. A la fin Sa Majesté s'estant
souvent enquise pourquoy telles allégresses se faisoient, ledit
laird la vint trouver en sa chambre, et luy demanda si elle ne
se vouloit pas resjouyr avec eulx de la coronamment de son
filz, qui estoit à présent leur Roy, et que pour elle on pouvoit
bien dire *Deposuit potentes.* Les assistans se moquèrent de
Sa Majesté, qui d'une façon qui d'une aultre, la bravans que
son authorité estoit abolie et qu'elle n'avoit plus de puissance
de se vanger d'eulx. Surquoy Sa Majesté répliqua qu'ils
avoient un Roy qui la vangeroit, lequel elle prioit Dieu de luy
conserver et deffendre de leur meschantes et damnables trahysons; s'asseurant bien que s'ils avoient le moyen ils ne le
laisseroient jamais venir en aage de s'en ressentir.

Et estant extrêmement ennuyée se meist au mylieu de [3] la
chambre, près de la table, à genoux, pleurant incessamment et
fort amèrement, les [4] mains estendues et levées en hault, feist
une prière à Dieu; duquel le sommaire estoit qu 'il Luy pleust,
voyant les indignitéz qui luy estoient très injustement faictes,[5]
mesmes par ceulx auxquels elle avoit le plus faict de bien, et

---

[1] No such letters are entered in the MS.

[2] The folio numbered 116 in the original here ends, the reverse of which
is blank ; on folio 117 the text is resumed, as above.

[3] . . . de la chambre, près de la table . . . an addition between the
lines.

[4] . . . les mains estendues et levées en haute . . . an interlineation.

[5] . . . mesmes par ceulx qu'elle avoit le plus fait de bien . . . between
the lines.

avoit tousjours eu compassion des innocens affligéz, luy fere la
grace de voir avant[1] que mourir ses ennemys et rebelles subjectz aussi faschés, tristes, et desoléz qu'ilz la rendoient lors.
Et principallement qu'avant l'an, elle veist ledit laird aussi
triste qu'elle estoit, donnant sa malédiction sur luy et sa maison.
Ce que entendu par ledit laird, il luy print une frayeur, et
devenant tout pensif se retira de la chambre de Sa Majesté ;
la prière de laquelle eust effect sur luy.   Car avant l'an, lors
qu'elle fust sortie, ledit laird se[2] feist tuer sans l'empesche-
ment de ses serviteurs, et fust fort longtemps comme désespéré
en la plus grande rage qu'homme fust jamais.

Peu après ladite coronamment le comte de Murray, voyant
toutes choses menées à son point et tout bien préparé pour
l'establissement de sa tyrannie, avança son retour de France ;
et de prime abordée en Escosse il fust rencontré par plusieurs
du party de Sa Majesté, sur l'espérance qu'ils avoient en ses
promesses, joinct qu'à plusieurs il avoit tenu langage fort à
l'advantage de Sa Majesté, protestant qu'il moyenneroit sa
délivrance ; et monstroit porter un grand regret de l'estat
présent des afferes et de ce que s'estoit passé.   Mais l'intention
du bon personnage estoit bien au contraire, et commença à la
fere paroistre à Georges Douglas, son frère naturel, lequel Sa
Majesté avoit envoyé au devant de luy pour scavoir la volonté
en laquelle il estoit de la secourir, et de pourvoir à sa nécessité ;
luy ramantevant ce que luy mesmes avoit souventes foys advoué et publiquement confessé qu'il estoit sa créature ; les
honneurs et biens qu'il avoit receu d'elle, et ceulx qu'il méri-
teroit de plus en plus par les services qu'il luy pouvoit fere en
un tel besoing sur toutes choses ; elle l'advertist qu'elle avoit
signé quelques lettres contre sa volonté pour le fere Régent, et
que suivant ce ladite Regence luy seroit offerte.   Mais qu'il
se gardast bien de l'accepter, s'il avoit envie de s'entretenir avec
Sa Majesté, et avoit aucun respect à leur ancienne[3] amitié.
Sur quoy ledit Seigneur de Murray respondist assez froidement, et demeura troys ou quattre jours avec les ennemys de
Sa Majesté devant que la venir visiter.

[1] . . . avant que mourir . . . an interlineation.
[2] . . . se vouloit tuer . . . original.
[3] . . . ancienne . . . an interlineation.

Les meubles de la Royne, habits, tapisseries,[1] licts, vaisselle
d'argent, chevaux, mullets, et tous aultres équipage d'escurye,
avoient esté dispersés, qui à un qui à l'aultre, ces misérables
jouans à bon escient au Roy despouillé. Et mesmes ledit
Seigneur de Murray vint trouver Sa Majesté sur la hacquenée
qu'elle avoit ordinairement accoustume de monter, dont elle
fust fort malcontante ; s'appercevant par là, oultre ce qu'on
luy en avoit ja rapporté, que puisque ledit Seigneur Comte se
saisissoit de ses meubles, ce n'estoit pour les luy rendre. Sa
Majesté pria que ladite hacquenée luy peust rompre le col ; et
de fait elle le jecta en une eaue, où il pensa se noyer.

Ce bastard arriva à Lokleving sur l'heure du soupper, Sa[2]
majesté estant preste se mectre à table, accompagné du comte
de Morton, laird de Tuliberne, et quelques gens aultres ; et du
commancement qu'il aborda Sa Majesté, il ne parla que très
hault et se tournant toujours devant ceulx de sa compagnie,
comme s'il eust esté par eulx soubçonné. Mesmes à la fin le
traistre leur demanda congé de parler à part à Sa Majesté, les
asseurant avec un demyris qu'il ne les trahyroit point. Toutes
foys ils luy portoient tous un tel honneur et respect, l'appel-
lans du nom de Grace, qui n'a acoustume se donner qu'au
Roys, ou leur enfans et bien proches, que Sa Majesté se confirma davantage en la deffiannce qu'elle avoit ja prise de lui.

Ledit Seigneur Muray refusa de soupper avec elle, et ne
s'offert à luy bailler la serviette jusques à ce que Sa Majesté
l'en advertist ; luy ramentevant qu'il ne l'avoit aultres foys
desdaigné.

Après soupper ils entrèrent tous deux au jardin, où ils se
promenèrent longuement. Et ledit Seigneur de Murray,
aussi dissimulé[3] que jamais, se meist à remonstrer à Sa
Majesté le malcontantement que ceulx du pays avoient de
ses déportemens durant qu'il avoit esté absent, dont ores
qu'elle fust innocente devant Dieu elle debvoit avoir eu
esgarde à la reputacion du monde, qui jugeoit par l'apparance
et non par l'intérieur. Particularisant ce discours sur le

[1] . . . tapisseries, licts . . . above the line.
[2] . . . Sa Majesté estant preste se mettre à table . . . not in the original
text, and added above the line.
[3] Dissimulé et hypocrite, originally.

mariage d'elle et du comte de Bothuel, qui estoit cause à plusieurs d'entrer en soubçon qu'elle eust esté consentante avec luy de la mort du feu Roy, son mary; que ce n'estoit pas assez d'éviter la faulte, mais aussi les occasions d'en estre soubçonné; que les bruits importent bien souvent de plus que la vérité mesmes; avec aultres discourses d'un vray hypocrite, tel qu'il estoit en toutes ses actions, qu'il cherchoit seulement de fere approuver pour bonnes, sans respect de sa conscience.

Sur quoy Sa Majesté répliqua que se sentant innocente de tout ce qu'on luy pouvoit imposer, et estant tousjours preste de s'en justifier devant ses subjects propres, encores qu'elle n'y fust tenue;[1] elle ne craignoit toutes les impostures et calomnies de ses ennemys, s'asseurant que[2] Dieu, auquel elle n'a jamais voulu, comme dist, fere masque, feroit à la fin paroistre son innocence et leur faulses trahysons. En somme, qu'elle aymoit mieux ouir dire d'elle[3] le mal qu'elle n'avoit point faict que d'avoir faict le mal qui ne seroit jamais dist, ayant plus d'esgard à Dieu, lequel on ne pouvoit tromper, qu'aux hommes. Et pour ce que luy mesmes, qui avoit tant de sang de l'honneur de ce monde, advisast de n'oublier soubz[4] ce prétexte son debvoir envers Dieu et elle, qui estoit sa Royne, et plus que sœur en affection et bienfaictz, que lors l'occasion se présentoit de s'en revancher envers elle, et luy fere paroistre par effects le ressentiment qu'il avoit de tel obligation sans se desguyser, comme il pouvoit faire envers ceulx qui ne voyoient si clair qu'elle.

De ce propos tumbans en divers aultres, ledit Seigneur de Muray requist à la fin Sa Majesté de luy donner son advis sur l'offre qui luy avoit esté faicte de la Régence, laquelle on le pressoit d'accepter; alléguant que ce ne seroit jamais de sa bonne volonté, ny pour le respect de sa grandeur particulière qu'il y entreroit, veu que son naturel estoit totallement allevé de telles grandeurs et ambitions, ainsi qu'elle scavoit. Mais bien que s'il pensoit en ce fere service Sa Majesté,

---

[1] N'y fust tenue, between the lines; originally, qu'elle n'eust a en rendre compte qu'à Dieu.

[2] . . . que la verité à la fin . . . originally.

[3] . . . d'elle. An addition.

[4] . . . soubz ce pretext . . . between the line.

puisqu'il estoit besoing que quelq'un y fust placé, il seroit bien aise de s'en servir pour remectre les afferes avec le temps en meilleur estat, au lieu qu'un aultre poursuiveroit la totalle ruine de Sa Majesté.

Sur ce Sa Majesté, faisant estat de luy parler librement comme elle avoit accoustume, luy respondist sommairement que ce n'estoit chose qui luy fust propre, tant pour sa grandeur particulière que pour son debvoir vers elle. Et pour ce, qu'elle prioit de ne prendre une telle charge, d'autant qu'il ne seroit jamais en sa puissance de voir de bon oeil celluy qui usurperoit son authorité, avec quelque intention que ce fust, et quoy qui en peust réussir. Oultre ce, qu'il debvoit penser que si ceulx qui dès leur naissance ly estoient obligéz d'entière obéissance, et par ordonnance de Dieu lu debvoient honorer et respecter comme leur Souveraine, s'estoient si malheureusement oubliéz en son endroit (sans les avoir jamais fouléz ny oppresséz d'un seul denier extraordinaire, mais plustost enrichiz du sien propre), il ne debvoit dis-je espérer qu'ils luy gardassent aucune fidellité, n'estans aucunement à luy donner ceste[1] juiste authorité, sinon par la crainte qu'ils avoient lors d'estre punyz de leur rebellions contre la légitime, laquelle pour ceste occasion, ils tascheroient d'abollir et esteindre ; de façon que ceste crainte leur estant une foys ostée de devant les yeux, et n'ayans plus de besoing de son support, ils leveroient par mesme moyen le respect qu'ils luy professoient lors et sur le moindre malcontentement qu'ils prendroient; à quoy il les congnoissoit assez promptz, le débouteroient plus licentieusement qu'ils ne faisoient elle, attendu qu'il estoit bastard et de nativité et de commencement, sur[2] eulx qui ne luy debvoient rien ; ceste maxime estant très véritable qui celuy qui ne garde la foy où il la doibt, difficilement la tiendra-il où il n'est point obligé.

Le comte de Moray, après divers discours pleins de dissimulation, entrant tantost en ouverture de celluy qui seroit le plus propre pour ladite Régence, et nommant ceulx qu'il congnoissoit les plus séditieux et opinastres en leur rebellion,

[1] . . . ceste juiste . . . an interlineation.
[2] . . . dans le royaume sur eulx . . . originally

comme le comte de Morton, affin [1] d'induire Sa Majesté de le
proposer à ceulx la qu'elle avoit occasion de craindre, voyant
qu'il n'en pouvait tirer aultre résolution à son advantage,
s'advança de luy dire qu'il avoit jà promis d'accepter ladite
Régence, et qu'il ne pouvoit contrevenir à sa promesse. Ce
néantmoins, qu'il luy feroit tous les plaisirs qu'il pourroit;
admonestant Sa Majesté de prendre cependant patience, et se
consoler en ce que le Roy de France, son voysin, dedans
peu de temps seroit en pire estat [2] qu'elle n'estoit, ce qu'il
confessa avoir sceu de Colligni [3] l'Admiral, lequel il avoit
visité, et avoit trouvé grand ennemy de Sa Majesté. Mais
sitost il ly estoit certain, pour l'inimitié et partialité d'entre
luy et la maison de Lorraine, de laquelle Sa Majesté estoit
descendue.

Sa Majesté le pria en fin de [4] se tenir audit Loklevin un
jour ou deux, pour communiquer plus amplement des afferes
avec elle, ce qu'il refusa, alléguant qu'il estoit jà soubçonné
qui fust occasion que Sa Majesté luy recommanda le payement
des gaiges et entretènement de ses pauvres officiers, principalement les Françoys, qui estoient espars d'un costé et
d'aultre, et en grande désolation pour l'adversité de leur
bonne maistresse. Mais on y eust fort peu d'esgard, et a fallu
que Sa Majesté ayt faict payer jusqu'à leur despense de
bouche des deniers de son douaire depuis qu'elle a esté en
Angleterre. Je croy que c'estoit pour la fidellité que ces
bons serviteurs gardèrent vers leur maitresse, et les fere
participer à son ennuys.

Oultre ce Sa Majesté parla audit Seigneur de Muray de
ses bagues, qui estoient en grande nombre et beaucoup fort
excellentes, le priant de les conserver pour Monseigneur le
Prince, son fils, auquel elle estoit contante d'en fere don, et les
unir à la coronne d'Escosse, sans qu'il fust loysible à ceulx
du conseil [5] de les alliéner, d'autant qu'elles n'estoient de la
succession des feus Roys d'Escosse, mais acheptées par Sa

[1] Affin que Sa Majesté vint, originally.
[2] . . . en pire estat . . . an interlineation.
[3] . . Colligni . . . added between the lines.
[4] Originally, demeurer en ce lieu.
[5] A ceulx du conseil, an interlineation.

Majesté, ou qui luy avoient esté données, comme par le feu Roy Henry II., son beaupère, et le Roy Françoys, son Seigneur et mary. Sur quoy ledit Seigneur Muray luy dist que cela n'estoit raisonnable, d'autant que les Seigneurs en pourroient avoir affaire pour le bien du royaume ; jusques à luy particulariser si on faisoit contre eulx quelque entreprise pour retirer Sa Majesté de leur mains. Vous voyez l'impudence de ce malheureux, qui ne craignoit de détenir le bien propre de Sa Majesté contre elle mesmes.

Le xv de Décembre ensuyvant le Parlement fust assemblé à Edinbourgh, et fust tenu y commandant ledit comte de Muray. Dont Sa Majesté estant advertye, et voulant en ceste publique assemblé fere paroistre son innocence, escripvist une longue lettre audit Seigneur de Muray, luy ramantevant l'obligation qu'il luy avoit, comme il avoit recogneu par lettres escriptes à Baruik, où il se nomma la créature de Sa Majesté ; les grandes faultes et rebellions qu'il avoit commises contre elle, dont il avoit eu pardon ; le traictement qu'elle luy avoit faict, non comme à bastard mais comme à son frère légitime, luy ayant donné en effect l'entier gouvernement du royaume lors qu'elle avoit authorité ; les promesses qu'il avoit faictes au Roy de France et à Messieurs de Lorraine, ses parens, et ses protestacions en la dernière visitation au lieu de Lokleving. Et en fin requéroit qu'il luy fust accordé d'estre ouye, ou en personne ou par un députté,[1] audit parlement, pour respondre au faulsses calomnies que depuis son emprisonnement on avoit publiés d'elle, et esclaircir les estatz du pays de toutes choses qui pourroient de sa part importer au bien public du royaume ; offrant à cest effect de se démectre volontairement de l'authorité de Royne, et y intervenir seulement comme personne privée, se soubmectant pareillement à toute la rigeur des loix,[2] selon lesquelles elle désiroit instamment[3] qu'il fust proceddé à la punition de quiconque seroit trouvé coulpable du meurtre du feu Roy. Mesmes s'advança jusques à là que si après avoir esté ouye, il estoit résolu par lesdits

---

[1] Par advocat, un députté, added above.
[2] Originally, des loix et s'obligeant.
[3] Originally, desiroit et consentoit ; instamment, an interlineation.

estats que pour le bien du royaume[1] elle leur remeist
l'authorité que Dieu luy avoit donné sur eulx dès à présent,
elle y consentoit ; protestant au refus de ce que dessus de
la nullité dudit Parlement et de tout ce qui s'en ensuy-
veroit en vertu des lettres qu'on l'avoit contrainct passer
et signer, d'autant qu'il n'y a loiz qui approve aucune condamnation[2] sans cognaissance de cause quand il n'yroit que
du bien du moindre subject qu'elle eust, à plus forte raison ce
respect luy debvoit estre porté, elle estant leur Reyne, et en
une cause où il alloit de son honneur, qu'elle tenoit plus chère
que sa vie propre ; joinct que jamais elle n'avoit fermé
l'aureille au moindres plaintes que ses dits subjects luy
avoient faictes, ny refusé justice à personne d'eulx, sur quoy
elle desduisoit la douceur et clémence avec laquelle elle avoit
gouverné, sans que aucun d'eulx se peust justement plaindre
qu'elle leur eust faict tort d'un seul denier, s'estant contanté
de son revenu ordinaire, sans les charger d'aucun enprunt,
charges, ou imposts extraordinaires, mais plustost s'estoit
despouillée pour les enrichir ; et ainsi persistoit d'estre
deschargée ou condamnée de ce qu'on luy vouloit imposer.

A quoy pour toute response, ledit Seigneur de Muray
manda en troys ou quattres lignes et termes généraux,[3] que
ce que Sa Majesté demandoit ne luy pouvoit estre accordé,
sans spéciffier[4] ce que estoit, d'autant qu'il avoit encores honte
d'estre veu refuser une chose si juste et raisonnable.   Or le
dit Seigneur de Muray (ayant faict choisir les Seigneurs des
Articles dudit Parlement à sa dévotion, horsmis deux ou
troys, pour fere umbre aux aultres, qui ne deppendoient tant
de luy adherens seulement,) il feist secrettement proposer[5]
que par ledit Parlement il luy fust donné toute authorité de
disposer de la personne de Sa Majesté pour la seureté de
ceulx qui avoient esté en armes contre elle ; son intention
estant, comme il a esté dist cy dessus, de la fere mourir.
Mais aussi tost que cela fust esventé, il s'y trouva de grandes

[1] Originally, elle se demeist de son authorité.
[2] Originally, la condamnation d'une partye, aucune acte public.
[3] Generaux sans specifier la requeste de sadite Majesté.
[4] Originally, ayant honte de speciffier.
[5] Proposer audit parlement, erased.

contradictions, mesmes de la part d'aucuns qui soubçonnoient ce que ledit Seigneur de Muray avoit au cœur, et scavoient l'instance que plusieurs des siens luy avoient faict de se déclarer dès lors Roy, et les aultres plus prudens (voulans procedder moins odieusement du degré en degré)[1] héritier du royaume après la personne du Prince, duquel il se pouvoit par après deffaire.

Sur quoy ledit Seigneur de Muray avoit employé diverses personnes pour rechercher les moyens de se fere déclarer légitime, et trouver preuve au mariage qu'on luy conseilloit alléguer avoir esté secrettement contracté entre le roy James V., et sa mère, ores qu'elle fust lors mariée à un aultre, et que depuis la mort dudit Seigneur Roy elle ayt vescu longuement avec luy, sans aucune mention qui aye jamais esté[2] de divorce, ou séparation entre eulx. Ceste proposition donc fust délaissée pour le peu d'espérance que ledit Seigneur de Muray veist d'en venir à l'effect qu'il prétendoit, et fust[3] faite un acte pour l'indamnité et garantie de tous ceulx qui s'estoient mis en armes contre Sadite Majesté, icelle prise à la montagne de Carbarrie, et oultre pour la détention de sa personne au château de Lokleving. La démission de sadite Majesté et résignation de la coronne en faveur de Monseigneur le Prince, son fils, fust la pareillement ratiffiée, et le comte de Muray estably ou plustost confirmé Régent, d'autant qui dès le moys d'Aoust précédent il avoit pris ladite régence.

Mais lors que les lettres de ladite démission, résignation et régence furent leues audit Parlement, plusieurs seigneurs et barons assistans audit Parlement feirent instance d'estre plus au vray esclaircyz de l'intention de Sa Majesté. Et entre les aultres my lord d'Heris prenant la parolle se leva, et après avoir remonstré l'importance de ceste affaire, tant pour eulx qu'à l'advenir pour tous leurs successeurs, requist qu'il luy fust permis avec deux ou troys aultres, tels que le Parlement depputeroit, d'aller pardevers Sa Majesté pour scavoir son

---

[1] Et les aultres plus prudens . . . de degré en degré, an addition between the lines.

[2] Qui aye jamais esté, an interlineation.

[3] . . . fut seulement, originally.

intention, et si de bonne et franche volonté, sans aucune contraincte, elle avoit passé lesdites lettres, lesquelles ne pouvoient suffir pour ce regard, d'autant qu'on pouvoit alléguer que, veu le lieu où Sa Majesté estoit détenue, et ce qui s'estoit passé au paravant contre elle, on l'avoit forcée d'y consentir, ou qu'elles estoient faulses et sa signature [1] contrefaicte, de façon que sur icelles il ne pouvoit ratiffier ce qui estoit proposé ; et de ce, demanda acte ou instrument, jectant publiquement à la mode du pays une pièce d'argent au greffier dudit Parlement.　　Et à son example plusieurs refusèrent de signer les Actes dudit Parlement, dont on ne les pressa, craignant de fere trop paroistre la contradiction qu'estoit entre eulx. Ainsi la plus grande et pire part surmonta la meilleure.

Au dit Parlement furent faictes quarante une ordonnances, tant pour exterminer l'authorité du Pape que pour annuller certains actes faicts au paravant au parlement avec consentement desdits seigneurs [2] par Sa Majesté à son arrivé en Escosse, pour faire cesser toutes recherches [3] et persécutions contre les Catholiques, ce qui tendoit au repos du pays et bien d'icelluy.[4]　　Et sur ce feirent dresser et confirmer par ledit Parlement une Confession de la Foy et doctrine tenues par les Protestants d'Escosse.

Mais ne fault oublier qu'encores que la Royne d'Angleterre feist démonstracion apparente d'intrevenir avec lesdits seigneurs en faveur et pour le rétablissement des afferes de Sa Majesté, son Ambassadeur ayant eu souvent charge de recommander en son nom lesdites afferes de Sa Majesté, comme à la vérité il feist publiquement, ce néantmoins en secret elle s'aydoit d'eulx mesmes pour diminuer leur forces et puissance, qui a servy anciennement de bride à tous les Roys d'Angleterre.　　Et se souvenant de l'advantage que les Françoys avoit récemment pris contre elle par leur intelligence audit pays en les fortresses qu'ils y tenoient, elle moyenna que par ordonnance dudit Parlement le chasteau de

[1] Sa signature, interlined.

[2] Avec consentement desdits seigneurs, an interlineation.

[3] Pour la liberté de conscience touchant le service, has been cancelled and pour fere cesser toutes recherches, added above the line.

[4] The passage from ce qui to d'icelluy, is an interlineation.

Dumbar, qui avoit esté longuement tenu à la dévotion des dits Francoys, et la forteresse d'Inskeith (appellée par lesdits Françoys l'Isle aux Chevaux) seroient démolyz et abbatuz[1] rez de terre. Ce qui a esté exécuté contre tout debvoir de subjects et vrays Escossoys[2] et la fidellité qu'ils debvoient à leur patrie ; car ledit chasteau importoit grandement à la seureté du royaume contre les Angloys.

Peu de temps après ledit Parlement le dit Seigneur de Muray, accompagné du comte de Morton et divers aultres seigneurs, vint à Loklyving avec une très grande magnificence, et là visita Sa Majesté, mais avec tel mespris et desdaing que les choses s'en aigrirent tousjours depuis davantage. Car ayant par diverses foys conféré avec Sa Majesté sur l'instance que sa mère luy en faisoit, désirant infiniement que quelque bon appoinctment s'en ensuyvist, il luy parla fort discourtoisement et audacieusement, sans avoir aucun esgard aux overtures dont Sa Majesté le recherchoit, grandement à l'advantage et asseurance dudit Seigneur Comte, et sur tout ne vouloit jamais permectre qu'elle feist plus grande pursuitte pour la descharge de ce qu'on luy imposoit, dont elle faisoit continuellement instance, plus que du restablissement de son authorité et de sa liberté. Quand Sa Majesté eust bien considéré la détestable opiniastreté[3] du dit Seigneur de Muray, resolu de[4] n'entendre à aucune pacification ains de procedder par toute voye d'ennemy mortel et conjuré, ne pouvant supporter si prodigueuse[5] ingratitude, luy déclara ouvertement[6] que puis qu'il luy usoit de si grande injustice et indignité en tout ce qu'elle avoit requis de luy trop juste et raisonnable, elle n'avoit intention de le rechercher jamais pour quelconque occasion que ce fut ; ains plustost de consumer sa vie en perpetuelle prison que d'en sortir par son moyen, espérant que Dieu juste et vangeur des oppresséz l'en déliveroit à sa honte, dommage et ruine ; et là dessus luy ayant touché la main se départist d'avec luy, protestant en présence des

---

[1] Originally rasiz.   [2] Vrays Escossoys, appears to be cancelled.
[3] Et malheureuse resolution, cancelled.
[4] Originally dudit Ser de Murray, sourd a toute persuasion ne voulant resolument entendre.   [5] Originally, enorme.
[6] Ouvertemente . . . en luy touchant en la main, cancelled.

Seigneurs à quelque prix que ce fust [1] que tost ou tard il s'en repentiroit.

Il ne sera impertinent de remarquer que en ceste visitacion au mesme instant que James Bafour, (lequel avoit vendu [2] le chasteau de l'Islebourg, [3] à luy commis en garde, et tous les meubles et bagues de Sa Majesté, [4]) entra dedans la chambre de Sa Majesté, le temps estant fort calme au paravant, [5] une bourrace de vent s'esleva, qui feist ouvrir avec ung grand bruit toutes les fenestres de ladite chambre, de sorte que Sa Majesté, voyant entrer ledit Bafour, dist tout hault [6] qu'il falloit bien que ce soudain accident si violent fust pour quelque architraistre, dont ledit Bafour rougist bien fort, se retirant derrière parmy [7] la compagnie qui estoit là avec lesdits Seigneurs. Le comte de Morton parla fort courtoisement à Sa Majesté et luy promeist de fere tous les bons offices qu'il pourroit pour sa délivrance ; laquelle ce néantmoins il empeschoit plus que personne.

Or ledit Seigneur de Muray avant qu'il partist dudit Lokleving feit deffense à son frère maternel, George Douglas, puisné du laird de Lokling, de rentrer [8] jamais en ladite maison, après divers propos fort braves le manassa s'il faisoit aultrement de la fere pendre. Ce que ledit George, gentilhomme bien nay et de bon cœur, print en fort mauvaise part, concepvant lors une hayne contre ledit Seigneur de Muray, lequel il avoit tousjours respecté autant que son père propre ; et [9] lors voyant qu'on se deffioit de luy, il [10] délibera d'attempter par tous moyens délivrance de Sa Majesté ; ce qu'il n'avoit peu resouldre en soy mesmes auparavant, car encores que par debvoir de subgect il s'y recongnust obligé, ce néantmoins d'autant que c'estoit en la maison de son frère, où

[1] A quelque prix qui ce fust, an interlineation.
[2] Originally, vendu et trahi.
[3] A luy commis en garde, an interlineation.
[4] De Sa Majesté . . . qui estoient dedans . . . cancelled.
[5] Le temps estant fort calme auparavant, added above the line.
[6] Tout hault . . . qu'elle scavoit, originally.
[7] Parmy, added above the line.
[8] Originally, revenir.
[9] Et . . . se departant de toute l'intelligence amitié . . . cancelled.
[10] Originally, il resolut d'executer la delivrance de.

l'on se fyoit entièrement de luy, il avoit tousjours faict scrupules de décepvoir, comme il disoit, son dit frère. Bien s'estoit[1] il desjà employé pour moyenner quelque appoinctement entre Sa Majesté et les dits Seigneurs fastueux. Ainsi se voyant déchassé de sa maison paternelle et d'auprès ses plus proches parens, il commença à travailler entre les principaux fidelles subjects de Sa Majesté pour le rétablissement de ses afferes.

Depuis ledit George ayant communiqué avec ledit Seigneur de Muray pour les afferes de Sa Majesté, il eust permission de luy d'en aller porter la response à Sadite Majesté. Mais ledit Seigneur de Muray dépescha sur le champ un sien maistre d'hostel à Loklevyngh pour adviser le laird qu'il n'eust à recepvoir chez luy[2] sondit frère; lequel ayant descouvert ce secret message devança ledit maistre d'hostel, et s'estant arrivé audit Loklyvyng print le dernier congé de Sa Majesté après l'avoir particulièrement informée des moyens qu'elle debvoit tenir pour exécuter l'enterprise par luy mise en avant[3] de sa délivrance, et principallement comme elle debvoit practiquer et gaigner celluy qui avoit la charge des basteaux, estant du surnom du laird[4] du lac, comme estant necessaire plus que nul aultre à cest effect. Aussi que par luy elle pourroit tousjours entendre ce qu'il négotiroit avec les Seigneurs du party de Sa Majesté, mesmement avec le Seigneur de Seton, mectant a part pour le respect de sadite Majesté quelque différent qu'ils avoient ensemble. Et en fin luy jura de luy garder inviolablement toute la loyauté et fidéllité d'un bon subject tel qu'il protestoit luy demeurer le reste de sa vie. Porta à Monseigneur de Seton un mot de lettre escripte de la main de Sa Majesté, si estroitement gardée qu'elle fust contrainte fere de l'ancre du charbon qu'estoit en la cheminée, d'autant qu'on ne luy laissoit pappier ny ancre.[5]

Comme ledit Georges partoit de Sa Majesté son frère le laird le vint trouver, qui luy feist la deffense que ledit

[1] Bien s'estoit . . . Seigneurs . . . an interlineation.
[2] Chez lui . . . an interlineation.
[3] Entree et resolue . . . originally.
[4] Estant du surnom du laird . . . an interlineation.
[5] Originally, apres le conge pris de Sa Majesté il s'en vint trouver son frère qui luy signiffia.

Maistre d'hostel luy avoit signiffié de la part dudit Seigneur
de Muray, et dès lors luy commanda de partir sans jamais
retourner ny approcher de sa maison.   Sur quoy ledit George
se monstra fort offensé, et protesta par diverses foys à sondit
frère que tost ou tard il s'en vangeroit, et que doresnavant il
eust à se garder de luy ; dont leur mère fust extrêmement
ennuyée, portant grande amitié audit Georges, et d'aultre
part craignant la ruine de l'aisné et de sa maison.

Peu de temps après Georges [1] faisant semblant de passer
seulement près dudit Lokleving, et s'estant advancé dans le
lac le plus avant que son cheval pouvoit porter pour fere
quelque signal à Sa Majesté, son frère commanda qu'on
luy tirast un coup d'artillerie, ce qui fust promptement faict,
et lors il y eust de luy plusieurs parolles fort aigres et
menassées [2] entre lesdits frères, de sorte que Georges irrité
plus que devant, commança à battre le fer plus chaudement
qu'il n'avoit encores faict ; et pressant particulièrement les
seigneurs du party de Sa Majesté pour l'establissement de
ses afferes lors qu'il l'avoit mise hors de sa prison, essaya de
fere condescendre par diverses persuasions le batellier à luy
conduire un coffre dans ledit Lokling, et le luy rapporter ; luy
faisant entendre que dans icelluy estoient plusieurs pappiers
pours les afferes de Sa Majesté, laquelle avoit besoin d'iceulx.
Ce garçon, qui avoit ja porté quelques pacquets, soubçonna
promptement l'intention et effect de ce desseing, et estant de
longue main gaigné à la dévotion dudit George, lui dit
librement qu'il voyoit bien à quoy il tendoit, mais que tel
moyen ne valloit rien, ains de très grand hazard.   Partant le
prioit de luy déclarer franchement ce qu'il disiroit de luy en
cet endroict, et qu'il s'y employeroit jusques au hazard de sa
vie.   Georges se voyant de soy mesmes si fermement résolu
s'advança de luy descouvrir le fonds de l'affere, et luy advoua
que son intention estoit de fere rapporter Sa Majesté dans
ledit coffre, sur quoy ayant communiqué avec ledit batellier,
ils résolurent en fin d'emmener Sadite Majesté desguysée par

---

[1] Originally, George, estant revenu . . . faisant semblant de passer
seulement près du dit Lokleving . . . au interlineation.

[2] Et menassées, an addition.

un habit emprunté à la veue d'un chascun, tous aultres moyens estans de trop longue menée, et subjects à estre descouvertz. Là dessus Georges estant party alla droit solliciter les Seigneurs appoincter[1] un certain jour, et en l'attente se trouver avec toutes leurs forces en armes près dudit Lokling pour recepvoir Sadite Majesté, qui fust advertye de tout par lettres que luy porta ledit battellier.

Laird de Markyston, ayant réputation de grand magicien, voulust gaiger avec plusieurs jusque à cinq cens escuz, que dans le v. May Sa Majesté sortiroit hors de Loklyng ; sur quoy, et quelques advertissemens secretz qu'on disoit se donner par quelques uns du party de Sa Majesté, il fust mandé au laird de Loklevyngh qu'il se tint sur ses gardes et pourveist exactement à rompre l'effect de ce desseing. Et oultre il luy fut particulièrement mandé qu'il print garde à Guillaume Douglas.

Je ne veulx oublier à dire que le comte de Muray, commanceant à soubçonner Ledinthon, d'autant qu'il scavoit qu'il recherchoit Sa Majesté, pour sonder en quels termes il estoit, feist donner un fauls alarme dans la ville où ils estoient, faisant crier que Sa Majesté estoit sortye hors de Loklyving. Sur ce Ledinthon et plusieurs aultres montèrent à cheval et délibéroient de s'en fuyr, craignans la juste punition de leur rebellion ; et principalement ledit Ledinthon, encore qu'il recherchoit Sa Majesté, ne laissoit tousjours de se maintenir avec le comte de Muray, comme le voyant le plus fort ; et pour ce n'ayant encores aucune asseurance de Sa Majesté (laquelle il entretenoit seulement de belles paroles) doubtoit d'estre payé de ce qu'il avoit mérité.

Lesdits rebelles ordinairement se reprochoient les uns aux aultres leur trahysons et mauvais déportemens à l'endroict de Sa Majesté, et ce par manière de moquerie, se menassans les uns les aultres au nom de Sa Majesté d'en estre punyz comme de chose qu'ils pensoient ne debvoir jamais advenir, à quoy ils pensoient avoir bien pourveu. Mais Dieu, qui confond tousjours les meschans, en disposa aultrement qu'ils n'avoient proposé.

[1] Originally, pour s'assembler.

Il vint donc fort à propos que la femme du laird (laquelle estoit mise pour fere continuelle compagnie à Sa Majesté, l'espier et garder), vint à accoucher, et par ce moyen Sa Majesté eust plus de liberté de pourvoir à son affaire ; lequel, voyant une si belle occasion, elle pressoit avec la plus grande instance qu'elle pouvoit.   Car si l'aultre eust esté relevé auparavant, l'entreprise eust esté rendue de moictié plus difficille.   Le laird et la dame de Loklyvingh se moquoient de Sa Majesté en sa présence mesmes, sur le bruict qui courroit de sa sortye et se vantoient d'en bien respondre.   Toutesfoys à la fin ledit Guillaume Douglas fust fort soubçonné, tant pour ce qu'on le voyoit jouer, comme il y esté fort addonné, une grande quantité des pièces d'or, qu'il avoit eu en don de Sa Majesté ; aussi qu'une foys luy délivrant un nombre de lettres mal empaquetées, lesdites lettres tombèrent en présence de la fille et une niepce du laird, qui couchoient ordinairement avec Sa Majesté et luy faisoit continuelle compagnie.

Ces deux jeunes damoiselles, aagées d'environ quatorze à quinze ans, portoient une fort grande amitié et respect à Sa Majesté, et principallement la fille du laird ; laquelle un jour ou deux après la réception desdites lettres, et comme il y a apparence sur le bruict qui couroit de la sortie de Sa dite Majesté, songea que ledit Guillaume Douglas avoit apporté un corbeau noir en la maison, et que Sa Majesté, estant allée sur le bord du lac, ledit corbeau l'avoit emmenée.   Ce songé estant venu aux aureilles de Sa Majesté, et craignant que s'il estoit publié il ne servist à confirmer[1] le soubçon ja pris de sadite sortie, et mesmement la deffiance qu'on avoit dudit Douglas, feist telle instance envers ceste petite fille (qui regrettoit principallement la sortie de Sa dite Majesté, de peur d'estre esloignée d'elle), qu'elle luy promeist de n'en parler point, ny desdites lettres qu'elle avoit veues, moyennant que Sa Majesté l'emmenast avec elle quand elle sortiroit. Ce que Sa Majesté luy promeist, desniant ce néantmoins qu' elle eust aucun espérance ou moyen.[2]

---

[1] Originally, confirmer, les indices.

[2] . . . Davantage, ledit Guillaume. . . . chassé, this passage forms a note written in a blank space in MS.

T

D'avantage ledit Guillaume fust veu parler à Sa Majesté par l'une des petites filles, qui la rapporta au laird, et la dessus Guillaume estant interrogé confessa promptement, par crainte, qu'il avoit esté praticqué pour emmener Sa Majesté ; mais il ne scavoit encores le temps ny le moyen, de sorte qu'il ne peust rien descouvrir qu'en general ; et la dessus il fust chassé.

Ce néantmoins cela ne peust estre tenu si secret que le laird en ayant eu quelque vent ne chassa hors de sa maison ledit Guillaume Douglas, et n'escripvist à son frère George qu'il n'eust doresnavant sur peur de la vie d'approcher de sadite maison, ny du village qui estoit au delà du lac. Sur quoy le dit Georges print occasion de feindre estre résolu se retirer en France, et vint audit village, tant pour en advertir sa mère et son frère, que pour requérir lettres de faveur et quelque support de Sa Majesté. Ledit laird et sa mère furent fort ennuyéz de ceste rèsolution, ne voulans entièrement perdre[1] ledit Georges, auquel ils conseilloient se retirer avec Monseigneur de Murray. Mais n'y voulant aucunement condescendre, ladite dame pria Sa Majesté d'escripre audit George pour luy commander de leur obéyr en cet endroict ; et en ce faisant elle s'offrist de luy porter les lettres, lesquelles furent par Sa Majesté amplifiées de diverses nouvelles et discours en termes couverts, spéciallement pour le presser de l'effect de l'entreprinse avant que sa belle soeur fust rellevée. George Douglas y ayant faict response, travailla tant que par l'intercession d'une sienne soeur, Guillaume Douglas fust rappellé le dernier d'April [2] en la maison, où estant remis en sa première charge il commenca à préparer tout son faict pour le jour appoincté,[3] qui[4] estoit le second de May. Or Georges se servant de l'occasion qui se présentoit, voyant ledit Guillaume chassé, vint fort souvent au village parler et communiquer avec luy, de sorte que ceste inconvénient servit grandement à le remettre et résouldre de nouveau de toutes

---

[1] Originally, leur dit frere.
[2] Le dermer d'April, above the line.
[3] pour le jour appoincte, an interlineation.
[4] Et de bonheur il advint qu'un jour Sa Majesté s'etant allée promener sur le lac avec le laird, cancelled.

choses nécessaires pour ladite entreprinse, ce qui n'eust peu
si facillement si ledit Guillaume fust demeuré en la maison,
lequel pleurant incessamment du regret qu'il avoit d'avoir
descouvert ledit George, on l'imputa à repentance d'avoir
consenty auxdites pratiques, et à regret d'avoir perdit le
service de son maistre, ce qui ayda beaucoup à son retour.

Sur ces entrefaictes Sa Majesté s'estant un jour allée
esbattre[1] sur le lac avec le laird, et au retour les serviteurs de
la maison se moquans du bruit qui couroit de la sortye de Sa
Majesté, feirent semblant d'assailir la maison et d'attaquer
quelques uns qui estoient sur le bord du lac avec la vielle
dame, qui jectoient a ceulx qui estoient dans les batteaux de
la terre. Ce jeu veint à la fin au dommage des deux principaux gardiens, et espions et ennemys, que Sa Majesté eust
en ceste maison; car[2] celluy qui avoit la principalle charge là
dedans, d'aussi mauvaise volonté qu' aucun des deux aultres,
print une longue harquebuze qu'il pensoit n'estre chargée que
de pappier, et l'ayant tirée droict à la trouppe assez grande,[3]
qui estoit sur le bord de lac, blessa particulièrement, comme
s'il les eust choisye, les deux susdits, perçant la hanche de
l'un de sept on huit dragées, et la cuisse de l'aultre avec une
grosse balle, dont luy mesmes entra en telle rage qu'il se
pensa tuer. Sur ce le chirurgien de Sa Majesté, homme fort
excellent en son art, fust mandè, lequel commanda à ses patiens
de tenir le lict, où il les tient tant qu'il fust besoing.[4] Et
ainsi Georges Douglas, adverty de cest accident facilitant de
beaucoup son entreprinse, se hasta,[5] et tous ceulx de son
party, pour se trouver, comme ils avoient desseigné, au jour,
lieu et équipage entre eulx appointéz.

Or le premier desseing estoit que Sa Majesté debvoit
saulter une muraille du jardin, haulte de sept ou huit pieds, à
quoy craignant de s'adventurer elle feist semblant de jouer
troys ou quattre jours au paravant, avec ses deux femmes de
chambre se suyvans l'une l'aultre, pour passer par tout ou là

[1] Originally, alle promener.
[2] Car—leur Cappitaine, cancelled
[3] Assez grande—above the line.
[4] Ou il les tient tant qu'il fust besoing—an interlineation.
[5] Pour estre prest—cancelled.

première d'elles passeroit. Et ainsi estans venues en un aultre quartier de la maison vers une muraille de pareille haulteur que celle où elle debvoit passer, l'une de ses femmes de chambre ayant ja saulté, quand Sa Majesté fust sur la muraille pour saulter après elle, elle eust crainte de se blesser. Ce néantmoins, forçant ses forces[1] en cela par la nécessité où elle se voyoit, elle saulta. Mais ores qu'à demysault elle fust receue par un des gentil-hommes de la maison qui la receust, elle se blessa fort à une des joinctures des pieds qu'elle a fort faibles, de sorte que doubtant qu'il ne luy advint en saultant la muraille appoinctée de se blesser de sorte qu'on ne la peust enlever, elle feist advertyr ceulx de son party qui la debvoient attendre au delà du lac, qu'au cas qu'elle se blessast soudainement l'une de ses femmes, qui debvoit demeurer en la chambre, leur feroit un signal de feu pour se retirer, mesmement ledit Georges et mylord de Seton, qui avoient un navire prest pour s'embarquer et se sauver en France.

Guillaume Douglas, voyant la crainte ou estoit Sa Majestè pour saulter ladite muraille, se meist en debvoir de chercher[2] une aultre voye plus facile et moins dangereuse, et se proposa de fere sortir Sa Majesté par la grande[3] porte au logis. Pour à quoy parvenir ayant receu argent, il délibéra de convier le 2 de May tous ceulx de la maison a un desjeuner, qu'il debvoit fere au quartier plus esloigné de ladite porte; et mesmes Sa Majesté s'y trouva avec le laird, en présence duquel de toute l'assemblée le dit Guillaume, baillant un rameau à Sa Majesté comme aux aultres, se disant l'Abbé de la Folie, luy feist jurer et promectre qu'elle le suyveroit ce jour là quelque part qu'il allast; et là dessus s'estant mis à bout à Sa Majesté, il appresta à chacun occasion de rire comme d'un homme enyvré ou fort simple.

Sa Majesté demeura tout le reste du jour audit quartier du logis, tant pour y arrester le laird et sa femme que pour leur éviter le soubçon[4] qu'ils eussent peu prendre si elle se fust rétirée.

[1] Ses forces—above the line.
[2] Originally—de chercher tous moyens.
[3] La grand—above the line.
[4] Originally, pour leur donner moins de soubçons.

L'aprèsdisner elle se jecta sur un lict, donnant à entendre qu'elle vouloit reposer, dont elle n'avoit lors grand envie, encores que la niuct précédente elle n'avoit aucunement sommeillé. Et comme elle estoit sur ce lict, la femme du laird estant auprès, devisant avec une hostesse de village, qui luy comptoit comme ce jour mesme une grande compagnie d'hommes de cheval avoit passé par ledit village, qui disoient s'en aller à une assise, (jour de loy, comme il parle au pays,)[1] mesmement my lord de Seton, pour accompagner James Hammelton de Ormiston ; et que Georges Douglas, son beau frère, estoit demeuré audit village, qu'on disoit estre venu pour prendre congé de sa mère pour s'en aller en France. Et à la verité ladite dame fust voir son filz et persuader par luy qu' à fault de partir pour France il se retiroit publiquement vers le Mon[r.] de Muray, luy donna quelques sommes d'argent, et luy porta (pour le confirmer en ceste délibéracion) lettres de la royne qui luy commandoit expressement de s'en aller droit et en la plus grande dilligence qu'il pouvoit vers Glasgo, qui estoit le chemin entre eulx appoincté.

Or, oultre ce que la femme du laird estoit rellevée ce jour là, les deux soldats blessés estoient pareillement guérys ; et ung Draysdel, qui servoit là dedans de double espion, debvoit le mesme jour retourner de Lislebourgh, où Sa Majesté l'avoit exprès envoyé pour recepvoir quelque somme d'argent dont elle luy avoit faict don. Mais avant que partir elle l'avoit chargé d'un eschantillon pour en avoir une pièce de toille de linomple, auquel elle avoit escript à ses officiers qu'ils eussent à retenir ledit Draysdel le plus longuement qu'ils pourroient, ce qu'ils firent fort à propos.

Je ne veux oublier deux particularitéz assèz remarquables. C'est que la mère du laird, estant tumbée en propos avec Sa Majesté du bruict qui courroit de sa sortye, et luy remonstrant que ce seroit la ruine d'elle et des siens ; au lieu qu' avec le temps on pourroit moyenner quelque bon accord entre sadite Majesté et Monseigneur de Muray, pour assèurer les ungs et les aultres. Sur quoy Sa Majesté répliqua franchement que puisqu 'on la tenoit là contre sa volonté et injustement, elle

---

[1] Jour de loy, comme il parle au pays . . . an interlineation.

mectroit peine d'en sortir en despit de ceulx qui la détenoient par quelque moyen que ce fust. Et tant plus en parloit-elle librement moins y adjoustoit-on de foy, comme à chose estant véritable on pensoit que Sa Majesté n'eust voulu déclarer.

Or ladite dame se promenant au jardin avec Sa Majesté[1] vist une grande trouppe d'hommes à cheval passans de l'aultre costé du lac. Sur quoy[2] s'estant escriée, et disant qu'elle vouloit envoyer les recongnoistre Sa Majesté, pour la détourner de ceste délibération, feignoit se mectre en grande cholére contre Monseigneur de Muray, de sorte qu' entrant de propos en aultre elle retint ladite dame jusques à l'heure de soupper, lequel fust retardé expressément jusques à ce que toutes choses fussent prestes.

Le laird peu après, ayant conduict Sa Majesté en sa chambre et regardant par la fenestre,[3] advisa Guillaume Douglas, qui mectoit de petits chevilles de boys aux attaches et chaines de tous les aultres batteux hors mis un,[4] pour empescher qu'il ne fust suyvy. Ce qu' aperceu par ledit laird, il commenca à manasser ledit Guillaume, l'appellant poltron. Sur quoy Sa Majesté, se doubtant de ce qu 'estoit, feist semblant de se trouver fort mal, et demanda du vin, le quel le laird, n'y ayant aultre en la chambre, alla querir luy mesmes, et là dessus perdist la souvenance de ce qu'il avoit veu. Mesmes estant à son soupper feist fermer la fenestre, laquelle on avoit accoustume de laisser ouverte ordinairement, pour regarder de foys à aultre sur le lac, et scavoir ce que venoit du village.

Georges Douglas, ayant pris congé de sa mère, envoya à Sa Majesté par une damoiselle de la maison, qui avoit accompagnié sadite mère, une perle en poire, que Sa Majesté avoit accoustume de porter en l'une de ses aureilles, qui estoit pour servir de signal que tout estoit prest : et luy manda qu'un bastellier avoit trouvé ladite perle et l'avoit voulu vendre ; mais l'ayant recongnue appartenir à Sa Majesté luy renvoyoit avec promesse que ce soir mesme il partiroit sans faillir pour s'en aller à Glasgo sans jamais plus revenir.

[1] Originally ladite dame . . . regardant à la fenestre . . . vist.
[2] Quoy ayant commandé, cancelled.
[3] Originally Le laird . . . aussi ayant mis le nez à la mesme fenestre.
[4] Aux attaches et chaines . . . et hors mis un . . . interlineations.

Une heure avant le soupper Sa Majesté estant retirée en sa chambre print une cotte rouge appartenante à l'une de ses femmes, et dessus se couvrit d'un sien manteau. Puis après s'en alla parler dans le jardin à la vielle dame, où elle veist ceulx qui passoient au delà du lac.

Quand toutes choses furent prestes Sa Majesté, qui tout expressément jusques là avoit fait différer son soupper, commanda qu'on alla à la viande. Et après son soupper le laird, qui avoit accoustume de la servir ordinairement à table, se retira en une salle basse pour soupper avec sa femme et le reste de la maison, et un nommé Draisdel, (qui avoit la principalle charge en ladite maison et se tenoit ordinairement en la chambre de Sa Majesté pour la garder), s'en alla avec ledit laird[1] et s'amusa à jouer à la paulme à la main.

Cependant Sa Majesté, pour se deffaire des deux petites filles qu'elle avoit avec elle, se retira en une chambre haulte au dessus de la sienne,[2] où logeoit sondit chirurgien, soubz prétexte de dire ses prières, comme à la vérité elle les dist fort dévotement, se recommandant à Dieu, qui monstra bien lors avoir soing et pitié d'elle. En ladite chambre ayant laissé son manteau, et s'estant coiffée à la mode des paisantes de ce quartier, la feist accoustrer de mesme façon une sienne damoiselle pour l'accompagner, ayant laissé son aultre femme de chambre pour amuser lesdites petites filles, qui s'enquéroient fort de l'occasion que Sa Majesté tardoit tant à retourner.

Or durant que le laird souppoit, Guillaume Douglas en luy donnant à boire, luy desroba subtillement la clef de la grande porte, qu'il avoit sur la table devant luy ; dont il feist advertir promptement Sa Majesté, à ce qu'elle descendit au mesme instant. Et tost après, estant sorty hors la porte, il feist signe à ladite damoiselle, qui debvoit accompagner la Royne, regardant lors à la fenestre, ce que entendu par Sa Majesté elle descendist incontinant, et estant au pied du degré, apperceust dans la cour plusieurs serviteurs de la maison qui passoient par là, de sorte que s'estoit tenue quelque temps

---

[1] Laird, et luy feist compagnie, cancelled.

[2] Au dessus de la sienne, an interlineation.

près de la porte du degré. En fin, à la veue d'eulx tous, passa à travers ladite cour, et estant sortye à la grande porte Guillaume Douglas la ferma[1] avec la clef, laquelle il jecta dans une artillere braquée là auprès. Sa Majesté s'estant tenue quelque temps avec sa femme de chambre tout contre la muraille, de peur d'estre aperceue par les fenestres du logis, entra en fin dans le basteau et se coucha au dessoubz du siege du bastellier, à ce conseilliée tant pour n'estre recongneue[2] que pour n'estre offensée si l'on tiroit quelque coup de canon après elle.

Il y avoit plusieurs lavandières et aultres serviteurs qui s'esbatoient en un jardin près du lac quand Sa Majesté entra au basteau, et mesmes une desdites lavandières recongnust Sa Majesté et feist signe audit Guillaume Douglas, le quel luy criast tout hault qu'elle se teust, l'appellant par son nom.

Or quand la basteau fut près de l'autre bord, ledit Guillaume Douglas, ayant aperceu un serviteur dudit Georges, il le mescongneust, d'autant qu'il estoit armé, et pour ce feist difficulté d'aprocher davantage, craignant d'estre abusé. Toutesfoys à la fin ledit serviteur ayant parlé il aprocha, et lors survindrent Georges Douglas et Jehan Beton, qui receurent Sa Majesté, lesquels avoient forcé à la soudain l'escurie du laird et s'estoient saysis de ses meilleurs chevaux.

Sa Majesté s'estant montée au mieux qu'on peust, ne vouloit jamais partir qu'elle ne veist pareillement ledit Guillaume à cheval,[3] qui avoit tant hazardé pour sa déliverance, et laissa derrière elle sadite femme de chambre, donnant ordre qu'incontinent après elle fust équipée pour la venir trouver.

Deux mille de là Sa Majesté rencontra My lord de Seton et laird de Ricarton, accompagnéz, en compagnie desquels elle passa à Queenes ferry, qui est un bras de mer, où toutes choses avoient esté à cest effect bien ordonnéez par ledit Seigneur de Seton ; et de là elle arriva vers la mynuict à

---

[1] Originally, referma.
[2] Tant pour n'estre recongueue, above the line.
[3] A cheval, above the line.

Nidry, maison appartenant audit Seigneur de Seton, où elle fust fort honorablement receue et festoyée et équipée d'habits et aultres choses propres à son sexe et qualité. De là elle s'achemina à Hamilton, où elle demeura jusques au xiij jour du May 1568, assemblant les plus grandes forces qu'elle pouvoit.

Cependant tous ceulx du village de Loklein, ayans veu passer Sa Majesté la bénissans et prians Dieu pour sa sauveté, sans que aucun feist jamais semblant de luy donner aucun empesche-ment; mesmes l'oncle du laird recongneust Sa Majesté. Un paysan entra promptement un basteau, auquel Sa Majesté avoit passé, et le remena au chasteau de Loklyving pour annoncer par mesme moyen le partement de Sa Majesté, qu'estoit ja descouvert par le rapport desdits filles qui estoient en la chambre de Sa Majesté; lesquelles estans montées en la chambre haulte, et ayans trouvé le manteau de Sa Majesté, après l'avoir cherchée, soubçonnans qu'elle s'estoit expressé-ment cachée et ne la trouvans point, descendirent en bas pour advertir le laird. Mais de prime face ayans rencontré Drysdel, dont j'ay cy dessus parlé, ils luy dirent qu'elles ne pouvoient trouver la Royne, et qu'elles avoient opinion que Sa Majesté s'en estoit allée. Ledit Drysdel s'en moqua, et dist qu'il la trouveroit tantost bien, et qu'il luy donnoit congé de s'en aller, tantost sifflant, tantost gambadant. Mais durant telles moqueries survint le paysan avec le basteau, lequel ayant frappé à la porte leur cria comme il avoit veu la Royne passer par le village.

Sur ce laird estant adverty entra en telle rage qu'il tira sa dague pour se transpercer, dont il fust empesché par les assistans. Et désespérans de pouvoir ratrapper Sa Majesté, qui estoit jà plus de six mille loing, dépesche un poste vers le comte de Muray pour luy donner advis de cest accident.

Le comte de Muray estant lors à Glasgo, et ayant eu les nouvelles de la sortie de la Royne, dont il se trouva merveil-leusement estonné, fust en délibération de se retirer vers Strivelingh. Mais par après ayant considéré que si reculoit en façon que ce fust, il descourageroit tous ceulx de son party et donneroit cœur à ses ennemys, il se résolut de demeurer à Glasgo, distant seulement de Hammilton de 8 milles.

Sa Majesté estant à Hammilton, intervindrent plusieurs difficultés entre les Seigneurs et aultres des principaux de sa court, plusieurs ne trouvans bon qu'elle demeurast entre les mains des Hammiltons; à l'occasion desquels, oultre le danger qu'ils remonstroient y estre pour sa personne, les ennemys de leur maisons refusèrent de venir trouver Sa Majesté. Et sur ce fust conclud qu'elle se retireroit à Dumbarton, où un chacun pourroit avoir libre accèz vers elle. De faict Sa Majesté s'achemina vers Dumbertan le 13me de May, avec les comtes d'Arghil, Cassilles, Eglinton, et Rothes, Claud Hammilton, fils du duc de Chastelherault, lequel commandoit à l'avant garde; les Seigneurs de Seton, Flamingh, Sommerville, Yester, Borthwike, Levingston, Heries, Maxvel, Sanqhar, Boid et Ros; lairds de Lochinvar, Bas, Wartiton, Dalhowsay, Roslen, Sir James Hamilton, et pluseurs aultres; ausquels en bref se debvoient joindre les forces assemblées au north soubz le comte de Huntley et my lord d'Oliphan, qui furent un peu retardées par une assemblée des Forbes armés, ennemys de la maison de Huntley Gordons, lesquels, s'eslevèrent à la dévotion du Regent. Du costé duquel estoient les comtes de Morton, Mar, Glencarne, Monteith, Maistre de Graham, les Seigneurs de Hume, Lyndsay, Ruthven, Simple, Ogiltree, et Cathcart; lairds de Bargony, Blackcquam, Drumlanrig, Sesford, Lus, Buchannane, Tullibardin, Petcur, Grange, Lochlevin, Ledinthon, et Sir James Balfour.

Les deux armées marchans l'une vers l'aultre, de celle du Régent partirent quelques trouppes qui s'embusquèrent parmy quelques vielles maisons estans sur le chemin fort estroict[1] où debvoient passer les forces de Sa Majesté, laquelle cependant s'estoit arrestée avec quelque cavallerie sur une montagne voisine là auprès, plus pour fere monstré qu 'aultrement. Du commancement l'escarmouche s'attaqua entre quelques harquebusiers, qui feirent tant d'une part que d'aultre extrêmement bien leur debvoir, encores que du party du Régent quelques Francoys eussent promis de fere voye sitost qu'on viendroit au joindre. Mais le malheur voulust que ceulx du party de la Royne s'advançans trop avant qu'estoit adver-

---

[1] Fort estroict, an interlineation.

tye et les chargèrent, et par ce moyen les contraignirent de se
deffendre. My lord Claude monstra lors son bon coeur et
fidellité vers sa princesse, soustenant l'effort de ses ennemys
jusques ce qu'il se veist environner de tous costés et charger
par derrière de laird de Granges a faulte que la bataille de Sa
Majesté ne peust à temps le secourir, soit par peu de coeur de
ceulx qu' y commandoient ou aultre practique secrette à la dévotion des ennemys. Tant y a que ce pauvre jeune seigneur,
se voyant toutes les forces des ennemys sur les bras, fust en
fin contrainct de reculer, et rentrant vers la bataille il fust
si vifvement pursuyvy que tout le reste de l'armée fust à la
fin mise en fuyte, et furent tués xiiij du surnom des Hammiltons. My lords Seton, Ros et Sir James Hammilton furent
pris prisonniers. Du costé du Régent lord Hume fust blessé
au visage et en une jambe, et lord d'Ogltry au col, par my
lord d'Heris.

Je ne veulx oubleir que sur le partement de Sa Majesté de
Hammilton résolution avoit esté prise entre ceulx du party de
Régent de se retirer ; et de faict plusieurs estoient jà bottés
quand le vieux lord de Simpil, aagé de 80 ans ou environ,
Catholique en relligion mais fort factieux, vint les remonstrer
le tort qu'ils feroient à leur affaires s'ils fuyoient devant
Sadite Majesté, et ne se monstroient en la campagne,[1] au
lieu que se remparans dans ce vielles masures ils pouvoient
saluer et braver[2] leur ennemys sans estre contraincts de venir
à une bataille, et qu'ils avoient tousjours la ville de Glasgo
pour leur retraicte, en laquelle ils seroient assez asseurés.
Que d'aultre part, si les forces de Sa Majesté ne passèrent
par le chemin desdits masures, ains prenoient droit celluy
de Dunberton, ils leur pourroient donner à doz, ou pour le
moins s'exempter de honte de n'avoir paru en campagne.
Par où ils s'acquièrent ceste victoire si importante sur le party
de Sa Majesté.

Entre ceulx du party du Régent il y avoit un gentilhomme
sauvage nommé Makfarlane, suyvy de deux cens hommes de
ses amys et parens, lequel feist rage de combattre ; et depuis

---

[1] Et ne se monstroient en la campagne, an interlineation.
[2] Et braver, above the line.

en souvenance de ce service la vie luy fust sauvée par le comte Muray à la requeste de sa femme ; estant ledit Makfarlane chargé de plusieurs crimes.

Le chemin que Sa Majeste feist depuis la perte de ce bataille pour passer en Angleterre,

Comme elle beust de laict aigre en la maison d'un pauvre homme.

Emprunta du linge.

Se feit raser la teste.

Fust 24 heures sans boire ny manger.

Laird de Lokinvar luy bailla des habits et une damoiselle. Sa[1] Majeste ayant passé la mer et descendant de basteau tumba à terre, ce que plusieurs prindrent à bon augure, l'interprétans selon la façon commune qu'elle prenoit possession de l'Angleterre, où elle pretendoit droicts. Elle arriva en un petit hameau où le soupper se preparait. My lord d'Heris envoyà vers le laird de Korwen, qui estoit de ses amys ; luy donnant advis de son arrivée en Angleterre, et qu'il avoit amené avec luy une jeune damoiselle héritière, laquelle il avoit enlevée en espérance de la fere espouser à son fils ; et pour ce le prioit de le recepvoir chez luy. Fust rapporté que ledit laird estoit à Londres, et fust la maison offerte par un des principaux serviteurs dudit laird, entre lesquels un Françoys se trouva, qui recongneust Sa Majesté si tost qu'elle s'entra en ladite maison, et dist à my lord Flamyng qu'il avoit veu aultres foys Sa Majeste en meilleur estat. Sur quoy le bruit s'estant espandu, arrivèrent là le lendemain près de quatre cens chevaus. Sa Majesté se voyant descouverte trouva bon de declarer comme elle estoit venue sur la promesse de la Royne d'Angleterre, qui en fust soudainement advertye. Et de là Sa Majesté fust menée par[2] les gentilhommes de la alentour, où elle se feist faire une robbe de drap noir, qui luy fust baillée à crédit, avec quelques aultres estoffes pour quelques uns de ses gens[3]

[1] This passage, which occurs out of place in the original manuscript, is here restored to its true position in the narrative.

[2] Originally, pour ses gens.

[3] Here a blank space occurs after the word "par." The words, "les gentilhommes de la alentours," is an interlineation. The sentence appears

à Carlel, ou elle fust receue par les habitans de la ville et par Monsieur Lauder, lieutenant en ladite ville de my lord Scroop, qui pressa fort Sa Majeste de loger dans le chasteau, ce qu'elle feist. Là la vindrent trouver my lord Claude et plusieurs aultres de ses subgects. Le comte de Northumberland y arriva avec commission du conseil d'York, portant commandement audit Lauder de luy delivrer Sa Majeste, laquelle en estant advertye, et de ne sortir du chasteau de peur qu'on ne l'enlevast de force, moyenna avec ledit Lauder qu'il alla en extrême dilligence vers la Royne d'Anglererre pour scavoir son intention; sur quoy furent dépeschés soudainement my lord Scrup et Monsieur Knooles. Ledit comte de Northumberland estoit aucunement ennemy de Sa Majesté, tant à cause de la comtesse de Lenox, avec laquelle il avoit intrinseque amitié, que pour XV. M.Δ., envoyées par le Pape à Sa Majesté; lesquels ledit comte avoit rétenuz, souz prétexte que le navire estant rompu arriva au port de Tynmouth, que ledit comte avoit en garde.

Sa Majesté avant que donnoit la dernière bataille, pour pourvoir à la mauvaise issue qu'en pourroit advenir, dépescha vers la Royne d'Angleterre Jehan Beton, son gentilhomme servant, avec une bague de diamant faict en roche, qu'elle avoit au paravant receu de ladite Royne d'Angleterre, en revanche d'un cœur diamant; luy donnant advis de sa délivrance hors de Lokleving,[1] et que si elle se trouvoit pressée par ses subjectz, sa délibération estoit de venir en Angleterre pour requérir son ayde. Et sur ce luy ramentevoit la promesse que ladite royne aultresfoys luy avoit faicte envoyant ladite bague, portant expressément que toutes et quantes foys que Sa Majesté auroit besoing de son ayde, qu'elle luy renvoyast ladite bague pour token, et que soudainement, ou elle yroit elle mesmes en propre personne la secourir, ou y envoyroit. Ce que encores elle confirma audit Beton, l'asseurant que Sa Majesté seroit la bien venue, et qu'elle luy feroit tout le meilleur traictement et réception qui seroit en sa puissance.

to have been rewritten. As it stands, something is wanting to complete the sense.

[1] De sa délivrance hors de Lokleving, an interlineation.

Sur cet asseurance Sa Majesté vint en Angleterre, comme nous avons dist cy dessus, et envoya vers ladite Royne my lord Flaming et my lord Herys pour lui fere entendre son arrivée en son royaume, et l'occasion d'icelle, tendant principallement à avoir le support promis contre ses rebelles. Et ce[1] pendant qu'il luy fust permis de passer jusques à Londres pour visiter ladite Royne sa bonne sœur, ce que ne fust trouvé bon, ains fust Sa Majesté arrestée encores à Carlel pour quelque temps, et là fust dépesché vers Sa Majesté monsieur Mydelmor, avec lettres de crédit, pour passer en Escosse et requérir Sa Majesté, pour advancer quelque bonne pacyfication,[2] de fere quitter les armes à ceulx de son party, qui estoit lors en campagne et les plus fortz, à la charge que la Royne d'Angleterre entrevenant en feroit fere de mesmes aux rebelles.[3] Mais Sa Majesté, qui ne vouloit manquer à chose quelconque concernant le repose de son pays, ayant satisfaict à cest article fust déceue. Car au lieu d'effectuer ce qu'on luy avoit promis, tous ceulx qui l'avoient aydée et rendu le debvoir de fidelles subgects en sa fuyte furent ruinéz et pursuyviz à mort,[4] les uns ayans esté extraordinairement exécuté, comme fust un pauvre homme yvre, le quel pour avoir servy de guyde à Sa Majesté, chose deue aux ennemys propres par humanité,[5] fust mis en quattre quartiers; et un aultre, nommé Moor, qui receust (ne pouvant aultrement fere, d'autant qu'il n'estoit le plus fort[6]) Sa Majesté une nuict devant son foyer en une pauvre logis, fust pendu et sa maison bruslée. Crauté très exécrable et auparavant non ouyè.

[1] Here the narrative breaks off abruptly in the MS. Cal. B. iv., but is resumed in the MS. Cal. B. v., fol. 202. It will be observed that the separation takes place in the middle of a sentence, the connexion of the two fragments having hitherto escaped notice.

[2] Pour advancer quelque bonne pacification, an interlineation.

[3] Here occurs a cancelled passage, written partly in the margin, and partly as an interlineation. Lettres de la Royne d'Angleterre sur ce, ou se déclareroit contre eulx, si après les avoir semoncer ils ne cessoient leurs excès. . . .

[4] originally. . . par justice, a mort.

[5] chose deur aux enemys propres par humanté, an interlineation.

[6] Nommé Moor. . . ne pouvant aultrement fere, d'autant qu'il n'estoit le plus fort, an interlineation.

Sa Majesté ayant séjournée à Carlell environ 3 sepmaines, ou un moys, luy fust envoyée une compagnie de cent cinquante soldatz entretenue à Barwick (qui estoit, comme nous disons en France des vielles bandes), soubz le commandement du cappitaine Read. Ces soldatz luy furent envoyéz soubz prétexte de sa garde sur la frontière contre ses propres subjects, alléguant la Royne d'Angleterre, qu'elle vouloit la préserver suyvant sa promesse contre sesdits subgectz.

Et sur ces entrefaicts luy envoya dans une petite cassete d'un pied et demy de quarré, vij yerdes de taffetas et autant de satin, avec quelque toille de linomple, et de outre soullierz de velours noir pour l'accomoder, entendant qu'elle n'avoit rien apporté avec elle d'Escosse. Sa Majesté fust là longuement à ses propres despenses et deffrayoit les seigneurs d'Angleterre, speciallement Monsieur Knooles, qui luy avoit esté envoyé.

En fin la conclusion prise de retenir icelle Royne d'Escosse, luy fust sa despartie ordonnée par ladite Royne d'Angleterre, et par son commandement fust menée dudit Carllel à Bowton, plus avant dans le pays, contre le gré de Sa Majesté, laquelle desclara publiquement qu'en ce on la forçoit, contre la promesse de leur Royne, à laquelle elle désiroit estre audevant, si on la vouloit fere passer plus avant ; et de ce demanda acte, et feist protestations devant le baillif et les principaux officiers de la ville. Ce néantmoins sur la fin du moys de Juillet elle fust amené audit Bowton, où elle sejourna cinq moys après, ou environ, lequel temps fust employé aux négotiacions, tant en Escosse pour paciffier ces choses qu'en Angleterre à ce mesme effect, entre les commissaires et depputéz des deux roynes et les depputéz des rebelles d'Escosse.

Icy fault prendre le discours de Monsieur de Rosse pour ce qui s'est passé avec lesdits commissaires, et du mariage du duc de Northfolk, de son procès et de sa mort, à quoy firent le livre.

Sa Majesté sur l'ouverture qui luy fust faicte du mariage dudit duc, envoya certains Articles[1] aux principaux du conseil d'Angleterre, tenus en party, pour bien asseurer la négotia-

[1] In the margin occurs the note:—Faut faire entrer icy les dits Articles ; but none have been inserted.

tion; protestant speciallement ny vouloir entendre sans que ladite Royne d'Angleterre y consentist et leur agréable [estoit],
ce que luy fust promis par les dits conférences les plus privéez
avec ladite Royne, comme il apparoit par les lettres escriptes
et signées de leurs mains.

Les lettres se pourront icy inserer.[1]

Ledinthon en Escosse, voyant que la balance ayant renversé
d'un costé où il s'asseuroit le plus, il n'estoit plus capable d'en
tenir le mylieu, comme c'estoit son desseing, pour avoir
tousjours les choses en contrepoix, commença fort à trafficquer
pour avoir la Royne en Escosse, et fust un des principaux
entremecteurs du mariage du duc.

D'aultre costé le bastard de Moray, qui appelloit ledit
Ledinthon un mal nécessaire, voyant qu'il n'alloit sinon pour
avoir toujours toutes choses en sa main, chercha les moyens de
s'en deffaire.　Et pour ce feist venir un jour en plein conseil
un des gens de Monseigneur de Lenox pour accuser le Seigneur
Ledinthon du meurtre du feu Roy, et luy feist sur ce garder
son logis par forme d'obeyr à justice, laquelle il ne pouvoit des-
nyer, et sur ce ostit son desseing de s'en deffayre habillement.[2]

La dessus les choses venans à s'aigrir d'une part et
d'aultre, et Ledinton se voyant en danger prochain de sa vie,
commença plus précipitamment que jamais à dresser un party
pour se fortiffier, ce que ne pensa pouvoir mieux effectuer que
soubz l'authorité de la Royne, laquelle il vouloit remectre sus.
Entra en pratique avec tous ceulx qui tenoient ce party, y
attira laird de Granges, et aultres ses amys et alliéz; de façon
que comme il estoit homme d'intendement et subtil, ayant
gaigné le chasteau d'Edinbourg tenu par le Seigneur de
Granges, il se releva.

Le siége du chasteau.

Le séjour des Angloys.

Du Crok envoié et Verac par le Roy de France.

Service d'argent pour Monsieur de Fleming.

Monsieur de Seton et le frère du laird de Grange.

---

[1] A note in the margin of the original.

[2] The sentence is apparently defective.

La composition de ceulx qui estoient dans le dit chasteau, et de les adhérens estans dehors.

Le Comte de Muray, qui avec Ledinton avoit faict semblant d'approuver le mariage du duc, entra en la practiqne, puis la descovrist à la Royne d'Angleterre.

Après la mort du duc.

Le Comte de Shrewsbury monstra de la part de la Royne d'Angleterre à la Royne d'Escosse un regret ou estoient, et disoit il plusieurs discours et remonstrances envoyées de plusieurs princes[1] en divers endroicts de la Chrestienté à la dite Royne, mesmement de France, pour la persuader à fere mourir ladite Royne d'Escoce, pour ceste principalle considéra-tion qu'elle estoit la colonne et totalle espérance du restab-lissement de la relligion papistique[2] de ceste isle, et qu'élle estoit bien obligée à ladite Royne d'Angleterre, qui luy faisoit grace.

Sa Majesté demanda à voir ledit discours, ce que luy estant refusé, elle protesta que tant s'en fault qu'elle tint à destourber ce tiltre qu'on luy donnoit d'espérance et defensa-trice de la relligion Catholique, qu'au contraire elle l'acceptoit en bonne part et trés volontiers. Au reste, estant Royne souveraine, ne pouvoit recepvoir ny recongnoistre aucun espèce de grace de personne vivante, quelle qu'elle fust; et pour ce prioit ledit comte de n'user de ces termes, car elle pouvoit licitement fere ce qu'elle avoit faict. Et que pour le regard du duc, puis qu'il estoit traicté à ceste façon à son occasion seul, qu'elle auroit faict ancore davantage si elle eust peu fere le délivrer, comme elle y estoit obligée, ayant tousjour persévéré à le recongnoistre pour son fiancé et quasi mary asseuré.

[1] Plusieurs princes en—above the line.
[2] Papistique—added above the line.

U

MEMOIRES DE L'ESTAT ET SUCCES DES AFFAIRES D'ECOSSE DURANT LA REGNE DE MARIE STUART.

L'AN[1] 1542 le vij^me du moys de Decembre, jour de Vendredy, veille de la Conception Nôtre Dame, nasquist Marie Stewart, fille de Jacques Vme, roy d'Escosse, en la ville de Lythcou, au pays de Escosse.[2]

Le xiiij^me de Decembre au mesme an 1542, mourut Jacques 5me, roy d'Escosse, aagé de trente troys ans, au chasteau de Falkland, lequel il avoit faict bastir, au pays de Fyfe.

Le Cardinal de Beton, archevesque de S. André, voyant les affaires du royaume en mauvais estat par la mort du Roy, moyenna avec la faction des Francoys, desquels il estoit partisan, que la regence luy fut delaissée, et appella avecques soy les comtes de Murrey (frere bastard du feu Roy dernier), d'Arghyle et Huntley, sans faire mention des contes de Lenox et Arraine, les plus proches héritiers de la coronne.

Le   de   l'an   [3], la Royne fut coronnée en la ville de Stirlin.   Le conte de Arrene, gouverneur, porta la coronne et le conte de Lenox porta le sceptre.

Le Roy Edward vj^me rechercha de mariage la Royne d' Ecosse.

L'an 1547 le roy Henry 2, soudain après son advènement a la coronne de France, despecha en Escosse, avec xvj. navires bien equipées d' hommes et toutes sortes de munitions, le sieur

---

[1] These notes are written, in Nau's best hand, on some sheets of paper which now form part of the Cottonian MS., Calig. B. v. 191. The reverses of the folios marked 191, 192, 193, and 196 are blank, as is the whole of 195.

[2] Between this and the following entry Phelippes, Walsingham's decipherer, has interpolated the following passage:—L'an 1586, le viij^me du moys de Februrier, jour de Mercredy, fut decapitée la dite royne d' Escosse au chasteau de Fodringhey, au pays d' Angleterre.   Hence we have evidence that Nau's historical papers came into the hands of Phelippes.

[3] Blank in the MS.   The Battle of Pinkey.

de Strosse,[1] prieur de Capue, pour restablir les affaires d'
Escosse. Estans en grand trouble par la mort du feu Cardinal
Beton, qui avoit esté, l'an auparavant, massacré en sa maison
archiépiscopale de S. André. Sitost que le dit Sieur Strossé
fust arrivé en Escosse il met le siége devant la dite ville de
S. André, tenue par les ennemys et meurtriers du dit Cardinal;
et se rendist maistre en 14 jours, tant de la ville que du
chasteau, le 29 Juillet au dit an 1547. Envoya les dits
meurtriers en France, et entre aultres le principal autheur
Normand Lesley, lequel depuis fust tué en la bataille de
Renty, pres de Montreal sur la Mer, le xj[me] d'Octobre,
1554.[2] Il commandoit à une compaynie de cent chevaux
légers.

Le 10 de Septembre an dit au 1547 fust donnée bataille
entre les Angloys et les Escossoys, soubz la conduict de James
Hammilton, conte d' Arrane, pres de la ville de . . . .[3] La
victoire demeura aux Angloys. Y fut pris Georges de Gordon,
comte de Huntly.

An moys de May 1548 fust envoyé par le roy de France,
Henry 2, le sieur Dessay,[4] chevalier de son ordre, avec 4
galères soubz la conduicte de Nicolas de Villegaignon, chevalier
de l'ordre de S. Jehan de Hierusalem; lesquels de leur
première abordée recouvrirent l'Isle de Chevaux,[5] occupée par
les Angloys, située entre le Leith et Kyngorn.

L'an 1550, le 20 de Fevrier, le sieur de Thermes, chevalier
de l'ordre du roy, prend la fortresse de Borthycrag[6] en
Escosse, et tue tous les Angloys qu'il trouva dedans.

Le xvij[me] de Septembre au dit an 1550 la Royne[7] dour-
airierére d'Escosse, fille du duc de Guyse, arriva en France avec
plusieurs seigneurs d' Ecosse, et le conte de Huntly, y estant
appelléz par le Roy Henry 2.

La[8] Royne d' Angleterre Marie, fille d'Henry 8 et de

[1] See Lesley, ap. Jebb, i. 163.

[2] According to Leslie he died on August 29 of a wound received at the battle of Renty, which was fought on the 13th of that month.

[3] Blank in the MS.   [4] See Lesley, ap. Jebb, i. 169.

[5] Id. p. 177.   [6] Id. p. 179.   [7] Id. p. 180, 181.

[8] From the Cottonian MS. Calig. B. ix. fol. 67. See Lesley, ap. Jebb i. 188.

Catherine fille du Roy d'Arragon, laquelle avoit esté répudiée par le Roy son mary, succéda en ce mesme temps à la coronne par la mort d' Eduard VIme.

Ceste mort apporta de grands troubles en Angleterre pour la succession de la coronne ; car la plus grande part du conseil, manié à la dévotion du duc Northumberland, déclara Royne Jehanne fille du duc de Suffolk et femme du fils aisné du duc de Northumberland, au surnom de Dudeley.

En fin, du commun consentement des seigneurs, elle fust couronnée, d'autant que Anne de Boulen, mère de la Royne Elizabeth à présent regnante, avoit esté convaincue d' adultère dudit vivant de son mary, et eust pour cela teste tranchée.

Toutesfoys [1]

L' an[2] 1558 au mois de Décembre la Royne douairière assembla le parlement à Edinburgh, où par consentement des estatz furent choisiz Jacques Beton, archevesque de Glasgo, Robert Read, évesque d' Orkney,[3] (premier président du sénat d' Escosse, qui mourut à Diepe retournant en Escosse, le 16 Septembre ensuyvant), Georges Lesley comte de Rothes, Guilbert Kennedy comte de Cassels, Jacques Stueuart prieur de Saint André, qui depuis a esté comte de Meurrey, Georges seigneur de Seton, et Jacques seigneur de Flemmyng, et Jehan Herkyn, baron,[4] seigneur de Dun, ambassadeurs depputéz vers le Roy, pour contracter et sollenniser le mariage d' entre Marie leur Royne et Françoys dauphin de France, sur quoy leur furent données amples instructions.

Partirent au moys de Fébvrier ensuivant, et après avoir esté fort longuement tourmentéz sur mer, de sorte que plusieurs de leur vaisseaux feirent naufrage, ils arrivèrent en France et furent receuz au moys de Mars à Fontaine-belleau.[5]

---

[1] The page to which this is the catchword has not been recovered.
[2] From the Cottonian MS. Cal. B. ix. 31.
[3] Here there is a mark referring to the note in the margin giving an account of his office and death, which follow.
[4] Baron, added above the line.
[5] The following clause is cancelled, having previously undergone several changes :—Le mesme jour ayant en audience de— estans venuz trouver leur, Royne la chambre ou elle estoit.

Le contract du mariage fut passé à Paris le[1] jour de Apvril 1558. Fust faict ligue entre les estatz d'Escosse et France, et luy fut assigné soixante mil livres de douaire sur les contés de Pontieu et duché de Touraine avec vingt mil livres de pension.

La[2] Royne d'Angleterre Marie décéda le xvij^me Novembre l'an 1559, à laquelle succéda Elizabeth sa soeur, combien qu' elle eust esté déclarée bastarde dès le vivant et par commandement du Roy son père. Mais la nouvelle relligion, dont elle avoit fait profession durant le règne de sa soeur, fortifia de beaucoup son party.

La Royne[3] d'Escosse, ayant entendu les nouvelles de la mort de sa bonne soeur et cousine, se vestist en deuil et le porta six sepmaines, comme parente et proche héritière de la Royne deffuncte, à laquelle légitimement elle debvoit succéder. Sur ce elle receust commandement du Roy son mary de prendre les armes d'Angleterre, lesquelles furent adjoustées à celles de France et d'Escosse. Qui a depuis esté occasion de grandes querelles entre ces deux Roynes.

La[4] maladie estoit une apostume . . . grande resverie deux jours avant sa mort. La royne feist sa quarantaine en sa chambre, ou elle fust visitée des roy, royne, prince . . . . des roys estrangers, et entre aultres de celuy d'Angleterre. Pluseurs entrirent en extreme jalousie, craignans . . . aisné d'Espagne avec la Royne Blanche.[5] A quoy [le] Cardinal de

---

[1] Le 24 cancelled. The contract of marriage, dated 19th April 1558, is printed in the Acta Parl. Scot. ii. 511, and in Keith i. 353. See Lesley, ap. Jebb, i. 198, 199.

[2] From the Cottonian MS. Cal. B. ix. fol. 66. See Lesley, ap. Jebb i. 203.   [3] Jebb, p. 205.

[4] The present section, extending to the arrival of Queen Mary in Scotland, is transcribed from Nau's autograph in the Cottonian MS. Calig. E. V., folios 119, 120, 121, the reverse of which last leaf is left blank. This volume suffered severely in the disastrous fire of 1731, the margin of many of the leaves having been totally destroyed. In the translation here given the imperfections of this text have been supplied by the help of Leslie's original Latin, and occasionally from other sources.

[5] The widows of the kings of France were so styled because they wore a white stomacher and veil during their widowhood. See Lalaune's " Dict. Historique de la France," p. 302.

Lorraine, son oncle, ne fauldroit de présenter . . . de regne qui s'ensuyvist soudain après la mort . . . . Car soudainement l'Admiral et ceulx de sa faction . . . . court, et fortifians de jour en jour leur party, soubz ceulx qui envioient le gouvernement entier des affaires, co . . . . . . l'ont toujours possédé, donnèrent le sault à ceulx . . . lesquels en fin se bannyrent volontairement de la court. . . . Royne Blanche.   Laquelle voyans les indignités qui luy estoient . . . et les deportemens de ses ennemys et de ceulx d . . . retira avec eulx à Nancy.[1]

Ce departement apporta davantage de soubçon à la . . . . mere, quy la renvoya soudain quérir pour avec tant . . . de bonne volonté qu'il fust aisé à ceste jeune Royne ʼ. . . . ce que moins estoit.

. . . grandes occasions de se . . . Escosse, ou elle estoit appellée par les . . . venu quérir soudain après la mort de son mary . . . estoit d'opinion de ce partement, alleguant qu'il . . . seant d'estre première personne en son royaume que seconde . . . d'aultry . . . principallement les affaires y estans en l'estat . . . de Guise son frere y contredisoit plainement, et disoit que . . . . comme la brebis en la geule des loups, à cause . . . qui estoient en Escosse.[2]

. . . avec ledit sieur l'amb . . . Blanche demanda audience d'elle pour . . . poincte d'importance sur [le passage] de la par. . . . De prime abordée il luy remonstra la jus . . . Royne sa maistresse avoit de rester offensée . . . pris le nom et armes de Royne d'Angleterre contre . . . succession naturelle, et que sans se demectre de . . . ne falloit point qu'elle esperoit aucune amitié d'. . . . . . Bref, qu'estoit nécessaire qu'elle accordast certaines . . . . . lesquelles elle se pouvoit asseurer de [n'arriver] . . . passage libre en Escosse.[3]

¹ See Q. Mary to Throckmorton 1561, April 22. R. O. Foreign Cal., No. 130, 131, 155, 158.

² Her settling in Lorraine, there to have lived amongst her own kin and parents of the mother's side, until she had been provided of some Catholic prince, or honourably qualified person for husband, was vehemently urged by the Duke of Guise, her uncle, but the resolution to the contrary was carried by the Cardinal of Lorraine, his brother, which was, all other things set apart, to return into her own country, whereunto likewise the Queen herself most inclined. Anon. Hist. Cal. B. iv. f. 138b.

³ This and the following clause have reference to the conversation be-

La Royne Blanche soudainement luy respondist qu'elle avoit pris les armes d'Angleterre après la mort de la . . . et ce par le commandement du feu roy son mary, en obeissance l'advis de son conseil et commun conse . . . d'Escosse, sans lesquels, comme en chose qui leur . . . au bien commun au royaume d'Escosse, elle ne voul . . . en ceste endroit.

Que pour le regard du passage, elle l'avoit deman . . . d'Angleterre, sa bonne sœur et cousine, pour les pays des . . . la recongnoissoit seulement avoir puissance . . . . de la mer estre libre à un chacun, de sorte qu'elle se deliber . . . . en Escosse par ceste voye, esperant de passer, nonobstant les . . . le pourroit efforcer de luy donner.

. . . en donna ce . . . tresse qui [arriva] meist soudain quelques . . . . rencontrer la Royne d'Ecosse. Mais le brouillard . . . . . qu'ils ne sceurent se recongnoistre l'ung l'aultre de . . . . Angloys retournèrent à leur grande honte . . . . . d'Escosse approcha fort près de la terre d'Angleterre jusques . . . et plusieurs de sa compagnie parlèrent à ceuls qui estoient.

. . . . general[1] en Escosse pour le feu Roy . . . pour luy demander passage par son royaume, ce que ladite Royne refusa tout à plat et en . . . . de passer en Escosse ou il avoit esté pareillement . . . . départir hors d'Escosse ce que y restoit des forces, ou remectre les places fortes qu'ils tenoient . . . . naturelz Escossois.

La Royne fut accompagnié de Paris jusques à Calais . . . le Duc d'Aumale, le Marquis d'Elbeuf, et le Grand P . . . . d'Anville, le Duc de Nemours, et grande partye de la noblesse de France ; et passèrent avec ung bon nombre de gentilz-hommes en Escosse, et y sejournèrent quelques moys. Toute cest compagnie passa en deux galères et deux . . . eurent le temps et le vent fort a-gré, de sorte qu'en se . . . arrivèrent de Calais au Petit Liet, que fust le xix Aou . . . les huit heures du matin.

Sa Majesté fust la receue par le Seigneur de Sainte Croix,

tween Queen Mary and Sir Nicolas Throckmorton, for which see the letter written by that ambassador to his mistress, and dated 1561, Aug. 11, R. O. Foreign 395, and Cal. E. x. 94.

[1] See Lesley, ap. Jebb, i. 230.

son, ... avec une bonne partie des gentilshommes du pays circonvoisin et les habitans . . . principalle ville du royaume.

La dit Seigneur de Sainte Croix luy donna à disner et à sa suytte à l'abbaye de Sainte Croix, en attendant que la maison de la royne . . . . préparée, à quoy on n'avoit donné ordre, d'autant que la Royne estoit arrivée fort inopinement non attendue, et moins au . . . des rebelles et factieux de la nouvelle religion.

Quatre [1] ou cinq jours après l'arrivée de la Royne D'Escosse à l'Islebourg le duc de Chastelhéraud, le conte d'Arghil, le prieur de St André, bastard du feu Roy Jacques 5me et plusieurs aultres gentilzhommes de leur faction et relligion, feirent grande instance avant toutes aultres choses [2] pour asseurer l'estat des affaires et de leur relligion, tel qu'ilz l'avoient au paravant establly. Et comme ceuls du conseil estoient à leur dévotion, il leur fut aise par leur commun advyse [3] résolution de faire approuver certain acte sur ce dressé avec le consentement de la Royne, portant qu'il ne seroit directement ny indirectement rien innové par quelque personne que ce fust au faict de la relligion receue dans le royaume pour éviter aux troubles qui l'en pourroient ensuyvre, avec deffenses sur grandes peines de ne rien attempter publiquement ou privément au contraire.

Fut ce néantmoins réservé à Sa Majesté, qui protesta de quitter plustost la coronne que l'exercise de sa relligion, de pouvoir sollennellement faire dire Messe par chacun jour en sa chapelle, et y faire célébrer le service divin à la forme de l'Église Catholique, Apostolique et Romaine, avec permission d'y assister par tous ses subjects qui n'avoient fait profession de foy au contraire. Fut aussi permis aux chanoines de la Chappelle Royale de Sterling de faire dire et célébrer le service divin comme dessus en l'absence de la Royne.

Nonobstant ce premier accord passé en conseil, le Dimanche

[1] From the Cottonian MS. Cal. B. ix. f. 32. See Lesley, ap. Jebb, i. 230, who shows at some length the drift and results of this decision.

[2] Avant toutes aultres choses, added above the line.

[3] Advyse, an insertion above the line.

ensuyvant My lord de Lyndsay, accompagné de quelques aultres sédicieux de pareille humeur, vint trouver le chappellain de Sa Majesté en la chappelle, et l'espée au poing avec grand tumulte et rumeur chassa ledit chappellain de l'autel, qui se sauva dans le revestiaire, quoy voyant ledit seigneur de Lyndsay renversa scandaleusment tous les ornemens qui estoient en la chappelle ; dont la Royne, sur l'advis qu'elle en receust, feist appeler les seigneurs, leur commandant de réprimer telles insolences qui contrevenoient grandement à l'establissement de la paix.

Peu après [1] furent choisiz, pour estre du conseil secret de la Royne, douze Seigneurs et un évesque,[2] qui auroient l'entier maniement des affaires, et par l'advis desquelz la Royne en ordonneroit selon les occurrences. Six d'iceulx estoient officiers de la coronne, comme chancelier, grand trésorier, secrétaire, controuller, et aultres, pour demeurer continuellement près de la Royne.

Le duc de Chastelhérauld.

Le comte de Hunteley, chancelier.

Le comte d'Ergheil, grand steuart.

Le comte de Athol.

Le comte Mareschal, du surnom de Keith.

Le comte de Glencarne.

Le comte de Morton.

Le comte de Montrose.

Le comte d'Erol, connestable.

Mr Henry Sinclair, évesque de Rosse.

James Steuuart, bastard, prieur de Saint André.

Le Seigneur Erskyn.

Mr Robert Richarson fut continué en son office de Grand Trèsorier.

Laird de Ledinthon, Guillaume Maitland, secrétaire de la coronne.

Thomas Grahame controlleur du Royaume, très homme de bien et bon Catholique.

[1] See Lesley, ap. Jebb, i. 234.
[2] Originally, par l'advis.

SKETCH OF THE HISTORY OF SCOTLAND DURING THE MINORITY OF QUEEN MARY STEWART.[1]

Après la mort de Jacques V luy succéda Marie, aagée de sept jours, son unique fille et héritière, le 18 de [2] Décembre l'an 1542, estant lors au chasteau de Lythguo en la garde de la Royne sa mère, laquelle se trouva en grande peine à cause des divisions et partialitéz nouvellement survenues, tant pour le gouvernement du royaume que pour la garde de la jeune Royne, qui fust occasion de différer le coronement jusques au moys d'Aoust ensuyvant.   Cependant le comte d'Aran fust déclaré Gouverneur du royaume et tuteur de la Royne selon les loix et coustume du pays; sa régence ayant esté publiée dans Edimbourgh, nonobstant les oppositions formées par le Cardinal de St André, et quelques aultres, qui alléguoient le feu Roy dernier avoit institué par son testament quattre administrateurs du royaume durant la minorité de sa fille. Ainsi le Régent entrant en sa charge se saysit du palais [3] de Sainte Croix et du chasteau de Fakland ; et ayant en sa main le trésor de la corone, il contraignist les Trésoriers, Controlleur et aultres officiers de rendre compte de leur charges, y continuant les uns et cassant les aultres.   Par après il fust pourveu tant à la garde qu'à la despence ordinaire de la maison [4] de la Royne, sans que près d'elle [5] aucun y peust estre receu de la part de la Royne sa mére à sa dévocion que le Seigneur de Levingston.

Sur ce le Roy d'Angleterre, considérant l'occasion qui se présentoit de réunir les deux royaumes de l'ile Bretagne par

[1] From the original draft, in Nau's hand, in the State Paper Office, Mary, Queen of Scots, vol. xxi., No. 46.

[2] The Laud MS. 538 (an uncollated copy of Lesley's translation of his Latin original of his Scottish history) gives the date of 24th December, but afterwards alters it to 14, confirmed by the original Latin in Jebb i. 149.

[3] Originally Chasteaux.

[4] De la maison, an interlineation.

[5] Près d'elle, added above the line.

le mariage de son filz, aagé de 5 ans, et de la Royne d'Escosse,
se résolut de la mener à effect; et pour y commancer il communiqua particulièrement sa délibération aux contes de Cassils
et Glencarne, aux seigneurs de Maxwel, Fleming et Grey, et à
quelques aultres seigneurs et gentilhommes Escossoys,[1] detenuz
prisonniers en son royaume; leur remonstrant le bien qui pourroit reussir à toute l'isle par ce mariage, et les moyens qu' il
conviendroit tenir pour la seure garde de leur Royne jusques
à l'accomplissement d'icelluy. A quoy trouvant lesdits seigneurs inclinés d'eulx mesmes sur l'espérance de leur liberté;
il les depescha en Escosse pour commancer cette négotiacion,[2]
et par mesme moyen envoya le comte d'Angus et Georges
Douglas vers le Régent[3] avec lettres fort favourables pour le
prier de restablir lesdits bannys en leur biens et dignitéz.

Le Régent ayant amplement[4] entendu par les dessusdits
l'intention du Roy d'Angleterre feist assembler les principaux
de la noblesse[5] au 3 des calends de Mars [27 Feb.] et publia[6]
le Parlement au moys ensuyvant pour prendre résolucion sur
les ouvertures que leur estoient faictes. Mais[7] pour obvier que
le Cardinal ne les traversast en ceste affaire, ilz le tindrent
quelque temps prisonnier à Dalkeit, et depuis au chasteau de
St André, où le seigneur de Seton fust depputé pour le garder;
tous les prestres du diocèse de St André cessans pour ceste occasion de célébrer le Divin Service. Ce fust en ce temps que la
relligion Catholique commenca à s' ébranler en Escosse soub-
la faveur du Régent, persuadé par ceulx qui estoient nouvellement retournéz d'Angleterre, et par les prédicacions d'un
Jacobin[8] tant contre l'autorité du Pape que plusieurs aultres
ordonnances de l'Eglise; permectant à un chacun de lire la
Bible traduite[9] en Angloys, et de choisir telles prières que
bon luy sembleroit.

---

[1] Bannys de leur pays, written above the line and then cancelled.
[2] Pour commancer . . . . . . negotiacion, an interlineation.
[3] Originally gouverneur.   [4] Amplement, added above the line.
[5] Originally seignieur—principaux de la noblesse, an interlineation.
[6] Publia le, added above the line.   [7] Prevoyant, cancelled.
[8] The Laud text (fol. 75) calls him a Dominican (or Black Friar) named
William, as also does the Latin original, p. 150.
[9] Traduite, added above the line.

Le Roy d'Angleterre, pour advancer sa délibération et favoriser la rèsolution que s'en debvoit fere au Parlement[1] Escossoys, y envoya en qualité d'Ambassadeur le Sieur Rodolph Sadler, chevalier; après l'arrivée duquel et à la pursuitte desdits nouveaux[2] restablyz, le mariage dessusdit fust conclud[3] et trèves pour dix ans accordées entre les deux royaumes par le commun consentement des estatz, ce que le Roy d'Angleterre confirma depuis par ses[4] lettres patentes en date au premier Août, délivrées aux ambassadeurs qui luy furent envoyéz, c'est à scavoir, le conte de Glencarne, Georges Douglas, Guillaume Hamilton et James Lermond, chevaliers, au retour desquels, toutes choses semblans à ceulx de ceste faction bien asseurées, le Cardinal fust mis en liberté et le comte d'Angus, George Douglas, my lord Glames, héritier de Jacques Hammilton, avec quelques aultres, furent remis en leur biens et honneurs par le Parlement.

Jehan Hammilton, frère du Régent, en revenant de France, où il avoit longuement estudié, visita le Roy d'Angleterre ; qui le receust et plusieurs hommes doctes de sa compagnie, fort courtoisement.   Soudain qu'il fust arrivé en Escosse, il eust l'estat de Trésorier lequel il tint avec fort grande reputacion tout le temps de la régence de son frère, l'assistant de son conseil au gouvernement de toutes afferes.

Le comte de Bothuel revint en ce mesme temps de Venize, où il avoit demeuré durant son bannissement.

Le Roy tres Chrestien, ayant eu advis de ce qui se passoit entre le Roy d'Angleterre et le Regent d'Escosse, en[5] demeura fort malcontant ; et pour ce[6] avec la meilleure dilligence qu'il peust il dépescha en Escosse le comte de Lenox, qui avoit esté nourry en France et l'avoit servy aux guerres d'Italie,[7] avec

---

[1] Que se debvoit tenir, cancelled.   [2] Nouveaux, an interlineation.
[3] Au dit parlement, cancelled.   [4] Ses, added above the line.
[5] Fust eu fort grand . . . . . peine, here cancelled.
[6] Originally, pour ce envoya.
[7] Et l'avoit servy aux guerres . . . . . d'Italie. La remonstrance . . . . que le Roy luy interlineation. Lennox's Italian service is not mentioned in the Latin original, nor in Lesley's translation. The former of these passages is an interlineation ; the second is apparently intended to become the heading of a chapter on the revision of the text.

lettres tant au Régent qu'aux principaux de la noblesse, par lesquelles Sa Majesté leur mandoit qu'ils n'eussent à rompre l'ancienne alliance qu'ils avoient avec la France ; demeurassent constans en leur foy et promesses, ne conclussent aucun accord avec l'Angloys, contre lesquels il leur offroit ses forces et moyens s'ils en avoient besoing.

Le comte arrivé, qu'il fust en Escosse[1] feist entendre sa charge à plusieurs, sans en avoir receu aucune favorable response ; et s'apercevant que le Régent avec plusieurs aultres estoient entièrement à la dévocion du Roy d'Angleterre, par l'advis du Cardinal de St André, du comte de Huntley et aultres[2] de ce party il se retira au quartier d'ouest vers la Royne mère, laquelle feist assembler tous les partizans de l'alliance de France pour donner ordre promptement à retirer la Royne sa fille d'entre les mains du Régent, qu'on soubçonnoit avoir délibéré la délivrer à l'Angloys. Et pour authoriser ceste entreprise il fust advisé que le comte de Lenox, comme le premier légitime prince du sang, prendroit la garde et tutelle de la jeune Royne contre le comte d'Aran, lequel ils alléguoient estre venu d'un second mariage non vallable ; et de là prevint une inimité tres grande entre les deux familles, qui dure encore aujourd'huy.

Au moys d'Aoust la Royne mère, ayant faict venir près de soy à Lythguo les comtes de Huntley, Lenox, Mont Rosse, Mountheyth, le Cardinal et aultres de mesme faction, se feist accompagner par eulx à Strivelingh, où elle amena sa fille, et furent depputez pour leur sauve[3] garde les seigneurs de Levingston, Flemingh, Erskyn et Ruthven. Le reste de la noblesse fust appellé pour assister aux cérémonies du coronement le moys de Septembre prochain, où le Cardinal et comte de Huntly persuaderènt le Régent de se trouver, comme il feist, y portant la corone,[4] mais non sans grand malcontantement des comtes d'Angus et Glencarne, des Seigneurs de Maxuel, Gray et quelques aultres, qui favorisoient le party d'Angle-

---

[1] Et ayant faict, the original reading.
[2] The words, fidelles subjects de la Royne, are here cancelled.
[3] Sauve, added above the line.
[4] Y portant la coronne, an interlineation.

terre ; lesquels ayant attiré[1] à eulx le comte de Lenox[2] le firent départer de Strivelingh soudainement après la coronement, où ledit comte de Lenox porta le sceptre.

Le chasteau d'Edanbourgh fust vers ce temps[3] surpris sur Piere Chreiton[4] par la pratique de l'abbé de Pesley, frère du[5] Régent, lequel y estant entré soubz prétexte d'amitié et conférence[6] s'y rendist le plus fort.

Le Roy d'Angleterre, adverty par les seigneurs de son party et par Raf Sadler, son ambassadeur, de l'inconvénient survenu pour la personne de la Royne, pour prévenir qu'elle ne fust transportée en France, manda soudainement au Régent et seigneurs du conseil qu'ils eussent a amener ladite Royne en son royaume, ne pouvant estre en aultre lieu plus seurement jusques à l'accomplissement du mariage entre eulx arresté.   Ce que luy ayant esté refusé, il envoya lord Thomas Wharton avec deux mil hommes ; et Lord Euers avec autant, pour se joindre au[7] Régent contre ses adversaires.   Mais la Royne douairiere travailla tellement avec les parties du Cardinal et du comte de Huntley qu'ils gaignérent à leur cordelle le Régent, lequel en ce faisant fust continué en sa régence.

Le Roy de France, pour ne perdre l'occasion que le pressoit de pourvoir à la rupture de la ligue passée entre les Escossoys et Angloys, dépescha les seigneurs de la Brosse, Menage, et Jacques Anort, en compagnie de Pierre Françoys Contareni, Patriarche de Venize, Nunce en Escosse pour le Pape Paul 3, et envoya par eulx environ soixante mil escuz avec grandes munitions[8] pour ayder ceulx de son party contre l'Angloys. Ilz arrivèrent en la bouche de la rivière de Cloyde avec cinq navires,[9] mais le comte de Lenox en ayant esté adverty enleva par ruse tout cest argent, et le retira pardevers luy au chasteau de Dumberton, ayant[10] pour satisfaire à la despense et entre-

[1] Originally attirerent ayant written in the margin.
[2] Soudain a se, cancelled.   [3] Entré, cancelled.
[4] Sur Piere Chreiton, an interlineation. The name does not occur in the Latin text.   [5] Gouverneur, cancelled.
[6] En chassa, cancelled.   [7] Originally gouverneur.
[8] Avec grands munitions, an interlineation.
[9] Ils arriverent . . . navires, an interlineation.
[10] Au chasteau de Dumberton ayant, an interlineation.

tienement des forces qu'il levoit de jour à aultre en intention
d'aller attaquer en bref le Régent, son principal ennemy.
La principalle occasion de malcontantement dudict seigneur
comte de Lenox estoit pour ce que, en un Parlement[1] tint à
Edimbourgh en présence du Nunce du Pape et des ambassadeurs de France, ledict comte d'Aran fust confirmé Régent
comme plus proche prince du sang, et que en ceste qualité la
corone luy fust baillée à porter au coronement. Ce que fust
faict par le Cardinal, parent dudict comte d'Aran, lequel gou-
vernoit entièrement toutes les afferes en ce temps là, de sorte
que ledict comte de Lenox, se voyant frustré de l'espérance
dont on l'avoit repeu jusques alors, escripvit au Roy de France
pour luy fere entendre la juste occasion qu'il avoit de se mal-
contanter et luy déclarer l'intention en laquelle il estoit
d'abandonner son service, comme il feist avant qu'il avoit eu
responce, et arriva avec toutes ses forces en Lyth[2] distant
d'un mil ou environ d'Edimbourgh, où estoit lors le Régent.
Mais accord, intervint entre eulx, et furent délivréz pour
ostages George Douglas pour son frère le comte d'Angus,[3]
pour le comte de Glencarne, son père, son filz aisné, et l'abbé
de Cassaghole pour son frère, le comte de Cassils, qui de-
meurérent en la garde à eulx appoinctée par le dict Régent.

Le comte de Lenox vint trouver le Régent à Lislebourgh,
et après plusieurs promesses d'amitié confirmées par serment
d'une part et d'aultre, demeurèrent là près de six jours.
Mais tost après ledict comte de Lenox, allant de compagnie
avec ledict Régent à Lythguo se[4] desroba secrettement et se
retira à Glasguo, où il se[5] fortiffia et ayant laissé le conte
de Glencarne pour commander en l'armée là assemblée, il
s'en alla à Dumbertayne pour amasser de plus grandes forces.

Le Régent, ayant eu les nouvelles du département et dé-
portement dudict comte de Lenox assembla les plus grandes
forces qu'il peust; et accompagné[6] de plusieurs de la no-

[1] Originally, en parlement où assister.
[2] Le Regent, cancelled.
[3] Originally, le jeune Glencarne pour.
[4] Originally, se departit.
[5] Se, added above the line. Le chasteaux et le clocher, cancelled.
[6] Originally, principaux.

blesse, spéciallement de my lord Boyd, duquel il se servoit
en ses plus secretz conseilz et afferes, tira droict à Glasguo.
A un mil près il trouva en teste ses ennemys lesquels il
rompist et meist en fuyte; demeurans sur le champs du party
dudict comte de Lenox[1] le filz dudict seigneur de Glencarne,
et le seigneur de Monipenis, cappitaine des gens de pied, avec
plusieurs aultres non signaléz. Le Régent, avec peu de perte
des siens, entra dedans la ville de Glasgo, où il se comporta
fort doucement à l'endroict des cytoyens, se contentant de
punir les principaux séditieux et rebelles par la perte et confiscacion de leurs biens.

Cest accident estourna merveilleusement le comte de Lenox,
et ce neantmoins ayant receu au chasteau de Dumbertayne le
comte de Glencarne et quelques aultres, qui s'estoient sauvéz de
la bataille, par leur persuasion il fortiffia de nouveau le
chasteau et le clocher de Glasgo, lesquels furent peu après
assiégéz par le Régent, et en fin à luy[2] renduz par ceulx qui
estoient dedans, desquels il feist pendre dix huit des principaux pour servir d'example à tous aultres.

Le comte de Lenox, se voyant fort bas de ses afferes,
dépescha le comte d'Angus et my lord Maxwel vers le Régent
pour traicter d'accord avecques luy; mais comme ils estoient
en conseil avec ledict Régent au convent[3] (monastère) des
Cordelliers, ilz furent secrettement emmenéz au chasteau
d'Hamilton; et depuis le comte d'Angus à Blaknes, où ilz
furent gardéz fort longuement en très grand hazard de leur vie.

Ledict comte de Lenox, ayant entendu l'emprisonnement
de ses envoyéz, et considérant le peu d'apparence qu 'il y avoit,
d'entrer en seure pacificacion selon le chemin qu 'il avoit com-
mancé à tenir, il dépescha vers le Roy d'Angleterre le comte
de Glencarne et un gentilhomme nommé Thomas l'Evesque,
pour luy offrir de sa part son service, requérir son ayde et le
mariage d'entre luy et Madame Marguerite Douglas, fille du
comte d'Angus et niepce dudict seigneur Roy; lequel (ayant
particulièrement entendu les doléances dudict Seigneur de

[1] Du party dudict Conte de Lenox, an interlineation.
[2] A luy, added above the line.
[3] Convent, written above monastère, and neither word cancelled.

Lenox, ses pretensions au gouvernement et tiltre de seconde personne en Escosse, avec le mauvais traictement qu'il se plaignoit avoir receu du party François) pensa se pouvoir servir de l'occasion présente pour se vanger du Régent, maintenant contre luy ledict Seigneur de Lenox. Ledict mariage et support requis furent enfin accordéz audict comte, et le traicté faict à Carlel[1] entre le seigneur Wharton au nom du Roy d'Angleterre et l'évesque de Cathenes, frère dudict comte, et le comte de Glencarne pour ledict seigneur de Lennox.

Cependant le Royne et ceulx de son[2] conseil advancèrent en ce qu'ilz pouvoient le party du duc, le voyans entièrement résolu à leur dévocion et pour luy complaire davantage en un parlement assemblé à Strivelingh ilz firent condamner le comte de Lenox du crime de Leyz Majesté et trahison, avec confiscacion de tous ses héritages. D'aultre part Jehan Steuwart, seigneur d'Aubigny, frère dudict comte de Lenox, fust mis en prison en France par le commandement du Roy, et privé de tous ses estatz, tant de cappitaine des Gardes que des Cent Hommes d'Armes Escossoys, des ordonnances de sa Majesté très Chrestienne.

Je ne veulx oublier[3] que ledict Patriarche, Nunce de sa Saincteté, fust fort honorablement receu par la Royne et tous les seigneurs du pays, mesmement par le comte de Murray[4] oncle bastard de la jeune Royne, lequel en un banquet qu'il feist audict patriarche de Venize, feist charger un grand buffet de toutes sortes de vases de cristal de Venize, ou de Muray,[5] quelque le lieu où il se feit, donnant charge à un de ses sommeilliers qu'il feist renverser ledict buffet après le premier service, ce qu 'estant advenu, et toute la compagnie fort déplaisante de tel accident, soudainement le buffet fust

[1] A Carlel, interlined.
[2] Party cancelled. Conseil, written above.
[3] A remantenir, cancelled.
[4] Frère bastard, cancelled.
[5] Glass manufactured in the island of Murano, near Venice. "The glass manufactures of Murano were the most renowned in Europe, not only during the middle ages but even until the beginning of the present century. Mirrors, flasks, drinking cups, and an infinite variety of small articles for which Venice was so celebrated, were made here."

rechargé d'aultres vases plus beaux et en plus grand quantité, avec grand admiracion dudict Patriarche, lequel fust les jours ensuyvans servy de vaisselle d'or et d'argent doré en très grande quantité. Ledit seigneur comte estoit seigneur de fort grande prudence, sincérité et expérience, ayant esté employé en plusieurs importans ambassades avec grande réputacion et heureux succèz. A la fin il mourut de la pierre en son chasteau de [1] . . . . .

Ledict Patriarche estoit depputé Légat à Latere durant son séjour en Escosse, et depuis il feist donner la mesme authorité au Cardinal de St André. L'occasion pour laquelle expressément il avoit esté envoyé estoit pour divertir les Escossoys de l'alliance de l'Angleterre, et par ce moyen obvier[2] au changement de l'ancienne relligion, ja abolie en Angleterre, avec l'entière ruine de tous les monastères.

Sur le printemps le Roy d'Angleterre, résolu d'obtenir par la force ce que par practiques il n'avoit peu gaigner, prépara jusques à deux cens vaisseaux bien équippéz pour descendre en Escosse, et ẏ feist embarquer dix mil hommes à Tynmouth soubz la conduicte du comte d'Herford et du seigneur Lisle. L'armée arriva à Forth, au dessoubz de Wendy Chasteau[3] un mille et demy au dessoubz de Leyth, environ le 3 de May, et print terre au Havre Neuf.

Le Régent, estant lors à Edimbourgh, ayant entendu l'arrivée de l'armée Angloise, leur alla au devant avec quelques légères forces ; mais congnoissant qu'il n'estoit pour leur résister, il se retira et envoya Mr Adam Otterburn, Prévost d'Edimbourgh, et deux des baillifs vers le comte d'Herford pour luy demander la cause de sa venue, et luy offrir de réparer toute injure, si aucune il prétende avoir esté faict au Roy son maistre ; l'admonestant en procedder par voye de douceur plustost qu'aultrement.

Ledict seigneur comte respondoit n'avoir aucune charge

---

[1] Tarnoway, mentioned in Lesley's Latin Text, p. 155, and p. 179 of the Scottish translation.

[2] Obvier que la, originally.

[3] Au dessoubz de Wendy Chasteau, an interlineation. The embarcation of the English troops at Tynemouth and their disembarcation at Wendy Castle are facts added by Nau to Lesley's history.

d'entrer en quelconque appoinctement, mais de vanger la faulseté
et rupture des promesses faictes par aucuns au Roy, son
maistre, mesmement pour la délivrance de la jeune Royne ;
laquelle il demandoit luy estre mise en main, pour la transporter en Angleterre ; qu'aultrement il estoit déliberé de
mectre à feu et à sang Edimbourg et toutes les aultres villes
de l'Escosse ; commandant pour ceste occasion aux habitans de
se venir soubzmectre à luy comme lieutenant général du Roy
d'Angleterre pour en fere à son bon plaisir.

Le Prévost respondoit que les Escossoys estoient résoluz
d'endurer plustost toutes extrémitéz que de patir une si injuste condition, et làdessoubz se retira en la ville. Le Régent
informé de la response faicte par ledict comte d'Herfort,
ayant faict fortiffier le chasteau d'Edimbourgh, se retira à
Strivelingh.

Les forces Angloyses, demeurèrent toute la nuit au Leyth,
et le lendemain s'estans joinctz à six mille hommes de cheval,
qui estoient venuz de Berwick souz le commandement de sir
my lord William Euer et son filz,[1] prindrent leur chemin à Lislebourg de costé de Canigatte, où ilz furent arrestéz[2] par quelques
Escossoys, de sorte qu'après quelques escarmouches ils se retirèrent sur la nuit en leur camp auprès de Lyth. Le jour
prochain ensuyvant, avec toute l'armée marchant en bataille et
toutes leur artillerie, ilz vinrent à Edimbourgh, où ilz entrèrent
sans aucune résistance, et là ayant l'intention de planter leurdite
artillerie pour assiéger le chasteau, le cappitaine Stenhouse,
qui estoit dedans, le chargea si rudement de coups de canon
qu'il les contraignoit de se retirer, en laissant sur la place
plus de sept ou huit cens des leur ; en revanche de quoy
ilz meirent le feu dans le ville, pillans et saccageans tout le
plat pays.

En ce temps le Regent[3] meist en liberté le d'comte Angus,
my lord Maxwel, Mr de Glencarne,[4] sir George Douglas, et
quelques aultres de leur faction ; s'assemblant les plus grandes

---

[1] Soubz le . . . . . et son fils, an interlineation, added by Nau to
Lesley's Latin text.

[2] Assailléz, cancelled.   [3] Originally, gouerneur.

[4] Glencarne's name does not occur in the Latin text, but is given in
Lesley's translation, p. 182.

forces qu'il peust pour chasser les Angloys hors de leur royaume, comme il feist. Car vers le 14 de May les Angloys, emmenans avec eulx la Salemandre et la Licorne,[1] après avoir bruslé et pillé tout ce qu'ils avoient peu, séparans leur forces en renvoyèrent une partye par mer et l'aultre par terre, qui ne fust sans avoir continuellement les Escossoys à la queu, et avec diverses escarmouches. Le conte de Lenox avoit aussi une armée dans le pays à la dévocion desdicts Angloys.

Les Escossois sauvages[2] avoient jà monstré leur naturel inconstant et cruel ; car ceulx qui du règne de Jacques 5 estoient assubjectéz aux loix se comportoient paisiblement, et payoient leur cens[3] et arrentemens sans aucune contradiction, vivans soubz un Roy[4] grand justicier, dès aussitost qu'ilz veirent le pays en combustion par les factions et partialitéz des nobles, ilz commencèrent de mesme à courir par tout licentieusement, saccageant et pillant tout ce qui se trouvoit à leur rencontre. A quoy pour obvier et refréner une telle audace, le Gouverneur depputa le comte de Arguil en son pays, et les adjacens et le comte de Huntley au quartier du north, et aux iles d'Orcade et Shetland. Ledict comte ne faillist d'assembler soudainement ses forces, et avec la meilleure dilligence qu'il peust aprocha de l'assemblée des . . . . . .[5] joinctz et confidenz ensemble, lesquels s'enfuyrent[6] avant que voir l'ennemy, et laissèrent les maisons des seigneurs de Grant et Lovet, qu'ils avoient auparavent occupées. Ledict seigneur comte ne peust suyvre les fuyans, d'autant que le pays où ils estoient retiréz est fort marescageux et montagneux, les chemins y estans difficilles, mesmement pour une armée.

Le seigneur Lovet tirant vers sa maison, rencontra ses ennemys en teste, et se trouvèrent si près les uns des aultres que de tous les deux costéz on fust contrainct de venir aux mains, après avoir combattu quelques temps avec l'arc et les flesches. Le combat dura jusques à la nuit, et y fust faict

---

[1] Emmenans avec eulx. In the manuscript as originally written the text was somewhat differently arranged, but it is here restored to the directions finally marked by the author. [2] Boudouilliers, cancelled.

[3] Rectes, cancelled. [4] Roy juste, originally.

[5] " Against the Glenchameron and Glenronell, Mudyard and Kundyard," in *Lesley's Vernacular*, p. 184, names which Nau did not venture to encounter. [6] Originally, promptement.

tel carnage d'une part et de l'autre qu'on ne peust scavoir
à qui la victoire estoit demeurée jusques au lendemain matin
en recongnoissant le nombre de ceulx qui avoient esté tuez.

Du costé des . . . . .[1] plusieurs furent emblessés, mais[2]
plus de 3000[3] manquèrent du costé des Frassars dessoubz
ledit Seigneur Lovet, jeune gentilhomme, nourry aux escoles en
France, estoit chef. Et comme quasi tous ceulx de ce surnom furent tués en ceste rencontre, aussi Dieu voulust que
les femmes des décédéz se trouvent toutes grosses de filz, de
sorte que la famille se remist sus par ce moyen.

Le comte de Huntly porta fort à regret ceste desfaicte des Frais-
sars, et pour les vanger assembla telles forces que, demeurant
maistre de la compagne, il print Euen Allanson et Renauld,
ausquels il feist trancher la teste ; punissant les aultres selon
la sévérité des lois ; et à la fin[4] remist tout ce quartier la en
bonne paix par sa prudence et bon debvoir. Le comte
d'Arghil n'y procedda pas moins sagement en ce que luy
estoit ordonné, mais il trouva les afferes plus heureusement dis-
posées à son intention. Car devant que frapper coup les
rebelles se vindrent rendre à luy et avec ostages promecterent
de vivre[5] doresnavant en paix et tranquillité.

Vers la fin de Penthécouste le comte de Lenox, l'évesque de
Cathnes et quelques[6] aultres seigneurs et gentilhommes de leur
compagnie, suyvirent le camp des Angloys, et estans arrivés
avec le vent fort favorable à West Chester ; furent receus par
le comte de Shrewsbury, qui les feist conduire fort honorablement à la Court : où estans le comte de Lenox environ la St
Jehan [24th June] espousa[7] Mad. Marguerite, niepce du Roy,
qui luy donna pour son dot l'abbaye de St Servius[8] avec quelque aultre bien, promectant à son mary de le restablir en[9] ce
que luy appartient en Escosse.

[1] The Glencamerons and others are again omitted by Nau.
[2] Originally, il mourut.   [3] A mistake for 300.
[4] Reduisit, originally.   [5] De vivre, added above the line.
[6] Originally, plusieurs.   [7] Originally, espousa la niepce du Roy.
[8] The correct reading is Jervois, or Joreval, a Cistercian abbey in Yorkshire. The last abbot was hanged in June 1537, for opposing the measures of Henry VIII., by whom the site was granted to Matthew earl of
Lennox and Margaret his wife.—See Dugdale's Monast. v. 567.
[9] En ses biens, cancelled.

MEMORIALS OF THE STATE AND PROGRESS OF EVENTS IN SCOTLAND DURING THE REIGN OF MARY STEWART.

In the year 1542, on Friday, December 7, being the Vigil of the Conception of our Lady, Mary Stewart, daughter of James the Fifth, King of Scotland, was born in the town of Lythcow, in the country of Scotland.

On December 14, in the same year 1542, James V., King of Scotland, aged thirty-three years, died in Falkland Castle, in the county of Fife, which he had built.

Cardinal Beaton, Archbishop of St Andrews, seeing that the affairs of the realm were in a bad state, by reason of the king's death, so arranged matters with the French faction, of which he was a partisan, that the regency devolved upon him. He associated with himself the earls of Moray (a base brother of the late king), Argyll, and Huntley; making no mention of the earls of Lennox and Arran, who were the nearest heirs to the crown.

On . . . of . . . in the year . . . the Queen was crowned in the town of Stirling. The Earl of Arran, the Governor, carried the Crown, and the Earl of Lennox the Sceptre. King Edward VI. sought the Queen of Scotland in marriage.

In 1547, King Henry II., shortly after his accession to the crown of France, sent into Scotland the Sr. de Strossi, prior of Capua, with sixteen ships, well manned, and provided with munitions of all kinds. He came to re-establish the affairs of Scotland, which had fallen into great disorder in consequence of the death of the late Cardinal Beaton, who, in the course of the previous year, had been murdered in his archiepiscopal palace of St Andrews. Immediately upon his arrival in Scotland, Strossi laid siege to the said town of St Andrews, then held by the enemies and the murderers of the Cardinal, and within fourteen days (viz., 29th July 1547) he made himself master of both town and castle. He sent the said assassins into France, among whom was Norman Lesley, the originator of the crime, who was afterwards killed at the battle of Renty, near Montreuil-sur-Mer (11th October 1554), where he commanded a troop of one hundred light horse.

On 10th September 1547, a battle between the English and the Scotch, under the command of James Hamilton, Earl of Arran, was fought near the town of   . The English gained the victory, and George Gordon, Earl of Huntley, was taken prisoner.

In the month of May 1548, Henry II., King of France, sent into Scotland the Lord d'Essay, a knight of his order, with four gallies, under the conduct of Nicolas de Villegaignon, Knight of the Order of St John of Jerusalem. Immediately upon their arrival they retook l'Isle de Chevaux [Inchkeith], between Leith and Kinghorn, which had been occupied by the English.

On 20th February 1550 the Sieur de Thermes, Knight of the King's Order, took the fortress of Borthycraig, in Scotland, and killed all the English whom he found in it.

On 17th September 1550 the Queen Dowager of Scotland, daughter of the Duke of Guise, arrived in France, to which she had been summoned by King Henry II. She was attended by the Earl of Huntley, and many other Scottish lords.

Mary Queen of England, daughter of Henry VIII. and of Catherine, daughter of the King of Aragon (who had been repudiated by the king her husband), succeeded about the same time to the crown by the death of Edward VI. Edward's death occasioned great troubles in England for the succession to the crown; for the greater number of the Council, won over to the party of the Duke of Northumberland, declared in favour of Queen Jane, daughter of the Duke of Suffolk, and wife of the Duke of Northumberland's eldest son, of the surname of Dudley. At length, however, by the common consent of the nobility, Mary was crowned Queen; Anne Boulen, the mother of Queen Elizabeth, now upon the throne, having been convicted of adultery during the life of her husband, in consequence was beheaded.

In the month of December 1558 the Queen Dowager assembled a Parliament at Edinburgh, in which, by the consent of the Estates, were chosen certain Ambassadors, viz., James Beton, Archbishop of Glasgow, Robert Read, Bishop of Orkney, and first President of the Senate of Scotland (who died at Dieppe on 16th September following, as he was returning home), George Lesley, Earl of Rothes, Gilbert Kennedy, Earl of Casselis, James Stewart, Prior of St Andrews, who afterwards was Earl of Moray, George, Lord Seton, James, Lord Fleming, and John Erskine, Baron of Dun. They were Ambassadors deputed to the king to contract and solemnise a marriage between Mary their queen, and Francis Dauphin of France, respecting which they were provided with ample instructions.

They set out in the month of February next following; and after having been tossed about at sea for a long time, so that many of their vessels were wrecked, they reached France, and in the month of March were received at Fontainbleau. The contract of marriage was dated at Paris on . . . April 1558. A league was made between the estates of Scotland and France; and a dowery of 60,000 livres, from the comté of Ponthieu county and duchy of Touraine, was assigned to the queen, a pension of 20,000 livres.

Mary, Queen of England, died 17th November 1559, to whom succeeded her sister Elizabeth, although she had been declared a bastard during the lifetime of her father, and by his orders. But the new religion, of which she had made profession before the reign of her sister, much strengthened her party.

When the Queen of Scotland heard of the death of her good sister and cousin, she put on mourning, which she wore for six weeks as the relative and next heir of the deceased queen, to whom by right she ought to succeed. She was ordered by the king, her husband, to assume the arms of England, which were added to those of France and Scotland, which afterwards was the occasion of great disputes between these two queens.

. . . . His illness was an imposthume . . . . . great trance for two days before his death. The queen kept her chamber for forty days, during which she was visited by the king, queen, prince, [and the ambassadors] of foreign princes, among others by the ambassador of England . . . many became exceedingly jealous, fearing a marriage between the eldest son of the King of Spain and "the White Queen." . . . The Cardinal of Lorraine, her uncle, could not . . . . which should follow immediately after the death. . . . For presently the Admiral and those of his faction . . . . and strengthening their party day by day . . . . with those who desired the entire government of affairs . . . always possessed it, gave these a check . . . who at length voluntarily banished themselves from the court . . . "the White Queen" noticing the indignities

which were . . . and the behaviour of her enemies . . .
retired with them to Nancy.

Her departure still further increased the suspicion . . .
mother, who immediately sent to seek her with so much
. . . the good will this young queen, . . . which was
less . . . great occasion to . . . Scotland, to which
she had been called, by the . . . came to visit her
shortly after the death of her husband . . . thought
about her departure, saying that it . . . [was more]
becoming to be the first person in her own kingdom than
second [in that of any] other person, chiefly as matters
then stood . . . of Guise, his brother, was clearly of the
contrary opinion, saying that . . . like a sheep in the
jaws of the wolves. On account of . . . which were in
Scotland . . . with the said D'Oysel . . . Blanche" asked
for an audience with her . . . matter of importance regarding the passage of . . . He at once pointed out the
. . . queen his mistress to continue displeased . . . taken
the style and the arms of the Queen of England against
. . . natural succession, and that unless she laid them
down she need not expect any friendship . . . In short,
it was necessary for her to grant certain . . . she might
assure herself of having a free passage into Scotland.

"The White Queen" promptly answered that she had
assumed the arms of England after the death of . . . and
that she had done this by the orders of the late king,
her husband, in obedience to the advice of her counsel,
and with the general consent of Scotland, without
which, as this was a matter of . . . common good of the
realm of Scotland, she would not . . . in this business.

In respect to the passage she had asked . . . of England, her good sister and cousin, for the countries . . .
would own only that she had power . . . of the sea was
free to every one, so that she determined . . . into

Scotland by that way, hoping to cross, despite the obstacles which they might attempt to interpose.

. . . gave . . . which happened . . . speedily some . . . to meet the Queen of Scotland. But the fog . . . so that the one could not see the other . . . the English returned, to their great disgrace. The Scottish ships came so near the English coast . . . and many of the company spoke to the persons on shore.

. . . general in Scotland for the late king . . . to ask leave to go through her kingdom, which the said queen absolutely refused . . . to pass into Scotland, where he likewise had been . . . to remove from Scotland what yet remained there of the forces, or to place in the hands of the natives of Scotland, the fortified places which they (the French) held.

The queen was accompanied from Paris to Calais, by the Duke D'Aumale, the Marquis D'Elboeuf, and the Grand Prior . . . D'Anville, the Duke de Nemours, and a great party of the nobles of France, and they journeyed with a great number of gentlemen into Scotland, where they remained for some months. The whole company crossed over in two galleys and two . . . the weather and the wind were in their favour, so that they went from Calais to Leith, which was the nineteenth of August . . . eight o'clock in the morning.

The queen was received there by the Lord of Holyrood, her . . . with a good number of the gentlemen of the neighbouring country, and the inhabitants . . . chief town of the kingdom.

The Lord of Holyrood entertained her and her suit at dinner in the Abbey of Holyrood, waiting until the queen's house should be ready, for which no order had been given ; although, indeed, she had arrived very unexpectedly . . . chiefly by the rebels and turbulent followers of the new religion.

Four or five days after the arrival of the queen in Edinburgh, the Duke of Châtelherault, the Earl of Argyll, the Prior of St Andrews (bastard of the late King James V.), with many other gentlemen of their party and creed, were very urgent with the queen that before doing anything else, she should decree that the state of affairs and their religious matters should continue exactly as they had been already established. As the members of the counsel were of this way of thinking, it was easy for them, by their common advice and resolution, to cause the queen to give her approval of a certain act upon this matter already drawn up for her acceptance. It provided that, in order to avoid the troubles which hereupon might ensue, no person howsoever should, directly or indirectly, make any innovation in the religion received in the kingdom. It was also forbidden, under heavy penalties, to attempt anything in public or private to the contrary.

The queen having protested that of the two she would rather lose her Crown than the exercise of her religion, an exception was made in her favour. She was allowed to have solemn High Mass daily in her chapel, and might there cause Divine Service to be celebrated according to the form of the Catholic Apostolic and Roman Church, with permission for all her subjects to assist thereat, who had not made a profession of faith to the contrary. The canons of the Chapel Royal of Stirling were also allowed to celebrate the Divine Service, as above, in the queen's absence.

Notwithstanding this first agreement passed in council, on the following Sunday, Lord Lindsay, sword in hand, accompanied by some other seditious people of opinions like his own, came to seek the queen's chaplain in the chapel, and drove him from the altar with great tumult and con-

fusion.   The chaplain took refuge in the sacristy ; seeing
which Lindsay scandalously overthrew all the ornaments
which were in the chapel.   When the queen heard of
this, following the advice which she received thereupon,
she caused the lords to be assembled, and ordered them to
check such insolences, which greatly hindered the
establishment of peace.

Shortly afterwards twelve lords and one bishop were
chosen to be the queen's Privy Council, who should have
the entire management of affairs, and by whose advice
the queen should govern according to circumstances. Of
these, six should be officers of the crown, viz., the
Chancellor, Great Treasurer, Secretary, Controller, and
others ; and these should continually reside near the
queen :

The Duke of Châtelherault.

The Earl of Huntley, Chancellor.

The Earl of Argyll, Grand Steward.

The Earl of Athol.

The Earl Marshall, of the surname of Keith.

The Earl of Glencarne.

The Earl of Morton.

The Earl of Montrose.

The Earl of Errol, Constable.

Mr Henry Sinclair, Bishop of Ross.

James Steward, bastard, Prior of St. Andrew's.

The Lord Erskine.

Mr Robert Richardson was continued in his office of
Grand Treasurer.

The laird of Lethington, William Maitland, Secretary
to the Crown.

Thomas Graham, Controller of the kingdom, much
respected ; a very good man and a good Catholic.

SKETCH OF THE HISTORY OF SCOTLAND DURING THE MINORITY OF QUEEN MARY STEWART.[1]

Upon the death of James the Fifth, Mary, his only daughter and heir, succeeded to the throne on 18th December 1542, being then but seven days old. At that time she was in the castle of Linlithgow, under the charge of the queen, her mother, who found herself in great difficulties, by reason as well of the feuds and factions which had sprung up of late regarding the government of the realm, as for the custody of the young queen. This caused the coronation to be delayed until the month of August following. In the meantime the Earl of Arran was declared to be the governor of the kingdom and the protector of the queen, in accordance with the laws and custom of the country. The regency was proclaimed in Edinburgh, notwithstanding the opposition made by the Cardinal of St Andrews and certain others, who affirmed that the late deceased king by his will had appointed four administrators of the realm during the minority of his daughter. The regent entering on his office took possession of the palace of Holyrood and the castle of Falkland, and having in his hands the treasury of the crown, he compelled the treasurers, the controller, and the other officers of State to render an account of their charges. Some of them he continued still in office ; others he discharged. Provision was further made as well for the custody of the queen's person as for the ordinary expenditure of the household, so that no representative of the queen-

[1] From Nau's Original French, given at p. 308.

mother, devoted to her interests, could be admitted near the queen except Lord Levingston.

Hereupon the King of England, taking note of the opportunity that presented itself for uniting the two kingdoms of the Isle of Britain by the marriage of his son, then but five years old, with the Queen of Scotland, decided to put this project into execution. By way of taking the first steps he privately communicated his design to the Earls of Cassilis and Glencarne, to the Lords Maxwell, Fleming, and Gray, and to certain other Scottish lords and gentlemen, then held prisoners in his kingdom. He pointed out to them the good that might result to the whole island from this marriage, and the measures which it would be well to take for the custody of their queen until the accomplishment of the plan. When he found that the said lords were inclined of themselves to this arrangement (hoping thereby to obtain their liberty), he sent them into Scotland to commence negotiations. With the same object he sent the Earl of Angus and George Douglas to the regent, who were provided with letters strongly urging him to reinstate the said exiles in their possessions and dignities.

When the regent had been made fully aware, by the persons aforesaid, of the purpose of the King of England, he summoned the principal nobility to meet him on 27th February, and he announced that parliament should meet in the ensuing month to take some resolution on the overtures that had been made to them. But by way of preventing the cardinal from crossing them in this matter, they held him prisoner for some time at Dalkeith, and afterwards in the castle of St Andrews, where Lord Seton was appointed to guard him. Here-upon all the priests of the diocese of St Andrews ceased to celebrate the Divine service. From this time the

Catholic religion began to decline in Scotland under the adverse influence of the regent, who was persuaded thereto partly by those who were lately returned from England, and partly by the discourses of a certain Jacobin, who declaimed as well against the authority of the Pope, as also against several other rules of the Church, permitting every one to read the English version of the Bible, and to choose such prayers as he pleased.

In order to advance his purpose and further the decision which was to be taken upon it in the Scottish Parliament, the King of England sent thither, as ambassador, Sir Ralph Sadler, knight. His presence, joined to the influence of the nobles who had lately been restored, led to the conclusion of the marriage at the said parliament. A truce for ten years was agreed upon between the two realms by the common consent of the Estates, which the King of England afterwards confirmed by his letters patent, dated on 1st August, and delivered to the ambassadors sent to him, namely, the Earl of Glencarne, George Douglas, William Hamilton, and James Learmonth, knights. On their return, as those of that party thought their success assured, the cardinal was set at liberty; and the Earl of Angus, George Douglas, the Lord of Glamis, heir of James Hamilton, and certain others were restored to their property and honours by the parliament.

John Hamilton, the regent's brother, as he was returning from France, where he had studied for a long time, visited the King of England, by whom he was very courteously welcomed, as were also the many learned men by whom he was accompanied. Immediately on his arrival in Scotland he was appointed Treasurer, an office which he filled with very great reputation as long as his brother continued to be regent, aiding him with his advice in the management of all his affairs.

About this time the Earl of Bothwell returned from Venice, where he had resided during his banishment.

When the Most Christian King was advised of these dealings between the King of England and the Regent of Scotland, he was much displeased, and with all possible haste he sent the Earl of Lennox into Scotland, who had been brought up in France, and had served in the Italian wars. He was the bearer of letters not only to the regent but also to the chief nobility, in which his Majesty told them not to break the ancient alliance which they had with France, but to remain constant to their faith and their promises, and to abstain from concluding any treaty with the English, against whom he offered them his men and money, should they be needed.

On his arrival in Scotland, the earl explained to several persons the objects of his mission. Receiving no encouragement, and perceiving that the regent, with many others, was entirely devoted to the King of England, he acted upon the advice of the Cardinal of St Andrews and the Earl of Huntly, and of others of that party, and retired to the western parts to join the queen-mother, who assembled all who favoured the French alliance, with a view of taking prompt measures for withdrawing the queen, her daughter, out of the hands of the regent, as he was suspected of an intention to deliver her to the English. To give weight to this conclusion it was decided that the Earl of Lennox, as the first lawful prince of the blood, should take on himself the custody and protection of the young queen against the Earl of Arran, who, as they alleged, was come of a second and irregular marriage. Hence sprung a deadly feud between the two families, which endures even to the present day.

In the month of August the queen-mother, having

summoned the Earls of Huntly, Lennox, Montrose, and Monteith, the cardinal, and others of the same party, to meet her at Linlithgow, went with them to Stirling, taking her daughter with her. Lords Levingston, Fleming, Erskine, and Ruthven were appointed guardians. The rest of the nobles were summoned to assist at the ceremonies of the coronation in the month of September following, at which the cardinal and the Earl of Huntly persuaded the regent to be present. He came, and carried the crown, whereby the Earls of Angus and Glencarne, the Lords Maxwell, Gray, and a few others, who favoured the English faction, were greatly offended. These latter having drawn the Earl of Lennox to their side, caused him to leave Stirling abruptly after the coronation, at which he had carried the sceptre.

The castle of Edinburgh was surprised at this time and taken from Peter Christon by the treachery of the Abbot of Paisley, the regent's brother, who having gained admission under pretence of a friendly conference, made himself master of it.

The King of England, being informed by the nobles of his own party, and by his ambassador, Sir Ralph Sadler, of the mischance which had happened as regards the custody of the queen, in order to prevent her removal into France instantly directed the regent and Lords of the Council to bring the said queen into his realm, seeing that she could nowhere be in greater safety until the accomplishment of the marriage agreed upon between them. This request being rejected, he sent Lord Thomas Wharton with two thousand men, and Lord Evers, with as many more, to act with the regent against his opponents. But the queen dowager so managed with the parties of the cardinal and the Earl of Huntly, that they won over to their side the regent himself who thereupon obtained a confirmation of his regency.

In order not to lose the opportunity which presented itself for bringing about the rupture of the league which had been made between the Scots and the English, the King of France despatched M. de la Brosse, M. Menage, and James Anort, accompanied by Pierre Francis Contareni, Patriarch of Venice, nuncio in Scotland for Pope Paul the Third. They were the bearers of about sixty thousand crowns and a large store of ammunition to help his party against the English. Their five ships arrived safely in the mouth of the Clyde; but the Earl of Lennox having been apprised of it, contrived to carry off the whole of the money by stratagem, and took it with him to his castle of Dumbarton, having to meet the expense and maintenance of the troops which he was raising from day to day with the view of shortly setting out to attack his principal adversary, the regent. The chief origin of Lennox's hostility was this: that in a parliament held at Edinburgh, in presence of the pope's nuncio and the ambassadors of France, the said Earl of Arran had been confirmed in the regency as the nearest prince of the blood, and in this character had been appointed to carry the crown at the coronation. All this was brought about by the cardinal, who was nearly related to the said Earl of Arran, and at this time absolutely ruled all the affairs of the kingdom. The Earl of Lennox seeing himself cheated of the hopes with which they had amused him so far, wrote to the King of France, giving him to understand the just cause he had for discontent, and to inform him of his intention of quitting his service, which he did before receiving an answer. He arrived with all his forces at Leith, about a mile from Edinburgh, where the regent then was. Matters, however, were arranged between them, and there were handed over as hostages George Douglas for his brother, the Earl of Angus, for the Earl of Glencarne, his eldest son, and the Abbot of Crossraguel for his brother the Earl of Cassilis, who remained thenceforth in the custody appointed for them by the regent.

The Earl of Lennox came to visit the regent at Edinburgh, and after many promises of friendship, confirmed by oath on either side, they remained there nearly six days. But shortly after, the said Earl of Lennox having gone to Linlithgow in company with the regent, secretly withdrew and retired to Glasgow, where he fortified himself. Then he left the Earl of Glencarne in command of the army there assembled, and went himself to Dumbarton to collect greater forces.

The regent being informed of the departure and behaviour of the said Earl of Lennox, collected all the forces he could, and accompanied by many of the nobility, and especially by Lord Boyd, whom he employed in his most secret councils and affairs, he marched straight to Glasgow. About a mile from there he found the enemy awaiting him, whom he defeated and put to flight. Of the partizans of the Earl of Lennox there were left on the field the son of the said Earl of Glencarne, and Lord Monipenny, captain of infantry, together with many others not noted. The regent having lost few of his men, entered the town of Glasgow, and behaved with great consideration towards the inhabitants, contenting himself with punishing the leaders of the sedition and revolt by the loss and confiscation of their goods.

This mishap signally disturbed the plans of the Earl of Lennox, but nevertheless, having received the Earl of Glencarne and some others who had escaped from the battle into his castle of Dumbarton, he fortified anew, by their advice, the castle and belfry of Glasgow, which were soon afterwards besieged by the regent, and at last surrendered to him by those who held them, of whom he caused eighteen of the principal men to be hanged, to serve as an example to all others.

The Earl of Lennox, seeing that his affairs were in a desperate condition, despatched the Earl of Angus and Lord Maxwell to meet the regent, to treat of an agreement with him ; but when they were in council with the said regent in the convent (or monastery) of the Grey Friars they were secretly carried off to the castle of Hamilton. Afterwards the Earl of Angus was removed to Blackness, and they were both kept a long time in very great peril of their lives.

The said Earl of Lennox having heard of the imprisonment of his envoys, and taking into consideration the small appearance that there was of securing peace by the course he was pursuing, sent the Earl of Glencarne and a gentleman named Thomas Bishop to the King of England to offer him his services, and to ask in return the king's assistance and a marriage with Lady Margaret Douglas, daughter of the Earl of Angus, and niece of the said king. Having fully heard the grievances of the said Earl of Lennox, his pretensions to the government and to the title of the second personage in Scotland, together with the bad treatment he complained of having received from the French party, the king thought he might avail himself of this present opportunity to avenge himself on the regent, by maintaining the Earl of Lennox against him.   The said marriage and required assistance were accordingly conceded to the earl, and the treaty was concluded at Carlisle between Lord Wharton in the name of the King of England, and on the part of the Earl of Lennox by his brother the Bishop of Caithness, and the Earl of Glencarne.

In the meantime the queen and her advisers did their utmost to advance the duke's party, seeing he was entirely devoted to their service ; and in order to please him still more, they had the Earl of Lennox condemned for lesemajesty and treason, in a parliament held at Stirling, confiscating all his inheritances.   Moreover, John Stewart, Seigneur d'Aubigny, brother of the said Earl of Lennox, was put in prison in France, by command of the king, and deprived of all his appointments, that of captain of the guards, as well as of the command of the hundred Scottish men-at-arms at the orders of His Most Christian Majesty.

I must not omit to mention that the patriarch nuncio of his holiness was very honourably received by the queen and all the nobles of the country, especially by the Earl of Moray, bastard uncle to the young queen ; who, at a banquet which he gave to the said patriarch of Venice, had a large sideboard charged with all kinds of vases of glass of Venice, or from Murano, or from any other place where it was made, giving orders to one of his butlers that he should upset the said sideboard after the first course.   This having happened, all the company was much troubled at such an accident ; but the sideboard was speedily again filled with other vases more beautiful and more numerous than at first, to the great admiration of the patriarch, who on the following days was served on a great quantity of gold and silver gilt plate.   The said earl was a nobleman of very great prudence, sincerity, and experience, having been employed on several important embassies with great credit and happy success.   He at last died of stone in his castle of (Tarnoway).

The said patriarch was deputed legate à latere during his stay in Scotland, which authority he afterwards caused to be conferred on the Cardinal of St Andrews. The purpose for which he had been especially sent was to prevent the alliance between the Scotch and English, and so avoid the change of the old religion, already abolished in England, together with the entire ruin of all the monasteries.

In the spring, the King of England determined to obtain by force what he had been unable to gain by intrigue. He prepared as many as two hundred well equipped vessels to make a descent on Scotland, and embarked ten thousand men at Tynemouth under the command of the Earl of Hertford and Lord Lisle. The army arrived at the Forth below Wendy Castle, a mile and a half above Leith, about the 3rd of May, and landed at Newhaven.

The regent, being then at Edinburgh, hearing of the arrival of the English army went to meet them with a few light troops, but becoming aware that he was not able to face them, he retired and sent Mr Adam Otterburn, provost of Edinburgh, and two of the baillies to the Earl of Hertford to ask the cause of his coming, and to offer to repair all injuries, should he say that any such had been offered to the king, his master; admonishing him to proceed in the matter by the way of conciliation rather than by force.

The said earl answered that he had no commission to come to any agreement, but to punish the treachery and the breach of the promises made by certain persons to the king, his master, concerning the deliverance of the young queen, whom he demanded to have placed in his hands, in order to carry her into England; and that otherwise he was determined to put Edinburgh and all the other towns in Scotland to fire and the sword. In the meantime he ordered the inhabitants to come and make their submission to him, as lieutenant-general of the King of England, to be disposed of according to his good pleasure.

The provost answered that the Scotch were resolved to suffer any extremity rather than submit to so unjust a condition, and thereupon he retired into the town. The regent being informed of the answer given by the Earl of Hertford, fortified the castle of Edinburgh, and withdrew to Stirling.

The English forces remained all the night at Leith, and next day, being joined by six thousand horsemen who had come from Berwick under the command of Lord William Euer and his son, took the road to Edinburgh by the way of the Canongate, where they were brought to a stand by some Scots, so that, after some skirmishing, they retired at night to their camp near Leith. The next day, with all the army marching in battle array, and with all their artillery, they came to Edinburgh, which they entered without any resistance, intending to put their artillery in position there for the siege of the castle. But Captain Stanhouse, who commanded within, attacked them so violently with his artillery that he forced them to retire, leaving seven or eight hundred of their company on the spot; to avenge which they set fire to the town, and sacked and pillaged all the open country.

About this time the regent set at liberty the Earl of Angus, Lord Maxwell, the Master of Glencarne, Sir George Douglas, and some others of their faction; and assembled all the forces he could to drive the English out of the kingdom, which he did. For about the 14th of May the English, after having burnt and pillaged as much as they were able, separated their forces and sent back one portion by sea, taking with them the *Salamander* and the *Unicorn*, and the other by land ; which was not accomplished without having the Scots continually upon their rear, and after many skirmishes.   The Earl of Lennox also had an army in the country at the disposal of the English.

Meanwhile the wild Scottish clans had already shown their inconstant and cruel disposition.   From the reign of James the Fifth, they had been subject to the laws, and had conducted themselves peaceably, and had paid their taxes and assessments without dispute, living under a king who was a great administrator of the law. But now, as soon as they saw the country aflame by the factions and feuds of the nobles, they also commenced to overrun it, everywhere lawlessly sacking and pillaging all that came in their way.   In order to hinder and restrain such audacity, the governor appointed, as deputies, the Earl of Argyll in his own country and the neighbourhood, and the Earl of Huntly in the north and the islands of Orkney and Shetland.   The latter earl did not fail to collect his forces at once, and with all the speed he could advanced against the gathering of the (highlanders,) who were united and confident in their union, but they fled before seeing the enemy, leaving the houses of the Lords Grant and Lovat, which they had previously occupied. The said earl could not follow the fugitives, inasmuch as the country to which they had withdrawn is very marshy and hilly, the roads there being very bad, especially for an army.

Lord Lovat, drawing towards his house, met his enemies face to face, and they found themselves so close together that both sides could not avoid coming to close combat, after having fought for some time with bows and arrows.   The battle lasted until night, with such terrible slaughter on both sides, that it could not be known with whom the victory rested until the following morning, when the number of those killed was ascertained.

Several were wounded on the (adverse side,) but more than three thousand of the Frasers were missing, besides the said Lord Lovat, a young gentleman brought up in the schools in France, who was their chief. Since almost all of the name were killed in this encounter, so God willed that the wives of the deceased found themselves all pregnant of sons, and by this means the clan recovered itself.

The Earl of Huntly greatly regretted this defeat of the Frasers, and to avenge them he assembled such forces that, remaining master of the country, he took Euen Allanson and Ronald prisoners, whom he caused to be beheaded, and punished the others according to the severity of the laws; and so in the end he reduced all that part of the country to good order by his prudence and conscientious discharge of his duty. The Earl of Argyll proceeded no less wisely in what had been appointed to him. But he found matters more fortunately arranged to his wishes, for before striking a blow the rebels came and surrendered themselves to him, giving hostages and promising to live henceforth in peace and tranquillity.

About the end of Whitsuntide the Earl of Lennox, the Bishop of Caithness, and some other nobles and gentlemen of their party followed the camp of the English, and having arrived with a favourable wind at West Chester, were received by the Earl of Shrewsbury, who conducted them with great honour to the Court. While they were there, the Earl of Lennox, about the feast of St John, married Lady Margaret, the niece of the king, who gave her the abbey of Jervois as a dowry, together with some other property, promising her husband to reinstate him in all that belonged to him in Scotland.

INDEX TO NAU'S NARRATIVE, AND
ILLUSTRATIVE DOCUMENTS.

letter to him, 189, 190 ; Bishop Chisholm sent to him, 198, 202, 210

Haddington, Mary at, 19, 44

Hamilton, 91, 92, 94, 167, 170, 171

Hamilton, the family of, support the queen, 43, 55, 92, 173 ; at Langside, 94 ; their title to the crown, 142, 143

Hamilton, Lord Claude, of the queen's party, 167, 172, 173 ; distinguishes himself at Langside, 92, 93, 94 ; visits Mary at Carlisle, 96

Hamilton, James, eldest son of the Duke of Châtelherault, returns from France to Scotland, 112 ; joins the reformers, 112

Hamilton, Sir James, at Langside, 93

Hamilton, James, of Ormiston ; see Ormiston

Hamilton, John, Archbishop of St Andrews, his early history, 330, 332; accompanies Mary to Edinburgh, 19 ; joins her at Hamilton, 167 ; opposes her going into England, 128, 129 ; his death, 133

Hamilton, Sir William, 330

Hay, Alexander, draws up the bond for Darnley's murder, 35

Henry VIII. of England, his dealings with Scotland, 321, 329, 330, 337

Henry II. of France, 320, 337

Hepburn, John, executed for the murder of Darnley, 150, 151

Herries, Sir John Maxwell, lord, 13 ; his character, 129 ; joins the queen, 167 ; his speech in parliament, 74, 75 ; at Langside, 92 ; opposes her going into England, 129 ; accompanies her to Carlisle, sent by her to Elizabeth, 97, 175-187 ; his property in Galloway, 174

Hertford, Edward Seymour, earl of, invades Scotland, 337, 338

Highlands, insurrection in the, 339, 340

Holyrood, 18, 190, 193 ; seized by Arran, 328 ; James VI. at, 33; Mary's last visit to, 54 ; riot in the chapel there, 326, 327

Holyrood, Robert Stewart, abbot of, receives Mary on her arrival, 325 ; captures Bothwell's servants in Orkney, 149

Hume, Alexander, fifth lord, accompanies Mary to Edinburgh, 19 ; joins the party against Bothwell, 41 ; besieges Borthwick castle, 42 ; at Carberry, 43 ; takes the oath to James VI., 63 ; wounded at Langside, 94

Huntly, George Gordon, fourth earl of, opposes the reformers, 112 ; his claims to the throne, 117 ; ruined by Moray, 15, 43

Huntly, George Gordon, fifth earl of, 139, 140 ; escapes from Holyrood, 204 ; aids Mary's escape from Holyrood, 10, 17, 204, 205 ; returns with her to Edinburgh, 19 ; remains with her there, 23; incites Darnley against Moray, 20 ; goes with Mary into Meggotland, 29 ; joins in Darnley's murder, 35 ; joins Bothwell's party, 39 ; at Carberry, 43 ; why he becomes Bothwell's enemy, 41 ; in danger of his life, 142 ; attends Parliament, 146 ; brings troops for Mary, 93

Huntly, the countess of, aids Mary in her escape from Holyrood, 5, 10

Inchkeith, fortress of, taken from the English, 321 ; destroyed, 76

James V., king of Scotland, 74 ; besieged in Stirling castle, 138 ; said to have married Moray's mother, 127 ; his zeal against heresy, 105 ; poisoned, 106 ; his death, 320

James VI. king of Scotland, his birth, 27, 121 ; it strengthens Mary's claim to the Crown of England, 26 ; plans of the lords respecting him, 23, 134, 135 ; taken to Stirling, 30 ; his illness, 32 ; Mary recommends him to the king of France, 33 ; placed under the care of the earl of Mar, 133 ; his conference with F. Gordon, 139, 140 ; persecutes the Catholics, 141 ; his marriage, 142

Jervois abbey, 340

Jesuits in Scotland, 138, 139

Justice-Clerk, the, advises Mary to marry Bothwell, 37

Keith, earl Marshal, see Marshal

Kennedy, earl of Cassilis, see Cassilis

Kennedy, Quintin, abbot of Crossraguel, 113

Kerr ; see Carr

Killigrew, Henry, his missions to Scotland, 22, 28, 153

Kinghorn, 321

Kinross, 159, 162

Kirk of Field, Darnley at, 33

Kirkaldy, Sir James, of Grange, a tool of Moray, 36, 40 ; joins the conspiracy against Bothwell, 40 ; at Carberry, 43 ; Mary surrenders herself to him, 47 ; her letter to him,

TURNBULL AND SPEARS, PRINTERS. EDINBURGH.

315

9 781293 762882